D1440928

Alone against Hitler

Alone against Hitler

Kurt von Schuschnigg's Fight to Save Austria from the Nazis

Jack Bray

Prometheus Books

Guilford, Connecticut

Ⓟ Prometheus Books

An imprint of The Rowman & Littlefield Publishing Group, Inc.
4501 Forbes Blvd., Ste. 200
Lanham, MD 20706
www.rowman.com

Distributed by NATIONAL BOOK NETWORK

British Library Cataloguing in Publication Information available

Library of Congress Cataloging-in-Publication Data

Names: Bray, Jack, author.
Title: Alone against Hitler : Kurt von Schuschnigg's fight to save Austria from the Nazis
/ Jack Bray.
Other titles: Kurt von Schuschnigg's fight to save Austria from the Nazis
Description: Guilford, Connecticut : Prometheus Books, [2020] | Includes
bibliographical references and index. | Summary: "*Alone against Hitler* tells the lesser-
known but pivotal story of former Austrian Chancellor Kurt von Schuschnigg. As one
of the first leaders to defy Adolf Hitler during the build-up to WWII, his is a story of
lasting importance. Though young and untested upon entering office, von Schuschnigg
courageously rejected the rising tide of Austrian Nazism, insisting on equal rights and
respect for the Jewish minority. Author Jack Bray surveys the geopolitical conditions
in Austria during the march to war, highlighting Von Schuschnigg's valiant four-year
struggle to prevent his nearly defenseless small nation from being taken over from within
by unrelenting, violent Austrian Nazis."—Provided by publisher.
Identifiers: LCCN 2019056385 (print) | LCCN 2019056386 (ebook) | ISBN
9781633886124 (cloth) | ISBN 9781633886131 (epub)
Subjects: LCSH: Schuschnigg, Kurt, 1897-1977. | Austria--Politics and
government—1918–1938. | World War, 1939-1945—Austria. |
  Statesmen—Austria—Biography. | National socialism—Austria—Vienna.
Classification: LCC DB98.S3 B73 2020 (print) | LCC DB98.S3 (ebook) | DDC
  943.605/12092 [B]—dc23

LC record available at https://lccn.loc.gov/2019056385
LC ebook record available at https://lccn.loc.gov/2019056386

Contents

Part VI: Invasion

Part VII: The Jaws of the Nazis

Illustrations

Acknowledgments

$\mathscr{I}$ am profoundly grateful to many talented people and to a number of academic and history institutions for the help and resources they provided in the creation of this manuscript. My son, John, is chief among many. His support and constancy kept this project going, and his sound judgment and crisp writing skills added immensely to the story.

I owe a great deal to Dr. Carole Sargent, director of the Georgetown University Office of Scholarly Publications. Her talents, support, and keen intelligence about publications made this book a reality.

James Conaway, a brilliant author and a creator of language starbursts that I can only envy, has been a generous advisor and the wisdom of Finlay Lewis has guided me for decades.

My agent, John Willig, a consummate professional and gentleman, guided the book to shore with wisdom and assurance. Jake Bonar at Prometheus Books shepherded the manuscript with professionalism and patience. Others at Rowman & Littlefield and Prometheus, especially editors Andrew Yoder and Nancy Syrett were exceptionally skillful and perceptive and proved to be devoted caretakers of the manuscript.

Ideas and suggestions of many others helped shape key pieces of this history. Some of the best came from the love of my life, my wife, Joan. Some came from voracious readers, and other historians who helped me choose where to dig deeper, when to think again, and when to question conventional wisdom.

Some of the events could merit a place in the popular realm of historical fiction. This, however, is a history, not a novel. Nor is it subjective commentary. The many tributes and many criticisms of the central characters are the recorded judgments of their contemporaries and the rest are the views of respected scholars, historians, and journalists. Not all tributes could be included. Similarly, no criticism was intentionally omitted.

Witnesses to stories almost a century old are hard to find. I am especially grateful to Ellen Shafer for her guidance and enthusiasm and for her help finding some keen observers whose firsthand information and astute observations were very enlightening.

I am especially grateful to Chancellor Schuschnigg's extraordinary son, Kurti, who, with his wife, Janet, were kind enough to spend many hours with me and with my son, John. Their thorough critique, their stories about the chancellor, and Kurti's recollections of prewar Austria helped bring that world into vivid relief.

Thanks also to the chancellor's grandson, Marc de Kergariou of Vienna, for recounting his days with his grandfather and his mother.

Several readers of the manuscript provided helpful guidance, including Robert Muse, Hank Gutman, Jack Lewis, Dr. Britta McEwen, Alexander Shakow, and others. Many who knew Chancellor Schuschnigg as a professor provided useful recollections and anecdotes of his time in America—James Murphy, Gerald Ortbals, Dr. Daniel Schlafly, Seneca Nolan, Pat Rice, Sarah Fehlig, Donna Marting Hamilton, Robert Proost, Dr. Peter Heinbecker, and others.

Special thanks are due to Anne Gutman for her enthusiasm for this story and for her insistence that it be published. And for their help, outreach, and encouragement, I am also very grateful to David Hensler, Esther Foer, and Dennis Drabelle.

My wonderful secretaries of many years, Margaret O'Brien and Deborah Yates-Carney, were masterful in the revision of this complex manuscript, and both were cheerful companions as it took shape.

Several institutions and their staffs provided major assistance. Foremost was the staff of Saint Louis University's Pius XII Library where the Schuschnigg Archive is housed. The library's staff and the archivists were always ready for visits from me and my son, John, and for years they have been prompt, cheerful, and effective in fulfilling our many requests. The University of Delaware, home to the Ambassador Thomas Messersmith Archive, was a very useful resource for this book.

My time at the Heeresgeschichtliches Museum of Military History in Vienna was a rich immersion into the political and military world of the Habsburg Empire and early twentieth-century Austria. The National World War I Museum in Kansas City, Missouri, was another special resource for understanding the Great War that shaped the people in this story. The staff at the Lauinger Library at Georgetown University made available to me the library's fine collection of German and Austrian histories, and I am grateful for their unfailing hospitality and assistance.

The US Holocaust Memorial provided both museum exhibits and research resources that helped bring to life the history of the murdered Jews of Europe. Special tribute is due to the wise and determined people in Central and Eastern Europe who succeeded against the odds in preserving the graphic evidence of that era—the buildings of Auschwitz, Birkenau, Sachsenhausen, and Dachau, as well as the many other Holocaust sites. They deserve the gratitude of all of us. The historians at Yad Vashem spent the time and effort to unearth and preserve the magnificent stories that today justify hope despite this grim history. Their chronicles of the "Righteous" demonstrate there is nobility in human conduct; they found the participants in time to preserve those stories and present them in moving exhibitions at Auschwitz and elsewhere.

Introduction

$\mathcal{T}$he first chapter of history's worst bloodbath, World War II, began on a deceptively quiet day with no sounds of explosions. The invasion took place on March 12, 1938; it was the day Hitler first erupted on the rest of the world, sending troop trucks rolling out of Nazi Germany across the border into Austria. A correspondent covering Europe called it "the most cataclysmic event of modern history."[1]

The Third Reich did not fire a single shot.[2] No country declared war, yet the heavily armed invaders captured their first independent nation, claiming that Germany had been implored by Austrians to rescue them. Austria's chancellor broadcast defiance and condemned Hitler's pretext for invading, crying out to tell the world the truth—Austria was under attack by overwhelming force. Only later would the Moscow Declaration of the Allied Forces provide the verdict that Austria was, in fact, Nazi Germany's "first victim."[3] Those who saw only a story of a small, massively outgunned nation overrun by a powerful tyrant were to miss the more ominous point. They may be next.

The overpowered Austrian chancellor, Kurt von Schuschnigg, had spent the last four years fighting violent Nazis inside Austria and fending off Hitler's moves to force Austria to merge with Germany. For several years, Europe had lived with anxiety about the growing possibility of another European war to match or even surpass the Great War. On February 12, 1938, Hitler disclosed how close he was to starting his war when he threatened Schuschnigg with invasion during an explosive tirade at Berchtesgaden in Germany's Bavarian Obersalzburg.

By the time of that early 1938 meeting, Hitler had been the dictator of Germany for five years. He had massively rearmed the Wehrmacht, murdered his political enemies, and saw that most of Europe was cowering before him; his Third Reich was frightening even those in the far reaches of the world. Two years earlier, in 1936, he had marched troops onto the French border in the Rhineland in a blunt violation of the Treaty of Versailles, and no one raised a finger to stop him. His enablers in Europe came in many stripes, ranging from unvarnished Nazis in several countries to impressed observers, admirers, fellow anti-Semites, anti-Bolsheviks, and antiwar isolationists. Most were simply appeasers terrified he would attack them. All of them contributed in large and small ways to encouraging him—some by their fearfulness, and some by their tolerance. This could be seen in places as diverse as Italy, Britain, and America.

Most memorable was Britain's prime minister, Neville Chamberlain, the archetype of appeasement. His fearful fecklessness was for the most part conveyed to Hitler by the toadying of Britain's foreign minister, Lord Halifax, and its ambassador to the Third Reich, Neville Henderson. More enthusiastic was the former King Edward VIII, a true Hitler fan and a chummy visitor to Berchtesgaden in 1937. Former prime minister David Lloyd George fairly gushed with praise of Hitler.[4]

In Italy, Benito Mussolini at one time was openly hostile to Hitler's murders and an early opponent of his plan to take Austria; but that was before 1938. By then, Il Duce had blundered his way into a difficult predicament, one in which he desperately needed Hitler's support; and, to keep it, he swung sharply about and fully embraced the Nazi regime.

America provided its share of timidity. Some prominent Americans dished out applause for Hitler's Reich. Others, including America's ambassador to Britain, Joseph P. Kennedy, were outspoken isolationists, repeatedly warning Europe and the world that the United States would not take sides in the looming struggle. Ambassador Kennedy and others were accused of fostering defeatism. Kennedy was accused of providing comfort to Hitler after he speculated publicly that democracy appeared finished in England.[5] He was also accused of anti-Semitism as a result of his message that Hitler need not fear any American resistance to his racial persecution or aggression.[6]

Even America's reigning celebrity, Charles A. Lindbergh, who visited Germany at the request of the US military, enthusiastically complimented the German armaments he saw, and in 1938, he accepted a medal gratefully bestowed upon him by Hermann Göring.[7] Lindbergh's vocal isolationism elevated him to leadership in the America First movement while he spouted ideas that caused many to call him anti-Semitic; President Roosevelt and others called him a "Nazi."

At this point, President Roosevelt himself was still unwilling to become an open critic of Hitler's persecution of German Jews.[8]

★ ★ ★

Inside Austria in the 1930s, a core of unruly, violent Hitler supporters cheered the Führer on; they constantly bellowed their admiration for him, their hatred of Jews, and their hatred of Schuschnigg. This raucous Nazi support was gaining momentum, and the Austrian landscape was quite discouraging for any who would dare to resist Hitler's determination to capture Austria.[9]

It fell to Schuschnigg alone to try to stop Nazism at the German border. As one commentator has said: "[T]he fate of the world . . . found itself . . . for a fleeting instant in Kurt von Schuschnigg's hands."[10] To resist Nazism, he would have to row against the strong tide of Europe's festival of appeasement. He would need support from countries that had once solemnly committed to preventing a German takeover of Austria, countries whose own best interests were to stop Hitler at his own border; but when it mattered most, all of them refused. At the crucial hour, Schuschnigg received no encouragement, and his pleas were rudely rebuffed. Yet he pushed forward; he resisted Hitler, stubbornly refusing to adopt the Nazi racial policies in Austria. Contrasted with all other leaders in the world of 1938, his was the story of one leader entirely out of step with the seemingly unstoppable parade toward a Nazi Europe.

Ten days after Schuschnigg defied Hitler, *Time* magazine paid him tribute, proclaiming his reputation as a "statesman of commanding powers" and elevating the little-known Schuschnigg to its cover.[11] He alone had done something to clear the fog that had allowed appeasers to pretend that Hitler was something crass but normal. Schuschnigg lit the only spark of hope amid a darkness that was about to engulf the civilized world. He did it wrestling against the leaders who had allowed Hitler's rise. Too late, even some of those appeasers came to appreciate that his call to reject the Nazis was a momentary triumph of morality, an act of personal courage, and a lesson for the days to come.

★ ★ ★

I first saw the former Austrian chancellor when he was a professor at Saint Louis University. Walking across campus, he was barely shielded against the cold sunny day; he wore a woolen suit but no overcoat. Thin, erect, and dignified, he lacked the haughty demeanor one might expect of a successor of sorts to the Habsburg emperors. We students were curious about him; we were intrigued that this professor once had direct encounters with the monsters of the Third Reich—more personal contact with them than Churchill, Roosevelt, or Stalin had—and that he once had it out, face to face, for several hours with Adolf Hitler, and yet he had somehow managed to survive seven years as a Gestapo prisoner. Here he was, in 1950s America, sporting an air of humility unusual for someone who had stepped right out of the history books.

He rarely spoke about any of that. There was controversy, we knew. He was hated by Nazis and ultranationalists on the Right and by communists and radical socialists on the Left. He was criticized by unembarrassed anti-Semites in Austria, and there were many who charged he had sold out to the Jews when he ended the traditional techniques of discrimination. By the time he was thrust into office, Austria, in its desperation to stop the violence and propaganda of the Austrian Nazis, had already resorted to a unique form of government, one fairly labeled as autocratic. By 1934, Austria's leaders were shocked by the Nazis' success at the polls; the governments were afraid to call elections since the Nazis had expedited their political rise and achieved astonishing, propaganda-fueled success in Austrian elections in 1932 and had gone right on to hijack Germany's government in 1933. We knew that Austria was not alone in these uncomfortable trappings of authority. More than a dozen European countries had consolidated power in their executives when faced with the triple crises of Hitler, communism, and the Great Depression. Historians had judged that only a few were justly labeled dictatorial. Schuschnigg had emerged with a reputation as an honest, incorruptible adherent to the rule of law who respected human rights despite the hatred that racked Austria. European anxiety had created political divisions during the Depression years, and those divisions lingered even after the war, but for him the historical issues of 1930s Europe had seemingly disappeared into the mists; he was now in academia focusing on contemporary issues—whether containment was the wisest policy for dealing with communism or whether communist China should be allowed into the United Nations despite US policy to the contrary. We did not learn much beyond sketchy renditions about prewar Austria; we saw even less the full color of his epic adventure at the center of Europe's turning point in 1938. But that was the story we ached to hear.

We knew he was imprisoned by the Gestapo and that, just as the war was about over, the Third Reich was annihilating its prisoners. We were keen to learn how he, of all Hitler's prisoners, could possibly have escaped death. Many of us were especially curious how it was that one of our fellow students, his daughter, Maria (Sissi), had been born during his captivity and spent her early years in the Nazi concentration camps of Sachsenhausen and Dachau, while the rest of us had endured only prosaic wartime hardships no more bothersome than the rationing of meat.

★ ★ ★

It was not until many years later that I began to look into Kurt von Schuschnigg's story, initially intending to write an article about those events to answer the questions that had made me so curious over the years. That deeper look revealed one dramatic surprise after another—gruesome battles in one world war, confrontation with the Third Reich in another, frightening encounters, and years facing daily violence. But he had also left behind a warm and interesting story of the love he shared with two unique women who sustained him.

Most compelling, however, was the story of Schuschnigg's resistance—standing entirely alone. When Hitler set out to manipulate Austria's political apparatus, Schuschnigg was the one who saw that taking Austria was the crucial start to Hitler's campaign, and he figured out why Hitler wanted to take Austria from within. Hitler feared launching an attack to conquer Austria; he wanted to take it from within primarily to avoid prematurely provoking the wider European war before his military buildup was complete. His generals were pleading that they were not ready for the war plans he disclosed to them in 1937. Schuschnigg, however, disrupted Hitler's gambit in Austria. He turned on the lights. He exposed the lies shrouding the Führer's effort to camouflage his conquest of Austria as a rescue.

Along that path, Schuschnigg also dealt with most of the leading Nazi protagonists and others who opened the door for them—Heinrich Himmler, Rudolf Hess, Hermann Göring, Joachim von Ribbentrop, Mussolini, and Paul von Hindenburg. The setting for these events could not have been more grand: post-Habsburg Austria, home to the glitter and music of old world Europe. But that ornate era had a tainted heritage of racial and religious biases and bitter class warfare, afflictions that seemed benign traditions to many Europeans, but were ripe for exploitation by a demagogue. By the time Schuschnigg came to office, those weaknesses had grown so malignant that they provided the catalyst to the Nazis' rise to power and helped make a monster acceptable to millions of otherwise civilized, intelligent, religious people.

At every turn of these events was this reserved, provincial lawyer, a man utterly without political ambition. Young Kurt von Schuschnigg had to be pushed hard to stand for election to Parliament. That eventually would lead to the awful afternoon when he was asked to become the chancellor of Austria. If he accepted, it would be up to him to save Austria from the Nazis—and to do it with no help from any allies in Europe or anywhere in the world.

Dramatic twists would hardly seem necessary to enhance such a saga, but as the climax approached, Schuschnigg called out to the nation. He summoned Austrians to resist Hitler and choose independence. He delivered a public shaming of Hitler even as the Nazis pushed their way into the chancellery screaming for his head.

What had begun as an article insisted on becoming this book.

The Prelude to Austria's Crisis

$\mathscr{A}$fter its defeat in World War I, Austria was intentionally crippled. The once powerful empire was extinguished, and the new Austria's borders were reduced to make it a small, landlocked nation. Its new government began life saddled with a heavy war reparations debt. Unemployment and inflation soared. Dystopia gave rise to armed militias marching in the streets, threatening civil war. By 1933, Austria was nearly disabled by the Great Depression and the threat of revolution by Austro-Marxists on the left. In this environment, the Nazi Party flourished trumpeting propaganda promising to crush enemies—Jews and communists—and using murder and assassination freely.

In January 1933, Hitler and his Nazis stunned Europe—they seized power in Germany and began arming to deliver on Hitler's pledge to acquire living space to feed Germans by reclaiming Germany's "lost territories." Austria was to be the first.

The fate of the Jews of Austria suddenly hung perilously in the balance. The Nazi program branded Jews as foreigners and as an inferior race, stripped them of their rights and their citizenship, and marked all of them for banishment. By 1935, Hitler had made these policies the law in Germany, and he was determined to spread this, the essence of Nazism, to Austria.

But in anti-Semitic Austria, Schuschnigg rejected Nazi racial policy outright, suppressed the Nazis, and insisted on full equality for the Jews. Jewish leaders in Austria reported in diplomatic circles that they had rarely been treated with such respect. But other Austrians accused him of selling out to the Jews. And the Nazis decided they had to kill him.

Three nations had pledged to protect Austria's independence—Britain, France, and Italy. The League of Nations subscribed to the same pledge. But Britain and France were visibly war weary and refused to take any real steps to stop Hitler when he began rearming Germany, obviously preparing for war. Sensing a green light, he decided very early that it was time to confiscate Austria.

I

COMING TO POWER

• 1 •

Sarajevo in Vienna

$\mathcal{O}$n the afternoon of July 25, 1934, Adolf Hitler made certain that he was visible. He wanted to be seen by the formally dressed audience attending, as he was, the Wagner festival's performance of *Das Rheingold* at the Bayreuth Festspielhaus. The dictator of Nazi Germany loved opera, but on this day, he had an added reason to attend—it established his alibi. He needed to be seen so the world would know where he was, would know that he was casually enjoying an opera and not off somewhere orchestrating the Nazi putsch under way in Vienna.

In mid-afternoon, a group of Austrian Nazis exploded into action to seize power in Vienna. Hitler wanted to portray it as a spontaneous eruption of Austrians. He would have gladly invaded Austria if his army had been ready to defeat Britain, France, and Italy were they to challenge him now, in 1934, over taking Austria.[1] And if Soviet Russia joined the Western powers, he would surely be defeated. Instead, he decided to try to lull them into believing that Austrians had rebelled against Chancellor Engelbert Dollfuss's suppression of Austria's Nazis.

Wagner's granddaughter, Friedelind, was watching Hitler from her own seat in the Wagner family box, growing more curious by the minute over what excitement was afoot, anxious to find out why Hitler's aides kept appearing at his side, kneeling, trying to be unobtrusive as the performance thundered on in the great opera house, whispering to the riveted Führer, then slinking away, then scurrying back to his side with more exciting news.

When Albrecht and the Rhinemaidens at last took their bows, Friedelind navigated to get near Hitler as quickly as she could glide her way through the small crowd in the elite boxes. She hoped to overhear some hint about the intrigue. But there was no need to crane her neck to hear Hitler; he was fairly bursting with joy, unable to contain the news the aides had delivered to him.[2]

Austria, he announced, had been overthrown. Chancellor Engelbert Dollfuss was dead.[3] A Nazi coup had just delivered Austria to the Third Reich on a silver platter. His European strategy had begun—and he had scored a major success in his first attempt. From the comfort of his seat enjoying an opera, the Führer had effortlessly conquered his first European nation. Better still, it would look like an Austrian uprising. His Bavarian Regiment could stand down. His troopers had spent the day crouched with their eyes toward the Austrian border, with their Panzers' engines idling, checking that their weapons were locked and loaded, anxious to show the world for the first time what blitzkrieg warfare could do.[4] There was now no need to invade and risk a wider war. Within minutes, they would be invited in as guests of the new Nazi Austria.

Hitler made not the slightest attempt to conceal his delight from his friends. Young Friedelind herself was no fan of the Nazis, and she took it all in and saw it for what it was. They all proceeded as scheduled to the Wagner home, where he could revel further in the inestimable glory beginning that night for his Thousand Year Reich.

Josef Göbbels was elated; he distributed a press release to the Berlin radio stations applauding the Nazi triumph in Austria.

★ ★ ★

In Vienna, where the coup had been unfolding, passersby near the Austrian chancellery had halted their strolls to make way for a dozen quick-stepping policemen in smart uniforms. The small crowd puzzled at the spectacle of these scowling men speeding up the few steps and virtually bursting into the central building of Austrian government. This anxious bustle of police hurrying into the seat of officialdom seemed odd, but law enforcement in nervous times occasionally called for sudden musters.

Inside the chancellery building, the small security detail was slow to react, barely suspicious of the platoon of loudly clattering police whose familiar uniforms signaled them as allies, clueless that these were costumed Nazis until the Nazis had disarmed them. The faux police headed directly to the chancellor's ground floor suite of gilded rooms where in 1815 dignitaries at Metternich's Congress of Vienna once danced.

★ ★ ★

The chancellor they sought was Austria's head of government, hardly an imperial or imperious figure in the style of the imposing, regal, and very tall Habsburg emperors. Engelbert Dollfuss had been chancellor for a little more than two years. He was an outgoing, likable farm economist who was unfailingly kind and gentle to most people and very approachable. Despite his small stature, standing just under five feet, he was a strong leader and a wounded, decorated combat veteran of World War I. Unlike the emperors of old, he was known for his self-effacing, down-to-earth style, as well as his devotion to his family.[5]

The Nazis had tried before to kill him. He had cracked down on the Nazis, and in June 1933, he banned the Nazi Party,[6] and they had promptly shot him. However, he recovered and seemed utterly unfazed by them or by the threats of the Marxists, his political opponents he had also banned and who ridiculed his height at every meeting. The Marxists also at times resorted to violence, but Dollfuss was devoutly religious and not one to dwell on such threats. Austria, after all, had a history of assassinations—the 1914 assassination of Archduke Franz Ferdinand, the 1916 assassination of Prime Minister Karl von Stürgkh, the attempt to assassinate Prime Minister Ignaz Seipel in 1924, and the wave of recent Nazi bombings.[7] Less than twenty-four hours previously, as Dollfuss dined with his minister of justice, he had seemed cheerful and unconcerned.[8]

★ ★ ★

Dollfuss heard the commotion as it approached his door, but how alarming could it be in the presumptively safest spot in Austria? This time he had no chance to reassess his initial surprise. The Nazi leader, Otto Planetta, burst through the door, walked right up to him, and, without a word, shot him twice in the neck; the chancellor of Austria collapsed unconscious.[9] When he awoke many minutes later in severe pain, soaked in blood, he saw he was surrounded by these fake police and was being attended by two trusted aides. The police were barking as if from a distance demanding that he sign a document they held appointing Anton Rintelen as the first Nazi chancellor of a new Austria. Dollfuss's aides raised him to his sofa, but he could not feel their grip. He asked Police Sergeant Johann Griefeneder to move his arms and legs. When he did, it confirmed the chancellor's worst fear: "I can't feel anything, I am paralyzed."[10]

The Nazis refused pleas for a doctor. Dollfuss whispered to his aides— had the government been overthrown? Was the president dead? What about the other ministers? They did not know. Gathering his wits, Dollfuss gave his aides an order he hoped could save Austria. He told Griefeneder that he wanted Schuschnigg to form a government.[11] Dollfuss ignored the demands by the Nazis standing over him that he name their man Rintelen as chancellor, and he mustered enough strength to say: "Minister Schuschnigg is to be entrusted with the government, or in case he is dead, Police President Skubl."[12] Shortly, Dollfuss lost consciousness, and at 3:40 p.m.,[13] he began a several-minute death rattle.

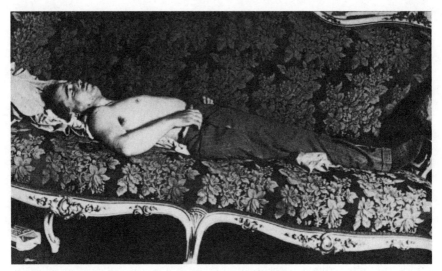

The death of Chancellor Engelbert Dollfuss, July 25, 1934.
Source: Alamy.

★ ★ ★

By the time Hitler arrived at the Wagner estate, his aides were radiating far less optimism.[14] They did not rush to his side with the same eagerness to bring news. Instead, with halting gestures, glancing at their feet, they delivered a blow to the flying-high Führer. The Nazi coup had failed.

True, the Austrian Nazis had assassinated Chancellor Dollfuss, but they had failed to kill the other government leaders or to gain the support of Austria's military. They attacked the radio station at Bisamberg, but they had been unable to hold it.[15] Only the chancellery had been taken, and the Nazi assassins were now trapped inside by Austrian troops.

★ ★ ★

Kurt von Schuschnigg, Austria's minister of justice and of education, was at his office at the Ministry of Education in the nearby Minoritenplatz when the attack occurred. As a junior member of Parliament, early on he had earned the respect and trust of its leaders, including Dollfuss and President Wilhelm Miklas, and they had appointed him to the cabinet at a young age. He went immediately to the Stubenring and gathered with other cabinet officials at the Ministry of Defense.[16] The initial reports they received were confusing. The assassins at the chancellery were claiming they had taken other sites, and the ministers[17] were left uncertain about Dollfuss's condition. They put a call through to Minister Emil Fey, the state secretary for public security affairs, at the chancellery. While Nazi gunmen nestled their ears close to the phone,

Fey was asked, "Is the injury difficult?" Fey nervously answered, "Yes, rather difficult."[18] After the call, Fey stepped out on the balcony and shouted that Anton Rintelen should come into the chancellery, raising suspicion that Fey had joined the putsch.[19] Other ministers eventually concluded that Fey was not involved.[20] Those who found Fey's actions suspicious likely did not know that when he appeared on the balcony in the company of Nazis, one Nazi behind him was holding a gun at his back and another was stooped low holding his ankles so he could not jump from the balcony to safety.[21]

The cabinet members were able to rally the military, stabilize the government, and demand that the conspirators surrender. Before they learned that Dollfuss's wounds were fatal,[22] and while the putsch conspirators held the chancellery building and were still claiming they had taken control of the government,[23] a discussion began about safe conduct for the conspirators to Germany. To negotiate on behalf of the conspirators, a surprising intermediary appeared—Kurt von Reith, the German ambassador to Austria.[24] The US ambassador observed in his report to the State Department that this was, in diplomatic circles, proof that the putsch had Hitler's approval. President Miklas and the cabinet members, however, insisted on the surrender of the conspirators.[25] The vice chancellor, Ernst von Starhemberg, was away in Italy meeting with Benito Mussolini, and the president called on Schuschnigg to take control of the crisis. The attackers were soon taken into custody.

Chancellor Dollfuss and several cabinet members, including Minister Schuschnigg in the rear to the right of Dollfuss and Vice Chancellor Ernst von Starhemberg to the left of Dollfuss.
Source: Getty Images.

The president and cabinet members agreed that Schuschnigg, not Vice Chancellor Starhemberg, should become the new chancellor. With considerable trepidation, Schuschnigg accepted the perilous assignment despite the personal risk and the dire predicament that Austria faced.

By choosing Schuschnigg, the president and the cabinet had passed over an imperious figure. The events that day had certainly not helped Prince Ernst von Starhemberg. All the ministers were aware that Starhemberg had once supported the candidacy of the man the Nazis had insisted become the new chancellor that day, Anton Rintelen. Several of them knew that Starhemberg had been an ally of Hitler in the early 1920s, and they suspected that Starhemberg was growing closer to Nazism every day. Many were aware that he embraced fascism, and they were wary of his oversized ambition. These worries were focused on the leverage he could wield through the militia he commanded. The Heimwehr was a private army capable of holding its own against Austria's meager armed forces; Austria's Bundesheer was still severely weakened by the limits the World War I victorious Allies had imposed. Moreover, by this point, many Heimwehr members were now believed to be Nazis.

Schuschnigg presented an especially stark contrast with the ambitious Starhemberg. He was a pacifist, and he had not wanted a life in politics in the first place. As the dust settled around the new chancellor of bloodied Austria, Schuschnigg would be facing off against powerful forces threatening Austria's ability to continue as an independent nation—Adolf Hitler's Nazis, violent communists, and the Great Depression. And lurking in the shadows would be the snubbed Starhemberg, still vice chancellor, ready to second-guess the new chancellor—or worse.

★ ★ ★

Schuschnigg never learned precisely why he was chosen to succeed Dollfuss, although Dollfuss had once told Schuschnigg early in his administration that he wanted him as his successor.[26] By right, the succession should have gone to the vice chancellor.[27] Starhemberg borrowed one of Mussolini's planes for a quick return from Italy, arriving in Vienna in just a few hours; there he faced the news that it was Schuschnigg, not himself, who was the consensus successor to Dollfuss. Starhemberg's initial response was that he had the superior claim to the position and that his Heimwehr supporters were clamoring for him, not Schuschnigg, to become chancellor.[28] He boasted that if he chose to take the chancellor's post, he could, but he said he would not oppose the wishes of the president.[29] Miklas let Starhemberg know that he did not support him, and Starhemberg became oddly less assertive in laying claim to the post.[30] By then, Starhemberg realized that the other cabinet members were aware that Miklas did not want him as chancellor, and many agreed with Miklas.[31] The fact that Dollfuss himself had told his aides, Rudolf Messinger and Johann

Griefeneder, that it should be Schuschnigg who succeeded him was apparently no surprise to Starhemberg.[32]

His Heimwehr was the strongest of several homeland defense organizations, and a powerful political group, but most other factions in the novel political umbrella organization that replaced the political parties, the Fatherland Front, opposed Starhemberg. Tension between the Heimwehr and Schuschnigg was particularly great.[33] The Heimwehr wanted control over the Fatherland Front, and Schuschnigg was totally opposed to that. Even some of the ministers who had been opponents of Schuschnigg, including state secretary for work creation Odo Neustädter-Stürmer,[34] endorsed him at the crucial moment. Some ministers saw in Schuschnigg the firmness needed for such an extreme national crisis. Contemporaries who dealt with him closely, both in the Austrian government and foreign governments, respected his quiet strength. As one diplomat put it, Schuschnigg was an intellectual but "by no means weak."[35]

★ ★ ★

In Bayreuth, as international denunciations poured in, it became clear to the depressed Führer that any Wehrmacht entry into Austria would be seen as a naked invasion and could start a European war. Hitler ordered the troops to stand down. In Berlin, Göbbels sent Nazis scrambling off to all broadcast locations trying to retrieve every copy of the press release applauding the coup, and replacing it with a message from the Third Reich condemning the revolt.[36] Few were fooled; it was clear that Hitler had ordered the Nazi violence in Austria despite the pretense. Mussolini realized it immediately: "Hitler is the murderer of Dollfuss, Hitler is the guilty man, and he is responsible for this."[37] Hitler continued to pretend that the Austrian Nazis were some entirely independent patriotic organization insulated from control by the Third Reich. The next day, however, documents were found concealed on a German courier caught near the border revealing the coordination with Hitler. The Kollerschlag Documents even listed the coded message telling Hitler of the successful assassination—"Old cutlery samples arrived."[38] Later, Austrian Nazi leaders would let slip the nearly automatic signals by which the German Nazis controlled the Austrian Nazis.[39]

★ ★ ★

The announcement was broadcast that the new chancellor was Schuschnigg. What the Nazi violence of that night had proven was just how unpredictable their ambitious moves could be. The Nazis had elevated not their chosen man, Rintelen, but the minister who was as firmly opposed as Dollfuss had been to the Nazis and Anschluss. Schuschnigg's appointment also helped install Schuschnigg's loyal supporter, Guido Zernatto, as the chief officer of the Fatherland Front. Thus, Starhemberg's consolation prize as the titular head

Funeral cortege of Engelbert Dollfuss.

Source: Alamy.

of the Fatherland Front was diluted by the daily presence of a Schuschnigg loyalist at his elbow.[40]

Schuschnigg entered office knowing that he was now at the top of the Nazis' list for assassination. He was also inheriting all the bitterness the Left harbored over its treatment. Even centrists and moderates were in their own state of anxiety over the continued depth of the Great Depression. He had to decide quickly how to deal with this complex ecosystem of political anger. For now, he would continue the Dollfuss policies.[41]

★ ★ ★

The very first decision that confronted Schuschnigg was whether he should attempt to appease Austrian Nazis or continue repressing them. He chose to hit back hard. Dollfuss's murderer, Otto Planetta, plus a dozen of the other ringleaders of the putsch were tried and sent to the gallows.[42] Their conspirators, including Anton Rintelen, the former governor of Styria and the hand-picked choice of the Nazis to take over the Austrian government, were charged with treason and sentenced to long prison terms.[43]

Schuschnigg's sentiment on that evening—when bloodstains still covered the chancellor's sofa and gunpowder residue wafted in the air inside the chancellor's private office—was great reluctance to take the office of chancellor of Austria.[44] Whoever stepped into the shoes of the assassinated chancellor knew all too well that the Nazi murders in Austria were far from finished.[45] An omen had already appeared at his doorstep—a February 12, 1934, bombing of Schuschnigg's Innsbruck apartment. The bomb caused considerable damage, but no one was home.[46]

★ ★ ★

Many saw his selection as chancellor as a reason for hope. This new chancellor who reluctantly accepted the burden of leading Austria was a man viewed by some as a "courageous and determined" leader[47] and a political figure with the rarest motivation—"devoid of the personal ambitions."[48] He convened the diplomatic community that night to report to them in person what was known. The US ambassador, George S. Messersmith, was quite moved by Schuschnigg's words and very impressed by how he handled so fresh a tragedy; he felt that "it gave promise for the days to come."[49]

★ ★ ★

The list of priorities was lengthy, but his highest priority was to strengthen Austria, to give it a chance to resist the Nazis. That could not be done alone. It required enlisting help from outside. Articles 10 and 16 of the Covenant of the League of Nations and Article 88 of the Treaty of St. Germain contained guarantees of support for Austria. However, it was now essential that the stronger nations step forward in the wake of this Nazi coup and reaffirm to Hitler that Austria's independence was important to them, to make those guarantees believable. In September, Schuschnigg went before the League of Nations and in his address urged them to show their support for Austria.[50]

★ ★ ★

Many were now willing to be patient with the government's slow effort to complete a new constitution. Schuschnigg obtained welcome breathing room when the international community reacted with outrage to the assassination.[51]

★ ★ ★

When he became chancellor, Schuschnigg was thirty-six.[52] In the shadow of the energetic Dollfuss, it was inevitable that observers would compare the two personalities. Ambassador Messersmith, who dealt closely with both, had given Dollfuss the ultimate accolade: "One had to know him only a few hours to realize that he was a great man."[53]

Charisma is not a transferable asset, and Schuschnigg did not set out to compete with the vibrant, outgoing Dollfuss. He was more reserved, fascinated by such tame pursuits as the poetry of Goethe and Hofmannsthal, and the music of Strauss, Bruckner, and Mozart. Some noted that Schuschnigg was more inflexibly Catholic and aloof. He was well aware that he lacked the dynamism of Dollfuss, but he was every bit as resolute.[54] All could see he had the same devotion to country, and before long, Ambassador Messersmith reported his assessment to Secretary of State Cordell Hull that Schuschnigg was a "wise" man, "essentially a scholar," a "very intelligent, decent and fine man," a "very fair person," and a "great patriot."[55] This portrait matched his early reputation—a good person thrust by circumstance into high office he had never sought, lacking guile, willing to consider the contrary opinions of others, not gullible, but trustful that most people were telling the truth and pursuing goals in which they believed. Others who dealt with him, including some who disagreed with his political moves, came to echo the exceptional praise of his character and morality. Cardinal Eugenio Pacelli, who became Pope Pius XII, concluded as the turbulent rise of the Nazis continued, that Schuschnigg was a very "courageous person."[56] One of the most vocal critics of anti-Semitism, Dietrich Hildebrand, who railed against any anti-Semites in Germany and Austria, viewed Schuschnigg from his vantage point as a "noble person with the best of intentions," as "decent, pious, and dutiful," and as a "clean, elegant, and cultivated" man.[57]

But when it would have helped to convey that, Schuschnigg sometimes lacked Dollfuss's oratorical skill. His speeches were delivered with a matter-of-fact demeanor. The speeches he most admired were ones without "dramatic gesture and cheap pathos,"[58] but to some, his speeches just seemed cold and distant.[59] Nor was he as shrewd politically or as personally dynamic and tireless as Dollfuss, who had reveled in "the joy of work."[60] One historian summed up the public persona of Schuschnigg as rather rigid.[61]

His cabinet selections reflected his lofty goals. Ambassador Messersmith reported to Secretary Hull that the Schuschnigg cabinet members uniformly enjoyed good reputations for competence and honesty and that the new cabinet and councils were bodies "of a deliberative nature which more or less take the place of Parliament."[62]

★ ★ ★

Kurt von Schuschnigg grew up in what for a time seemed an entirely comfortable Austria, in a culture of old-world Europe, a place ruled by a revered emperor of a centuries-old dynasty, among people bound to their traditions. His fellow Tyrolers had no suspicion in 1897, the year Schuschnigg was born, that the timeless empire would soon be over.

His youth was far different in every respect from the classic tale of a poor, tortured childhood. He grew up in a happy home, full of music, raised by parents who often expressed their gratitude for the comfortable life they enjoyed. His mother and father were bourgeoisie, both from the Tyrol, and both were very fond of the history and traditions of the Tyrol. The breathtaking mountains and valleys were an irresistible spectacle, and the terrain laid a powerful claim to their hearts. Their patriotism was rooted in the history and heritage of their Germanic ancestors and their respect for the storied Habsburg Empire.

His father, General Artur von Schuschnigg, was a career Habsburg army officer, as the general's own father had been. Kurt's grandfather had been the military commander of a large area in Tyrol and Vorarlberg, so a military career and government service seemed natural for Kurt and his brother, Artur.[63] Kurt assumed that he, like his ancestors, would eventually enter the service of the Habsburg emperor's army.

Their mother, Anna, had been a serious student who loved music and inspired her sons to do so. Anna von Schuschnigg played the piano at home for her children, and Kurt, from an early age, was extraordinarily fond of great music.[64] Anna and her husband were devoutly Catholic; through the influence of these very observant parents, and reinforced by a profoundly conservative Catholic country, Kurt too became a devout practitioner of Austrian Catholicism throughout his entire life.[65]

Austria was not merely home to an abundance of Catholics. It was, despite the presence of a large minority population of other Christian denominations, as well as a significant population of Jews, a country so wed to the Catholic Church that Catholics and institutional Catholicism became part of the fabric of the post-Habsburg experiment in government. Indeed, priests were sometimes government officials. A bishop became a cabinet minister in the 1920s, and a Catholic priest became chancellor of Austria in 1922 and a leader of the conservative parliamentary republic that was formed in the aftermath of the Great War.

Much of Kurt's youth was spent in Innsbruck, the capital of Tyrol. There he enjoyed a cultured upbringing. The music he loved was heavy in opera and traditional Tyrolean ballads and choruses. He was especially fond of the music and ceremony of the grand Tyrolean events like the annual Kaiser Parade and the many religious festivals. He was a patriotic Austrian, an Innsbrucker, and a son of the Tyrol; he was proud to be an Austrian German.

An army career in the Habsburg Empire caused periodic absences for General Artur von Schuschnigg, and Anna became the guiding parental influence on Kurt and his brother Artur, eight years younger than Kurt. There came times, however, when his father was reassigned to posts far from Innsbruck, which required the family to relocate. During Kurt's preteen years, the family decided that it would be less disruptive to his life and schooling if he were in a boarding school free from the impact of moving at the call of the Austrian military.

The Jesuits were the great teachers in Austria. Their priests and scholastics were among the best educated of Austria's Catholic clergy. The Jesuits, Kurt said, "constantly hammered into our minds" that even a "praiseworthy end in no circumstances justified a prevarication . . . untruth, injustice, or the viola-tion of conscience."⁶⁶ They were dedicated to classical scholarly training, and places in Jesuit schools were coveted for the educational rigor and the devotion of the faculties. The Jesuit curriculum was the widely admired *Ratio Studiorum*, a legacy of the sixteenth-century pedagogy of their founder, Saint Ignatius de Loyola, a Basque soldier. The Jesuits in Austria ran a particularly fine school at Feldkirk named Stella Matutina. This scholarly *gymnasium* (as Germans called schools offering education in the classics in preparation for advancement to university) was a very strict academy devoted to educating talented boys.

The best fit for such an academy was a disciplined, intelligent student. Kurt was exceptionally intelligent, but he was not an exceptional student. Moreover, at Stella Matutina he was homesick, and he found himself miserable many times during the long school year. In Germanic style, the boys would remain at school from the early fall, returning home only for the summer.⁶⁷

The teachers at Stella Matutina were all ethnic Germans; they showed a strain of Pan-German patriotism but no note of religious intolerance.⁶⁸ They attempted to motivate students to expend greater effort in their studies by reminding lackluster students, Kurt among them, that in Germany the boys would all master these lessons and become superior students. This plume of "Great German" influence was constantly in the air at the academy and inces-santly called to the attention of the underperforming students.⁶⁹ The technique was successful with Kurt. He came to realize his shortcomings as a student and responded to the severity of the academic discipline. As a result, he soon be-came a far better student than when he began, and in later years, he expressed gratitude for the fine education he received there.⁷⁰

That education included Shakespeare and music. The all-boys school conducted performances of Shakespeare's plays, but they omitted the female roles; they simply wrote the women out of the plays or substituted male parts where feasible. Changing the role of Portia in *The Merchant of Venice* to a man was easy compared to presenting *Macbeth* without Lady Macbeth.⁷¹

Music was a welcome friend at the school for the lonely boy, and his knowledge of music was expanded there. He played in the school orchestra, and he waded enthusiastically into the study of orchestral composition and musical variety.⁷² His fascination with music drove him to an ever-deepening lifetime of learning music, and in later life, his fondest pastimes were listening to music and conversing with fellow knowledgeable music lovers.⁷³

★ ★ ★

Kurt's father, General Artur von Schuschnigg, never pushed his sons to enter the military, yet Kurt envisioned a military career almost as a reflex because his ancestors had included many officers. He loved the stories of the great hero of the Tyrol, Andreas Hofer, the son of a Tyrolean innkeeper who rose to lead the

1810 uprising against Napoleon's French army, and who faced a firing squad refusing to be blindfolded, admonishing his executioners to shoot straight.[74]

Kurt did not, however, elect to enter any of the military academies that youths with such ambition attended. Just as he reached the school level where a career path would have to be chosen if he wanted a military career, the Great War exploded across Europe.[75]

He was hurried off to artillery training in the Habsburg army.[76] Kurt was sent to Pola for two years to attend the school for the Fourth Fortress Artillery Regiment, and, during that time, was promoted to the rank of lieutenant.[77] He began the war infused with his family's military tradition committed to serving in the Austrian cause of the moment, filled with affection for his soldier-father, and brimming with the lore of the Austrian military; he began his training with unquestioning esteem for soldiers' values. But in May 1916, he was sent to the front. His unit was designated for the Italian front—the Isonzo front and the Doberdo front.

Even at these fronts, miles from the incredible carnage of Verdun and the Somme, the Great War subjected the troops to enough horror to provide enduring trauma for the young Innsbrucker. In the heights of Isonzo, Austrians spent the winter in frozen trenches. The Battle of Isonzo became a second battle, then a third battle, and, eventually, more than a dozen battles with major artillery bombardment. Kurt was in the thick of the fighting in several battles. He fought at the twelve-day-long sixth battle of Isonzo, at the Battle of Doberdo, and at the storied river Piave.[78] By the time of the twelfth battle of Isonzo, the encounters degenerated to gruesome hand-to-hand combat with knives and scraps of metal and hideous wounds. The twelfth was also called the Battle of Caporetto, made memorable by Ernest Hemingway's *A Farewell to Arms*. The story of the Italians' fighting withdrawal and their stand at the river Piave gave rise to a legend and to the first Italian national anthem, "La Leggenda del Piave."[79] The Battle of Doberdo in August 1916 was one of the bloodiest of the war. Kurt was revolted when he saw war close up, a reality that was far different from heroic soldier stories and far more gruesome than sanitized reports of battles. There, his childhood illusions of the military—an institution draped with grand imperial ceremony, stirring marches, and air-brushed tales of gallantry in thrilling combat—were demolished by the horrors of mechanized death and the grotesque mutilations he encountered. He arrived at a single resolve—this must be mankind's last war.[80]

★ ★ ★

When the war suddenly ended with the November 11, 1918, Armistice, Kurt was near Codroipo in Italy between Piave and Tagliamento. The surrender added to his disillusionment with the Great War, a feeling shared by many Austrian soldiers. Now, in addition, they had been misled by their high command. They had been told, at first, that the armistice meant they could immediately go home; but when they disarmed, they were marched off in captivity. This startling deceit gave rise to serious alarm and lasting resentment among many Austrian soldiers.[81] By then, there had been abundant shocks and enough executions and murders to raise alarm over such seeming treachery. Just four months earlier, after the war seemed over for Russian czar Nicholas and his family, the worst fears had come to pass. While in the custody of the Bolsheviks and within reach of potential rescue by the Whites, the Romanovs and their children were suddenly murdered without warning.

Kurt and his colleagues in the Austrian artillery battery were sent to Italy where they remained prisoners of war for some ten months. Kurt and his father were housed in an officers' prison camp. In the camp, they were treated humanely. Kurt mixed with soldiers of the other Central Powers, and he learned through them about life outside Austria.[82] One of the memorable lessons of these months with other populations from around Europe was how dominant was the "Great German" vision held by other Habsburg nationalities, especially the Sudetens of German descent whom he met. He saw that they viewed themselves first and foremost as Germans, and they viewed Austrians as fellow Germans as well.[83]

★ ★ ★

The dictator who presided over the murder of Dollfuss was born and raised alongside the river Inn not many miles north of where Schuschnigg himself grew up, but he seemed to have evolved from an entirely different world. Hitler's childhood had been nearly friendless, and his home life in Braunau am Inn and Linz on the German border was tense and dominated by stormy arguments with his father, Alois. Adolf was determined to live life as he wished as an artist. His father told him repeatedly what foolishness this was, but the young Adolf would not budge, and the relationship between the two became extremely unpleasant.[84] Adolf's father beat him almost every day, on one occasion rendering him unconscious.[85] His mother and his older half brother Alois were also beaten. His mother, however, doted on Adolf.[86] As for his siblings, his half brother Alois detested Adolf's flashes of temper,[87] but Adolf seemed to have a good relationship with his sister Paula. At school, he played with other children and invented games for schoolmates to play, but his half brother Alois said that he did not develop real friends.[88] According to one friend, he was given to "sudden bursts of hysterical anger" and grew alienated from the other children.[89]

Whatever respect for authority he might have had disappeared somewhere in his childhood, and he formed his own firm opinions and decided himself how life should be lived. He grew to loathe the Habsburg world and detested the emperor with particular intensity; he developed what he termed "a profound hatred for the Austrian State."[90]

Hitler was an unusually spotty student. He was capable on occasion of very good work, but he was more often prone to abject failure, refusing to work or attend classes. The classical studies of a Lyceum were of no interest to him, so he was sent to the *Realschule*.[91] When he was about to finish *Realschule*, he abruptly refused to take the final test and received no diploma and was unable to advance to *Oberrealschule*.[92]

★ ★ ★

After his mother's death in late 1907, Hitler spent several years in Vienna, some of the time sharing a vermin-infested room with August Kubizek, a young Austrian friend who mostly served as a passive audience willing to listen to young Hitler reciting heroic fantasies. He would work himself to high animation then abruptly leave Kubizek and go off to climb a hilltop to enjoy alone the rapture of his images of pagan Germany in a private reverie of Wagner's music.[93]

Hitler's great ambition from his childhood was to become an artist. However, he was twice rejected by the Vienna Academy of Arts.[94] His paintings were said to be quite good as architectural renderings of the buildings, but his humans were poorly drawn. Disappointed, the once aspiring painter decided he should become an architect.[95] With entire days and years on his hands in Habsburg Vienna, Hitler would attend debates in the House of Deputies.[96] There he observed the political world in action; he became an admirer of Vienna mayor Karl Lueger, leader of the Christian Social Party and a vocal anti-Semite.[97] Long before he met Josef Göbbels, he marveled at the gullibility of the public; he concluded that people were stupid, and he watched with amazement the effectiveness of demagoguery and propaganda.[98] He thought Parliament was a "turbulent mess"; he said it was a "hideous spectacle."[99] He concluded that Parliament was a major cause of the Habsburg decline[100] and decided that the Austrian Parliament should be overthrown.[101]

His life in Vienna was that of a vagabond dreamer and street derelict. For a brief period, he worked as a manual laborer in the building trade.[102] However, he took to arguing with his fellow workers, and they attacked him and threatened to throw him from the scaffolding; so in 1909, he simply quit work.[103] Thereafter, he inexplicably refused to seek employment, though jobs were available, preferring to do as he wished yet hating the miserable lifestyle it caused him. He lived variously in night shelters, group flophouses reminiscent of skid row, and, at times, on an outdoor bench in Prater, the Vienna amusement park. For a time, he took to begging to sustain himself.[104] He described the housing he endured as "loathsome filth" and "appalling misery."[105] His closest flirtation with employment after that was painting postcards and some small watercolors at the suggestion of another resident of a flophouse who assisted with the sales.[106]

His few acquaintances found his tirades against the mongrels of the mixed races of the Habsburg Empire wearisome at best. His entertainment was the Vienna opera house where he somehow found it possible to spend many evenings at Wagner's operas romanticizing pagan Germanic heroic tales. He spent many of his days devouring anti-Semitic pamphlets, and many of his later, most toxic anti-Semitic phrases are traceable to those materials.[107]

His Vienna years were, he said, the most miserable time of his life.[108] And so, on May 24, 1913, he left, hating "repugnant" Vienna with its "mongrel depravity" and Jewish element, to resettle in Munich.[109] There, in the capital of Bavaria, he was delighted to find an entirely German city vastly more pleasing than the mixed-race, multiethnic Vienna. He found even the air and the sounds of Munich instantly refreshing.[110]

★ ★ ★

In 1914, the young Adolf Hitler continued to live a grungy vagabond existence in Munich; he spent many hours reading about Marxism and came to the view that Marxism was a terribly pernicious movement.[111] Those leisurely pursuits were interrupted by a notice from his Austrian past. He was ordered to report for military duty in the Austrian army. His disgruntlement was short lived, however, for when he reported to Salzburg, he was so run down that Austria rejected him as unfit to serve.[112] It was not long, however, before the assassination of the heir to the Austrian throne had Germany mobilizing for war, and when war started, Hitler was delighted. To him, it meant a chance to fulfill his youthful Pan-German dreams—but in a German uniform. He chose a grandiose method to volunteer for the German army; he posted a personal letter to Bavarian king Ludwig III at the Wittlesbach Palace. Soon enough he was enrolled in the First Bavarian Infantry Regiment,[113] which brought him quick and plentiful combat, and all the misery of life in the fetid, cold trenches. Hitler narrowly escaped death many times, performed bravely at every chance, and received citations including the Iron Cross.[114] In combat at the Somme, he suffered a shrapnel wound in the thigh and was evacuated to a hospital near Berlin, where he was treated and sent right back to the front.[115] Hitler received one promotion despite alienating many in his barracks. His diatribes against Jews and Marxists regularly drew shouts and curses from his fellow soldiers.[116]

Hitler fought in the first battle of Ypres and fought there again on October 14, 1918, in the third battle of Ypres[117] when he was blinded by gas in an attack near Werwick. At a hospital near Pasewalk, he slowly began to recover his sight, but suddenly, he lost his vision once again. It happened on November 9, 1918, moments after he heard the jarring news that Germany was surrendering.[118] He thought his world had collapsed and his dreams ended. This blindness was diagnosed as psychosomatic; it was determined to have been a hysterical episode of a psychopath.[119] He soon recovered his sight.

★ ★ ★

Back in Munich after he returned from the war, Hitler found himself confronted by Marxism when communists staged uprisings in Germany. To him, as to many Germans, the Marxists and Jews were viewed as synonymous, and together they seemed to him to pose an existential threat to German tradition and to his Wagnerian dreams.[120] And, like many Germans, he blamed the terms of the Treaty of Versailles and the November criminals who caused it.[121] Hitler was convinced that someone had sabotaged the valiant military with the humiliating armistice. He found Munich overflowing with disillusioned, outraged veterans, many of whom shared this view, and he determined, somehow, that he would get into politics and form a new political movement.[122]

Field Marshall Paul von Hindenburg and General Eric Ludendorff had called with the utmost urgency for an armistice, but neither of them was willing to be the public face of such defeatism. If Hindenburg had at war's end been willing to attest that the army was still capable of defending Germany, President Friedrich Ebert would have refused to sign the Treaty of Versailles.[123] Instead, Hindenburg discreetly went to meet with the kaiser at Spa on September 28, 1918, and insisted that he must accept that the war was lost and seek an armistice. Ludendorff told the foreign minister that the western front was about to collapse.[124] And yet, without missing a beat, they became the loudest condemners of the "November criminals" who had sold out Germany. Both Hindenburg and Ludendorff connived to get others to step out front and become tainted with the appearance that they were the sources of the unpopular decision. Here in 1918, and again in 1933 at the twilight of the Weimar Republic, tragic consequences would flow from Hindenburg's devotion to protecting his own legend at all costs.[125]

Even though Ludendorff and Hindenburg realized that the war was lost, they nevertheless prolonged the fighting briefly and sought to buy time because the Allies refused to negotiate an armistice with, in essence, a German military dictatorship. To mislead the troops to believe continued fighting had a legitimate purpose, Ludendorff spread the false story that the French army was about to collapse due to a sudden epidemic of pneumonic plague.[126] Both Ludendorff and Hindenburg must have been surprised and delighted, if a bit puzzled, to see how easy it was a short time later to manipulate public opinion to reposition themselves and condemn the very armistice they had sought.

Hindenburg and Ludendorff carefully collaborated in preparing the testimony they gave to a committee of the Reichstag, and the testimony of those two major figures helped assure perpetuation of the stab-in-the-back myth (the *Dolchstosslegende*). More important, they shielded themselves from blame

Field Marshal Paul von Hindenburg and General Erich Ludendorff, 1916.
Source: Wikimedia, Creative Commons. Photographer: Ginschel.

for the loss of the war. The false story that Germany was winning the war but had been sold out by the political elites, the establishment, became a powerful tool of Hitler and the Nazis. It is unlikely such falsehood could have gained traction if the two trusted generals had been candid. Indeed, it has been said that Hindenburg's "fatal flaw" was his "inability to take responsibility for Germany's collapse in 1918."[127] Later, Hindenburg would succumb to that flaw again when, in 1933, he made a tragic decision aimed at saving himself, as president, from embarrassing accusations and blame for the collapsing Weimar Republic government.

Before long, Ludendorff would become the leader of the disillusioned veterans chanting the stab-in-the-back myth. Before much longer, Hitler and Ludendorff would be arm in arm.

★ ★ ★

Postwar Munich became a violent place. The streets of the capital of the province of Bavaria were battlegrounds for Marxist revolution. The resulting chaos and barbarity raised a new level of fear of the Left.[128] Radical revolutionary surges seemed to follow one after the other in Bavaria: a takeover attempt by democrats led by Ernst Toller; uprisings of Spartacists, the Whites, and anarchists; formation of a socialist revolutionary government led by Adolph Hoffmann and the overthrow of his government; a revolution led by Kurt Eisner and Eisner's assassination; a Red revolution led by a Russian, Eugen Levine; intrigue by the anti-Semitic Thule Society; and the execution of many of the Thule Society's members.

All these sparked the formation of a Free Corps of ex-soldiers and the hoarding of weapons, mainly to fight the greatest perceived threat to Germany—the Marxist-Leninists.[129] By May 1919, the Free Corps had formed a strong and well-organized paramilitary form of conservative control in Munich and elsewhere. When the signing of the Treaty of Versailles took place on June 28, 1919,[130] the dictates of the treaty limited Germany's army, the Reichswehr, to 100,000 men, and Hitler was one of them. The reduced German army was given the task to maintain peace in Bavaria, a society on the brink, with armed groups forming on the Left and on the Right, a world in which revolutionary plots were reported every day, as communists vied for control against a new right-wing government led by Gustav von Kahr. New groups began to form, and the army found it difficult to determine which groups would require serious surveillance.

★ ★ ★

Stationed in Munich, Hitler was sent one day to the Furstenfelder Hof restaurant to conduct surveillance on a small political party that was to meet there—the German Workers' Party, a group founded by Anton Drexler and philosophically guided by a zealous anti-Semite, Dietrich Eckart. Its membership totaled six people.[131] In September 1919, Hitler dropped in unannounced on the meeting of the group, and he listened with little interest to their speeches. Suddenly, the words of one speaker sent him into a flare of anger and out came one of the tirades he had inflicted on his fellow soldiers so many times in the barracks.

A window into what Hitler's views were at that stage first appeared in a September 16, 1919, letter Hitler drafted to one Adolf Gimlech memorializing the essence of the beliefs that formed his tirades. The letter contains the earliest known written expression of his hatred of the Jews—and the first ominous portent of the Holocaust. He proposed that the state's ultimate goal must be the "*entfernung der Juden*" (the irrevocable removal of the Jews).[132]

The army remained suspicious of the tiny fringe party, so Hitler was sent to a second meeting, held at the Sterneckerbrau.[133] The fervor and intensity of Hitler's words, or his voice, or his manic style, or all of them, had captivated Drexler and Eckart. As he left that meeting, Drexler approached Hitler and handed him a party pamphlet. That night Hitler took the time to read it, and he saw they were of like mind. There he also saw for the first time the label "National Socialism."[134] The pamphlet made clear that Drexler and Eckart were zealous purveyors of a hate-filled agenda that resonated well with Hitler and enticed him to attend a third meeting at the Altes Rosenbad.

The next week his commanding officer asked Hitler to join the German Workers' Party to help the army gain support from workers.[135] He became the party's seventh member.[136] Eckart envisioned that a messianic leader would one day appear to bring his wild ideas to life, and to him, Hitler was a godsend. There is little to indicate that Hitler was a source of significant information or knowledge that would galvanize such people to fall in behind him for intellectual reasons, but his fervent speeches captivated this group. Indeed his close friend, Putzi Hanfstaengl, observed that Hitler was not only quite ignorant but also had a complex that compelled him to reject the very idea of learning anything.[137] Yet, by 1920 Hitler had been made the leader of the renamed party, now called the National Socialist German Workers' Party, and that year, Hitler chose their symbol—the swastika with the crossed *hakenkreuz*, the Z-like symbol of the ancients.[138]

★ ★ ★

Kurt von Schuschnigg spent his postwar years in a starkly changed Austria; the loyal Habsburg youth—who had marched off proudly in 1914 to a seemingly justifiable brief skirmish with little Serbia over its role in the assassination of his future emperor—came shuffling back home in 1919 from a prisoner-of-war camp to a destitute Innsbruck with no employment and no prospects.

The returning veterans found that the life they knew was gone.[139] Kurt was no exception. Innsbruck had little to provide; and even his warm family home was cold and bare. Their furniture had disappeared during the brutal war. There was scant chance of employment, and what few jobs could be found were temporary. Their modest savings could not support the bourgeois life they had enjoyed and hyperinflation ravaged Austria from 1919 to 1922.[140] As with other Austrians who had survived, the war had stolen their youth, and the poverty that resulted from it was strangling their transition to adulthood. The little money any Austrians might have would quickly dissolve in their purses while they slept, eaten by the termites of the breathtakingly quick inflation, forcing most to sell or barter whatever they owned just to have food, requiring many to rent out rooms, turn kitchens into extra bedrooms, and double up to make housing affordable.[141] However, unlike the millions left in muddy graves, the Schuschniggs were alive and well, and this fact was never lost on them.[142]

Despite the need to start life over, Kurt was still a young man—and a resilient one.[143] Even a healthy family had to eat, and food was extremely scarce. General von Schuschnigg's small pension was all they had. Kurt was determined to avoid burdening his parents, but he had no money to enable him to strike out for the capital of Vienna where opportunity was greater.

His first priority was to find a way to complete his education in order to attain relief from the postwar chaos surrounding him. Fortunately, Innsbruck, though small, was home to a fine university,[144] and he began the study of law. He also fell in with the evolving sociopolitical organizations in Innsbruck,[145] a city filled with veterans, many of whom were overcome with malaise and anger over the war.[146]

In 1925, he finished his legal studies, ranking first in his class. Armed with a degree from the University of Innsbruck, he passed the required exam and began practice in Innsbruck under the guidance of a well-established lawyer.[147] He undertook additional studies at the Academy of Commerce, anticipating a business practice.

★ ★ ★

Kurt's personal life received a welcome boost when he met a young woman from Bolzano, Herma Masera. From their first meeting, he found it easy to converse with her and was delighted to learn that her great interest was classical music. From that moment on, they shared the delight of listening together to the music that each loved the most. And, music aside, Herma was quite beautiful.[148]

He was encouraged by their initial encounters, and he traveled to Bolzano to see her again. Bolzano, however, had become part of Italy in the postwar division of spoils, and he had to deal with irritating burdens—not only the travel but also the tedium of completing visa forms, being asked the same questions over and over, and awaiting approval before he could cross the border.[149] Then, he did it again. He soon realized that these irritants were not dissuading him from going to Bolzano repeatedly. He was in love with his soulmate, and he repeated the treks to see her for two years.

Herma was equally taken with Kurt, and their romance blossomed into an engagement; they wed and began married life in Innsbruck. Herma was happy to look forward to a quiet future with a promising provincial lawyer. Their son, Kurti, was born in 1926, and at last, the Great War became a nearly forgotten adventure as a charmed future spread out before the lucky young family.

★ ★ ★

Kurt had no interest in entering politics; indeed, he had a profound aversion to the political world.[150] For the next five years, he enjoyed the practice of law in closely knit Innsbruck where his intelligence was on display and obvious to judges, to the influential clergy of Innsbruck, and to the political kingmakers.[151] Class warfare was fueling political bitterness in postwar Austria and driving Austrians into polarized groups. Attendance at discussion groups pulled Kurt into political debate. He detested the raucous politics of postwar Europe, but in time, colleagues put his name forward on a party list; those names on the list were put forward by a party for seats in Parliament. Young members of the Volkspartei, the Tyrol Christian Socials, nominated him in April 1927 for the Nationalrat, the House of Representatives or National Council, the more powerful lower house of the Diet (Parliament). In 1927, the list he was on was elected, and he was swept into the orbit of government.[152]

★ ★ ★

Austria's legislature was a very unpopular institution, and quite a different organ of government from some other parliaments. Votes were cast for lists of candidates who had been handpicked by party leaders. The Austrian public did not have a chance to pick and choose among the individual candidates party leaders selected.[153]

Worse, the Parliament he entered as a very junior member was fragmented and always near deadlock; both the Nationalrat (National Council) and the Bundesrat (Federal Council or upper house), were dominated by two almost equally powerful parties, the Christian Socials and the Social Democrats. The Christian Socials drew their support from the countryside and the Social Democrats from Vienna and industrial areas.[154] Those two parties each controlled roughly one-third of the seats in the Nationalrat. The final third for whose support they competed was chosen by the other parties and eclectic voters, mixed groups who based their votes for the smaller parties on many different issues—social strata, nostalgia for the Habsburg Empire, agrarian policies, different religions, and segments within religions. There were also a number of anti-parliamentarians, Marxists, and anti-Marxists.[155] The resulting Diet was made up of fragile coalitions sometimes held in power by a single representative's vote.

He found the Vienna government crippled by the frequent deadlock in Parliament. His party, the conservative Christian Socials, was stymied by the socialist and Marxist party, the Social Democrats. The gridlocked Parliament was unable to pass the measures that were needed to deal with the crises—unemployment, inflation, and the Great Depression. As a result, the Christian Social coalition government struggled against bank failures, violence from paramilitary groups, and increasing terrorism. The challenge was to make that government function and try to rescue Austria from a postwar economy on the brink of collapse. The nation was struggling to pay the crushing debt of the war reparations that had been imposed on Germany and Austria. Together, unemployment and the war debt threatened Austrians just as intensely as they threatened the German economy.

Catholics heavily supported the Christian Social Party, but they did not vote as a bloc; otherwise the Social Democrats and Christian Socials would not have been so nearly evenly matched in the Diet. In the act of voting, Austrians were inevitably guided far more by their personal circumstances: Were they poor or middle class? Were they rural or Viennese? Were they workers, clerks, laborers, or shopkeepers? Were they farmers or tradesmen? These economic political issues that directly affected a voter's own class and financial interests typically trumped the religious identity of a candidate or party on election day. This was so for Catholics, Jews, and Protestants.

For a brief period, immediately after the war, the Social Democrats had been able to lead coalition governments formed with the Christian Socials.[156] At that time, the Social Democrats had just enough popular political wind at their back. They benefited from the public's memory that they had been the people who opposed both the war and the monarchy.[157] However, the Social Democrats led by an Austro-Marxist, Karl Renner, as chancellor were only able to hold power for a short time, from 1918 to July 1920. The Christian Socials formed a coalition government on July 7, 1920, without the Social Democrats, and thereafter the Christian Socials ruled with the support of other coalition partners well into the 1930s.[158]

The Christian Socials' hold on government, however, was constantly in danger; the government could fall from power over any important issue, and their governments as a result were weak. They were firmly opposed to the socialist wing of the labor movement, and many Christian Social politicians berated socialists and opposed Marxism intensely.[159]

The Christian Socials attempted to form a coalition with the Social Democrats after July 1920, but their efforts proved fruitless.[160] They had to form their coalitions with the so-called bourgeois parties, the Pan-Germans and the Agricultural League.[161] Once the Social Democrats went into opposition, the party became more and more a determined enemy of the Christian

Socials. Before long the Social Democrats made a public vow to oppose totally the efforts of the Christian Social government.

Aggravating their social policy differences was the great divide—religion against atheism. The Social Democrats professed atheism while the Christian Socials were mostly Catholics. The two groups were so polarized that the Social Democrats became not merely the perennial opposition party; their most radical wing was angry, intransigent, and volatile.[162] The rhetoric of the Social Democrats and their Schutzbund paramilitaries was incendiary. As the years of Christian Social control rolled on, the socialists began to speak of civil war and appeared to be on the verge of taking to the streets.[163] The Christian Social coalition governments endured a daily barrage of the socialists' political attacks, and eventually, the rhetoric turned to sporadic violence.[164]

In that environment, the Nazis of Austria found electoral opportunity and made a startling breakthrough, gaining sufficient seats in the provincial and national parliaments to advance their aim to destroy the government entirely.[165]

★ ★ ★

The Austrian chancellors who were elected by the Parliament were virtually at the mercy of this "immobile" body[166] because most government power had been placed in the Parliament. A constitutional change would be necessary for reform, but no coalition could muster the two-thirds majority needed to enact it.[167] This hamstrung the chancellor and made the demands for abolishing Parliament popular throughout Austria.[168]

Although Austria's president was a respected and influential figurehead, he had no significant governmental powers.[169] Provincial parliaments and municipal councils suffered under the same system. The result was a government that had become a facade of democracy without the substance of a genuine people's voice. Most debilitating was that the president, chancellor, and cabinet even together lacked power to act decisively.[170] The government was never in a position to solve critical problems but, instead, repeatedly provided only unsatisfactory half-solutions to the postwar economic and political crises.

II

CRISES

Threats to the Independence of Austria

*P*ostwar Austria became a toxic mix of ideological, economic, social, cultural, and ethnic differences. Several segments of the population were at loggerheads with each other; their fights were fueled by perceived economic injustice producing class warfare and hyper-polarization of the Left from the Right. One overriding dispute emerged: many Austrian Pan-German nationalists called "Blues" were vocal political opponents of the "Blacks" who wanted continued independence for Austria.

The economic conditions Austria had to endure after the Great War heated these toxic ingredients to a boil. The toughest blow was unemployment at a dramatic level. Added to that was the financial drain of the war debt imposed by the Allies in the Treaty of St. Germain. Austria's government was unable to generate tax revenues to infuse the nation with financial stamina. Access to markets to export Austrian products was difficult for the small, landlocked country. Austria was dependent on good relations with the Weimar Republic. This awful economy made Austria exceptionally vulnerable to the Great Depression, which made the economic pain exponentially worse. An emergency loan was the only hope to keep Depression-era Austria afloat, but obtaining one from the international community for such an unstable borrower as Austria was extremely difficult.

The Soviet Union was pushing communist expansion in Europe, so a Bolshevik-style Marxist revolution was a constant concern and became the great fear of Austrians into the early 1930s. They saw how Germany had been racked by a Marxist revolt right after the war, and Marxists and socialists in Austria together supported a Far Left paramilitary called the Schutzbund. It was well armed but was being kept at bay by Ernst von Starhemberg's equally well-armed conservative Heimwehr paramilitary. Revolution was the government's constant worry. Until 1932, these other threats exceeded the Nazi threat.

* * *

It only took a few weeks in Vienna for Kurt von Schuschnigg to learn that the political world he had entered greatly magnified the intensity of debate over subjects he had discussed in relative calm in the coffeehouses of Tyrol. There, the issue of Pan-Germanism was white hot. Its most extreme element was found in the disorganized, violent Nazi Party. As the ultimate German nationalists, the Nazis championed Anschluss—union with Germany—as the solution to the Bolshevik threat and the answer to all of Austria's economic problems. They lobbied all nationalists to join with them, and they had a large target audience because a sizable portion of the Austrian population embraced some form of German nationalism. They ranged from those who merely reminisced about their German heritage to many others who wanted some special alliance. Many Pan-German Austrians were tempted to join the Nazi Party. The varying degrees of support for the Pan-German agenda all had roots in the Bismarck banishment of Austria.

* * *

Most Austrians were of Germanic stock and proud of it. Some 96 percent of them spoke German.[1] The heritage of the Germanic peoples was at the root of Austrian patriotism, nurtured by the tales of the tribes from which they descended. This was the heritage not only of people in Germany but also of many others of Germanic stock living in Austria, Hungary, Czechoslovakia, and elsewhere. However, the Germanic pride of those Austrians had suffered a powerful rebuke in the nineteenth century.

Until 1866, Austria had been the center of the German Confederation and the leading member of the Germanic states of Europe. While fervently Germanic, Austrians had a distinctly different culture, tradition, and religion. Austria was 90 percent Catholic[2] while Germany was more heavily Protestant. But in 1866, Germany's Iron Chancellor, Otto von Bismarck, put an end to Catholic Austria's leading role when he crafted the intrigue that started the Austro-German War and achieved his goal of vaulting Germany and its House of Brandenburg to the leadership of the Germanic people.[3] The war ended with the creation of a new North German Confederation and, in 1871, the adoption of the Constitution of the German Empire. The Habsburg Empire and Catholic Austria were excluded. Austria aligned with the far less Germanic monarchy of Hungary in the Austro-Hungarian Empire in 1867.[4]

That banishment, what Hitler would call "the humiliation of Austria," continued to disturb many postwar Austrian Germans; some never became reconciled to the exclusion of Austria from Germany.[5]

Austrians of German stock were never entirely comfortable with the multiethnic, multireligious society of Austria-Hungary; many Germanic Austrians longed for a country populated only by Germans and for a union of some sort with Weimar Republic Germany. Some Austrian Pan-Germans preferred what they termed *alliances*, informal special relationships among all heavily Germanic nations. However, many Pan-Germans feared that smaller Austria was not big enough to survive on its own without Germany. At the extreme edge were some radical Pan-Germans who were willing to use violence to force a union with Germany and thus accepted Adolf Hitler, who said he felt so intensely about the separation of the Germans that it caused him "perpetual heartache."[6] In reality, support for Anschluss by many Austrians was based on "Austrian anti-Semitism" (according to Jewish writer Oskar Karbach).[7]

Practical economics played a large role in the Anschluss debate. Austrian business had the potential to benefit from Anschluss. The empire lost 60 percent of its territory after the war, and Austria's economy was so weakened by its new national borders that some professors taught that Anschluss creating a single German state and a single large German market was an utter necessity for Austria.[8] Austria was heavily dependent on exporting to Germany and attracting Germany's citizens to vacation in the Austrian Tyrol, a magnet for German tourists. The Tyrolers' *Alpland* newspaper made it clear to Germans that the more Germans who came to Austria, the better.

Immediately after the Great War, a majority of Austrians, left adrift by the end of the empire,[9] wanted to become part of Germany just to survive. Both the Social Democrats and the Christian Socials had then favored Anschluss. Austria's first postwar chancellor, the Marxist intellectual Social Democrat Karl Renner, was then an especially outspoken proponent of Anschluss.[10]

However, in 1919 the Allies forbade Anschluss. When the Treaty of St. Germain was signed, the Allies rejected any union of Germany and Austria, and much of the pro-Anschluss sentiment waned after that. By the 1930s, the Christian Social Party had decided for its own reasons to oppose Anschluss; their reversal had two goals—keeping Austria independent of its larger neighbor and keeping Austria Catholic and free from the greater Protestant influence in Germany.

The attitudes of many Austrians began to change, however, as Nazism became more visible and more ugly. Many Austrian Pan-Germans came to realize that, if the Nazis actually seized power in Germany, they would have to reassess whether they wanted a union of any sort with a Nazi government. For some, any such affiliation would be out of the question. For others, Nazi control might not even dampen their desire for Anschluss. For the many Nazis in Austria, Nazi rule of Germany would make Anschluss all the more welcome.

★ ★ ★

When Kurt von Schuschnigg entered Parliament, Hitler and the Nazi Party were not in power or on the threshold. Weimar Germany was still controlled

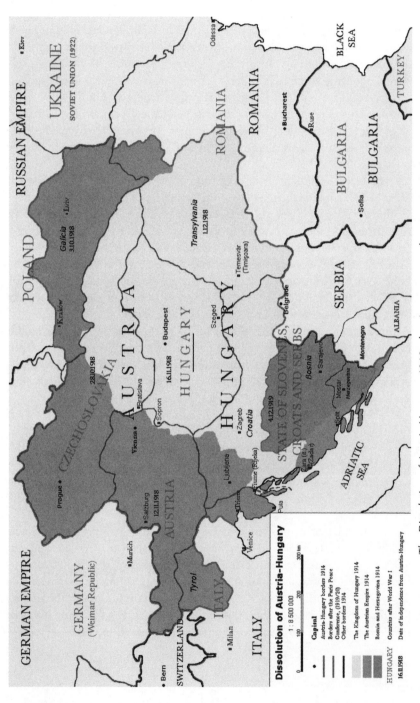

The Dissolution of Austria-Hungary, 1918, showing prewar and postwar territories.

Source: Wikimedia, Creative Commons. Modifications by P. S. Burton.

by other parties and other leaders, and the Nazi threat was still far behind the Marxist threat. Austrians were exceptionally anxious about such dangers. Less than a year before the overthrow of the czar, Austria's prime minister, Count Karl von Stürgkh, was assassinated, and it was a Marxist who murdered him.[11] So Austrian soldiers froze when news of the overthrow of the czar reached them on the battlefield.[12] Austrians at home had the same reaction; the thought of Marxist revolutionaries suddenly rising up as they had in Russia to overthrow their rulers and create a new world order in Austria and elsewhere solidified their fear of the Left.

The "Blues," Pan-Germans, faced off against the "Blacks," the Austrian Nationalists.[13] And their most heated disagreement was whether Anschluss was necessary, if for no other reason, to ward off the Bolsheviks. Conservatives wanted protection against chaos striking their world from the Far Left. The socialists in Austria wanted serious reform of that world. The Austro-Marxists wanted an end to it.

These political groups armed themselves, each planning to defend Austria against the threats that terrified them. Austria's postwar governments had to contend with armed camps of paramilitaries facing off against equally armed opposing camps. Daily life in Austria seemed unstable, with conservative Catholics, Marxists, communists, socialist workers, and Nazis all supporting paramilitaries with powerful supplies of weapons. Soon the paramilitary groups were flexing their own political muscle.

Austrians felt the need for the security of these paramilitaries in part because the severely diminished Austrian army looked too weak to defend against the Marxist threat. Fear of Marxists was enhanced when the Austro-Marxist, Karl Renner, succeeded in attracting enough support at the polls to form coalition governments from 1918 to 1920. Anti-Marxists armed themselves to prepare to put down a revolution. Though the Treaty of St. Germain severely limited the size of the Austrian military, it did not prevent political or religious groups from forming their own private militias, much as the German Nazis formed their SA Brownshirts squads, and others formed the German nationalist paramilitary group, the Steel Helmet (Der Stahlhelm).[14]

The Austrian army, the Bundesheer, was very small, as ordered by the victorious Allies; however, it was even further weakened by a fundamental disagreement between the two major Austrian political parties over the mission of the military. These parties were not just political enemies; they were pursuing entirely different national goals. They were unable to agree what the strategic purpose of the army should be, and neither side was willing to appropriate the funds to raise troop strength even to the size allowed by the treaty. Instead, they increased their own armed militias, which gave rise to a chronic condition of incipient civil war. This stalemate created what was termed a "half-way house between a parliamentary and a soviet republic."[15]

The conservative militia, the Heimwehr, and the socialists' Schutzbund were the dominant militias, but several other religious and splinter groups also formed their own. In its earliest days immediately after the war, the Heimwehr aligned with the Christian Social Party. In due time, however, it became a powerful political force, barely coexisting with the party. The dubious backgrounds of some Heimwehr leaders put off some of the leaders of the Christian Social Party it professed to support. As Nazis attracted more and more supporters in Styria where the Heimwehr also thrived, the Heimwehr followed a different path than the Christian Socials, and at the most crucial moments for Austria, the leaders of government came to distrust the Heimwehr leaders.

The Heimwehr insisted that it had no aggressive ideology but existed only to defend against a Marxist/socialist revolution. However, the Heimwehr became a political force of its own. Even while it ostensibly functioned under the tent of the Christian Socials, many of the Heimwehr members began to proclaim that parliamentary government was unworkable in postwar Austria.[16]

★ ★ ★

The Schutzbund was formed under the leadership of socialist politician Julius Deutsch; it too became a political power, and it was more loyal to the Social Democrats than the Heimwehr was to the Christian Socials. Both militias became demanding constituencies and, thus, were influential with the party leaders. Though each was an army of sorts, both militias eluded control by the successive Austrian governments.

The Schutzbund was especially alarming; it had a stockpile of guns, hand grenades, machine guns, and bombs in its strongholds in Vienna and other locales.[17] The Schutzbund and the Heimwehr launched assaults against each other usually attempting to find and decommission the weapons stashed away by the other. Eventually, by the 1930s these became near constant skirmishes. One newspaper described the resulting popular anxiety as "terror and counter-terror."[18] Despite relatively few deaths from this violence, the Schutzbund was feared by the Christian Socials as an "instrument of brutal force."[19]

Concern over the drift of the Heimwehr eventually caused Christian Social leaders to rethink their alliance. Some Heimwehr members were sounding similar to the fledgling Nazis in Styria where the Heimwehr was rooted. It had been founded in the 1920s by Innsbruck lawyer Richard Steidle, a skillful orator and agitator, who succeeded in bringing several such groups together and forming them into the leading force against socialists and communists.[20] Since many Jewish Austrians were also prominent leftists, the Heimwehr took on the appearance of hostility not just to the Left but also to the Jews. Steidle insisted, however, that he and his Heimwehr were not anti-Semitic; he opposed only those Jews who were in the Schutzbund but welcomed Jews into the Heimwehr. However, less temperate Heimwehr officials undermined his claim since not all Heimwehr leaders were as grudgingly tolerant. Walter Pfrimer, the Heimwehr leader in Styria, where anti-Semitism ruled the day, was widely considered an unvarnished anti-Semite.

★ ★ ★

The Austrian Heimwehr and Austrian Nazis were early on hostile organizations, yet similarities in their severely Pan-German and anti-Marxist propaganda blurred the lines between them. As some Heimwehr units became increasingly fascist, their members became sympathetic to the Nazis and more hostile to the government; they began to resemble the Nazis' SA (Sturmabteilung) and appeared to be supporting each other.[21] Some Heimwehr units took in individual Nazis and their fellow travelers as members,[22] and many Heimwehr members went on to become Nazi Party members.[23] The Nazis welcomed them and made overtures to the Heimwehr leaders to merge with them.[24]

The precise mission statement of the Heimwehr was difficult for others to deduce, and it changed with the leadership. Its early leader, Richard Steidle, promulgated a Heimwehr platform known as the Korneuberger Oath, announced in the city of Korneuberg on May 18, 1930. The oath enshrined Steidle's view of the Heimwehr philosophy and goals[25]—the support of fascism and the rejection of electoral politics as un-German. However, when many Heimwehr members disagreed with the oath, Steidle lost power.

When Steidle fell, the even more worrisome arm of the group, Walter Pfrimer and the Styrians, filled the void. Pfrimer and his associates attempted a putsch against the Christian Social government. He and his local cohort staged a "march on Vienna" in 1931 to echo Mussolini's March on Rome in 1922. They intended to bring down the government, but the march on Vienna failed. Pfrimer and eight of his associates were put on trial, but all of them were acquitted.[26]

★ ★ ★

Prince Ernst von Starhemberg became the new national leader of the Heimwehr.[27] He had lost his title as prince in 1919 when Chancellor Karl Renner abolished all hereditary titles, but he continued his ambitious advance in the leadership of the Heimwehr. Starhemberg added to the suspicion that the Heimwehr shared the Nazi ideology for he had once been an ally of Hitler and at least flirted with Nazism when living in Germany. Starhemberg claimed to have lost interest when Hitler's clownish Beer Hall Putsch was crushed in 1923. However, his bravado, body language, and dictatorial look called to mind the agitated style of Hitler and the daring puffed chest of Mussolini, and the taller, more imposing Starhemberg was at times even more charismatic.

His competition in the Heimwehr, Emil Fey and Odo Neustädter-Stürmer, were openly fascist and constantly plotting ways to best each other and move up to take the leadership.[28] Eventually, government leaders had to wonder whether this once friendly militia had become a group of armed-to-the-teeth Nazi sympathizers. Later they would learn that several Heimwehr leaders—including Fey, Steidle, Count Johann Alberti, and Starhemberg[29]—approached Austrian Nazi leader Theo Habicht with proposals for coordinating their efforts and to merge the Heimwehr and the Nazis to form an Austrian-Fascist Front.

Schuschnigg steered clear of the Heimwehr. Starhemberg, however, was a political force, and Schuschnigg had no choice but to deal with him and his Heimwehr constituents despite his dislike of Starhemberg's Pan-German fervor, his fear of Starhemberg's impulsiveness,[30] and the Heimwehr's fascist attitudes[31] that adorned its "shady side."[32]

After the Great War, Schuschnigg helped form a Catholic youth organization called the Ostmarkische Sturmscharen, an ideological counter to the Heimwehr, a Young Austria militia espousing Catholicism and opposing Marxism.[33] Its goal was to nurture Austrian ethnicity, Habsburg culture, and Catholicism in preference to the German National type of Prussian German ethnicity, Hohenzollern culture and Protestantism. This group opposed the Pan-Germanism rampant in certain parts of Austria.[34] While the other groups were stashing weapons, Schuschnigg saw this and other organizations with which he affiliated as little more than marching societies notable only for a vague longing for the restoration of the Habsburgs; by 1936, this group had declared itself a merely cultural organization.[35]

Restoration of the Habsburg monarchy, however, was more than mere nostalgia for some others; it was a point of serious dispute among many Austrians. Some believed that the only government that could be effective was a restored Habsburg monarchy led by an emperor who could brush aside the dysfunctional parliamentary regime. That was the goal of the Nibelungia; they hoped to place Prince Otto von Habsburg, the Pretender, on the throne.[36] The Nazis, however, were determined that this would never happen.

★ ★ ★

Often near chaos in their first decade, the Nazis, nevertheless, were a determined slice of society, and they began to grow in power not only in Germany but also in Austria. As vocal and violent as the Social Democrats of Austria and their Schutzbund paramilitaries were, they paled in comparison to the Nazis of Austria. As demanding as the Austrian Nazis were in the days before Hitler took power in Germany, from 1933 on they were awash in hubris.

Even before Hitler's breakthrough, Austrians could see that he had plans that might very soon lead to war. Many had read his disturbing diatribes and were alarmed when Nazis began achieving political success.

People began to realize that the goals he laid out in *Mein Kampf* were not merely provocative cant.

As early as 1925, Adolf Hitler's goal was Anschluss and nothing less. He wrote then that "Austria's dissolution as a State appeared to me only as the first step toward the emancipation of the German nation." And for him personally, the Anschluss would be "the fulfillment of what my heart had always longed for."[37] Hitler's determination to take Austria—to do it somehow, and with force only if necessary—was very clear to others. Mussolini warned Schuschnigg in 1934: "[Y]ou cannot hope that the Third Reich will ever leave Austria in peace."[38]

The appeal of Nazism had been strong in Austria for some time, particularly among the Pan-German population.[39] The appeal Nazis offered—pointing to the economic recovery of Germany under Hitler—fell on fertile ground in Austria.[40] The initial organization that became the Austrian Nazi Party predated the 1920 founding of the Nazi Party in Germany by more than fifteen years. Nazism also achieved a stronger grip on the irate psyche of those Austrians who were Nazis; anti-Semitism among Austrians who were Nazis was equally or more virulent than that of the German Nazis.[41] Most Austrians, however, were not Nazis, and their clashes with those who were made for considerable violence in Vienna, Innsbruck, and Styria.

Anti-Semitism was a remnant of Austria's history, but it remained widespread, and the Nazis' extreme anti-Semitism drew many Austrians to join the Nazi party and accept their hate-filled agenda.[42] They were a distinct minority party; nevertheless, in post-Habsburg Austria their influence was enhanced by terrorism and propaganda. The Nazis' willingness to assassinate higher officials and lesser opponents gave them the powerful weapon of fear, producing an oversized impact. In 1933 and 1934, the Austrian Nazis, guided by German Nazi officials in Munich, committed frequent bombings targeting tourist centers and railroads—treating the public to photos of trains derailed by bombs to make Austria appear unsafe and damaging its economy by frightening off tourists.[43] The propaganda they used was guided by the master of the era, Josef Göbbels.

In the social and political calculus, Austrian Nazis benefited from the fragmented opposition against them. Non-Nazi Austria was evenly and heatedly divided. Having the Christian Socials nearly at civil war with the liberals of the working-class Social Democrats paid dividends for the Nazis.

The secret sauce of Nazi propaganda was that their platforms were deliberately ambiguous and implausible, based not on truth but on promises—often incoherent, even contradictory promises. But they were always promises to take action, bold action, and always it was action against designated enemies. The enemies were Nazi constructs, but each targeted enemy was made to sound minimally believable to distressed angry segments of society.[44] They were willing to make dramatic promises that other politicians, constrained by reality, refused to make.[45] They made exhilarating economic promises to Austrians even as Hitler enforced his tourist boycott of Austria and his boycott of Jewish-made Austrian goods, both intended to hurt Austria's economy.[46] Hitler's focus on Jews and Bolsheviks and the international financial world was especially dishonest. Although Jews were only 0.76 percent of the German population, he attributed most societal ills to them; although Jews were only 2 percent of the bankers and brokers, he attributed financial hegemony to them.[47] Even before Hitler took power, Nazis in Germany and Austria were providing evidence that Hitler's madness, hatred of Jews, and other portents of what he came to be were every bit as grotesque as they sounded. In 1932, Jews were repeatedly attacked by Austrian Nazis.

One word began to underscore the prospect of coming conquest—Hitler's demand for *Lebensraum* (living space). This slogan of his expansionism sounded more and more like a muted warning of coming aggression to bring Austria and Czechoslovakia into the Third Reich. His threat, to his delight, was being met only by appeasement.

Concerned as they were, western Europeans were not sufficiently alarmed to overcome the paralysis that appeasement was causing, and none were preparing adequately for the possibility of war. European nations had once been enthusiastic about war, even cocky. That changed when the reality of the Great War turned their jubilant citizens into mourners. Instead of enjoying the short, glorious, and profitable war that many had imagined, they had instead suffered horribly for four years, and then recession and depression followed. By the 1930s, no European nation including Weimar Germany had any appetite for another war, and few in Europe could bring themselves to believe that the Nazis in Germany could want one either. And the reality was that virtually disarmed Austria was unable to wage anything remotely like a war against Germany. Prior to 1932, the fear of a Nazi war did not drive European or Austrian policy, for Europeans could quite reasonably believe that the Nazis would be unable to take over either in Germany or in Austria.

So Austrians were astonished when the Nazis made their breakthrough in the Austrian political arena in 1932. The Nazi Party enlisted Josef Göbbels to devise their campaign propaganda for the provincial elections in Lower Austria, Salzburg, and Vienna. Using his innovative techniques, the Austrian Nazis succeeded in electing a surprising number of deputies—including fifteen to the Vienna Provincial Council.[48] In Austria's last free local elections in 1933, Nazis, who had only been polling between 15 and 24 percent in the provinces where Nazism was strongest, suddenly reached 41 percent in Innsbruck. After that shock, the government refused to risk further elections.[49]

What had been concern about Nazis now became real alarm. The earthquake at the polls demonstrated the effectiveness of Göbbels's propaganda machinery and revealed that the Austrian electoral process was extremely vulnerable to being hijacked by Nazi Germany.[50] The underlying reality was that Nazism was growing; while a reliable count of party membership was not available at that time, later information showed that the Nazis were attracting a sizable new membership in Austria, growing from 69,000 in 1934 to 164,000 in 1938.[51]

The Austrian Nazis drew from many segments of the Austrian population, but they were largely a proletarian party, heavy in people from the border areas. Most were young; students made up most Nazi groups, and Nazi students gained control of many student organizations. Their professors also often joined the Nazis.[52] Nazi leadership in Austria included Josef Leopold, Alfred Proksch, Leopold Tavs, and Anton Rintelen. While Nazis were mostly men, they also boasted many women.[53] The Nazis presented a worrisome contrast with the demographic makeup of the Christian Social Party. The Christian Socials were older; they had become more upper class and included many military officers and clerics, and most of their votes were cast by women.[54] The youth of the Austrian Nazis added to the warning signs that they were growing in numbers and would continue to do so.

★ ★ ★

Postwar Austrian officials were strangers to self-government. When the Great War ended, the foundation of Austria's history and security, the centuries-old Habsburg monarchy, had disappeared, and the ensuing experiment with parliamentary rule did not go well. The glue holding the people together had been the patriarchal Emperor Franz Joseph. Without him, Austrians fumbled trying to discover a new self-concept and a new form of government that could get them through the crises of the 1920s.

Their first postwar chancellor, scholarly Marxist Karl Renner, pleaded for relief, telling the victorious Allies that Austria would not be able to survive under the burden of the debt being imposed as war reparations.[55] Renner argued that the aggressor in the war along with Germany had been the Habsburg regime; that their empire had come to an end; and that his Austria was an entirely new and much smaller country carved out of the German-speaking areas of Habsburg Austria. Renner implored that the War Guilt clause not be used to impose war reparations on this new country. He emphasized that Austria was central only to starting the war, and it did so only after it had suffered the provocation of an assassination. Ownership of the war, he explained, had been taken by Kaiser Wilhelm II of Germany, who changed the war to serve his own goal of European conquest.

The Allies, however, were unreceptive; they acknowledged many of the facts underlying Austria's plea but decided that none of it warranted any relief: "Austria should be held to assume its entire share of responsibility for the crime which has unchained upon the world such a calamity."[56] The new Austria was stuck with paying a full share of the war reparations.

★ ★ ★

By the 1920s, Austria's economy was as bad as predicted; economic instability led to hyperinflation. Unemployment was as high as 25 percent in the 1920s. Although the currency became stabilized by 1925, credit was virtually unavailable.[57] Violent protests erupted repeatedly, and the risks of violence and assassination were an everyday worry. This economic distress persisted into the 1930s and the Great Depression. When the Creditanstalt Bank failed, exports fell, unemployment rose dramatically, and industrial production dropped.[58] Nearly 600,000 people were out of work,[59] and tax revenue virtually dried up.[60]

After more than a decade of this misery, Austria also had to deal with the economic sanctions imposed by Germany to bully Austria into submission.[61] And Austria watched with a quickening pulse as Germany brazenly thumbed its nose and began to raise a powerful army.

★ ★ ★

These crises wore down one Austrian chancellor after another as a succession of coalition governments gained little purchase in the early 1920s. Parties changed leaders and coalition partners in rapid succession. As this continued, the "political machine ground to a standstill. The brakes were still functioning but the steering was dangerous."[62] The split placed the balance of power in the hands of one or more German Nationalist parties; whichever of the two dominant parties the German Nationalists decided to support would head future governments. Johannes Schöber took office leading a coalition of the Christian Social Party and the Greater German People's Party;[63] Schöber, however, died the next year.

★ ★ ★

A new era in the life of the fledgling First Republic of Austria appeared to have arrived when a strong figure, a priest, Monsignor Ignaz Seipel of the Christian Social Party, became chancellor of Austria in 1922 succeeding Schöber. Seipel was such a dominating person that he became the authoritative figure in government,[64] and others grew weary of trying to contest his rule. Seipel's hold over his party was due in large measure to the fact that he was widely respected and trusted by many Austrians at various levels of the classes that struggled with each other in the daily turmoil of Austria.[65] Not surprisingly, a conscientious cleric serving as a chancellor found that there were serious tensions arising from his two roles. Seipel could see this himself, and he recorded the stress he experienced in troubled terms in his diaries.[66] Seipel's resilience did not, however, translate to success in enlivening the economy.

★ ★ ★

It was during Seipel's last years that Schuschnigg became a member of the Diet. Though members of the same party, the two never became close; indeed, they had few significant conversations.[67] Schuschnigg envisioned that his unexpected stint in Parliament would be a short-term adventure, and he did not rent a permanent apartment in Vienna.[68] Seipel was the party leader, and to Schuschnigg, he seemed aloof; he never reached out to Schuschnigg nor encouraged a relationship. And Schuschnigg, as a junior legislator, lacked the assertiveness to approach the intimidating chancellor.[69] As a "freshman" legislator, he followed Seipel's political lead, and he did not find it easy trying to speak out from a most junior seat in the Nationalrat.[70] There were occasions on which Schuschnigg found that he and Seipel were on different sides of an issue, and Schuschnigg had to go against Seipel. He learned each time to his chagrin that it was Seipel who was the one in control of the Christian Social Party.[71] Seipel, nevertheless, formed a high opinion of Schuschnigg.[72]

As he led cobbled-together coalitions, Seipel was in and out of office more than once. Even his strong efforts to stabilize the currency, however, failed, and his attempts to inject momentum into a weak and chaotic economy were beginning to seem futile.[73] But other chancellors who tried—Carl Vaugoin, Rudolf Ramek, Ernst Steeruwitz, and Otto Ender—fared no better, and Seipel kept returning to leadership throughout the 1920s.[74]

The Great Depression, however, so devastated the economy that the powerful eventually lost faith in the party. Seipel then started to pull away from his dominant role. He concluded that the very structure of Austrian government must be entirely reformed in order to function, and he decided to resign. His withdrawal in 1929 was accelerated by failing health. Despite his illness, Seipel tried to form a cabinet composed of all parties, a so-called national government, in 1931. The failure was Seipel's last gasp, and it may have been the last chance to save parliamentary government in Austria.[75] Once the monsignor retreated from the leadership, others came forward to try to lead Austria out of the Great Depression.[76]

Three short-term chancellors followed Seipel's last term, and in 1931, Karl Buresch took office. Chancellor Buresch made an effort to bring new blood into the Austrian government, bringing in a younger generation of ministers. He formed a cabinet of the center and chose as his minister of agriculture a dynamic, agrarian economist, thirty-nine-year-old Engelbert Dollfuss.[77] For his minister of justice, Buresch made an especially interesting choice.

★ ★ ★

Kurt von Schuschnigg was surprised when Buresch named him minister of justice.[78] For one thing, he was young at thirty-three years old. For another, the post of minister of justice was usually slated for a Great German, and Schuschnigg did not fit that mold.[79] He felt the kinship traditional among Germanic people, but his goals were not the goals of Great Germans, and he was no Anschluss supporter.

Once in the cabinet as Minister Schuschnigg, his contacts grew, and his visibility greatly increased. Leading representatives he had come to know only slightly now became his colleagues. One of them was Engelbert Dollfuss, who had scarcely been an acquaintance before, but once they served together in the Buresch Cabinet, Dollfuss became an ally and perhaps chief among Schuschnigg's admirers,[80] greatly impressed with how well informed he was.[81] Many came to see him as a highly intelligent man, and they appreciated that he was not distracted from duty by political ambition.[82]

Eventually, Buresch, like Seipel, failed to stabilize the economy and he interacted poorly with the Social Democrats. After less than a year in office, he saw the Nazi Party score its first startling victory in provincial elections. The following month, Buresch wound up in a nasty political head-butting over his resolution calling for a vote of mistrust of the Social Democrats; his proposal was rejected, and Buresch resigned.[83]

The jockeying to select a new chancellor began immediately, and the Austrian Nazis sponsored a strong candidate, Anton Rintelen. The most conservative members, especially the Styrian members of the political arm of the Heimwehr, the Heimatbloc, led by Prince Starhemberg, joined in support of Rintelen.[84]

Buresch had realized that new leadership was necessary; the old guard in the party could not interact successfully with the increasingly radicalized Social Democrats. Buresch gave his support to the agriculture minister, Engelbert Dollfuss. President Miklas agreed with Buresch; he too felt that the Christian Socials had to find someone to improve the terrible relationship with the Social Democrats; otherwise, the Parliament could not enact essential measures needed to improve the economy. The personable and charismatic Engelbert Dollfuss seemed to enjoy a better relationship with the Social Democrats than his predecessors, and so Miklas asked Dollfuss to form a government.[85]

Dollfuss had the good sense to be very apprehensive. A succession of capable leaders, even the powerful Seipel, had all failed. He was hesitant to accept the position as head of government. He agonized over it; he went off to his church and spent the night in prayer. By morning, he had found his confidence. He agreed to try to form a new coalition—Christian Socials, the Agricultural League, and the Pan-Germans, but he also needed the Heimatbloc votes. Achieving that difficult coalition, Engelbert Dollfuss became chancellor of Austria on May 21, 1932.[86] He invited Schuschnigg to join his cabinet as minister of justice and minister of education.[87]

Schuschnigg's rise to the cabinet under Buresch and again under Doll-fuss had come about because he was called there by them, not as a result of any campaign of his own. By 1930, during his three years in office, he had been entrusted with important parliamentary committee work on the key constitution and judiciary committees,[88] and had demonstrated that he was a knowledgeable public servant.[89] He also was a good public speaker,[90] while a reserved and scholarly one. He had shown potential to gain the support of some public constituencies, including some of the Jewish leaders.[91]

The reins of Austria's government were being shared with a new genera-tion. Dollfuss and Schuschnigg were promising young men, largely untried, but determined to bring about economic recovery. Most of all, both Dollfuss and Schuschnigg were strongly committed to independence for Austria.

★ ★ ★

Dollfuss set out to be a coalition builder and political peacemaker. He called for a balanced budget and tried gamely to make peace with the socialist lead-ers. He committed his government to fairness to the workers, and he promised innovative agricultural trade policies to rural Austria.[92]

Seipel remained a strong presence as a member of Parliament, and Chan-cellor Dollfuss well knew that he needed Seipel's support. At times, Seipel and Dollfuss clashed, but their disagreements were over agricultural policy, a subject on which the farmer Dollfuss was far more knowledgeable than the priest Seipel.[93] But on most issues, Dollfuss got along well with Seipel and with most others—except for the Social Democrats.

Dollfuss achieved his subsequent successes because the "Millimet-ternich," as he came to be called, was a gregarious and very likable man.[94] He was not weak; indeed, he often had strong political disagreements. He formed firm opinions of people and thereafter rarely changed his view of them. Once he saw a person prevaricate or blunder seriously, his low opin-ion would not change.[95]

He also displayed no arrogance. One correspondent of the day observed that Dollfuss at times even seemed timid.[96] He succeeded in suppressing that air of superiority that often attaches itself almost uninvited to powerful office-holders. He lived very simply, occupying a small, sparsely furnished apartment in a modest part of town.[97] As chancellor, he would be found cheerfully per-forming such self-effacing chores as cleaning up the ashtrays in his office after cabinet members finished a smoky meeting.[98]

He failed, however, to solve the hostility between Christian Socials and Social Democrats. Moreover, his trouble on the right grew as well. The Nazis and Prince Starhemberg's Heimwehr both made his work difficult. When

they did, Dollfuss could become rather sharp about his great cause—the independence of Austria.[99] His hearing became a problem at a young age, and it
affected his personality. A grenade explosion in the dugout in which he served
in the Great War caused the damage, and his difficulty hearing what people
were saying began to make him suspicious of what went on around him. On
balance, however, Dollfuss remained a kind person, a man from the farm
country who had a very positive impact on most people.[100]

★ ★ ★

When Dollfuss became chancellor, Austria was beyond mere economic hard-
ship, it was at the brink of disaster.[101] Amid the Depression, Austria suffered a
startling decline in exports and a resulting massive spike in unemployment.[102]
Complaints from city dwellers who lost jobs poured in. Dollfuss, viewed as a
supporter of the farmers, was accused by Social Democrats of favoring agricultural interests over the workers, and he was criticized for inadequate spend-
ing for poor relief and jobs stimulation.[103] Dollfuss did support several jobs
projects, including the major highway construction project and the Tyrolese
Glassworks, but these failed to satisfy the Social Democrats or the workers.[104]
To have any chance to lead and turn the economy around, Dollfuss needed
financial help and political cooperation to end the crippling rivalries in the
government that had led to the gridlock he inherited.

Only months into his tenure, Dollfuss faced increasing waves of violence
by newly emboldened Austrian Nazis and by socialists, making him all the
more determined to deal firmly with radicals and to execute some master
stroke to rescue the economy. He also hoped that time would strengthen the
will of Britain, France, and Italy to oppose the growing German thirst for expansion. But to acquire the time to pull Austria back from the brink, he first
needed that bold economic stroke.

★ ★ ★

In summer 1932, he thought he found it—a loan of 300,000,000 schillings
from the League of Nations. The so-called Lausanne Loan, if approved, could
stabilize the Austrian economy; without it, Austria faced "a gale of catastrophic
force."[105] The loan would also require reaffirmation of Austria's acceptance of
the league's insistence that there be no union of Austria with Germany.[106]If
the loan vote failed, factories would close, high unemployment would worsen,
and the social welfare apparatus would become insolvent.[107] Many more
would join the call for Anschluss with Germany as the only remaining hope
for Austria.

Despite these stakes, debate erupted in the Diet over the loan; Karl
Renner, still a leader of the Social Democrats, led his followers in bitter op-

position. The last thing that Renner and his Social Democrats wanted was a success in the Diet for the Christian Socials, and they set out to do everything they could to defeat the loan and finish Dollfuss. The debate in the Nationalrat was "an extremely shabby business."[108] In opposing the Lausanne Loan, the Social Democrats' "real aim was tactical: to break the struggling Dollfuss government at all costs and clear the way for new elections."[109] The Social Democrats well knew that the failure of the loan agreement could bring down not just Dollfuss but also Austria itself, yet they introduced a resolution of "no confidence," taking advantage of the fact that one key vote was unavailable to Dollfuss because Seipel was in failing health and unable to attend.

The date for the cliffhanger vote was August 2, 1932, and the "no confidence" resolution was set to pass 81 to 80 and defeat the loan and bring down Dollfuss as well, simply because Seipel was unable to cast his vote.

But when Parliament was called into session, Dollfuss had an eerie calm about him as he asked for the floor. Waiting for quiet, he looked out upon contemptuous faces and taunting shouts. The small chancellor betrayed no sign but the grave demeanor of a man bringing news that a distinguished statesman had passed away.

Dollfuss announced that Seipel had died during the night. Some members shifted in their seats—to assure they had heard his news—and were trying to calculate its effect. Dollfuss watched quietly for a moment until the light dawned on the faces of his opponents as they realized that the rules allowed Seipel to be replaced immediately. Dollfuss turned to introduce Seipel's successor, who was standing nearby, to have him sworn in, and to cast the vote that saved the loan, saved Dollfuss's government, and saved Austria from collapse. The dramatic vote resulted in a tie, defeating the resolution of "no confidence."[110] The Lausanne Loan survived and went on to be approved by the Diet.[111]

Once again, however, the nearly deadlocked Parliament had almost brought Austria to its knees. The loan proceedings in Parliament had underscored how "incompetent, formalistic parliamentarism had become in Austria."[112] Something had to be done before another crisis caused Austria to collapse.

It seemed for a time that this one financial infusion might provide the antidote needed to secure the survival of the economy and the independence of Austria. The July 15, 1932, loan began economic reconstruction.[113] Dollfuss's government, however, was still faced with an acutely crippling systemic financial difficulty; Austria was starved for taxes.[114]

In addition to surviving the Depression, Dollfuss had to survive the Marxists and the Nazis. His own beliefs and his government's policies were entirely hostile to Marxism and its Marxists, and to National Socialism and its Nazis. Dollfuss embraced the anti-Marxist teaching of Pope Pius XI.[115] But as late as 1927, National Socialism played hardly any part in the national dialogue; socialism, Marxism, and extremist violence were the daily front page issues.[116] That continued until worries grew at the very end of 1932 and early 1933. The Marxist threat was abruptly surpassed by the startling success of the Nazis.

III

THE NAZI ADVANCE

• _3_ •

Thirty Days from Pariah to Dictator

"In the Third Reich every German girl will find a husband."

—Adolf Hitler

$\mathcal{I}$n Germany, the Weimar Republic was likewise enduring legislative grid-lock in its Reichstag. Its president, Paul von Hindenburg, had been clothed with extraordinary powers to enable him to deal with the emergencies they faced. He was able to name and virtually install a so-called presidential chancellor when the Reichstag was unable to come to a consensus.

The Nazis were gaining strength in elections but had been unable to win enough Reichstag seats to form a government. Nevertheless, in 1932, even without a Nazi majority, Hitler decided it was time to make his move.

★ ★ ★

The world was very nearly spared the saga of Adolf Hitler and the horror of his Third Reich. But fortuity—the distance of a few inches on one day and the span of a few seconds the next day—saved him. Hitler was almost killed in 1923—twice in consecutive days. He had marched into a hail of machine gun bullets fired by the state police of the Weimar Republic during his ill-fated march to the center of Munich in the Beer Hall Putsch of November 9, 1923.[1] He and General Eric Ludendorff and Hitler's close colleague, Max Erwin von Schuebner-Richter, were marching arm in arm when the bullets killed Schuebner-Richter instantly. He fell and dragged Hitler to the ground, dislocating Hitler's shoulder. Neither Hitler nor Ludendorff was hit.[2] Hitler, with severe pain in his dislocated shoulder, however, fled to Uffing to the home of his friend and coconspirator, Putzi Hanfstaengl. Putzi was still at large with others from the putsch, but his wife Helen let the weakened Hitler in. He looked ghastly; very pale, he was covered with mud, and his left arm dangled helplessly.

Ernst (Putzi) Hanfstaengl, Hitler, and Hermann Göring, June 21, 1932.
Source: Wikimedia, Creative Commons. Bundesarchiv Bild 102-14080.

The next morning Helen awoke to find Hitler in a state of high anxiety. He grew worse when he learned that the police were about to arrive at the door. Standing in the upstairs hallway in a bathrobe, Hitler wailed, "Now all is lost—no use going on." He grabbed his pistol and appeared about to kill himself when Helen snatched the pistol from his hand. She chastised him, saying that he couldn't enlist all these people in his cause, promise to save the country, and then instead take his own life.[3] Moments later, the police arrived and marched him out wearing the blue bathrobe with just his coat draped over it, and he was charged with high treason.[4]

The trial of Adolf Hitler and the Beer Hall Putsch conspirators provided the dynamic orator a platform for his populist demagoguery; he used it effectively, swayed public opinion, and so hijacked the course of debate at the court that he received only a short jail term. His talent for such persuasion was not just style. He could sense audiences, and he had the skill to summon from somewhere within himself an oration that would inevitably thrill them and convince them. One of his adversaries, Otto Strasser, painted a vivid portrait of Hitler's oratorical magic:

> Adolf Hitler enters a hall. He sniffs the air. For a minute he gropes, feels his way, and senses the atmosphere. Suddenly he bursts forth. His words go like an arrow to their target . . . telling it what it most wants to hear. . . . [L]et

The defendants in the 1923 Beer Hall Putsch, including Ludendorff to Hitler's right, and forward, second from right, Ernst Röhm.
Source: Wikimedia, Creative Commons. Bundesarchiv Bild 102-00344. Photographer: Heinrich Hoffmann.

him throw away his crutches and step out boldly, speaking as the spirit moves him, and he is promptly transformed into one of the greatest speakers of the century. . . . [H]e responds to the vibrations of the human heart with the delicacy of a seismograph. . . . [He] only knows what he wants to destroy. He pulls down the walls without any idea of what he will build in their place.[5]

During his incarceration, Hitler and Rudolf Hess wrote *Mein Kampf*, a best-seller whose sales made Hitler famous and prosperous enough to finance the purchase of his Berghof at Berchtesgaden.

★ ★ ★

By 1932, however, Hitler was at the crossroads, hoping to achieve a break-through with the voters, but facing a serious risk of the end of his political career and rejection of his rage against communists and the Weimar Republic. In 1925, he wrote: "The German State is intensely overrun by Marxism."[6] Christians were a political bloc against communism, for communism professed atheism. Godless communism encapsulated a simple, clear message unacceptable to most religious. Moreover, a major papal encyclical, *Quadragesimo Anno*, was issued by Pope Pius XI on May 15, 1931, and a central thesis was the threat of Marxism. Christians were at first strangely tolerant of Hitler; perversely, they did not uniformly invoke religious-based opposition to pre-Holocaust Nazism.

The Communists had many opponents and were more than matched by nationalist right-wing groups, both radical and temperate. But the deep and angry divisions within the German population at this time were not just Left against Right. Germans were polarized along all segments of society: rural against urban, middle class against working class, Protestant against Catholic, and many more.[7]

Austria found it exceedingly difficult, however, to gain reliable political intelligence from the Weimar Republic to sort out the turmoil surrounding its looming showdown with Hitler's Nazis. Weimar officials themselves were perplexed and anxious as Hitler repeatedly rebounded from setbacks. Kurt von Schuschnigg gained insight into Germany when he found an opportunity to visit Hindenburg and other Weimar officials at the crucial moment of this political battle for the life of Germany. He hoped to be able to assess the viability of the Weimar government for he knew Austria faced the same economic and political forces.

The march toward Germany's 1933 crisis began with the 1918 revolution of the navy against the plan for an end-of-war "Death Ride." The ensuing revolutionary anxiety led to the abdication and flight of the kaiser and all royalty, as well as the selection of a moderate leftist leader, Friedrich Ebert of the Social Democrats, as the head of the Council of People's Deputies. On January 19, 1919, voters endorsed the creation of a national assembly, the Reichstag. The Social Democrats won 39 percent of the vote, and Ebert became Germany's first president. When Ebert died in 1925, there was one man who had emerged from the war with a lustrous image sufficient to win election as the second president, Field Marshal Paul von Hindenburg.

Germany during the 1920s was fortunate to have the leadership talents of a gifted chancellor and foreign minister, Nobel Peace Prize–winning laureate Gustav Stresemann, who served briefly as chancellor in 1923 and then far longer as foreign minister. Stresemann was instrumental in extracting Germany from its pariah status, negotiating a restructuring of the war reparations debt, securing German membership in the League of Nations, ending the Allied occupation of the Rhineland, and bringing an end to hyperinflation.[8] While he did not achieve all this alone, Stresemann "left the greatest mark on the Weimar Republic."[9] His premature death from a stroke in 1929 at 51 was a "crippling blow"[10] to Germany and a tragedy that helped create the vacuum ultimately filled by Hitler.[11]

★ ★ ★

The catalyst for the rise of the Nazis, the Great Depression, made many German voters desperate and reckless in the choices they made in search of relief. Some rank the Nazis during this period as essentially a protest movement against the capitalist and globalist system that had produced such a collapse of world economies.[12] But the Nazi movement began to grow among rural Protestants.[13] In 1930, the Nazis showed they were more than a fringe group; they scored electoral gains and became the second-largest party in the Reichstag and put Hitler in a position to run for president.

The political intrigue under way in Weimar Germany by 1932 was a saga unmatched in its unpredictable twists and turns, in the sudden coming and going of aspirants to power, in the rising and falling of candidates for the leadership of Germany, and in ruthless plots and conspiracies. When the dust had settled, that saga produced the worst outcome imaginable.

The Weimar Republic was floundering, but it was not clear that its final hours were ticking away when Adolf Hitler decided his hour was at hand; he would run for president of Germany in 1932 against Hindenburg. The eighty-four-year-old Hindenburg was vulnerable amid the Depression even to a madcap candidate like Hitler, and in a contested election, he presented a poor contrast with the dynamic Hitler because he had suffered a mental collapse of some sort in 1931. Yet, he was also a symbol of the establishment Right of Germany, and he insisted upon remaining president.[14] Chancellor Heinrich Brüning, a Catholic Center Party labor leader, supported Hindenburg, and much of the population supported them both. The conservative coalition of the Right needed the support of the German National Party led by several including Alfred Hugenberg. So far the coalition had not needed the votes of the radical Right Nazis to fight off the communists and socialists, but some among the establishment felt that the day was fast approaching. For the time being, there was enough establishment support for the Weimar government that Hindenburg and Brüning were able to govern using decrees rather than legislation from the Reichstag.[15]

Hitler's improbable effort to unseat Hindenburg in the election was surprisingly strong; he proved to be a far greater threat than expected. He and Josef Göbbels unleashed the full power of their manipulative techniques to gain votes, making relentless attacks on Hindenburg, renewing the stab-in-the-back fantasy (*Dolchstosslegende*) about the German surrender in the Great War, and pinning it all on Hindenburg.

Hitler had first been introduced to Hindenburg on October 14, 1931. Hindenburg was a legend of towering proportions—he stood six feet and five inches.[16] And Hitler was intimidated by the imposing figure. Afterward, however, he told his henchmen that Hindenburg was actually rather stupid.[17] Hindenburg, in turn, came away distinctly unimpressed with Hitler and thereafter long held him in contempt.[18] One Hindenburg supporter badly underestimated Hitler. General Kurt von Schleicher, Hindenburg's calculating advisor, recommended an alliance with Hitler because he had become awed by Hitler's speaking ability; Schleicher assumed that was the extent of Hitler's dynamism and expected he could manipulate and control Hitler like some puppet master.[19]

President Paul von Hindenburg.
Source: Wikimedia, Creative Commons. Bundesarchiv Bild 183-Co6886.

Hindenburg's advisors asked Hitler to throw the Nazi Party's support to Hindenburg, but Göbbels recommended against it; he urged Hitler, instead, to challenge Hindenburg and encouraged the race for president.[20] Hitler, however, had a unique problem for a presidential candidate. He was not a

German citizen; he was Austrian. But he quickly contrived a way to become a citizen and went on to campaign with his typical fervor. His platform was built around a simple slogan of freedom and bread. The anger of voters produced by the Great Depression—coupled with the Nazis' willingness to promise whatever might appeal to any constituency and the highly effective propaganda devised by Göbbels and Hitler—won the Nazis big gains in elections in the early 1930s. Göbbels had no hesitation to concoct false rumors and spread them effectively. He accused Hindenburg's son Oskar and his daughters of being socialists.[21] Films of Hitler's speeches were shown in town squares. Phonograph records of his speeches were distributed. Posters and leaflets were spread everywhere.[22] Hitler, however, finished a distant second, but his long-shot candidacy had kept Hindenburg from achieving the 50 percent majority required for election. Hindenburg's distaste for Hitler increased when he saw that Hitler had now made it necessary for him to endure another election.[23]

Straining to attract all possible votes in the second presidential election, Hitler revealed that he was willing to promise the voters the moon ("In the Third Reich every German girl will find a husband").[24]

The Sturmabteilung (SA), the rough and ugly private storm troopers of the Nazi Party, led by Chief Ernst Röhm, made plans to launch a coup if Hitler won the presidency, apparently viewing the presidency as only a partial fulfillment of their dreams for absolute power. On the eve of the first presidential election, Röhm mobilized 400,000 SA to surround Berlin.[25] However, on April 10, 1932, in the runoff election, Hindenburg broke through and won more than 53 percent of the vote.[26] With Hindenburg reelected, Gregor Strasser, Hitler's northern Germany competitor, and some other Nazis who had soured on Hitler, sensed that he might at last be washed up; they reevaluated their tenuous loyalty and began looking for someone other than the failing candidate Hitler to lead the party.

Throughout this period, the SA had been given a long leash; fistfights and pub brawls had become commonplace.[27] Chancellor Brüning and the army, led by the minister of defense, General Wilhelm Gröner, learned of Röhm's and his SA's coup plans, and they prevailed upon Hindenburg to crack down on the SA.[28] The attempt, however, backfired when the Nazis erupted in protest. Schleicher saw this was his opportunity to join forces with the irate Nazis and form a Far Right coalition government under his control.[29] Schleicher devised the steps he needed to take, starting with a show of support for Hitler. This was not pleasant for Schleicher; he had a low opinion of Hitler. He once remarked that "it's a pity that he's crazy." Unfortunately, the insult was reported to Hitler, and it remained in that dark file within his memory devoted to settling old scores.[30] Schleicher and Röhm both favored merging the SA with the Reichswehr, but they both knew that their plan was unacceptable to

Hitler; he wanted to control the SA. It was also unacceptable to the many career army officers who were revolted by the Nazi thugs who made up the SA.

With Hindenburg as president and no majority party controlling the Reichstag, approval of a coalition chancellor was difficult. Only Hindenburg could name a presidential chancellor, but the chancellor still needed the confidence of a majority of the Reichstag.[31] Schleicher was a perennial optimist, and he assured Hindenburg that he could assemble the political coalition Hindenburg wanted—a government unopposed by the Nazis but without Hitler in it. Schleicher was placing his hopes on Strasser's potential splinter group of northern socialist Nazis who had been at odds from time to time since 1925 with Hitler's conservative right-wing Nazis in the south.

Schleicher went to Hitler and promised that if he supported a regime of Schleicher's choosing, Schleicher would remove the ban on the Brownshirts.[32] Hitler was in no position to resist, and he consented. Schleicher believed he had worked out an accord on the SA with Hitler and could trust him to keep his word, and he believed that Hitler would lead the Nazis to support calling new Reichstag elections. Schleicher then went back to Hindenburg and convinced him to demand the resignations of Gröner and Brüning.

But Schleicher turned out to be a far less effective manipulator than Hitler. In the course of these maneuverings, Hitler learned all he needed to know about the weakness of Hindenburg—his ego; his malleability; his interest in land and money; his fear of scandal, indictment, and impeachment; his declining energy; and his near senility. These failings of the president into whose empty shell the circling sharks had bundled all the remnants of power of the government were to be Weimar Germany's Achilles' heel. The Nazis began scheming to "threaten or intimidate" Hindenburg into naming Hitler chancellor.[33] Hindenburg was about to be adorned with exceptional powers and then swallowed whole by Hitler and his Nazis.

The next player on the stage of this seemingly unscripted saga was Franz von Papen, a polished product of Westphalian nobility, a friend of Schleicher for a time, but an especially cunning deceiver. Schleicher realized that Hindenburg had taken to Papen, who was surprisingly little known by many in government. Most who did know the treacherous former diplomat also knew not to trust him. Many, including his own advisors, considered him rather dumb, and worse.[34] Schleicher handpicked Papen and proposed Papen rather than himself as chancellor.[35] Schleicher was a general and thus considered less appropriate to be chancellor. Hindenburg went along, revealing his passivity or worse at this stage of his life.

In accordance with the horse trades that had brought them this far, Papen reinstated the SA and dissolved Parliament. The folly of all this became apparent when Hitler unleashed the refreshed SA and let them take to the

General Werner von Blomberg, German chancellor Franz von Papen, Hitler and President Hindenburg.
Source: Alamy. Hefte fur Politische Bildung: Weimar Republic. Photographer: Mr. von der Dexter.

streets beating and killing communists, Jews, and others. He also withheld his promised support of Papen.[36]

In the next election, held on July 31, 1932, the Nazis won the most they would ever achieve in a free election, 230 seats in the Reichstag—37 percent. Growth, but no majority. The Social Democrats won 133 seats.[37] The gains were enough, however, to convince Hitler that his hour was at hand. He went to Schleicher, not to Papen, and on August 5, 1932, Hitler demanded that he be made chancellor with power to rule for a time by decree.[38] After several days, Schleicher agreed, but he insisted that Hitler rule with consent of the Reichstag. Hitler met with Schleicher and Papen and found that Papen had somehow changed the deal—only the vice chancellor post was offered to Hitler. The meeting that would count the most, however, was Hitler's with the president. They expected little resistance since earlier that year Hindenburg had suffered "a complete mental relapse lasting more than a week."[39] Hindenburg, however, by this time detested Hitler, referring to him as that "Bohemian corporal," and when they met, he suddenly awoke to full lucidity. His response to Hitler's impassioned demand that he be made chancellor was to stare down at him imperiously and growl "*Nein*."[40]

Hindenburg proceeded to give Hitler a solid scolding. He criticized the Nazi Party's misconduct and lack of discipline. The Nazi outrages during the last election had been more than a mere lack of control; some fifteen people had been killed by Nazis and sixty wounded on Bloody Sunday, July 17, outside Hamburg. Six more were murdered, and Social Democrats' offices were torched by Nazis on election night, July 31.[41] Hitler was surprised; apparently he had launched his demand too soon. Stung by the rejection by Papen and Schleicher and the disrespect shown him by the president, Hitler turned on Papen after the meeting and blamed him for the embarrassment.[42] Then he retired to Berchtesgaden where he continued railing against Papen and doubled down on his resolve to recreate the German nation.[43] Hindenburg and Papen, however, were not finished undermining Hitler; they infuriated and embarrassed him by releasing a report revealing that Hitler had met with them and demanded complete power, and that Hindenburg had turned him down.[44]

Business leaders were becoming acutely anxious amid the Great Depression over this deadlock in the Reichstag; it was bringing government to a standstill.[45] Early on, the Nazi Party's financial support had come from dues, sale of leaflets, and charging admission to rallies, but finally major industrialists and bankers petitioned Hindenburg to appoint Hitler as chancellor. They, too, underestimated him, calculating that all Hitler's socialistic talk was disingenuous and that he would serve their economic and regulatory wishes.[46]

Hitler still had to eliminate Hindenburg's personal favorite, the current chancellor, Franz von Papen. He began his takedown of Papen on September 12, 1932. He did it by maneuvering a vote of no confidence in the Reichstag to remove Papen as chancellor. The apoplectic chancellor screamed at the Reichstag president, Hermann Göring, that the move was illegal, waving Hindenburg's decree dissolving the Reichstag, but Göring ignored Papen as if he were nowhere in sight. The vote went overwhelmingly against Papen, and he was through as chancellor. Yet, in the election that followed on November 6, 1932, the Nazis lost ground. Hitler was again dejected. Another plan would have to be devised.

Schleicher changed his plan also; he decided at last to make his move and take the office himself. He, too, had turned against Papen. Using his stature as a general and minister of war, Schleicher convinced the army to withdraw its support for Papen. Schleicher believed he had succeeded in convincing Hindenburg that he himself could form a government—with the support of Hitler's Nazi rival, Gregor Strasser.

But Strasser had clashed with Hitler several years earlier at the Bamberg conference of February 1926 and had lost out.[47] His attempt to steer the Nazis to socialism with the government confiscating the property of the Wittelsbachs and Hohenzollerns had failed, and Hitler had so turned the event against Strasser that he was able to establish the *Führerprinzip* as the core of Nazism.[48]

Only the Führer ruled the party; he was not to be questioned or disobeyed, and no parliament or committee or court was to have any role in governing. Hitler's twenty-five-point program of Nazism was from then on unalterable. Schleicher's hope for support from a Strasser splinter group was to no avail.

The outraged Papen, however, would not go quietly. On December 1, 1932, Schleicher and Papen met with Hindenburg. Papen proposed that the Reichstag be suspended for a time and that he remain chancellor. Schleicher, however, offered himself as chancellor. Hindenburg paused and reflected; when he broke the silence, to Schleicher's surprise, the president turned to Papen and instructed him to form a new government.[49]

Angered and disappointed, Schleicher tagged along with Papen to confer with the cabinet, and once there, Schleicher renewed his attack; he argued that Papen could not lead the army or prevent a Nazi putsch and that civil war was imminent. Papen hurried back to Hindenburg, and the befuddled president inexplicably turned to Schleicher and asked him to form a government instead. Hindenburg was now so frustrated that he threatened that he himself would resign if a solution was not found.[50] Papen was shoved aside, and on December 2, Schleicher's slowly paced climb to power made him the chancellor.[51]

Hitler seemed on the ropes. Schleicher, not he, was the new chancellor. Even new elections offered no solution because the Nazis were virtually bankrupt and had lost ground in the November election when they did have money to spend. Adolf Hitler seemed about to drift into a political wasteland to wither and disappear.[52]

Schleicher did not even offer the vice chancellor post to Hitler; he offered it to Strasser, still thinking that Strasser, leader of the so-called Strasserist faction of the Nazi Party, was willing to challenge Hitler. However, Strasser's 1926 failed clash with Hitler left him with sufficient doubt of his support that he decided he had better consult with Hitler. When he did, Hitler did not see loyalty in Strasser's gesture; the old animosities that had nearly split the Hitler faction from the Strasser faction at the 1926 Bamberg conference sprung to life. Hitler accused Strasser of stabbing him in the back.[53] Strasser shot back, accusing Hitler of leading the party to destruction; but then Strasser surprised everyone—he quit. The end result, oddly, was that the hoped-for Nazi splinter group did not splinter, and the crucial Nazi who could serve as an opponent to Hitler did not materialize.[54] Schleicher was out of options, so he offered Hitler the post of vice chancellor. Hitler, however, again refused to settle for the second spot.[55]

★ ★ ★

It was in the midst of this historic joust that Schuschnigg paid his visit to Hindenburg, and then spoke with others in the Weimar government. He gained an unusual opportunity to learn about the jockeying for rule of Germany, as well as the chance to assess Hitler's prospects firsthand. Still just a young minister of justice, Schuschnigg visited Berlin on January 14, 1933. There he enjoyed an audience with the most iconic figure of the Great War. President Hindenburg, the victor of the legendary Battle of Tannenberg, received the former Habsburg artillery lieutenant, and the two men who had such very different roles in the Great War reminisced and enjoyed each other's company.[56]

On the same trip, Schuschnigg paid official visits to the other Weimar officials, one to recent chancellor Papen, and another to incumbent chancellor Schleicher. Schuschnigg asked them both about the prospects of the Nazis and their provocative leader. Over lunch, Papen told Schuschnigg that the Nazis were through. Chancellor Schleicher met separately with Schuschnigg and gave a similar assessment. Schleicher was still wincing after running afoul of the business community; he explained to Schuschnigg that he was now focused on trying to gain the support of all the trade unions and was taking steps to find common ground on which the trade unions and the Nazis could support his government. He, too, told Schuschnigg he was confident that "Hitler was no longer a problem" and that the Nazi movement could now be "numbered among the cares of yesterday."[57]

Schleicher's lack of concern about Hitler and the Nazis was typical; he was generally overly optimistic, and his view of Hitler's trajectory was no exception.[58] Whether he simply chose to dissemble, or else was inadequately prescient, Schleicher surely did not foresee that in two weeks he himself would be out of office and struggling mightily to try to figure out why Hindenburg, who had been so unremittingly hostile toward Hitler, could possibly have changed so abruptly.

Schleicher, however, alienated the farmer-landowners as well as business. The farmers wanted high tariffs so they could charge more for food; they wanted no part of free trade. Schleicher declined to impose the tariffs they wanted and, when he lost their support, he lost the support of Hindenburg, a Junker landowner himself. Hitler's prospects at that point seemed bleak. It was Hindenburg who would select the new chancellor, and it was well known that he loathed Hitler. Hitler decided to negotiate with Papen and to try to make a fresh start. On January 4, 1933, they met in Cologne but reached no agreement.[59] In the next election on January 15, the Nazis gained ground over their previous vote but still fell short of a majority; nevertheless, these gains elated the Nazis.[60] To end any chance that the growing Nazi movement might be splintered by Strasser, Hitler publicly denounced him, and Strasser resigned from the Reichstag.[61] Strasser finally saw that his former leader was a chronic liar. Moreover, Strasser began to hear that Hitler's close followers were accusing him of treason. He became fearful that Hitler was preparing to have him murdered.[62]

Hitler and Papen met again on January 18 at Joachim von Ribbentrop's home, but again, Papen refused Hitler's demand to be chancellor, emphasizing that Hindenburg was not willing to agree to that.[63] Hitler could see that he had no choice but to deal with Hindenburg, but he chose to do it in a more sinister fashion.

★ ★ ★

Hindenburg, it appears, had certain vulnerabilities, and Hitler was aware of them. Rumors abounded about corruption and allegations of Hindenburg evading taxes. His Junker landholdings were rumored to be the subject of shoddy maneuvers to escape inheritance taxes. And his son Oskar was a very ambitious but talentless army officer frustrated that he had little prospect for promotion. Hitler took advantage of these weaknesses; in fact, he had planned all along to overthrow Hindenburg if necessary, and impeachment or disgrace was part of his plan from their first encounter.[64] He approached the president through his son Oskar, and, he charmed, threatened, and offered bribes to the stolid colonel.

Oskar von Hindenburg and the president's state secretary, Otto Meissner, arrived confident and impatient, reluctantly tolerating yet another meeting with the tiresome Adolf Hitler, at the home of Ribbentrop, an up-and-coming Nazi. They hardly expected that the meeting was about to break the Hindenburgs' opposition to Hitler, but that night at the Ribbentrop home, Hitler unfurled his threat of scandal. He excluded the others who were there and pulled Oskar into a separate room where the two of them met alone for an hour. When they emerged, Oskar von Hindenburg had lost his appetite and likely showed it. He curtly summoned Meissner, and they hurried off into the night. As they rode back to the president's home, Meissner was curious, tense, and anxious to hear from Oskar what had caused the abrupt flight. Finally, Oskar glanced away and mumbled cryptically that Hitler would have to be allowed into the government. It couldn't be helped was all he would say.[65]

★ ★ ★

Six years earlier, the Hindenburg family had become great beneficiaries of a government program, the Eastern Aid Fund. The fund made it possible for Junkers, like the president, to improve and retain their properties. However, to avoid death taxes, Hindenburg had transferred the property to Oskar, allegedly without reporting or paying the conveyance taxes. Some feared that this may have amounted to an impeachable offense, and, in any event, it was enough to sully the great legend's legacy.

The Osthilfe (Eastern Aid) scandal was not a surprise to the Hindenburgs, if indeed that is what Hitler used to blackmail Oskar and the president. What

Colonel Oskar von Hindenburg.
Source: Wikimedia, Creative Commons. Bundesarchiv Bild 102-09560.

is known is that President Hindenburg was very concerned about the danger of impeachment over the allegations.[66] Press reports in the past had touched on the subject, but the full details relating to Hindenburg's involvement were in a report not made public, and the matter remained of immense concern to Hindenburg who was fixated on preserving his lofty image.[67] These allegations had been used to intimidate the Hindenburgs once before; Schleicher used them in a direct confrontation with President Hindenburg. Schleicher had alienated Junker constituents and businessmen, and Hindenburg had become angry with him; he started berating Schleicher over the political trouble he had caused. However, Schleicher had a weapon of his own to control the president. He knew the details of the secret Reichstag report on the Eastern Aid scandal, and he silenced the president by proposing to publish the report and the details about Hindenburg and his son.[68]

Schleicher, however, was now relegated to trying to save his government and the Weimar Republic itself. He made a last stab at blocking Hitler; he asked Hindenburg on January 27 to dissolve the Reichstag, but Hindenburg refused.[69] Lacking the necessary support to form a government, Schleicher returned the next day and conceded that his attempts had failed.

President Hindenburg's manor house in Hanover.
Source: Wikimedia, Creative Commons. Photographer: Bernd Schwann in Hanover.

★ ★ ★

The towering lion of the Great War was about to undo any good he had ever done in his long and illustrious life. He mused about his imminent approval of Hitler; Hindenburg said he may regret it in heaven later on. To this, Schleicher bluntly chastised the president: "After this breach of trust, sir, I am not sure that you will go to heaven."[70]

Hindenburg, however, had made his choice; he called in Papen and instructed him to form a government, and to do so in coalition with Hitler, the previously unacceptable Bohemian corporal.[71] Hindenburg's abrupt about-face raises the highest suspicion. Papen's willingness to bring Hitler into the government as its leader is also inexplicable, but Papen apparently felt that recent setbacks at the polls made Hitler so weak politically that Papen and members of the Reichstag could control him.[72] Papen was heard to remark with historic naïveté, "We have hired him."[73]

Franz von Papen and Hitler began the negotiations for the formation of a coalition government; they reached agreement, and on January 30, 1933, Adolf Hitler slithered through the final cracks in the crumbling edifice of the Weimar Republic and became the chancellor of Germany.

A few months later, once the Nazis controlled Germany, the Hindenburgs received 5,000 additional tax-free acres at the family property at Neudeck. In August 1934, Oskar was catapulted in rank from colonel all the way to major general,[74] despite Hitler's assessment that Oskar was one of the stupidest people he had ever met.[75] No complaints were raised against President Hindenburg based on the unpublished report on the inheritance tax allegations—indeed, Hitler saw to it that the Hindenburgs received even more land and more money later.[76] In fall 1933 when Hitler needed Hindenburg to acquiesce to Hitler's withdrawal from the League of Nations, he arranged to give two valuable properties to Hindenburg and appropriated 800,000 marks to spruce them up.[77]

★ ★ ★

Less than a month after Hitler took office, fire lit up the night sky above the Brandenburg Gate in central Berlin. On February 27, 1933, Marinus van der Lubbe, a communist provocateur fond of using arson, set the *Reichstag* building ablaze. He was caught in the building, and he submitted to a thorough interrogation and admitted to the arson. He acted alone; he set the fire as a protest. Although there was no evidence he was lying, or that any other communists were involved, Hitler pretended that the fire was part of a Bolshevik-style Marxist revolution erupting all across Germany. Communists took their guidance from Moscow, and there was no evidence that the fire had its origins there.[78] Regardless, the Nazis turned Göbbels loose to sell this event to Germany and to the rest of the world as a nation-stealing conflagration of historic impact. Subsequently, some have provided evidence that the fire was Göring's doing, that he had his own men load the place with flammable chemicals.[79] Göring joined in Hitler's excited exclamations to the cabinet that there was a wide conspiracy of which van der Lubbe was merely a part. No one demanded any evidence even when Hitler insisted that Hindenburg must issue a decree granting him emergency powers.[80]

The Nazis spread alarm ("This is the beginning of the Communist revolution"), and Göring demanded execution of every communist official.[81] Hitler, they insisted, must, of course, be given the emergency powers needed to stop it. Hitler stampeded Hindenburg into signing the decree that began Germany's free fall into dictatorship. The Reichstag Fire Decree was a blatant fraud; it was tyrannical and wildly excessive on its face. Marinus van der Lubbe was a Dutch communist, but no evidence surfaced that he had conspired with anyone else, let alone that this was a vast communist conspiracy to take down the Reich. Fundamental civil rights and freedom of communication by telephone and telegraph plainly posed no threat, but the Reichstag Fire Decree suspended all of them. The government in Berlin was granted power to take over the federal states. Confiscation of property without due process and warrantless searches were utterly uncalled for by what had happened, but the crafty Hitler had achieved control over President Hindenburg and got him to sign the decree ostensibly to save Germany from the fate of 1917 Russia.

Thousands were arrested by storm troopers racing through towns all over Germany. These arrests were far more brutal than police raids. By now, the sizable Prussian police force was under Nazi control and ruled by Göring, not Papen.[82] The Prussian police would not be sent out to stop the brutality as the SA gathered truckloads of supposed communists.

The full Göbbels propaganda apparatus was also unleashed. Göbbels's genius for the spectacle of torchlight parades, mass turnouts, huge swastikas, and loudspeakers everywhere sprang to life. Central to all of this was spectacular lying to the population in Nazi propaganda. They announced that communist atrocities were under way everywhere in Germany, and they muzzled the press that could have debunked these fabricated stories.

Even after the Reichstag fire extravaganza, the nationwide carnival of propaganda, and plentiful Nazi violence in pursuit of votes, when the next election day was over on March 5, 1933, the Nazis still had failed to secure a majority in the Reichstag. They received only 43 percent of the vote. They were the largest party but did not have the votes needed to end constitutional government even by the use of this fraudulent manipulation of the electoral and parliamentary process.[83] To eliminate the existing government and to make the dictatorship permanent, Hitler still needed Hindenburg and the votes of small allied parties.[84] Hitler proposed an innocuously titled Enabling Act on March 24, 1933. Title aside, in the Enabling Act the Reichstag gave away its legislative power to the chancellor—in literal terms, to his cabinet—for the next four years.

Hitler and Göbbels grandly staged a nostalgic ceremony in which Hitler publicly lathered unctuous praise on the doddering Hindenburg, using clever words that sounded as though it was Hindenburg who was being placed in charge of German government. The occasion for this ceremony of ultimate deception was the opening of the Reichstag, an overblown event held at the old Garrison Church in Potsdam near the tomb of Frederick the Great. Hindenburg, near his end from cancer, spoke and endorsed the historic death blow to Germany.[85] Through this series of failures, Germany was "betrayed by Hindenburg" acting in large measure in a foolish effort to preserve his overblown image, but he had instead "definitively and permanently ruined the reputation Hindenburg had always been so careful to guard."[86]

When the Reichstag assembled to vote on the Enabling Act, uniformed Schutzstaffel (SS) stood behind every row while the vote was taken.[87] In a session of the reconstituted Reichstag, held in Berlin's Kroll Opera House on March 23, 1933, Hitler assured members in several different ways that he would be restrained in the use of such powers and that he would respect the president's power of veto, though the act contained none. The necessary plurality of votes was then achieved by arresting the Communist deputies and some of the Social Democrats and preventing them from voting. Thereafter, the Reichstag was merely a Nazi ceremonial assembly.

Hitler bowing to President Hindenburg at Potsdam, March 21, 1933.
Source: Wikimedia, Creative Commons. Bundesarchiv Bild 183-S38324.

Hitler delivering the Enabling Act speech to the Reichstag, March 23, 1933.
Source: Wikimedia, Creative Commons. Bundesarchiv Bild 102-14439.

Others much closer to the horizon at that dawn of Nazi power failed to see what was falling upon them. The Prussian minister of finance, Johannes Popitz, who was not a Nazi, tried to reassure Schuschnigg that this terrible-sounding experiment with its serious chance of going woefully wrong would not actually be as bad as many feared. Popitz told Schuschnigg that he believed that the Nazis would slow down and calm down in due time.[88]

Hitler, however, did not slow down. His theft of power was further cemented by the January 30, 1934, Law for the Reconstruction of the Reich, abolishing the various states' popular assemblies. The provincial governments in Prussia, Bavaria, and other provinces were emasculated, and the nation's federal character ended by substituting Hitler's handpicked Reich governors to govern the states instead of their elected Diets. Thereafter, Hitler chose the members of the Reichstag and never again held real elections.

Hitler did not wait long to act upon his hatred for Jews. On April 1, 1933, he called for a boycott of Jewish businesses. To enforce it, he assigned SA Brownshirts to take up posts at most Jewish businesses to discourage customers.[89] For those businesses not boycotted, particularly the large industries, he lavished them with exaggerated promises of great things to come that would benefit their business interests. The bankers and industrialists rallied to his side and put abundant money at the disposal of the Nazis.[90]

★ ★ ★

Although Hitler now had total power and had silenced the free press who could have called him on his frauds, he knew he still had enemies, and he considered them very dangerous. Schleicher, Strasser, Röhm, and many others he saw as enemies, some who had been the other tarantulas in the bottle with Hitler, fell to his deadly sting beginning on June 30, 1934, in the so called Night of the Long Knives (Nacht der Lange Messer), a three-day festival of Nazi executions of personal enemies, even other Nazis,[91] set in motion by some complicated jockeying for power by factions of Hitler's top Nazis. It is said that the conservatives were both the targets and the audience for this brutal demonstration of terror and power.[92] Many of the four million Brownshirts of the SA had become disgruntled that Hitler had refused to convert them into Germany's national army. They were the revolutionaries who had brought him to power—as their leaders saw it. The leader of the SA, Ernst Röhm, held this view and the grudge that went with it. Röhm made the mistake of venting his spleen about Hitler in private, calling him a "traitor" and "that ridiculous corporal." Unfortunately, Röhm's enemies reported all that to Hitler.[93]

The Reichswehr, the army, felt threatened by the goon squads who made up the Brownshirts, and were ready to believe false rumors spread by Hitler's ambitious henchmen, Heinrich Himmler, Göbbels, Reinhard Heydrich, and Göring, that Röhm and the Brownshirts were about to launch a putsch and would attack the army very shortly.[94] They used fake memos and false reports to trick the army into believing that Röhm was about to move against it.[95] Röhm had no such plans.[96]

But Hitler seems to have been driven into a panic by his instinctive distrust of Röhm. He decided to take down Röhm and most of his political enemies on the same three days. Hitler traveled to Bad Weissee to lead a small squad to arrest Röhm on June 30, 1934.[97] He said whatever he needed to convince the army to buy in and help him, and they did.[98] Hundreds were arrested, and many were murdered on the spot. Early figures indicated that less than a hundred were murdered, but later objective analysis concluded that 116 identified victims were killed and that the real total appeared to be as high as 401.[99] Hitler ordered scores of SA leaders and personal and political opponents killed. Schleicher, Strasser, Röhm, and other formerly close colleagues of Hitler were taken and murdered on Hitler's orders, both by his henchmen and by duped military firing squads over the next few days. The full total is still not known.[100] Vice Chancellor Papen was placed under house arrest and nearly executed, but he survived.[101] Papen's top aide was arrested, and Papen's speechwriter was executed; many others were shot point blank at their homes and offices.[102] Those killed were selected for death by Hitler; no one had a trial of any sort.[103]

On the second day, Hitler had misgivings. He told his closest generals he had decided to pardon Röhm. That, however, produced immediate protests from Göring and Himmler who wanted their rival dead. Hitler relented, and Röhm was shot as he sat shirtless and sweating in his prison cell.[104]

The Nazis fed Hindenburg the story that this was done to stop the SA, but then they also had to disclose to Hindenburg that his former chancellor, Kurt von Schleicher, and Schleicher's wife had been killed. Hitler had obviously not forgiven Schleicher's quip years earlier that it was a pity that Hitler was crazy. The Nazis told Hindenburg a transparently false story that the Schleichers had been killed resisting arrest. Hitler knew, however, that he could not have the president condemning this orgy of murder, and he knew exactly how to prevent that. More money and land was given to Hindenburg. Instead of a condemnation, Hindenburg issued a telegram praising Hitler's "bravery," and his "gallant" and "decisive intervention" to save the nation.[105] It was not until near the end of the war that others learned how common Hitler's corruption of high officials and generals was. Former general Fritz Halder recounted that some were given stuffed envelopes with up to 500,000 reichsmarks in cash to buy their loyalty.[106]

This sudden rampage of killing by the leader of a European government astounded the rest of the world. The German government was plainly a despotic regime, savagely ruled by murderous tyrants. Mussolini was not taken in. He condemned the murders in the Night of the Long Knives in searing language both in private and in public.[107]

Now that Hitler had immunized himself from meaningful condemnation, he prepared to address the Reichstag. On Friday, July 13, 1934, he appeared at the Kroll Opera House before a handpicked *Reichstag* and claimed all those murders were justified by a wave of treason. No one presented any evidence, and no one so much as asked for any, before the men assembled passed a bill approving the murders as necessary to deal with some kind of emergency.[108] His claim was that he did all this to save the Reich from a conspiracy hatched by traitors, and his claim was not challenged in Germany. This grim criminality had the effect of increasing, not diminishing, Hitler's support.[109] When it was over, and no one rose up to condemn him for these murders, few remained who were willing to oppose him, and few who witnessed what he would do to an opponent were ever again tempted to cross him, attack him, offend him, or disagree with him.

Hitler followed these murders with political purges. By July 14, 1934, even Hindenburg's supportive German National Party was dissolved, and the Nazi Party was left as the sole political party allowed in Germany.

Hindenburg's health continued its obvious decline, and he died on August 2, 1934. After Hindenburg's death, a national referendum was held and 90 percent of the German people voted to approve Hitler as successor to Hindenburg and to approve the bill creating a new office naming him Führer and Reichskanzler.[110]

★ ★ ★

Many leaders, and clergy, and some surprising organizations, had expressed support for Hitler when he first took office in Germany. Even the Association of National German Jews issued an appeal in his favor when he succeeded Hindenburg.[111] Even more businesses threw their financial support to the Nazis.[112] Most of these same businesses had previously funded the Nazis' opponents.[113]

Later, during the war, as if his dictatorial power was still insufficient, Hitler had the Reichstag enact yet another law on April 26, 1942, giving him supreme command over every person in the Reich and exempting him from any restrictions of the laws or the constitution.[114]

★ ★ ★

The Nazi violence in Austria was also guided by Hitler and trumpeted by the propaganda of Josef Göbbels. Now that Germany and Nazism were synonymous, Nazi violence in Austria, where the Austrian Nazi Party was banned, became more common. In June 1933, members of Austria's Christian German Athletic Association were bombarded with hand grenades by the Nazis in Krems, Austria; one man was killed and several badly wounded.[115] From that moment on, Dollfuss banned all Nazi activity.[116]

By that time, the rest of Europe behaved toward Hitler as though it had already become seriously intimidated. Despite the desire of Europe and America to keep Hitler from conquering other European states, leaders everywhere refrained from public criticisms, which Hitler might view as provocative. European leaders all understood that something might at any moment trigger this strange man's vilest proclivities and, that he might well be willing to restart the industrialized mass murder that they had so recently inflicted upon each other.

Hitler's regime, for all its underlying evil, began to bring widespread relief and resurgence to economically devastated Germany. A year after taking power, the Führer was presiding over a population enjoying widespread prosperity. In February 1934, Hitler was able to boast that he had solved Germany's chronic unemployment.[117] Austria, on the other hand, still mired in the

Depression, presented a grim contrast to the bustle and activity of Germany. Austria still had several hundred thousand people unemployed.[118]

Dollfuss was determined to produce a similar economic miracle—but outside the regime of National Socialism.[119] He knew that it would take more than the Lausanne Loan to make the Austrian economy rebound as it struggled against the economic turmoil of the 1930s. To do so, he had to try to expand the economy beyond Austria's constricting borders. Germany was essential to that goal—Dollfuss's repugnance for Nazis notwithstanding. Dollfuss had to support close relations with Germany; he hoped he could do so by cultivating the two nations' common bond—their sentimental attachment to German culture and tradition.[120]

Hitler, however, had no stomach for independent Austria growing prosperous while he sought to capture it. He had already revealed his hostility to much of the international community by withdrawing Germany from the League of Nations, and he lost no time in instituting measures to weaken Austria from within.[121] On May 27, 1934, he imposed a 1,000 mark tariff on German tourists going to Austria—effectively a blockade—virtually halting Austria's German tourism.[122] Before the blockade, thousands of Germans every year had enjoyed their holidays in the splendor of the Tyrol, the Obersalzburg, Salzburg, Vienna, and villages of Austria. German tourism had become essential to the Austrian economy, and Hitler knew it was a weapon to punish the Austrian government.

A few years before Hitler's rise, the tourist industry had been hurt by the imposition in Germany of a mere 50 mark tariff; that modest added cost of a holiday in Austria was enough to deliver a hurtful sting to the Austrian economy. The impact of Hitler's 1,000 mark tariff was far worse. While tourists from other countries were not affected, most of the tourists who sustained the Austrian economy were Germans. Tyrol's tourists in 1932 had been 60 percent German. Other provinces had enjoyed comparable German tourist revenues, so Hitler's mischievous boycott soon was proving very harmful.[123]

Austrians could not mistake this for economic policy; it was naked political punishment for anti-Nazi policies.[124] The blockade also showed Hitler's readiness to hurt his native land. Dollfuss realized that the boycott was a very serious threat to Austria, and he sent Schuschnigg to negotiate some type of solution with Theo Habicht and Alfred Proksch, the Nazi leaders.[125] However, the Austrian Nazis' demands were excessive; they insisted on placing Nazis in the cabinet and holding a national election.[126]

★ ★ ★

By fall, the economic threat had become an emergency, and Dollfuss asked for a conference with Hitler; he was pleased to receive word that a meeting in Munich with Hitler was arranged for October 31, 1933.[127]

Dollfuss sent Schuschnigg and Leo Muller, an agriculture official, as plenipotentiaries traveling to Munich in secrecy on the overnight train. In the morning at the Munich station, they emerged to a sea of huge swastika flags and banners. Such displays were banned in Austria, and the scene shouted to the two Austrians that this was enemy territory.[128] Schuschnigg saw the menacing black uniforms of the Nazis everywhere. He noticed that unions had disappeared, their offices closed down. A new order of things was evident in Germany.

They were met by an unremarkable functionary in civilian clothes, greeting them through a pair of small eyeglasses above his spare mustache. He told them his name was Heinrich Himmler; he inquired politely about the purpose of their trip. Puzzled, Schuschnigg told Himmler that they were scheduled to meet with the Führer. But Himmler said that there must be a misunderstanding. The Führer was out of town. Himmler suggested they go to see Rudolph Hess at his villa.

Hess, by comparison, was a striking figure; he had a fanatical look and a wolf's eyes. Hess, too, professed that there must be a misunderstanding; but he took the opportunity to deliver to the two Austrians a withering diatribe spoken in a very soft voice against Austria's treatment of Nazis, and he demanded that swastikas be permitted in Austria. Schuschnigg barely had the chance to inject a brief profession that Austria wished to establish relations as a good neighbor. He and Muller returned empty handed to Vienna. Further attempts in the following weeks by Dollfuss and Austrian ambassador Theodore Hornbostel to engage the Reich in talks were also to no avail.[129]

Hitler had demonstrated that he could try other ways to force Austria to adopt his Nazi Party agenda,[130] and Austria saw the reality that Germany could shrivel Austria's economy without firing a shot. Central to his agenda was the Nazis' abuse of Jews. In addition to the tourist tariff, Germany made clear it was monitoring Austrian products created or financed by Jews in Austria and elsewhere. That boycott caused some of Austria's most creative figures to emigrate to find work. Movies were a special target. Such luminaries as Billy Wilder, Otto Preminger, Michael Curtiz, and Peter Lorre were squeezed out of Austrian film work and departed for Hollywood. The day would come, of course, when they would be grateful that such trouble had come early.[131]

★ ★ ★

Dollfuss had to turn elsewhere for help; he increased efforts to solicit support to cope with Hitler. His best hope was Mussolini. At the time, Mussolini still considered Hitler a copycat and viewed him as a likely enemy. He was happy to stage a lavish welcome in Rome for Dollfuss, then to promise help and to trumpet that he would assure the independence of Austria against any who threatened the country. Mussolini positioned himself as the chief protector of

Austria for several years while it suited his ambitions, but he exacted a price for doing it. He wanted assurance that Austria would continue to hold fast to anti-Marxist policies and would suppress the Social Democrats.[132]

Mussolini, however, did not want Italy to be the lone guarantor of Austrian independence, and then find himself a target of Hitler, for Hitler's ambitions in Austria were not lost on Mussolini.[133] It was clear to Mussolini that Hitler was determined to annex Austria, and he pushed Mussolini to support his plan.[134] Mussolini sought to delay it. He continued to play the elusive partner, and he valued the leverage he gained from being courted as an ally simultaneously by Austria, Germany, France, and Britain.

IV

THE AUSTRIAN RESPONSE

· 4 ·

Parliament Dissolved

$\mathcal{T}$he loan crisis in Austria had underscored the urgent necessity for government reform. It had already become clear that some regimes in Europe were courting extinction. France was unable to establish a government that did much more than bicker and recriminate. Austria had been little better. All parties wanted the unpopular Parliament ended, but they all wanted their own brand of reform. The socialists wanted a socialist regime, the Marxists wanted a communist regime, and the Nazis wanted a Nazi dictatorship.

Even before Hitler seized power in Germany, Chancellor Buresch had witnessed the rise of Nazi electoral power in Austria; he knew that a national election would only make things worse. The Austrian Nazis had found their stride when they made the 1932 election breakthrough, emphatically demonstrating the effectiveness of their volkisch anti-Semitic propaganda. They were poised to dominate the next national election, win seats in the Vienna Parliament, and eventually control of Parliament; Buresch saw the election landscape as hopeless and concluded the Nazi gains were the harbinger of a coming Nazi avalanche. So, with the threat of Hitler on the right and Stalin on the left, Buresch had delivered an emphatic "no" to the demands by the Nazis and the Social Democrats for an election in 1932.

The political landscape Dollfuss faced in 1933 was much worse. Nazism as a movement now possessed startling new power and Dollfuss could see that genuinely free elections were impossible in Austria. But the Social Democrats handed him an opportunity. They pulled an unusual stunt in the Diet, a procedural move that gave him the chance to make a counter move that might prevent the Nazis from taking power through elections.

★ ★ ★

As Engelbert Dollfuss awoke on the morning of March 4, 1933, with Adolf Hitler having just become the dictator of Germany, he faced a day on which he was barely clinging to his office. Just one week earlier, Hitler had used the Reichstag fire to seize the power of Parliament in Germany. Hitler was suddenly free to begin the conquests he planned. He was free to decide quickly and alone, and he was capable of making Germany act immediately.

In Austria, however, Dollfuss's hands were tied. The vote of any one member could block his program and drive him from office. The Social Democrats were pledged to bring him down and to resist everything the Christian Socials wanted. Every other party and its members could see what great leverage that gave them. Even the mavericks knew that any resolution in Parliament might bring a tie vote and thereby hand every representative a political dagger he could use to cut a deal or cast his one vote to drive the chancellor from office. As a result, "there was a constant state of crisis within the parliament."[1]

The Social Democrats also wanted a national election; they calculated that the threat presented by the new success of the Nazis would drive many Christian Socials to vote for Social Democrats as the best means of defeating the Nazis in new elections.[2]

★ ★ ★

But on March 4, 1933, a dust-up occurred over a procedural vote, and it changed Austria's Diet and turned Austria's political world upside down. Dollfuss found himself presented with an entirely unexpected opportunity. When the day began, he was hanging by the thread of a single vote majority.[3] A procedural vote was instigated by Otto Bauer and socialist supporters in the hope of bringing down Dollfuss's government. The vote, however, produced a stalemate. To break the stalemate, the three heads of Parliament—Parliamentary president Karl Renner and the two vice presidents in the Diet, Rudolf Ramek and Sepp Straffner—resigned,[4] a tactic that was intended to enable them each to cast a vote from the floor of the Parliament on the pending matter.[5] But what they did opened a trapdoor they had not seen.

Dollfuss was as surprised as anyone by their simultaneous resignations, but he saw the opportunity this presented. He took the position that the three resignations had dissolved Parliament. Dissolutions of Parliaments occurred in some countries rather frequently and for a great variety of reasons. However, Dollfuss pointed out that the rules did not cover this,[6] and there was no legal requirement to reconstitute the Diet. The three resignations that accomplished the dissolution had occurred entirely without his instigation, so he felt he would be justified in trying to rule, quite temporarily, without Parliament, using executive decrees instead of legislation.[7] The members of the Diet all left, and Dollfuss subsequently asserted with what one critic concedes was "at least a modicum of truth, that it had dissolved itself."[8] Protests over the dissolution were short lived, and the police helped prevent an attempt to reconvene Parliament.

The day after Parliament was dissolved, Dollfuss developed a plan; he would use this predicament to persuade the Social Democrats to agree to a revision of the Constitution.[9] The Wartime Economy Authority Law of 1917 (the *Ermachtigungsgetz*)[10] was still in force, an heirloom of the Great War, and Dollfuss invoked it when he issued executive decrees. At the outset, he had no expectation that this would last very long, and he set about planning a reorganization of the Austrian government along lines that would be workable, constitutional, and permanent.

The rest of the public was far more accepting of the concept of an end to the Parliament than the socialists. Prince Metternich had once ruled without a Diet for fourteen years, and the emperors had summoned and dismissed Parliaments with some frequency. This Parliament, moreover, was extremely unpopular. "Parliament had . . . never become respected, let alone revered by the nation at large." The Diet had long behaved "as though that assembly were Austria itself, and therefore answerable to nobody."[11]

Dollfuss scheduled a speech to explain what had occurred; as soon as he mentioned the dissolution of Parliament, "a roar of applause . . . from the public . . . took minutes to subside."[12] Many Austrians appreciated that this streamlining of government was necessary to deal with "the emergency created by Hitler's arrival to power," because Austria was already feeling "the Nazi grip tighten around her windpipe."[13] Many historians see this seizure of parliamentary power as a crisis-driven defense against the Nazis and communists. Some describe it as a desperate attempt to keep the Austrian Nazis from manipulating elections and seizing power in Austria as they had just done in Germany. Dollfuss would not let that happen. He prorogued the Diet and redoubled suppression of the Nazi Party, then he eliminated political parties and replaced them with estates, intending to conduct future elections using the medieval style of voting by estates and crafts. The hope he expressed was that the Nazi and communist threats would wane and that elections could safely resume.

One historian observes that the new advisory bodies that replaced the Diet "were meant to represent the new order of society more democratically than Parliament had ever represented the old, yet without impairing that strong centralized authority on which the country's best hopes of safety were thought to depend."[14] After dissolution, the government "enjoyed broad support both in the Christian Social Party and among economic interest groups."[15] The Social Democrats, however, condemned these moves as dictatorship.

★ ★ ★

Within days, a new model of government began to take shape as new councils replaced the old organs of government. On March 7, the Nationalrat (National

Council) was dissolved. The Bundesrat (Federal Council) remained but in a different form; it was now subject to the will of the chancellor. The judges of the constitutional court concluded that it would now be inappropriate for that court to issue constitutional rulings before the new constitution was drafted, and so each of the judges voluntarily resigned and the court was abolished;[16] all other courts remained open and independent. The Vaterlandische Front (Fatherland Front) was decreed to be the only legal political organization, and by September 11, 1933, it held its first roll call.[17] The other parties were dissolved. The Communist Party and the Nazi Party were banned. Voting would no longer be for political parties and their candidates but, instead, for representatives chosen by the members of the trades and professions.

Opponents of the government demonstrated, and dissidents of many different stripes were arrested. Some were, for a time, housed in detention centers and internment camps, usually for terms of a few months, a move some saw as having the "justification . . . that the country was virtually in a state of war."[18]

A year later, on May 1, 1934, some core provisions of the new constitution were ready, and the creation of the new government was declared. It was the Federal State of Austria (Bundesstaat Osterreich), a corporatist-style state that came to be called Ständestaat. This medieval form of government was inspired by the anticapitalist, anticommunist message of the papal encyclicals, *Rerum Novarum* and *Quadragesimo Anno*, proposing a third way of governance different from communism and capitalism.[19] The encyclicals left to political leaders exactly what form such a new state should take. Sympathetic historians have acknowledged that Dollfuss used the guidance found in the encyclicals as well as "Christian morality" to guide him.[20] Not everyone approved of the embedding of Catholicism in the fabric of government. Political opponents, moreover, disparaged his purposes and challenged his political and legal right to set up such a state.

The political elements of the new government were adapted from governments of old. The proposed new constitution created a parliamentary system of "medieval" style "estates."[21] Citizens would form and join together in interest groups based on their occupations or professions and would then participate in government through those groups rather than as individual voters or as members of a political party.[22] Pending the ratification of the new constitution, Dollfuss ruled with a provisional government of appointed councils and Diet overseeing his executive decrees.[23]

The parts of the new constitution completed by May 1934 were approved by a Parliament of sorts consisting of Dollfuss's allies. They also ratified the decrees he had issued. The courts remained open and able to outlaw decrees beyond the chancellor's newly expanded authority. The new constitution assured equal rights and a catalog of other civil rights for all citizens.[24] It also created a new federal Supreme Court and reaffirmed the independence of the judiciary.[25] Public votes in referendums were also preserved.[26] That same Parliament vested parliamentary power in the chancellor and the president for the time being. To some historians, the Austrian government had been transformed in the image of the Vatican's recommended corporatist state.[27] Opponents disparaged it as a fascist form of government.

The rest of the constitution would be drafted by respected former chancellor Otto Ender, president of the highest court, with recommendations from several other leading figures, and the new constitution would be confirmed in full when completed.[28] In the meantime, all laws and decrees were to be only temporary until the new constitution went into effect, phase by phase.[29] A parade of the newly formed corporations was held at a Vienna stadium to celebrate the announcement of the new constitution.[30]

The councils created to become the policy sources for the government were the Cultural Council, composed of representatives of the schools, sciences, cultural groups, and religions, and the Economic Council, consisting of occupational and professional groups from the trades and industry sectors—communications, banking, forestry, agriculture, credit, mining, crafts, insurance, the professions, and the civil service.[31]

The legislature, the Bundestag, was a fifty-nine-member Diet of delegates elected by the advisory councils.[32] The thesis of the encyclicals, and the goal Dollfuss expressed, was to make the government more democratic, not less,[33] and his hope was that Austria would have, at last, effective executive authority enabling prompt action to deal with the emergencies they were facing.[34]

★ ★ ★

The trappings of power the reorganization gave to the executive were quite fairly criticized as authoritarian, but they were still far less than Austrians were long accustomed to under centuries of "radical absolutism" and "neo-absolutist" Habsburg emperors.[35] Under Habsburg rule, the political activity that took place had usually been kept in check, at times fully repressed, by chancellors and the army. Prince Metternich had ruled with an extremely tight fist, and his legendary army leaders, Count Joseph Radetzky and Prince Alfred Windischgratz, kept the army loyal to Metternich and the emperor.[36]

Elsewhere in Europe, official reaction was calm; neither Britain nor France criticized the dissolution of Parliament.[37] Scholars in many countries continue to debate the merit, or lack of it, of a government operating temporarily without a parliament. Nevertheless, socialists and other political opponents in Austria were quick to hurl invective and attach harsh labels. But the complaints of political opponents did not resonate widely with the public. In 1933, large segments of the public could see that some of those opponents were disingenuous, perhaps hypocritical, when crying fascist, since they had been aggressive in their own machinations to end Parliament in order to acquire that same power for themselves.

Political opponents devoted much debate to comparisons to other authoritarian states, and there were abundant examples. Dollfuss's implementation of an authoritarian model for government was neither unique nor even unusual in 1930s Europe. This style was by then found in a "host of European countries"[38] besieged with many of the same threats to their stability from mass movements both Left and Right; many had formed authoritarian governments as an emergency action necessary to survive the similar combined financial and social crises. Some were responsible and fair, but some headed toward dictatorship. The number of such government conversions included not only Italy, Spain, Portugal, and Germany but also Poland, Lithuania, Albania, Serbia, Croatia, Slovenia, Estonia, Latvia, Bulgaria, and Greece.[39]

★ ★ ★

In 1930s Europe, the word *fascist* was commonly and cavalierly used to describe virtually any government opposed to the parliamentary system.[40] Mussolini embraced the label; he behaved as though he had made the label *fascism* oddly fashionable. He urged Dollfuss to become entirely fascist; but Dollfuss was a lifelong believer in democracy, and he refused.[41] Critics who thought that the fascist label was a stretch referred to the Dollfuss regime with new compounds—semifascist, gob-fascist, clerico-fascist, and Austro-fascist. Some impartial historians call him authoritarian but not fascist,[42] and other historians called his regime fascist in form only, "rather than the real thing," and acknowledge that it "never became anything resembling an all-out dictatorship."[43]

Dollfuss may, in the last analysis, be the prime example of what historians have in mind when they caution against using those classic labels as pejoratives regardless of context. As one put it, the labels *fascist* and *dictator*, as applied to some of these leaders, is "unjust and oversimplified" because some of these governments were "safeguards against other vicious, extremist mass movements."[44] Hitler grabbed power to use it for aggression; Dollfuss's actions were a defense to that aggression. He did not use frauds, lies, and murders of political opponents to gain power. He was neither corrupt nor dishonest, and he took very seriously the duties he owed to everyone in Austria.

Some others reject comparing the Dollfuss government with those others because it was unique. A modern evaluation by objective US analyst/historians concludes: "Although a variety of political labels have been applied to the Dollfuss regime, it eludes simple classification."[45] While the regime had elements of some of the governments in Europe that were called fascist, it lacked the "two features widely viewed as essential to fascism": the leadership principle (*Führerprinzip*) and the mass political base.[46] Never an unchecked ruler, Dollfuss was accountable to the cabinet and the president, and his actions were subject to the courts. In Austria, moreover, there remained very real opposition to Dollfuss.

★ ★ ★

Dollfuss did resort to stern police and military tactics to deal with the violence of both the Nazi opposition and the socialist Schutzbund. In that era when the death penalty was seen by the Vatican as morally permissible, he reinstated capital punishment for murder, arson, and malicious public violence.[47] Journalists whose sympathies lay with the working class referred to these actions, particularly against the Schutzbund, as excessive, counterproductive, and fascist.[48] Others, however, viewed such measures as appropriate responses to the strikes, revolutionary rhetoric, and violence of the Schutzbund.[49] All during this period, the Marxists and the more radical among the socialists threatened to bring down, at the least, Dollfuss's government, as well as to launch a civil war and destroy the bourgeoisie. This provocative bombast, to many, provided justification for Dollfuss's coercive measures.[50]

He was also criticized for press censorship, which was among the most troublesome points of comparison with the fascist regimes of Europe, and it was a great provocation to the press. The Dollfuss regime used censorship to limit, but not eliminate, publications containing prohibited material. It was used to curtail Nazi propaganda and, conversely, to curtail language that would provoke Hitler or alienate Mussolini.[51] It was also used, however, to tone down some criticisms of the government; a few critics for this and other reasons called the censorship severe.[52] It was far less, however, than Germany's total control of the press. It was more comparable to the heavy period of censorship in America during the Great War. Under Dollfuss and Schuschnigg, both the liberal and conservative press continued to publish with a significant level of freedom. Specific stories and editorials had words or lines removed by censors, and some publications and issues were confiscated.[53] The socialist papers, the *Arbeiter Zeitung* and *Das Kleine Blatt*, continued to publish, but the Nazi *Völkischer Beobachter* was outlawed.[54]

★ ★ ★

No censorship could curtail the shouts and insults hurled by all sides, often unjustifiably. Dollfuss was called a dictator, though he did not function as a dictator or attempt to appeal to a mass movement of radicals.[55] Even some critics of the Ständestaat acknowledge the "genuine differences" between it and Germany's government under Hitler.[56] Dollfuss's Ständestaat, in its structure and in his purpose, was "far from a dictatorship" and quite different from Mussolini's Italy or any concept of "state omnipotence" common to dictatorships.[57] Many have agreed that it is more accurate to call the Ständestaat in its temporary form in its provisional years an authoritarian government.[58] Others will not even go that far; they underscore that Dollfuss was a highly moral man with no outsize ambitions, utterly free of corruption, devoted to democracy, and strongly antitotalitarian.[59]

And this bulwark against the Nazi threat was not premature. Putsches and civil disorder were both very much in the air as Nazi support in Austria grew to capture 40 percent of the vote.[60] The Nazi threat, the principal force that led Dollfuss to seek to rule in an authoritarian mode,[61] grew like wildfire after Nazis seized power in Germany. The Great Depression provided the dry tinder to fuel their rise. At bottom, the reason for popular tolerance of the Ständestaat was that Austrians had seen enough; they saw that the deadlocked Parliament had failed them—that it was unable to protect them against Nazi Germany, that another election would increase Nazi power in the Diet, and that it was unable to deal with the Depression.[62]

★ ★ ★

Hitler's success with the German economy challenged Dollfuss to demonstrate to unemployed Austrians that it was not necessary to join the Nazis to save themselves from poverty.[63] He realized that many of the Austrians drifting toward the Nazis in the Hitler era did so primarily because they wanted work. Hitler had helped provide work for Germans by ending the payment of war reparations, by building the Autobahn, and by rearming. More difficult to see was that much of the economic success during Hitler's reign was due to initiatives of others before him, especially the currency stabilization work of Hjalmar Schacht, the restructuring of war debt and ending of Germany's pariah status led by Gustav Stresemann, and the job creation program of Kurt von Schleicher.[64]

Similar measures Dollfuss initiated once the gridlock ended proved very helpful to Austria's economy—industrial costs were lowered, the tourist industry was modernized, conflict resolution was improved, trade with western partners grew, exports from heavy industry increased, and the chemical, automotive, textile, and electrical industries all began to improve.[65]

But it was his personal conduct in office more than anything that demonstrated that Dollfuss was no dictator but, instead, an honest man whose focus was the welfare of Austria. He said exactly what he believed and intended, and he was a realist. Moreover, most were well aware of his background. From his youth under the emperor, he was "the product of an upbringing that was both democratic and authoritarian," and he was reluctant to depart from a democratic model.[66] Totalitarianism, however, was a world apart from his goals.[67] He was the polar opposite of Hitler, Mussolini, or Franco, rulers who employed very different personal styles and techniques to gain power, and whose every move was calculated to assure they retained it.[68] A crucial reason given by Mussolini when he pressured Dollfuss to adopt the Italian model of fascism was that *Il Duce* believed he had invented the self-perpetuating model.[69]

★ ★ ★

Some saw points of similarity between Dollfuss's Austrian government and the comparatively benign model of Antonio Salazar's Portugal[70] because of the Catholic social doctrinal origins of both. Salazar, however, wielded unchecked power whereas the Ständestaat did not arrogate total power to the chancellor. Salazar held complete power for decades and referred to himself almost casually as a dictator, but he insisted he was a progressive. He, too, based his government on the same encyclicals, behaved as a repressive but generally moral leader and not as a brutal tyrant. In twenty-first-century surveys, Salazar has been ranked as the greatest Portuguese of modern times[71] despite his fascist label.

Many Austrians wanted even more authoritarian government—a return to the regal days of the Black and Gold of the Habsburg Empire. Some historians applaud the creation of the more authoritarian government at that crucial juncture, believing it was necessary to keep peace internally, that Dollfuss was making a "valid attempt to institute an organic order," and that it was "the sole defense against the perils of socialism and capitalism."[72]

The Austrian public, on balance, acquiesced to Dollfuss's concentration of power in the Austrian executive because Dollfuss needed an independent hand to quell Nazi terrorism, rioting, and violent attacks. They appeared to trust his assurance that he was not driven by a desire for personal power but, instead, by the need to deal with the far more threatening dictatorial power of Hitler. It was clear from the outset, moreover, that Dollfuss was never bent on implementing any *Mein Kampf* agenda or destroying any race or population.

★ ★ ★

Dollfuss's vice chancellor and heir apparent was Prince Ernst von Starhemberg, a tall, energetic orator with an aristocratic pedigree and a mysterious blank expression. He was at times underestimated as a "playboy ignoramus";[73] however, Starhemberg was intensely ambitious, and he left little breathing room for other ministers like Schuschnigg to influence policy. He became the federal leader of the Heimwehr, winning a bruising struggle against his competitor, Emil Fey, the Heimwehr leader in Vienna, a hawkish commander described as a "hatchet-faced and brutal reactionary."[74]

Dollfuss was leery of Starhemberg, yet he needed his support, for it was Starhemberg who had helped Dollfuss bring the Heimwehr leaders and their political wing, the Heimatbloc, into the Fatherland Front, the umbrella organization Dollfuss had created as a substitute for political parties. He hoped it would become a bulwark against the Nazis whose Austrian followers were plainly growing. He knew he could not withstand the Nazi violence that would erupt if he banned only the Nazis, so he dissolved all parties, the Social Democrats as well as his own Christian Socials.[75] Former members of the parties or factions could either join in his Fatherland Front or live in a political wasteland as illegal, unorganized opposition voices.[76] His hope was that the Fatherland Front would realign Austrians and temper the hostility between political parties and reduce factionalism.[77] However, as some predicted, it did not produce unity; it fueled competition.

★ ★ ★

It had been clear from the start that the Ständestaat was created in a crisis[78] that had now dramatically worsened. It began days after the Nazi government became a dictatorship in Germany. That was reason enough for many contemporaries, and many later historians, to sympathize reluctantly with Dollfuss's authoritarian state. As one puts it:

> In the same way that the Nazis agitated in Germany, they agitated in Austria, forcing Engelbert Dollfuss . . . who opposed the Nazis, to institute in retaliation something of a dictatorship of his own. . . . Austria was beset by a Nazi terror that did not stop at the destruction of railroads and power stations, murder of supporters of Dollfuss, violent interference with parliamentary processes, and the distribution of anti-Semitic propaganda.[79]

While few nations have experienced a crisis of such intensity—or had so urgent a need to enhance their government with emergency powers like those then needed in Austria—the Ständestaat, some of its formal features notwithstanding, in actual operation "was far from being a dictatorship." In fact, the Ständestaat was "some distance removed from Mussolini's Fascism" because of its morality, because it "never preached nor practiced the doctrine of state omnipotence," and because it made no attempt to use extreme and dishonest means to "control the thinking of the individual citizen or to control every aspect of his private life," despite the powers available for emergencies.[80]

★ ★ ★

Executive decrees, moreover, were neither new nor unusual in Austrian government even after the empire. Long before the Ständestaat, Austria's chancellor had possessed the power to issue decrees and executive orders, and even in the new government, those orders were subject to oversight by the independent courts. Executive orders in many other countries often stepped onto the turf reserved for a legislative body, and political opponents predictably called such measures fascist. But the iron-fisted tactics of leaders in Germany, Spain, and Russia were making Austria's time without a parliament look benign by comparison.

★ ★ ★

And Europe was not alone in this era of authoritarian governments. United States presidents were repeatedly accused of fascism as well. Many called the New Deal of President Franklin Roosevelt fascist as he gathered unprecedented levels of power in the presidency through his Depression-fighting initiatives under the National Recovery Act and his attempts to reconstitute the Supreme Court by adding additional justices aligned with him. Later on, his controversial unilateral preparations for war would draw especially loud accusations of fascism in isolationist America.[81] President Roosevelt's orders, however, became significantly more authoritarian as crises raged; he issued one executive order in 1942 confining 110,000 Japanese Americans to concentration camps without trial or accusation. Even before America was attacked, Roosevelt was criticized for actions that amounted to, in effect, waging war without going to Congress to seek a declaration of war.[82] President Roosevelt's opponents were sometimes called fascist as well.[83]

Woodrow Wilson had endured withering criticism for many authoritarian actions before and during World War I—for his arbitrary rules for press censorship; for the mass arrests of 1,186 striking workers in Arizona; and for his defiance of Congress when it refused his request to arm merchant vessels in the Atlantic—and he issued an executive order and did it anyway.[84]

★ ★ ★

If conquest by Germany from the Right were not sufficient worry for Austria's government, civil war was always looming from the Left. The conservatives were constantly challenged by the workers to their left and far more stridently by the more extreme socialists and Marxists within the Social Democratic Party. Only the moderate socialists offered any hope for a coalition, but leadership of the Social Democrats and the Schutzbund was in the hands of the radical wing.[85]

In social and economic terms, in 1930s Austrian society the alienation of classes was nearing extreme. The propertied class and the working class were separated by more than conflicting philosophies of social justice; both groups were afire with a sense of injustice to them, and each was driven by a need to fight back against the other. This had become a virtual law of nature in Austrian society.[86] Neither constituency would relent—the propertied class, the bourgeoisie, would never voluntarily surrender the power, property, and overall ascendancy they enjoyed; nor would the socialists, Marxists, or even the less ideological in the working class, accept what the Austrian economy and class structure allotted to them.[87]

The hostility between conservatives and socialists was ingrained long before Dollfuss and Schuschnigg ever entered political life. It reached a new level in a violent clash in 1927 before either of them had become a member of a government. That violence occurred in the town of Schattendorf. Conservatives and socialists were converging on the town, planning competing demonstrations. But when the conservative Front Fighters group arrived at the train depot, Schutzbunders attacked and badly beat them.[88] Other Front Fighters in the town retaliated; they fired on a marching column of Schutzbunders, and two people were killed. The skirmishes ended quickly, but three Front Fighters were charged in the deaths.

Months later a jury acquitted the defendants, and the verdict set off a rampage; thousands of socialists and workers in Vienna shut down the transports and cut off electricity.[89] A mob marched to Parliament carrying tools as weapons. The police had great difficulty trying to restrain them, so a number of police charged trying unsuccessfully to disperse the mob. In the process, the marchers injured many of the policemen. Not all casualties were incidental to chaos. One dead policeman was found with his throat neatly slit.[90] Before the day ended, the mob sacked and burned the Palace of Justice.[91]

★ ★ ★

The violence of 1927 was still fresh in the minds of the government ministers when Dollfuss became chancellor five years later. Dollfuss wanted an end to the enmity, and he proposed to bring socialists into the cabinet and to forge the kind of coalition Chancellor Seipel had once achieved in 1918 with Karl Renner, the leader of the Social Democrats. But by 1932, Otto Bauer had gained control and moved the party further to the Left, and its program was more radical than ever.[92] Renner himself warned, "We socialists cannot hold Bauer back and the Right Wing cannot hold Fey back. Mark my words; there will be a blood bath. It just has to happen."[93]

At the same time, Nazis were staging marches[94] all over Austria and trumpeting their radical right-wing propaganda while the angry-looking Bauer trumpeted the radical Left agenda of the Social Democrats and the Schutzbund. At every opportunity, Bauer made it clear that the Social Democrats were sworn enemies of Dollfuss's government and were pursuing a radical Marxist ideology.[95] He rejected coalition with Dollfuss and the Christian Socials. He forbade any cooperation at all, and members of Parliament followed his lead. Both sides behaved outrageously in the Diet, throwing inkwells and shouting "strong denunciations, taunting witticisms, noisy applause, and boos and catcalls."[96] Bauer published the threat that the socialists and the Marxists would wage "a bitter, decisive and ruthless struggle against this government."[97] They spoke convincingly and often of the "inevitable" world revolution[98] and predicted civil war.[99]

Bauer associated his cause with the Russian image. He did it in Parliament, bellowing, "I respect every Bolshevik."[100] These threats echoed the Schutzbund's long-standing plan of action, the Linz program, which called their men to be ready for violent action to bring down the government. The Schutzbund's leader, the equally radical Julius Deutsch, shouted similar taunts in the Parliament. Bauer, however, saw all this talk somewhat differently; he denied conservatives' claims that in 1926 he had urged a socialist dictatorship in Austria; he said that he had envisioned establishing a dictatorship only if the bourgeoisie was so undermining democracy that the proletariat had to launch a civil war to take power.[101] The distinction failed to reduce the alarm. The Austrian public and the Austrian government were faced with a spectrum on the left that ran from Bolsheviks, communists, ideological Marxists, radical socialists, armed Schutzbunders, and moderate socialists to nonpolitical working-class citizens, and there was little clarity how many along that spectrum were ready to turn violent. It was, after all, fresh in people's minds that it had been a leading Social Democrat, Friedrich Adler, who had personally assassinated former prime minister Karl von Stürgkh, in 1916. As for the party itself, one Social Democrat leader, Mayor Karl Seitz, warned that for their party "democracy is not the final goal. It is a means to reach the final goal: socialism."[102] This rhetoric had been flowing for nearly ten years, and the Schutzbunders regularly marched around in helmets and uniforms through the streets of Vienna as though rehearsing for an uprising.[103]

Dollfuss was among the moderates who wanted very much to avoid bloodshed, and he made overtures to the moderate socialists to try to stave off what was coming.[104] Bauer did nothing to encourage Dollfuss's attempts to improve the relationship.[105] He would ridicule Dollfuss, disparaging his height in rude language[106] and addressing the chancellor to his face as "Little Dollfuss,"[107] and he called the rural Christian Socials "*Dorftrottel*" (village morons).[108] Bauer was seen by many as an intellectual among Austro-Marxists, in part because he had studied under Lenin himself, but Lenin referred to Bauer as an "educated idiot."[109]

★ ★ ★

It was in Vienna that the workers of otherwise conservative Austria held their most extraordinary sway. The capital had been granted *Lander* status in 1921 under the constitution, the equivalent of a state or a province, which conferred on the Viennese the power to impose taxes, approve their own budget, and provide for "cradle to grave" welfare and rent control programs.[110] Vienna's workers were especially insistent on public funds to build decent housing. When socialist budgets funded the huge Karl-Marx-Hof and other complexes, the bourgeoisie resented it, calling the expenditures a "soak the rich"[111] welfare move that fell in reality on the backs of the middle class. They complained that they could ill afford the taxes to pay for it, and they pushed back angrily against the workers' other demands. Vienna's leftist finance minister, Hugo Breitner, along with Otto Bauer and Julius Deutsch, bore the brunt of the criticism from the bourgeoisie.

Yet the socialist underground and the Schutzbund kept up the incendiary threats and propaganda.[112] One historian writes: "The Austro-Marxists clung to words which made violence inevitable."[113] That violence was seen in public street fights and armed clashes requiring police action to stop them.

In 1932 alone, there were twenty-four armed clashes and violent brawls just between the Social Democrats and the Nazis; several people were killed in these fights.[114] Bloody brawls also regularly occurred in municipal councils and at universities.[115]

All sides debated who was to blame. The Heimwehr took the position that it was acting in response to the Schutzbund's threats of revolution, while the Schutzbund took the position that its share of the violence was not spontaneous, that the Heimwehr intentionally provoked them. The Heimwehr did provoke at least some of the violence, but observers claimed that the Schutzbund did so as well; others said that once the violence commenced, both were culpable.[116] But each side would point the finger at the other asserting blame for the violence after every skirmish.

The government feared that this frequent violence posed an existential threat and began conducting searches for all the hiding places used by the Schutzbund for machine guns, bombs, and weapons. These arsenals were in heavily guarded locations throughout Austria. Meanwhile, the Schutzbund soldiers were told to wear their uniforms in public;[117] they had the look of a force able to begin a revolution at any moment. Since the Social Democratic Party had openly subscribed to the idea of commencing a civil war if necessary,[118] concern soared when police discovered a large stash of Schutzbund weapons in Styria. The Schutzbund had engaged in a particularly bloody clash on March 17, 1933, in Bruck an der Mur.[119] After that attack, the Nazis began a week-long binge of violence and murder from June 12 to 19, 1933.[120] This back-and-forth carnage became so frequent that it created the fear that Hitler might invade Austria using the pretext that Germany needed to restore order and put an end to the violence Austria's own government appeared unable to control.

★ ★ ★

The Schutzbund uprising finally began on February 12, 1934, provoked by a sudden government search of its meeting place, the Hotel Schiff in Linz, one of the arsenals where the Schutzbund housed weapons. It did not help that Emil Fey, the man ordering the search, wore two hats. He was the state secretary in charge of public security affairs, but he was also Vienna branch leader of the Heimwehr.[121] Fey decided that the Schutzbund, the Nazis, and the communists all must be disarmed and forbidden to hold parades or meetings.[122] The Schutzbund official in charge at the Schiff in Linz, Richard Bernaschek, was a vocal lightning rod on the left.[123] He and some sixty other members of the Schutzbund were in the hotel when the government's raid to confiscate the Schutzbund's weapons began.

Bernaschek had notified the Social Democratic Party leaders in Vienna that the Schutzbund had decided to start an uprising upon the next government search of one of the Schutzbund's citadels of arms. He insisted that the decision was unalterable. Exactly what the party leaders themselves decided is less clear, but in later court proceedings, a Social Democrat district leader testified that the top socialist leaders had decided the prior month to commence a socialist uprising against the government.[124]

The raid on the Hotel Schiff began, and Bernaschek shouted out a call to arms ("To the weapons"). That cry, and the call for a general strike, spread throughout Austria. Fighting broke out in many towns and cities.[125] Some radicals responded, but most workers did not. Some workers took only limited actions to support a general strike, but those steps were enough to shut down electricity, and late that morning Vienna went dark, transportation was interrupted, and some other services came to a halt. Members of the Vienna Schutzbund shot and killed a police inspector,[126] and police poured into the streets and faced armed resistance from socialists.

The Social Democrats and their Schutzbund finally had, in the Christian Socials' view, commenced the long-feared revolution and were heading into civil war.[127] Many Christian Socials felt sure that such an uprising would mushroom and mirror Russia's Bolshevik Revolution where the overthrow led to the execution of Czar Nicholas II and his wife and children, then to many more atrocities, and then to a long, murderous civil war.

The many causes of this tragic violence have long been debated. Documents confirm that the Schutzbund had planned to go on the attack when the next search occurred; however, they placed the blame on the government for provoking them.[128] The accusations of culpability for the violent revolt and the four-day civil war began immediately and continue to be heard today. The Social Democrats claimed that the documents did not show that the Social Democrat leaders had approved a national uprising. They also disputed evidence that was found showing that their top leadership had plans in place for establishing military headquarters for an uprising including tribunals to put the leaders of the government on trial.[129] One historian's analysis of the roles played by leaders on each side in lighting the conflagration concluded that blaming either side alone "would not only be patently unfair; it would also be utter historical nonsense."[130]

A more extreme claim was eventually articulated—that the Dollfuss government itself wanted or planned such an uprising against itself. That was not accompanied by evidence, and it appears far-fetched, for Dollfuss had just made a very public appeal on January 19 to the workers of Austria asking for their cooperation.[131]

The Heimwehr, however, was another matter; it had been a provocative force, particularly the forces led by Emil Fey. They had at least knowingly provoked the Schutzbund.[132] Fey had a strong hatred for Marxism, and he knew that Mussolini wanted Austria to put an end to the socialists' power. It appears doubtful that Fey knew that a socialist uprising was being planned by Richard Bernaschek's Schutzbund forces, but Fey's ambition and aggressiveness strongly suggest he welcomed a showdown.[133] Fey, however, was no confidant of Dollfuss; he wanted Dollfuss's job, and Dollfuss knew it. Fey was also a hostile rival of his Heimwehr colleague, Starhemberg, and was a man who blended "half loyalty and half treachery."[134] Dollfuss feared Fey not for the political competition; he feared assassination by Fey's many henchmen. Dollfuss had recently contemplated sleeping away from his own lodgings because of what Fey might do.[135]

Starhemberg was aggressive as well; he provided his own share of fascist forces. He professed to be able to field 30,000 Heimwehr fighters against the Schutzbund.[136] To add to the Heimwehr's considerable armament, Starhemberg covertly obtained large supplies of machine guns and rifles from Italy in the so-called Hirtenberg affair.[137]

★ ★ ★

Neither Dollfuss nor his closest government officials saw the uprising coming. On the day it erupted, he and several ministers were in church and were preparing for a full day of ordinary engagements; they were surprised and confused when lights went out in the Vienna church late in the morning of February 12.[138] The Schutzbund had cut electrical lines all over Vienna, which turned buildings in the capital into foreboding, darkened armed camps.[139] All six rail lines leading into Vienna were bombed.[140] A sizable bomb found its way to the desk of the vice chancellor, but it failed to explode.[141] Confusion reigned because Nazis also were suspected; they had recently committed scores of murders in Austria.

Dollfuss knew the Schutzbund's capability from the weapons searches already conducted.[142] He declared martial law in Vienna and in the specific provinces where Schutzbund fighting erupted.[143] They had fighters located throughout Austria, 60,000 strong, and somewhere they had huge supplies of grenades, rifles, ammunition, and machine guns.

When the uprising began, the Schutzbunders set up military positions in the sturdy workers' apartment complexes and began firing machine guns. Dollfuss had to bring such urban warfare to an end quickly—before Hitler invoked it as a pretext to take over Austria.[144] He was presented the difficult choice whether to direct the police to invade the workers' Vienna housing complexes—including the fortress-like Karl-Marx-Hof, whose cellars were the central arsenal for storing the Schutzbund's weapons[145]—or to fire artillery at the thick walls of the complex from which Schutzbund gunmen were firing their machine guns. Determined to do battle, the socialists had largely evacuated the families and had manned the housing complexes with gunmen.[146] Neither the police nor the army had tear gas that might permit them to evacuate the complex; tear gas had been banned by the Treaty of St. Germain. An eyewitness described the socialists opening continual sniper fire at patrols from the windows of houses; even some observers sympathetic to the socialists called the revolt criminal, unforgivable, and a self-destructive gift to Hitler.[147] Dollfuss's pleas to the rebels to accept amnesty and end the revolt were sincere and emotional. He knew that an infantry-style invasion would plainly produce the most casualties on both sides, so, when the rebels would not cease, Dollfuss approved the commanders' request to fire single salvos of artillery while offering amnesty for all but the ringleaders.[148]

Fighting raged in many areas throughout Austria; in some places, shooting lasted for sixteen days and resulted in many deaths—105 to 115 government soldiers, 137 to 270 Schutzbunders, and hundreds of civilians.[149] The violence left in its wake considerable destruction of workers' housing. Finally, the Schutzbund surrendered, and Dollfuss ended martial law on February 21.[150]

★ ★ ★

Dollfuss incurred the lasting enmity of the socialists, the workers, and those sympathetic to the plight of the workers who had viewed the socialists' revolutionary rhetoric more charitably. Some had not viewed it as a threat of revolution but, instead, as a cry for needed reform.[151] In Europe and America, commentators sympathetic to the Left condemned the government's violent response as "cold blooded slaughter of the Social Democrats."[152] However, in the heated debate, one charge—that the government fired on "defenseless workers"—has drawn particularly harsh rebuttal: "Like most of the party slogans of the day, the charge substituted emotions for facts."[153] Dollfuss insisted that his purpose, moreover, had been to disarm the Schutzbund, not wipe out the socialists.[154] He had directed that the government's response be humane,[155] and he professed sympathy for the workers and their families.[156] Those fired upon were predominantly Schutzbund gunmen who were armed and firing on the police; Dollfuss, nevertheless, said the order to fire artillery was "the most terrible decision of my life, but it was the only way to cut short the fighting."[157]

★ ★ ★

Schuschnigg had little to do with the field operations of the civil war, but he had a role as minister of justice in the prosecutions.[158] Military courts handed down twenty-one death sentences. Nine socialists central to the revolt were executed.[159] Twelve of the death sentences were commuted to life imprisonment.[160] Many other socialists were jailed, further polarizing the workers. Little has been proposed to show that those convicted were not culpable, but the executions in the wake of speedy courts-martial left an extremely bad taste. The later trials in civilian court were conducted under indictments carefully drawn in terms that removed any possibility of capital sentences for the socialist defendants.[161]

The United States ambassador, George H. Earle III, and the chargé d'affaires both voiced their support of Dollfuss's actions in reports to the secretary of state.[162]

The entire Left came under condemnation as well. Although Bauer, Deutsch, and Bernaschek were the firebrands of the Left,[163] Bauer and Deutsch were criticized for fleeing to Czechoslovakia on the second day of the fighting. In fact, not even all allies of the Social Democrats supported this radical conduct. Vienna's middle-class Jews largely rallied to Dollfuss's side, and the Union of Jewish War Veterans did as well.[164]

These events, nevertheless, sealed the hostility between the two populations. The socialists' call to arms was seen as a "strategic disaster," one that followed "mass inflammatory strikes, rhetoric, and occasional street violence by the left" leading not merely to violence but also to a national tragedy.[165] The socialist leadership under which this occurred has been branded as "flawed" by their critics and even by some who supported their larger platform.[166] The rigidity and radicalism of the Vienna Left, in the view of one generally sympathetic observer, had now "contributed significantly to its own destruction."[167]

★ ★ ★

At Christmas 1935, the government granted amnesty, freeing virtually all of the 1,521 prisoners, yet the alienation of the socialists was now permanent. Some workers even became Nazi supporters. Although socialists and Nazis were thought to be polar opposites, Richard Bernaschek, who had issued the call to arms and was already well known for making anti-Semitic remarks even against fellow Social Democrats,[168] defected together with some entire Schutzbund units[169] and became Nazis.[170]

Once Dollfuss, the creator of the new government, was killed, Austrians had to wonder what form government would assume under their new chancellor. Despite his distaste for the fascism of the Heimwehr and the Nazis, Schuschnigg inherited every criticism leveled at Dollfuss, warranted or not, from the socialists and other political enemies. They opposed the executive power that had been entrusted to Schuschnigg.[171] When he accepted it, he inherited not only the Ständestaat but also the label of fascism their opponents had applied to it.

★ ★ ★

Most Austrians had scant familiarity with Schuschnigg. As they began to take stock of him, it became clear that, though inheriting authoritarian tools, he was at least no Hitler, Mussolini, or Franco. Austrians took comfort in the quality of the members of Dollfuss's government and Schuschnigg's appointments as well. The appointed councils that supplanted the Diet were filled with respected members, and their reputations went a long way toward assuring the public that Austria was not suddenly going to veer toward dictatorship. It became clear to the diplomatic community that the Austrian population was behind the Schuschnigg government.[172] The international diplomatic community, including the United States embassy officials and their colleagues in that astute community, expressed their own virtually unanimous respect for Schuschnigg and for the members of his government councils. The US ambassador called for the United States to give its support to Schuschnigg; he warned Washington that Schuschnigg's government was "a necessity for European peace" and cautioned against holding public elections (" a return to elections and parliamentary government here now would only lead to internal chaos and upset the whole situation in this part of the world").[173] The two complaints about the continuation of the governmental form, aside from using councils instead of a parliament, were the lack of a Social Democratic voice and the heavier use of executive orders. From the outset, Schuschnigg issued predominantly rather ordinary executive orders and took no action to use power as a dictator would.[174] And the same United States ambassador advised Washington that the Social Democrats would be "distinctly worse."[175]

· 5 ·

Schuschnigg and the Jewish Question

"An absolute abyss separates Austria from Nazism."

—Kurt von Schuschnigg, January 5, 1938

*H*itler was using the Great Depression very effectively—he realized that the misery it caused his subjects fueled their gullibility for propaganda. He built upon a handful of lies that neatly satisfied the German public's thirst for vengeance against the villains who had caused their misery.

Hitler blamed everything he could on the Jews, which helped make his racial laws acceptable to a huge part of the German population. Once the Nuremberg Laws became acceptable in Germany, he tried to spread racial laws beyond Germany's borders to nearby Austria, Italy, and Hungary. It was becoming clear that these racial policies were the core of Hitler's mania and the point of the Nazi spear aimed at neighboring countries.

Schuschnigg refused Nazi demands that he adopt their racial policies. He forbade repression and discrimination against Jews. He repressed the Nazis instead. Nazis inside Austria tried to force these issues with violence and propaganda. They railed against Schuschnigg's anti-Nazi and pro-Jewish stripes, and they redoubled their efforts to assassinate him.

★ ★ ★

Hitler's first conquest was always going to be Austria when he finally was ready to launch his campaign to reclaim the "lost territories" of Germany.[1] The capital, Vienna, was his bull's eye. Hitler hated Vienna, scene of the misery of his teens and the rejections and failures that plagued his early twenties.[2] "Red Vienna" seemed to taunt him as a red flag does a bull. More than just "Red," to Hitler, Vienna was Jewish. He complained that Vienna had "the Jew here and there and everywhere."[3] His hatred of Vienna was often a source

Hitler, Göring, and Vienna Gauleiter Baldur von Schirach (in uniform at right rear) at
Berchtesgaden.
Source: Bundesarchiv.

of spontaneous bellowing. The Nazi Party's Vienna Gauleiter, Baldur von Schirach, recounted during his testimony at the Nuremberg war crimes trials that he had once witnessed Hitler in private at his Berghof estate raging with "incredible and unlimited hatred" against "the people of Vienna." Schirach testified that Hitler just "hated its people."[4]

Exactly how Hitler became obsessed with hatred of Jews[5] has perplexed many who studied him and has been attributed to several causes: his extremist view of racial traits and his fantasized exaggeration of both Aryan superiority and Semitic defects; his hysterical embrace of the anti-Semitism of the times; his lack of contacts with Jews in early life; and his immersion in anti-Semitic literature and periodicals—nineteenth-century anti-Semitic tracts of writers such as Theodor Billroth and Eugen Dühring—during his Vienna years.[6] His friend August Kubizek, however, wrote that Hitler had been an intense anti-Semite in his youth before he ever left home for Vienna.[7]

At that young age, Hitler was already spouting anti-Semitism freely. Many ignored him, but the anti-Semitism of the era helped Hitler spread his influence among Germanic peoples.[8] His rants were most effective with the like-minded haters he found among the seething outcasts of 1920s Bavaria. They craved affirmation of these views from someone impressive, a mentor who would encourage and guide them, a chorus to approve and embrace what he preached, and an outlet, a gang, to provide him the catharsis of action.

Whatever were the origins of Hitler's fanaticism, by the time Kurt von Schuschnigg came on the scene, the most provocative thing he could do to inflame Hitler was to defend or embrace the Jews of Austria.

★ ★ ★

By the 1920s, Hitler had found all of the ingredients he needed to become a racist political demagogue, and the Jews of Austria had begun to comprehend what Hitler and his Nazi gangs were willing to do to Jews in Germany—and to tremble during the 1930s as those Nazis circled around them getting poised to pounce on Austria. The Austrian Nazis were chanting anti-Semitism to mobilize receptive Austrians at election time, and they intimidated opposition voters by random violence. Officials who opposed them were often assassinated. Fear of Nazi violence silenced many Austrians; what those silent Austrians really felt is impossible to know. Some contemporary observers of the Austrians of this era believed that the vast majority were not extremists but, instead, decent and honorable people.[9] Many other Austrians, however, still reflected the anti-Semitic attitudes of their ancestors. In the eighteenth century, racial and religious anti-Semitism was approved by Emperor Leopold I and Empress Maria Theresa. Indeed, the empress herself led the way. Not only Jews, but Protestants became targets of her imperial religious discrimination. Strangely, for this zealous Catholic, she was hostile to Jesuits as well.[10]

However, her son, Emperor Joseph II, came to power in 1765, and the leadership message changed. Joseph promulgated the Edict of Tolerance in 1782 and dismantled some aspects of the apparatus of imperial discrimination against Jews and others. But Austrian Jews in the eighteenth and nineteenth centuries were not merely discriminated against; many Jews were considered illegal residents and thus were easy prey for extortion by public officials and opportunists demanding bribes just to allow them to stay.[11]

Franz Joseph became emperor in 1848, and, with some considerable prodding, he gradually became the most philosemitic of all the emperors. In 1849, he dismissed Parliament and decreed a new constitution enshrining equal civic and political rights for all regardless of religion; yet, at that time, the constitution notwithstanding, he ruled with "radical absolutism"[12] and refused to fully emancipate the Jews, to free them from restrictions on relocating, or to grant them the right to own property. It was not until the new constitution of 1860 and financial pressure that he changed his attitude. His financiers, the Rothschilds, told him "No constitution, no money," and Franz Joseph came around. With that motivation, he became a "neo-absolutist" and fully emancipated the Jews.[13] Eventually, Franz Joseph also insisted upon respect for Jews in Austrian society and helped dilute anti-Semitism. Gradually, many Jews came to revere him.[14]

★ ★ ★

The twentieth-century Jews of Austria did not withdraw in the face of discrimination. They were a robust, energetic population. Vienna was home to the third-largest Jewish population in Western Europe, behind Warsaw and Budapest.[15] The total Jewish population in the 1930s was difficult to measure; it was sometimes estimated as low as 200,000, but there was the belief that another 100,000 Austrians may have been Jewish, but not readily identified as such. Two-thirds of Austria's Jews lived in Vienna, and by virtue of that concentration, they ranked as the largest religious minority in the capital.[16]

Vienna's Jewish population was also diverse; it was composed of several social and religious components—a few wealthy bankers and businessmen, some prosperous chain store owners, academics, affluent doctors and lawyers,[17] clerical workers, and an abundance of immigrant peddlers and street hawkers. Prior to the Nazis, some Austrian Jews of the 1930s said they felt no overt disdain, hostility, or mistreatment in their daily lives even while others did.

Nor did they fail against these odds to obtain advancement and some great success. Jews played leading roles in academia,[18] the professions, and cultural circles, and many Jews in Vienna, such as Sigmund Freud, Theodor Herzl, and others, achieved great distinction. As distinguished as Freud was, however, late in his career he still had not been awarded fully advanced academic status at the University of Vienna.[19] Numerically, most Viennese Jews were bourgeoisie, and significant minorities of them were middle and upper class. There were few Viennese Jews among the most volatile group in the socialist ranks, the laborers. And there was also considerable Jewish poverty.[20]

The cloud of anti-Semitism covering the beauty of Vienna was comparable to that found in Germany.[21] Yet in Vienna, Jews provided 62 percent of the lawyers, 47 percent of the doctors, and 27 percent of university professors; in business circles, 85 percent of furniture dealers and 94 percent of advertising agencies were Jewish.[22]

National origin played a large role in defining Austria's Jewish social and political landscape. A marker for anti-Semitism was the failure to speak German, and many Viennese Jews were from elsewhere in Eastern Europe, especially Galicia and Bukovina. Polish and Russian immigrant Jews were separate populations, readily identified by their accents and distinctive dress. Most immigrants among them were poor, spoke Yiddish, and were Zionists.[23] Some Jewish immigrants, however, were the Jewish intelligentsia from those other European regions, those who fled pogroms and persecution at home and chose Austria as a comparatively better place. The Western Jews from Bohemia, Hungary, Moravia, and German regions spoke German and assimilated so well that they were referred to as "natives."[24] No community in Austria was entirely free of some type of anti-Semitism and some forms of discrimination. In Austria, as in Germany, prior to the propaganda campaigns of the Nazis, many Germans disliked Jews—"or rather the dominant cultural images of Jews"—not with an attitude of hatred but with a casual anti-Semitism with little political consequence because it was "too minor a problem to decide their vote."[25]

None among them seemed to see what was in store for a nation that let those attitudes grow.

★ ★ ★

As the increasingly tense face-off between Austria and the Third Reich approached its fifth year, the concessions made to appease Hitler were buying time but no relief. Schuschnigg continued to infuriate Hitler and provoke the Nazis by rowing against Austria's historic tide of anti-Semitism. Faced with the choice between embracing, tolerating, or condemning the Nazis' anti-Semitism, Schuschnigg grew more emphatic in rejecting it. He resisted all pressure to adopt the Nazi racial creed and, instead, condemned religious and racial intolerance.

In the 1930s, there were no major initiatives aimed at stamping out European anti-Semitism. Such progress would only find momentum after discovery of the Holocaust. Schuschnigg was taking a decidedly measured approach at a time and place when anti-Semitism had strong roots. He could expect only opposition from most Austrians to his stance against any official discrimination in Austria. That he did this with the most powerful anti-Semite in history breathing down his neck had to be refreshing to Jewish leaders, but it may have hastened the Austrian crisis to its conclusion.

★ ★ ★

Schuschnigg and Dollfuss had both been shaped by their Catholic upbringings and influenced by the papacy of Pope Pius XI. They both "repeatedly reaffirmed their commitment to the 1934 constitution, which . . . guaranteed the equality of all citizens before the law . . . and promised complete equality to all legally recognized religions."[26] Unlike Hitler, Schuschnigg respected the teachers of his youth, and even in anti-Semitic Austria, he had heard none of that religious intolerance from his Jesuit teachers.[27] The question about the new chancellor was whether he would practice what he preached.

The Dollfuss years as prologue to the Schuschnigg years had brought hope on race; they began a quiet break with Austria's intolerant past. Under Dollfuss, the year 1933 had "marked a major turning point for Austria and Austrian Jewry."[28] However, it was clear that not all change was going to constitute progress with Hitler in power in Germany and the Nazis with a dramatically increased presence in Austria.

Nevertheless, under Dollfuss and Schuschnigg, change had become visible to Jews. There were no longer signs of earlier governments' tolerance of the anti-Semitism indulged by some Christian Socials. Even though the Jewish leaders had little political leverage with which to motivate a chancellor to take unpopular positions on race, both of these chancellors refused to tolerate discrimination or even condone "verbal invective" when they heard it.[29]

★ ★ ★

One common thread heavily influenced the political and social choices of the Jews of Vienna—they were overwhelmingly liberals. The working-class Jews were mostly socialists, and a number were Marxists.[30] Vienna was the home base of the urban working class and was under the political control of the socialists, while the provinces were predominantly conservative. Socialism offered Jews a more inclusive political and social landscape.[31] Moreover, Jews obtained leadership positions in the Social Democratic Party.[32] While many socialists were peasants, some prosperous Jews were socialists. Even some Marxists joined the Social Democrats because few Austrians were willing to belong openly to the small Austrian Communist Party; many who might have joined it found the Social Democratic Party a palatable substitute.[33]

With these several communities on the Left, Vienna's local political control was dominated by workers and socialists.[34] That control was significant because of Vienna's *Lander* status—the stature of a province—and the ability to impose taxes for its own revenue.[35] That added to the power of the Social

Democrats, and the power of Vienna's Jewish leaders increased when the Jewish political activist Otto Bauer, one of the most visible Austro-Marxists, became a leader of the Social Democratic Party.

Viewed in terms of Left-Right politics, the Jews and the Catholics would appear to be in opposite camps; however, Austria was more complicated than that. Catholicism's numerical domination was stark. Some 80 to 90 percent of 6,775,000 Austrians were Catholic.[36] Many were conservative, and many, but not all, voted for the Christian Social Party. They, too, cast votes based on issues crucial to their pocketbooks, their divergent views on German nationalism, and the conflict between agricultural and urban interests, rather than on issues of religion.

As the Jewish electorate looked beyond Catholic politicians, they usually found no candidacy that was ideal for them and none that was utterly free of anti-Semitism; they had to assess the degrees of anti-Semitism. The Jewish working-class vote, potentially nearly 100,000, often went very heavily but not entirely to the Social Democrats. Some Jews supported the Christian Social Party just as some Catholics did not.[37]

Only intense anti-Semites were bent on repression or expulsion of Jews. Most Austrians were so-called moderate anti-Semites, who revealed "overtones" of "restrained" and "ambiguous" anti-Semitism; they were receptive to anti-Jewish rhetoric in political speech, and many Christian Social politicians of the 1920s used it.[38] Political, social, and public debates between the heavily Catholic countryside and the heavily Jewish Vienna political activists often led to accusations that the dialogue was moderately anti-Semitic, while the Christian Social politicians insisted that they were not anti-Semitic. But their image on this score was not helped by their association with the far more biased Heimwehr leaders. Many Jews saw the Heimwehr and its leaders, Ernst von Starhemberg and Emil Fey, as strikingly anti-Semitic.[39]

★ ★ ★

By the 1930s, attitudes had improved somewhat among members of both of the powerful parties. The succeeding generation of Christian Social leaders was not as biased and was even less commonly called racist.[40] For that and other reasons, more of the Jewish population supported the Christian Social government in the 1930s, including the better-informed Jewish industrialists.[41]

Moreover, the other main political choice, the Social Democrats, had never been a perfectly safe harbor for Austrian Jews. Socialism was weaker in the provinces; thus there was greater incidence of the less socialist provincial Jews voting for the Christian Socials.[42] Moreover, the Social Democrats at times showed antagonism to the Jews and used anti-Semitic rhetoric.[43] Some of the Social Democrat leaders had made anti-Semitic speeches over the years, and the party's publications had featured anti-Semitic writings and unflattering stereotypical cartoons of Jews and disparaging comments.[44] Generally, the leaders in the Social Democratic Party opposed anti-Semitism, yet they were hesitant to speak out boldly in support of Jews because some Social Democratic voters were fervently anti-Semitic.[45] These conflicted views coexisted despite the party's many Jewish supporters because party leaders feared that their non-Jewish voters would accuse them of "philosemitism." Many Jews saw lapses of sensitivity in the Social Democratic Party as a sign that the leaders took the Jewish vote for granted.[46]

Some segments of the Jewish population were leery of the party simply because they opposed the radical aspects of the socialist agenda; many middle-class Austrian Jews in particular sided with the Christian Social government during the socialist uprising in 1934.[47] The Social Democrats also had difficulty attracting religious Jews and Zionists because the socialists were anti-religion and refused to endorse Zionism.[48] Many Jews saw socialism as weakening Jewish cultural and family life.[49] Despite their imperfect racial history,[50] however, the Social Democrats, too, seemed less racist by the 1930s, particularly because of the prominence in the party of the Jewish leader, Otto Bauer.[51]

★ ★ ★

In addition to the divide between these two dominant parties, Austria had to face the increasing demands by the Nazis to allow their propaganda. Press censorship of the Nazis was popular among anti-Nazis, but as Germany's military strength heralded violent conquest, all of Austria's political parties had to choose their own public words very carefully. They all had to avoid provoking an invasion by the definitively more powerful Third Reich. Thus, both parties exercised self-censorship in this crossfire. The Social Democratic spokesmen, and the Christian Social spokesmen, for the most part avoided issuing ringing public condemnations of anti-Semitism. They also avoided bold public defenses of Jewish interests for fear of the inevitable backlash from Nazis.[52] Press censorship even when employed for these same goals, however, was more controversial.

Cultural anti-Semitism, so thinly veiled in ordinary times, became highly visible in the toughest economic times.[53] During the extremely poor postwar economy and the Great Depression, Austria faced severe austerity, rising food prices, and high interest rates. These conditions were accompanied by a steep rise of anti-Semitism.[54] Jewish employment suffered amid that economic misery due to the accompanying spike of anti-Semitism. When the Rothschild bank Creditanstalt failed in 1931, many Jews employed there and in related businesses lost their jobs.[55] By 1937, around one-third of Vienna's Jews were unemployed.[56] Even in better times, when the Jewish businesses in pre-Nazi Vienna thrived, Jewish businesses were far less successful in the more widely anti-Semitic countryside. Employment discrimination sometimes took the form of quotas for Jews in certain trades and professions.[57] Some politicians openly advocated imposing quotas.[58]

★ ★ ★

Although Dollfuss rejected anti-Semitism, many Jews in Vienna continued to be his political opponents. Many of them were stalwarts of the labor movement, or of the socialist campaigns, and a number were Marxists. Dollfuss's hostility to their very liberal politics and to the occasional violent tactics led some of them at first to doubt the sincerity of his opposition to anti-Semitism. However, the absence of anti-Semitism in his own words and his policies soon confirmed that his platform calling for religious freedom and racial tolerance by government and by society was exactly what he believed.[59]

Jews had historically been excluded from a number of organizations, but under Dollfuss's leadership, they were admitted to membership and participation in the Fatherland Front. The Union of Austrian Jews agreed to join the Front, but individuals' old biases died hard; no Jews held positions in the party's hierarchy.[60]

The message of tolerance Dollfuss expressed about Jews sharply exacerbated his troubles with Germany. Every sign of tolerance infuriated Hitler. The Austrian Nazis became more vocal and more violent with Dollfuss as the head of government, and Dollfuss's actions increased the Reich's urgency to put an end to Austria.[61]

★ ★ ★

As brief as Dollfuss's tenure had been, some leaders of the Jewish community had gotten to know Dollfuss well and to trust him. US ambassador George S. Messersmith kept a careful watch over Austrian Jewish affairs. He assessed Dollfuss in that sensitive context as "a very devout and very good man" and one who was "by no means an anti-Semite." Dollfuss, he said, had tried to follow a "neutral course."[62]

★ ★ ★

Schuschnigg was from the provinces where a tradition of anti-Semitism meant that some bias could virtually be assumed.[63] No one needed to be reminded that Hitler was a product of Austria's river Inn provinces. This led the US ambassador to harbor doubts about Schuschnigg, to question during the early months of his administration whether, as a Tyrolean, Schuschnigg might be "slightly anti-Semitic in his feelings, or if this not be so, that he does not have the understanding of the implications of discrimination and of the Jewish problem as a whole which his predecessor, Mr. Dollfuss, had. There was no reason, however, to believe that the new chancellor would tolerate any anti-Semitic activity or in any way permit the constitutional rights of the Jews to be infringed upon."[64] What he soon enough learned about Schuschnigg was that, despite that early provincial environment, he was an honest and devout man, a gentleman who showed no anti-Semitism in word or action, one who "is inclined toward tolerance and cannot be called a bigot."[65]

Like Dollfuss before him, Schuschnigg was a follower of the progressive papacy of Pope Pius XI, and he, too, embraced the Pope's encyclical *Quadragesimo Anno* as a call to treat all people fairly "irrespective of religious creed."[66] Schuschnigg emphasized that the purpose of the new form of government was to put the principles of *Quadragesimo Anno* into reality.[67]

Independent contemporary evaluations of Dollfuss and Schuschnigg, including a report by the British consul in Innsbruck, confirmed that, even in the provinces, their governments pursued a policy of undiscriminating liberalism and endeavored to prevent discrimination against Jews.[68]

★ ★ ★

In Vienna, however, where most Jews lived, they were less than comfortable with the anti-Semitism of local officials, especially Richard Schmitz, the Bürgermeister. Schmitz was a determined opponent of the Nazis as well as a Dollfuss appointee; he had become the "dictator" of municipal affairs in Vienna, including the hands-on implementation of laws and policies impacting the schools and the professions. Schmitz, however, had come to be seen as "an open and pronounced anti-Semite."[69] How Vienna would be run—by the Schuschnigg government's public stance of unequivocal opposition to discrimination or by Schmitz's tastes—remained to be seen. The Jewish leaders could anticipate that they might eventually have to seek the intervention of the chancellor himself in Vienna's municipal affairs.[70]

Many of Schuschnigg's government officials spoke out against violent anti-Semitism. Even that was a notable break with the resounding silence of the party's past.[71] No one expected them to be able to purge Austria of anti-Semitism; indeed it was gratefully acknowledged that Schuschnigg's policies and statements brought about a notable reduction in violence against Jews.[72] Refreshing as that was, far greater reform of Austrian society was a legitimate demand.

Resistance to systemic anti-Semitism, however, drew vocal opposition, and in many quarters, there were also attempts to sabotage efforts to end discrimination. Schuschnigg described to diplomats his frustration over the country's inability to eradicate anti-Semitic feeling among its people.[73] He emphasized the contrast between the anti-Semites and his government's policies, and he lamented the attitudes of old in his party. Before long, Jewish leaders confirmed that, as to Schuschnigg's own commitment and sincerity, they were "completely satisfied."[74]

If there were to be a confrontation, he would surely lose even more of his supporters to the Nazis. To avoid one, Schuschnigg had to express his public opposition to discrimination using politically calm language calling for religious freedom and equality, rather than delivering a lambasting to the anti-Semites.[75] He would caution that people should not judge him based on his affiliation with the Christian Social Party whose checkered history on this subject long predated his arrival in politics.[76] His messages still drew sharp reactions from anti-Semites. As for the most anti-Semitic faction connected to the party, the Heimwehr, his conflict with its biased leaders was far better known.[77] The public was used to helmeted, uniformed Heimwehr troops parading in Vienna chanting "Down with Schuschnigg! To the gallows with him!"[78]

Both Schuschnigg and Dollfuss had their critics, but some critics underscored just how opposed these two chancellors were to anti-Semitism by charging that they had sold out to the Jews. The insult spoke volumes; it trained the spotlight on Schuschnigg's opposition to anti-Semitism and lent emphasis to his words.[79] The Nazis virtually dared him to condemn anti-Semitism in emphatic terms. They spread venomous propaganda through a network of underground operations in Austria to coerce Schuschnigg to accept their racial ideology; they made Austria pay a price for his refusal by tightening the screws of Germany's boycott of Austria's Jewish products.[80]

★ ★ ★

Schuschnigg's determination to resist the Nazis' anti-Jewish policies had its roots in his view of Catholicism, a different moral base than that of many Austrian Catholics who were cavalier in their anti-Semitism.[81] The teachings of the reigning pontiff, Pope Pius XI, were central to understanding which type[82] of Catholic he was.

No other clergyman wielded social and political influence equal to that of the pope. Even non-Catholics were well aware that any pope was important to their lives because they could be indirectly impacted by a pope's influence on the huge European Catholic population. In the days of the empire, many Austro-Hungarian Jews had kept abreast of papal pronouncements for this reason, and many had supported earlier popes with great fervor.[83]

★ ★ ★

Jews everywhere would eventually have reason to rejoice at the elevation to the papacy in 1922 of Cardinal Achille Ratti as Pope Pius XI—he became the Jews' greatest Vatican ally. The then twenty-five-year-old Kurt von Schuschnigg became a fervent disciple, well before the events of the 1930s that set him and Pius XI on their paths toward their collisions[84] with the racial policies of Adolf Hitler and the detailed plans of his zealots—Alfred Rosenberg, Martin Bormann, Josef Göbbels, and Heinrich Himmler—to persecute Jews and rid the world of religion.

Although there had been popes who were anti-Semitic, Pius XI was not one of them.[85] He condemned anti-Semitism and was sometimes blunt and

Pope Pius XI.

emphatic when he did so.[86] Pius XI told Catholics—and the world—they must reject all forms of anti-Semitism on both a moral and an intellectual basis. As the Nazi movement showed its spots, he was appalled at their racial theories, and he condemned anti-Semitism publicly and privately in terms no Catholic could mistake. He was plainly troubled by Catholic anti-Semitism, and he pointedly reminded Catholics of the religious brotherhood of Jews and Catholics. This message undermined the rationale by which some Catholics had allowed their anti-Semitism to masquerade as mere doctrinal disagreement. Catholicism's roots, he said, include Abraham, and he preached that "Anti-Semitism is incompatible with the lofty thought which that fact expresses. It is a movement with which we Christians can have nothing to do. No, no, I say to you it is impossible for a Christian to take part in anti-Semitism. . . . [W]e are the spiritual progeny of Abraham. Spiritually, we are all Semites."[87]

In 1937, the pope decided it was time to deliver his condemnation of the Third Reich directly to Hitler's doorstep. He issued an encyclical directed at the Nazi regime, one subsequently seen as the Vatican's "first great assault on Nazism."[88] In a break with tradition, he gave it a German title, "*Mit brennender Sorge*" ("With burning anxiety"). Pius XI was fluent in German, and this encyclical became the first ever written in the German language. The angry pope smuggled 300,000 copies into Germany and ordered it read from every pulpit on Palm Sunday. The encyclical was a stinging condemnation of racism and a stirring tribute to the Old Testament; its astonishing crescendo was a warning against following a mad prophet. The Nazis exploded with outrage and rushed to confiscate copies throughout Germany. Hitler was beside himself and ordered a host of Catholics sent to prison camps, for the encyclical's support of Jews was clear.[89] In it, the pope condemned the mistreatment of people based on race and rejected the concept of a national religion.[90] Other verbal weaponry was less blunt, but it was rife with readily understood allusions. The Vatican, however, was loathe to speak in terms harsh enough to assure Nazi retribution against clergy in Germany. The pope had seen how swift and brutal Hitler's retribution against priests was going to be. Thus, even this provocative encyclical avoided the use of the name *Hitler* or the term *Nazi*, yet he accused them of deceit and mistreatment of Jews, Protestants, and Catholics. Still, the swiftness of Nazi reaction—the persecution of the Church[91] with searches, confiscation, and reprisals—was a shock.

Pius XI also began to take Mussolini[92] to task, insisting that he intervene with Hitler to stop the anti-Semitic abuses in Germany, only to have Mussolini begin his own repression of Jews.

★ ★ ★

Pius XI reigned all during Schuschnigg's public service and had a marked influence on the chancellor. Schuschnigg conceived of the new Austrian state as a product of Pius XI's teaching on governance and anti-Marxism. He also used his own pulpit to echo the pontiff's message against anti-Semitism.[93] Once Hitler began his conquests, Pius XI enlisted two Jesuits to begin drafting an even more powerful encyclical condemning anti-Semitism and a speech condemning Nazism and the anti-Semitic laws issued by Mussolini.[94]

Some Catholic clergy, however, revealed an uglier side, and some of them were high profile and influential. In Linz, Bishop Johannes Gföllner circulated pastoral letters to his congregation criticizing the Jews of Austria in iconic anti-Semitic tones. He used the wearisome money-loving tropes and made sweeping generalities attributing many of the world's ills to them. Gföllner did condemn persecution of the Jews; yet, in the same breath, he wanted to deny them the vote in Austria.[95] Others who knew Gföllner insisted he was not anti-Semitic, and a collective pastoral letter from the bishops of Austria with a clear condemnation of anti-Semitism helped ameliorate the controversy.[96]

Despite the messages of the pope or Dollfuss or Schuschnigg, discrimination in Austrian society and inequality in occupations and professions seemed certain to continue. The provinces had a history of boycotting Jewish doctors and lawyers, as well as a history of quotas limiting equal access to several types of opportunities and positions. The Christian Socials in the past had at times condemned racial anti-Semitism as un-Christian, yet many believed the party's governments tended to condone cultural anti-Semitism despite publicly disapproving it.[97] But when a conservative-leaning newspaper published an editorial in late 1933 expressing approval for quotas, the Dollfuss government repudiated the paper's position. These measures were no panacea, but they were not without effect. More Catholics began to distance themselves from the overt anti-Semites among them.[98] The Catholic aristocratic class responded in better fashion than some others, and Jews came to view them as more balanced and less tolerant of anti-Semitism than the bourgeoisie.[99]

That much more could have been done by Catholics, particularly by the senior clergy, as the historic developments of 1938 approached is obvious;[100] what more could safely have been done by Schuschnigg, when the existence of Austria might be imperiled by one provocative speech by its chancellor, is more difficult to determine. What the Schuschnigg government had to take note of, with any attempts at preaching, was that they would certainly alienate that crucial portion of "the Austrian populace, who they feared might otherwise be attracted to their [Nazi] adversaries."[101]

★ ★ ★

Pope Pius XI had no such electoral constraints, but top Vatican officials lobbied hard to tone down confrontational public statements that would provoke Hitler or Mussolini to persecute the church as an institution or persecute Catholic clergy inside Germany. Despite their obstructive efforts, the pope and his two Jesuit collaborators were drafting a blistering speech against anti-Semitism and Nazism. At last it was ready, and he ordered that it be printed and delivered to his desk on February 10, 1939. That night, however, the pope died. The speech was never delivered.[102]

Jewish leaders paid warm tribute to the late pope. A February 12, 1939, letter from Bernard Joseph for the executive of the Jewish Agency to the Latin Patriarch of Jerusalem said that "the Jewish people mourn the loss of one of the greatest exponents of the cause of international peace and goodwill." The executive expressed gratitude for the pontiff's concern for the Jews of Europe: "His noble efforts on their behalf will ensure for him for all time a warm place in the memories of the Jewish people wherever they live." Another rabbi praised him as "the first of all Christian voices in Europe to be raised against the general anti-Semitic policy of Nazism."[103]

★ ★ ★

A pope's condemnation of discrimination could not be ignored, but real equality required management day to day by people who would not sabotage progressive policies. Job discrimination had perhaps the most tangible impact on Jewish life in Austria, and the greatest impact was in Vienna where the powerful Bürgermeister, Richard Schmitz, had considerable authority over employment practices and education. Jews had great difficulty finding employment and gaining advancement all during the interwar period because of the plummeting job market, and they endured even greater difficulty when other events inflicted added blows on Jewish employment during the 1930s. In all those years, the employers who awarded the precious few jobs and promotions were predominantly non-Jews.[104]

Jewish leaders' uncertainty about Schuschnigg was brought to a head over an issue of discrimination in schools—as sensitive a nerve as discrimination can touch. In November 1934, the leaders of the Jewish community lodged a protest, and they brought it not to the Vienna Bürgermeister but directly to the chancellor. They were protesting the establishment of parallel classes separating Catholics and non-Catholics in schools.

The separation that had been ordered was a limited one; it was only for certain classes in those schools that had become sufficiently crowded that two classrooms were necessary to handle the students in a particular grade. The announced purpose of the regulation was to permit limited separation of Catholic students from non-Catholic in those parallel classes, a policy that the Jewish community and other non-Catholics had long approved in principle. Some correspondents endorsed the compromise of parallel classes as a satisfactory solution.[105] Indeed, several Jewish groups favored the separation. Though non-Catholic students were excused from Catholic religion class, some Jewish and Protestant leaders preferred separation of classes as a means of reducing the heavily Catholic atmosphere such instruction produced. Some of those groups wanted to go further and have entirely separate schools for Jewish children.[106] The implementation of the policy, particularly in Schmitz's Vienna, had caused some Jewish students to feel like second-class citizens, and Jewish leaders reached a consensus to protest the parallel classes. They requested a meeting on the subject and asked if the meeting could be with the new chancellor.[107]

Some of those leaders had their doubts as they arrived at the chancellery to brief him on the problems in Vienna. But that day they witnessed his reaction firsthand, and they were extremely pleased. Schuschnigg promised he would insist that the decree be changed. A new decree was promptly issued together with a communiqué emphasizing the full equality of Jews. Schuschnigg told the leaders that he had spoken with the Bürgermeister about the matter and assured them that he would follow up in the days ahead. Afterward, the Jewish leaders went to see US ambassador Messersmith to tell him of their complete satisfaction; they recounted Schuschnigg's assurance that he "would do everything in his power to stop discrimination." The ambassador reported the meeting to Secretary of State Cordell Hull: "They said that the Chancellor had been extraordinarily frank with them in telling them about his problems and that he has given them the most thoroughgoing assurances." They told the ambassador that Schuschnigg "had treated them with extraordinary consideration and courtesy.[108] . . . [T]hey told me that under the circumstances they had assured the Chancellor of the complete support in every way of the Jewish community in Austria." After that, they gave Schuschnigg "very whole hearted support."[109]

Schuschnigg lived up to his assurances to the Jewish community. There is no definitive poll because of the reluctance to call an election or a referendum while Nazism was being spread by Göbbels's propaganda machine. Many Jewish leaders, however, visibly supported Schuschnigg for the next four years.[110] The leaders among the influential Jewish merchant class supported him, and the ultraorthodox segment of the Jewish community did so "with the greatest degree of enthusiasm."[111] The ultraorthodox organization Agudat Israel supported both the Dollfuss and Schuschnigg governments and felt they well served the interests of Jews. Their community's *Agudah Press* repeatedly expressed their support for Schuschnigg's government.[112] At the opposite end of the spectrum, the Jewish liberals and their leaders, as well as the Alliance of Jewish War Veterans, publicly backed Schuschnigg to the end. Other leaders of the various constituencies in the organized Jewish community also voiced support for his government.[113] A scholar of the Jewish population summarized the response to Schuschnigg: "By and large the organized Viennese Jewish community outwardly supported [Schuschnigg's] government during the mid-thirties."[114]

★ ★ ★

Jewish loyalty to the Ständestaat included rendering service, and several Jewish leaders were appointed to the new National Council and other councils of government by Schuschnigg.[115] Schuschnigg's notable departures from the way Jews had been treated by the prior generation of Austrian political leaders brought about a more democratic approach than ever before: "Jews had greater formal representation on the appointed bodies of the thirties than on their elected counterparts a decade earlier."[116] Schuschnigg made it a point to hold regular meetings with Desider Friedmann, leader of the Israelitische Kultusgemeinde, and Hermann Oppenheim, the president of the Union of Austrian Jews.[117] Friedmann expressed the thanks of his followers to Schuschnigg and publicly praised the Schuschnigg government.[118]

Even with broad Jewish support, some Jewish groups were less open or less enthusiastic in their support than others. The Jewish Nationalists' organization seemed the most skeptical; it never became publicly allied with the Christian Socials or the Fatherland Front, but many of its members informally supported the party.[119]

There were also Jewish critics of the government, particularly the writer Oskar Karbach who was dissatisfied with some aspects of the Schuschnigg government and the conditions of Jews. But he acknowledged the nearly impossible conditions the government inherited, and he evaluated the Ständestaat as a "short lived innovation" devised as an "attempt to avert catastrophe at a tragic moment."[120] Karbach wrote that "[a] mighty opponent stood at the door; he had a numerically strong and fanatically devoted fifth column in the country; for a brief period it was thought that his [Hitler's] victory, which all feared, could be averted. . . . What began as an attempt to salvage Austria's independence was deliberately turned into a delaying maneuver for the benefit of the entire world."[121]

The gulf between the Nazis and the Schuschnigg government on the Jewish question was vast, but Austrian society still fell well short of the fairness, acceptance, and equal treatment the Jews had a right to demand. From the Nazis' perspective, one of their top foreign policy goals was to force the embrace of the Nuremberg Laws, for hostility to Jews was the core principle codified in Hitler's 1920 publication of the twenty-five principles of Nazism.[122] The leaders of some of the other countries—Mussolini in Italy and Miklós Horthy in Hungary—did adopt variants of the anti-Jewish laws at least in part to curry favor with Hitler.[123]

Schuschnigg had far more pressure on him than any leader to appease Hitler on race; nevertheless, he stubbornly refused anything of the kind. While Nazi Germany took away the citizenship of all German Jews and stripped them of their civil rights, Schuschnigg proclaimed that his government refused to go along. He said Austria would not treat any race or religion unfairly.

He made this clear to the Nazi surrogates and others. In 1937, Schuschnigg wrote Edmund Glaise-Horstenau bluntly reviewing the state of disagreements between his government and the Nazis. He said that Nazism is "incompatible"[124] with Austria's constitution (a word that Hitler would later try to force him to recant), and he denounced with strong language the teachings of *Mein Kampf* and the "gang murders" committed by the Nazis.[125] Schuschnigg's most emphatic difference with Hitler was his insistence on Austria's "rejection of German racial theory."[126] In Franz von Papen's 1935 letter to Hitler, he criticized Schuschnigg's "new Austrian ideology," and he vowed to overpower it.[127] The countries that did adopt anti-Semitic laws, Italy and Hungary, stayed in Hitler's good graces much longer than uncooperative Austria—whose chancellor publicly rejected Nazism to the very end.[128]

★ ★ ★

· *6* ·

The Solace of Music

𝒯hreats to Schuschnigg's life were palpable every day of his four years as chancellor. On the night of the Nazi putsch, after Dollfuss lay dead and he had been sworn in as acting chancellor, Schuschnigg and his family could hear the sounds of bullets all around their home. Nazi violence was virtually always nearby to remind him of the risk.

Austrian authorities found detailed plans revealing Nazi plots to assassinate Schuschnigg. The plots included a scheme to assassinate Papen, the Nazis' own ambassador to Austria. They planned to blame Papen's murder on Austria and to launch a German invasion in retaliation.[1] Schuschnigg had the two chief Nazis—the Gauleiter, or regional Nazi official, Captain Josef Leopold, and his cohort, Leopold Tavs, who were central to this plot—arrested for conspiracy to overthrow the government.[2] The evidence found against them in a raid left no doubt about their plot. Germany characteristically professed ignorance of the conspiracy. Tavs, however, was foolishly on record in an interview published in a Slovak newspaper that he and his men were completely obedient to Hitler and made their moves based on subtle hints conveyed by Berlin.[3]

★ ★ ★

Schuschnigg made it clear that the interim government was temporary; it was being called an "experiment" in government[4] using an incomplete, transitional constitution to deal with crisis conditions. Elections were planned, and in time, the schedule was announced. Schuschnigg did not rush the completion of the drafting of the new constitution; he hoped he would first be able to mend fences with the Social Democrats. And there were positive signs of progress with the workers of the Austrian trade union federation and with some of the workers aligned with the socialist movement, those Austrians who

114

had suffered the most in the 1934 civil war.[5] Schuschnigg "undertook guarded attempts toward reconciliation with the left wing."[6]

Criticism was bound to increase, however, as the suspension of the previous form of government dragged on. But completion of the constitution was imminent by late 1937. Former chancellor Otto Ender announced to the press in December 1937 and again in February 1938 that the drafting of the new constitution was progressing, that elections would take place in 1938, and that the new constitution would then take effect.[7]

Austrians were busy implementing the new institutions. The various trade groups were preparing for the coming elections, forming the organizations that were to represent them in the government (the corporate units of the corporate state). Business, agriculture, and public service groups were all working on the rules by which their representatives would sit in council within the new government, and those rules were near completion.[8] Schuschnigg was working on ways to "pluralize" the government and earn the trust of the workers.[9] In the adjustments he made, the fascist-like features of the Ständestaat were reduced, whereas a fascist would only have increased them.[10] History has left unanswered the question how well this new form of government Austria was creating would have worked.[11]

Schuschnigg assured Austrians that the government he inherited would never become a dictatorship and that the overriding purpose behind its design was to prevent Anschluss.[12] Yet he agreed that criticisms by its political opponents were made with "some apparent justification."[13] His writings, however, illuminated several elements of the interim regime that were entirely inconsistent with dictatorship as the modern world has known it.

The central difference was the rule of law. Just across the border in Germany, Hitler had declared himself above all law and free to do whatever he chose to do to anyone. Schuschnigg and everyone in his government, however, remained subject to the law, and the organs of law enforcement remained intact. The Supreme Court was not only independent and nonpolitical[14] but also the entire legal profession remained free and aggressive. Perhaps more telling is the fact that the courts and the legal profession did not have to launch any struggle to remain independent under Schuschnigg. Although the resignations of the judges[15] had ended the Constitutional Court, the Supreme Court remained active and independent and had the authority to sit as a Constitutional Court. The Supreme Administrative Court, the highest court with jurisdiction over public law, and the District Courts continued as well.[16] Schuschnigg, a scrupulously honest lawyer himself, was a firm believer in the rule of law and a principled former minister of justice; he made no effort to eliminate or undermine the legal branches or to raise any doubt about his own duty to obey the law. In this, his governance was the antithesis of the *Führerprinzip* that empowered the Hitler dictatorship. And he pointed out to critics of the Ständestaat that this "completely independent and apolitical juridical system" not only prevailed under his administration but also did so with his complete approval.[17] Ambassador Messersmith saw this firsthand. During one of their meetings, the chancellor was interrupted by a phone call; someone pressed him to take action he thought illegal, and he refused, saying in words not heard from dictators, "It would be unconstitutional." The ambassador reported the exchange to the State Department with the observation that "those who consider Austria such an autocratic state should have heard him."[18]

One historian says, "Schuschnigg was an authoritarian rather than a fascist."[19] Another labels Schuschnigg's administration "liberal authoritarianism" and calls it a government that "worked," for despite the Depression, some parts of the economy did show improvement under Schuschnigg.[20] Exports increased, and the trade deficit was reduced. Production of Austrian farm products was up sharply; iron and steel production showed a clear rise, and tourism was growing. The foreign debt and the cost of servicing that debt were cut in half by 1937.[21] "Economically and financially, conditions in Austria by the end of 1937 were markedly improved."[22]

Schuschnigg greeting Austrian youth.

That same historian also observes that Schuschnigg, and Dollfuss before him, "turned out to be the real opponents of the totalitarians" and they "turned out to be more courageous and more formidable opponents of Hitler and Stalin than many so-called democrats."[23]

★ ★ ★

Even in the face of threats and crisis, at home the Schuschniggs led a nearly ideal life. Those close to them said they "adored" one another; they had what others could see was "an unusually happy married life and their affection for each other was often a subject of comment among their friends."[24] They delighted in their young son, an imp of an eight-year-old, always into benign mischief, and devoted to his parents.[25] Discipline was the jurisdiction of the father, and Schuschnigg often had Kurti settle onto his knee to discuss in serious tone what there was they could learn from the difficulties of the day, and a great bond was established between father and son despite the heavy time demands of the chancellor's office.[26]

Herma kept her son active and happy. One friend in the international community said she was "like a child in her enthusiasm," "a very intelligent, pleasant, charming and simple woman."[27] Herma greeted the public in a friendly, gracious way; she participated in the community and attended many events, which endeared her to the Austrians. She particularly loved arranging events that would entertain a number of children. A friend of Herma's had a son Kurti's age, and the two boys became great pals and spent considerable time together. Rudi Fugger-Babbenhausen was the son of Herma's friend, Countess Vera Fugger-Babbenhausen, and Rudi's presence solved the difficulty of finding playmates for a chancellor's son.

Schuschnigg and Herma especially nurtured their passion for music.[28] The chancellor was expected to support the arts, and Vienna was awash in talented musicians eager to perform at the chancellor's residence. When the Schuschniggs moved into one of the buildings of the Belvedere Palace complex, a ballroom was available, and once each week they brought in great music. None in the audience enjoyed it more than the chancellor and his wife.[29]

The dark spot in Herma's life, however, was her abiding fear that the Nazis would assassinate her husband.[30]

★ ★ ★

Herma and Kurti were thrilled when Schuschnigg scheduled a family vacation. For the busy chancellor, it would have to be a working vacation, with ministers coming and going bringing him the government's flood of daily business, but it would mean time away at the lake house at St. Gilgen on the Wolfgangsee where the family could spend relaxed hours together. Kurti was especially excited. He knew this meant some time fishing with his father, and,

Chancellor and Mrs. Schuschnigg and son Kurti.

Source: Getty Images.

in a small boat, they could chat fully relaxed without ministers of state hovering nearby with papers to be reviewed.

Their devoted driver arrived at 5 a.m. to help pack the car for the long drive to the lake, and they set off along the road on a clear day, as happy as vacationers can be. But the car suddenly flew out of control and smashed into a tree. Schuschnigg was badly bruised. Kurti was seriously injured. Herma, however, was killed instantly.

The investigation revealed two highly suspicious signs of sabotage. Their driver was badly injured, and he remembered nothing of the crash itself, but he recalled that he had stopped off on the evening before the trip for his nightly one beer. He was well known to the innkeeper, and on this night, the innkeeper had noticed that the driver had been approached by a stranger who befriended him and had paid for the beer.

At closing time, as the establishment emptied, the innkeeper found the driver sound asleep at the table. He roused him and helped him out. The driver remembered heading home and returning early to the chancellor's home to pack the car for the trip. No other evidence could be found to explain the odd event. Nor were they able to identify the stranger, or to establish whether the driver had been drugged—but that was the suspicion.

Police who rushed to the scene of the crash arrested a suspicious onlooker, armed and apparently awaiting the Schuschnigg car just ahead along its route. He was a Nazi. Suspicious as he was, however, investigators could not link him to the crash.

Kurti had been foggy at the crash site, but before passing out, he had seen men carrying someone away. When he awoke in the hospital, he learned what tragedy was;[31] the eight-year-old boy was shaken to the core over the death of his mother. Schuschnigg did his best to provide comfort to his distraught son in the midst of his own grief.[32] They spent as much time as they could at the lake house on the Wolfgangsee.[33] However, even at the lakeside, a cloud of profound grief and serious depression virtually disabled the chancellor.

Herma had become a beloved figure to many Austrians. The US ambassador reported to Washington that her death produced "unusual manifestations of sympathy in the country."[34] When Kurti was able to walk again, he went on outings with his nanny, the very caring Fraulein Alice Ottenreiter. When Kurti was out of his father's hearing, Schuschnigg was all too often heard sitting in darkness sobbing. His hair turned white.[35] One of the few things that calmed him was music, even the music that he and Herma had so enjoyed when they sat together at home just listening. Now, alone, he listened long into the night.

★ ★ ★

The von Trapp family was also in love with music. Every one of them reveled in the liberating joy of singing. They felt a delicious satisfaction singing together spontaneously at home in Salzburg. They also loved to hike, and they spent many long hours singing outdoors in the meadows of the glorious hill-sides of the Obersalzberg. They constantly searched for new madrigals, church music, Bach fugues, and Tyrol folk music to add to the extensive repertoire they had assembled. They were very private people and intended their music only for their own enjoyment. They were not performers, not at all showy; indeed, they were all intensely shy. They valued their individual and family privacy and ultimately had to be thrust into performing in public.

It was the sheerest coincidence that brought them their first attention from the world of the performing arts, and then a fortuitous switch of one man's radio dial at just the right moment that brought them a summons from on high and vaulted them toward lasting fame.

A woman was approaching the von Trapp house one day, quite by chance, while Maria and the children were sitting among the pine trees out-side their home singing late on a Saturday afternoon.[36] The woman was look-ing for a home to rent. At the time, a local music competition was under way, but the family, as usual, had given not the slightest thought to participating. However, the approaching woman paused outside their home and drank in their music. She was Lotte Lehmann, the renowned opera diva. She stopped in her tracks when she heard their singing; she listened for a few minutes and was surprised to be so powerfully impressed. Ms. Lehmann, herself a seasoned critic of singers, instantly recognized that this family had gold in their throats.[37] She introduced herself and insisted that they enter the competition. But the von Trapps were not just reluctant; they were terrified of the idea of perform-ing in public. Lotte Lehmann must have sensed that stage fright was the reason for Maria's polite refusal because she took it upon herself to walk over and pick up their phone while the stunned family watched her. She placed a call and entered them in the next day's group competition.[38]

To the very proper Baron Georg von Trapp, it was unthinkable that his children should become performers and compromise the family propriety he valued, and he found it unacceptable that his children would be distracted from their studies by the glare of performing. But they did show up; they stumbled over each other's feet taking the stage, frozen by stage fright. With the baron sitting apprehensively in the audience, Maria and the children per-formed very well. When the judges ended their huddle at the conclusion of the competition, the announcement was: "The first prize is awarded to the Trapp family from Salzburg."[39]

They reminded themselves, however, that this was a one-time event; they saw it as an experience entirely foreign to the private life they loved. Yet, as the day went on and they laughed and teased about the exhilarating adventure, though they had been terrified on stage, they had somehow enjoyed the thrill. Still, they remained content and determined to spend life out of the public eye.

However, the head of a radio station from little Monchsberg had been in the audience, and he was enchanted. He called Maria and instructed her that the family was to sing on his station at a date and time he dictated.[40] The overly polite former nun, Maria, was beginning to say no, but he hung up too quickly for her to say it. Some mild teasing by the children followed, and this led Maria to relent and to muse that perhaps God might want them to do this just this once. The family went to the radio station on the day assigned, and they sang a touching "Hymn of Thanksgiving" by Bach.

By sheer coincidence, this radio program happened to be aired on an afternoon when the grieving chancellor of Austria had turned on his radio in search of the consoling balm of music.[41] Schuschnigg heard Maria and the children, and he was moved by their music's restorative message and by the lingering beauty with which they had caressed Bach's hymn. He sat down and wrote to them asking the family if they would sing at a national concert he was about to host in Vienna. The concert Schuschnigg was planning was to be his first public event since Herma was killed—a reception for the officials of the international community, the diplomatic corps, and the military. He hoped to make it an evening of memorable music. The program he wanted to present was to be built around the Vienna Philharmonic Orchestra, but Schuschnigg wanted to include another performance to accompany it—one that was uniquely Austrian.

Maria was startled by the chancellor's invitation. Baron von Trapp wanted very much to decline, but he felt it would be rude to turn down the head of the Austrian government in the midst of his period of mourning, and he gave his consent. Chancellor Schuschnigg himself took the microphone to introduce the von Trapp Family Singers at the concert.[42] This concert was broadcast throughout Austria, and the von Trapps' performance was as good as they or their audience could have wanted. Within hours, offers poured in for them to perform. The von Trapp Family Singers had been launched.

They were still very reluctant to entertain the notion of performing for money. However, Hitler's 1,000 mark penalty crippling the Austrian economy had struck the once wealthy Baron von Trapp very hard. He lost his wealth. The baron was a friend of the Lammers family, local Austrian bankers hard-pressed by the Great Depression and the sudden cessation of German tourism, and he tried to be helpful; he placed his investment funds in the Lammers' bank, but the bank failed.[43]

Maria recognized that the money they could earn from performing could go far toward restoring the family finances and curing Georg's depression over the loss. The von Trapps began to perform their unique harmony in Europe's most glittering capitals, and their performances were very well received by enthusiastic audiences. Before long, the revenue from their bookings made them realize that they had a new family career, and they began travels that introduced them to several kings and the pope.[44]

The von Trapp Family Singers.
Source: Wikimedia, Creative Commons.

Baron Georg von Trapp, Kommandant of World War I submarine SMU-5 in 1915.
Source: Public Domain. Wikipedia, Creative Commons.

★ ★ ★

Once Hitler began the covert military buildup, he issued a deadline to General Ludwig Beck, then chief of the General Staff, that the 100,000-man army must be increased to 300,000 by fall 1934; he told Beck that he was going to order conscription in the coming spring. Such a buildup of troops in defiance of the Treaty of Versailles would virtually dare the victors of World War I to try to stop him even as he, in an effort to dull the outrage in Britain and in France, blew a smoke screen of shameless lies claiming he harbored no ambition to acquire any territory to expand Germany.[45]

After Europe responded with only muffled protests over that military buildup, the lame reaction gave Hitler confidence. He decided he could launch his next far more daring, even foolhardy gamble of everything by marching troops into the demilitarized zone of Germany—the Rhineland on the border of France. Failure there could well have been the end of Hitler.[46]

In February 1936, General von Fritsch warned Hitler that the Wehrmacht was not at the strength needed for a war against France. Fritsch advised him to seek arbitration with the victors over remilitarization issues because the army could not prevail in the armed combat that would be provoked by stationing troops right at the French border in the Rhineland. General Beck agreed with Fritsch; Beck argued that France very well may fight. Few had forgotten how France had been the vocal proponent in 1919 at Versailles for establishing a demilitarized Rhineland as a buffer. If France resisted, Beck warned Hitler, the German army could not hope to defend against a French assault.

Hitler confided to Fritsch that if the French did resist, he would withdraw the occupying troops rather than engage in aggressive combat. Germany would at most, he said, conduct only a fighting withdrawal. Hitler did not, however, plan to retreat fully. His plan was that the troops would withdraw from their furthest advance back to previously prepared positions, still within the demilitarized Rhineland. This plan frightened even Hermann Göring.

★ ★ ★

Against the warnings of the top echelon of the military, Hitler ordered the launch of Operation Winter Exercise. On March 7, 1936, nineteen German divisions marched into the Rhineland flagrantly violating the 1919 Treaty of Versailles and the 1925 Treaty of Locarno. Germany simultaneously accused Britain, France, and Italy of violating the Treaty of Locarno by signing the Franco-Soviet agreement. Hitler proclaimed that Germany, therefore, was renouncing the Treaty of Locarno.[47]

France took the aggressive action seriously. The French did muster troops on the border, and war appeared imminent. When France seemed ready to attack, Hitler came perilously close to ordering the troops to withdraw. Ambassador Konstantin von Neurath, however, lent a firm hand to

General Ludwig Beck.
Source: Wikipedia, Creative Commons. Bundesarchiv Bild_146-1980-033-04%2C.

steady Hitler. He urged Hitler to stay the course while General Blomberg and others urged an immediate retreat.

It is now well documented that there actually had been no chance that France was going to invade Germany over its reoccupation of the Rhineland. There may also have been enough soft intelligence available to Hitler to make that assessment at the time. France was deeply committed already to an entirely defensive posture, and its army was wed to logistics and training that was almost entirely devoted to defending a German attack against France.[48] The planning and training that would have been essential for launching an attack in response to a German threat was well beyond the French army's mind-set, and in 1936, it was far beyond the army's readiness. The French army had no distinct mobile force at that time. France did have a larger military than Germany, but General Gamelin warned the government that, if armed resistance to Germany in the Rhineland was ordered, it would be twelve days before the largely static French army could be in position to go on the attack.[49] Moreover, he gave that assessment to French government officials who found that posture acceptable and were uninterested in challenging it.

France had tipped its hand a few years earlier, revealing to the plotting Führer that France had no stomach for a fight beyond its own borders. In 1934, when Hitler set startling new goals for the strength of Germany's armed forces, it seemed unlikely to him that France would react. And in March 1935 when Hitler calmly disclosed that Germany's sports flying group was actually a military air force of considerable strength, France merely protested. It was by then clear that the Treaty of Versailles was not a line in the sand.[50]

French lethargy was the result of the unique suffering of the French in the Great War. The war had ravaged the French countryside and scarred the French people. The French government shared and reflected the people's stress. The French had, after all, been required to host a large share of the carnage of the Great War and to bury a generation of their sons and the sons of their British allies at Verdun, the Somme, and other French sites. France appeared more war weary than any other nation.

France also lacked the strong and cohesive government that might have led the country to break out of its malaise in time to stop Hitler. In-fighting was intense among Paul Reynaud, General Maurice Gamelin, Édouard Daladier, and other French leaders. Governments were constructs of the most fragile coalitions.

Most French were content with inaction. The cabinet was uniformly opposed to military action. Likewise, the public, particularly the trade unions and the vocal veterans of the Great War, opposed any action by France that might lead to war. The French press reflected these attitudes; the newspapers strongly opposed an attack in the Rhineland.[51]

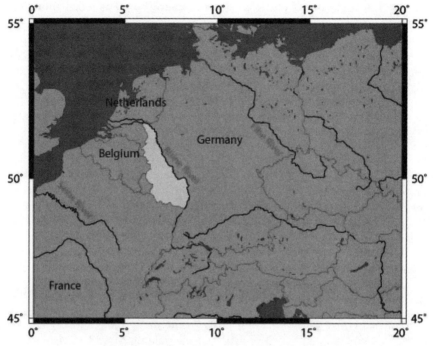

Remilitarization of the Rhineland of 1936.
Source: Wikimedia, Creative Commons.

Might a French decision to march across the border into the Rhineland in 1936 have brought Hitler down and prevented World War II in Europe? Information obtained after the war revealed that a French invasion might well have done exactly that. After the war, General Heinz Guderian asserted that if the French had responded by invading the Rhineland, Hitler would have been through.[52] Hitler knew the risk of his move into the Rhineland—the serious possibility that he would not survive if he were challenged by France. He knew that if he were forced to retreat and to withdraw his small force, he would most likely have been deposed by hostile career Wehrmacht generals.[53] He later acknowledged as much in an informal staff session in spring 1942, confessing that he had used lies, steel nerve, and his unique obstinacy to resist the pleas of many of his generals to withdraw the German troops when France gathered its force on the border and appeared ready to attack. Even when no French attack came, Hitler remained anxious for several days, but gradually his doubts evaporated. It became clear that the French government and the army's general staff were demoralized.

Once he completed the remilitarization of the Rhineland in the face of the French and British protests, the Treaty of Versailles he hated was just a shard of the broken glass of history. Hitler insisted that he was now entitled to the respect of the generals who had disdained him. He had been right; they had been wrong. But in Hitler's view, those generals—Beck, Blomberg, and Rundstedt—were not just wrong; Hitler had silenced them and could portray them as cowards.[54] Even more important than whatever limited esteem he actually had garnered from others was the enhancement of his own ego. He viewed himself as the greatest German general, perhaps the greatest general ever, and surely the equal of Napoleon.

Britain also refused to resist Hitler or embolden France in the Rhineland fiasco. Moreover, Britain's refusal was highly public, thereby undermining Pierre-Étienne Flandin, the French foreign minister, and the few influential French who favored sending three battalions forward to challenge Hitler's occupation.[55] Hitler may have, it seems, received additional back-channel assurance from Britain; King Edward VIII has been accused of letting the German ambassador know that he had threatened to abdicate if Prime Minister Baldwin attacked over the Rhineland occupation.[56] More relevant was Foreign Minister Anthony Eden's colossal misread of Hitler; Eden advised Parliament that Hitler's action gave no reason to think "that Germany's present action threatens hostilities."[57]

The British public heavily supported their successive prime ministers' rock-ribbed policies of appeasement. There was, of course, a powerful array of men like Harold Macmillan and Leo Amery who endeavored to change government policy in the 1930s but to no avail. Winston Churchill, too, was against appeasement, but his words were not enough to stir the British in the 1930s, and he was eventually muzzled by Chamberlain when the prime minister plucked Churchill from the Tory bench and made him first lord of the admiralty when war finally came.[58] Chamberlain himself refused to be moved, and he was quick to inflict political revenge on other members of Parliament to ward off their attacks upon his appeasement of Hitler. To be sure, there was no convincing Chamberlain that Austria was salvageable or that Austria's independence was so essential that it warranted Britain going to war with Hitler.

Trying to buy time, and lacking the allies Austria needed, Schuschnigg chose to pursue a "feigned friendship" with the Third Reich, while he tried to enlist international support. But, as Churchill later described the European nations who had failed to respond: "Each one hopes that if he feeds the crocodile enough, it will eat him last."[59] Schuschnigg feared all along that Austria was the food the appeasers had in mind.

The sound of those jackboots that marched into the Rhineland was the heraldry of Hitler's breakout move. That was just the beginning of the delivery on his threats, his writings, and his speeches. As shrill as his words were, it was his actions that would inflict a series of shocks so stunning that Europe was befuddled and incapable of reacting. There was no strong response or even limited resistance.

The lack of the bold action that was now needed to prevent another war was the worst sequela of the Great War. European nations had just missed the opportunities that could have prevented the catastrophe of Hitler; worse, their paralysis encouraged him. It also stilled the voices of any within Germany who might have opposed him. The paralysis hobbled Britain and France as they sat motionless in the months and years after Hitler marched in and remilitarized the Rhineland.[60]

To the rest of Europe, France had checked out. It was no longer the great bulwark upon which the crescent of small states had been relying. Before the Rhineland march, they had all looked to France.[61] All these nations now saw that France simply was not going to fight unless France itself was invaded. It was little consolation that the occasional ferocious voice or heroic-sounding protest from one French official or another was heard. Such voices were merely empty gestures by isolated outliers. The French government was unable to come to a consensus to try to stop the rise of Adolf Hitler. Other European nations, so accustomed to believing France was Europe's army in reserve, were left to fend for themselves.[62] And the inaction of the European powers taught Hitler all he needed to know. Behind the well-phrased protests of France and Britain, Hitler could see he had a green light.

In America, Hitler's action in the Rhineland was disturbing, but the Rhineland was, after all, a part of Germany. The United States government had no standing to take action against conduct by Germany entirely within its own borders; nor did it have standing to rally European nations to protest a violation of the treaties the United States had failed to ratify, nor any right to urge action by a League of Nations it declined to join.[63] Its separate war-ending treaties with Germany seemed not to be breached. At this juncture, most nations, the United States included, clung to a wisp of self-delusion, first, that they might still count on France and Britain to stop any German aggression beyond Germany's own borders and, second, that those two nations might have behaved in dramatically different fashion if Hitler had marched across the border of an independent nation—such as Austria.

Hitler, however, made the calculation that no one would fight to stop him from confiscating Austria. In 1936, during a raid by Austrian police on the home of Nazi provocateur Leopold Tavs, a document was found outlining the Nazi's "Action Programme" listing the steps the Nazis were planning to take to force Austria to fall into line. The document recited the Nazis' belief that Britain and France were not going to interfere in Austria.

★ ★ ★

Schuschnigg was shocked by Hitler's militarization of the Rhineland and dismayed by the lack of response.[64] One small dividend of the inaction of France and Britain was that it confirmed to Schuschnigg that neither of them would prohibit Austria from beginning to arm. Within weeks, on April 1, 1936, Schuschnigg ordered military conscription for men aged eighteen to forty-two years old.[65]

Conscription, however, did provoke opposition inside Austria, for it stepped firmly on the foot of Prince Starhemberg and his Heimwehr. Much of the criticism of the Dollfuss and Schuschnigg governments as fascist was based upon the fascist aura of the Heimwehr. The fascism of its leaders was evident in their goals, their rhetoric, and their style. Schuschnigg was splashed with all that when he became chancellor. It was said that he had inherited a government that was a "coalition government between the militant defense leagues and what little was left of the Christian-Socialist Party."[66] But once in office, he "pitted the rival forces within the government against each other."[67] The Heimwehr leaders, Starhemberg, Fey, and Odo Neustädter-Stürmer, were all rivals. Schuschnigg excluded the latter two from lead positions in government in fall 1935;[68] however, this move empowered the most formidable of the group—Starhemberg.

Tensions rose sharply between Starhemberg and Schuschnigg when Schuschnigg announced the demilitarization of the Heimwehr.[69] Starhemberg was irate; he began openly extolling a fascist platform.[70] He shouted: "Long live the fascist idea."[71] But on April 26, 1936, he went too far; he delivered a speech and warned that the Heimwehr would be disbanded only over his dead body. This was too much. Schuschnigg not only disbanded the Heimwehr but also dismissed Starhemberg and Fey[72] and folded the Heimwehr[73] members into the army.[74] Starhemberg's other portfolio, the Fatherland Front, also seen as an organization that could serve fascism, never became a serious force at all; Schuschnigg allowed it to wither until it became a "bureaucratic organizational shell with no dynamic development or significance."[75] These dismissals effectively gave Schuschnigg full power, but by these and other moves, he had purposely made the government distinctly less fascist.[76]

★ ★ ★

Grieving as a widower while overworked as chancellor, Schuschnigg had no desire to look for companionship. His conversations with Guido Schmidt and other colleagues who were friends were welcome distractions, but they were all business. He remained subdued even as foreign journalists began to praise his government. One wrote that he "assumed, modestly and unostentatiously, unrivaled power within the State—and gained the admiration of the world."[77] Others told the world he had turned out to be a great statesman. Yet, he seemed unwilling to reach out beyond the work of a busy chancellor even to escape his grief.

Kurti, however, needed and wanted friends. The only child of the nation's chancellor had limited freedom to mingle with neighborhood youths;

he kept the friendships he had enjoyed before Herma's death, including Rudi Fugger-Babbenhausen. The two boys were constant companions. Rudi would come to weekends at the lake where Schuschnigg was busy receiving a steady stream of his ministers with papers and issues to review. He barely was able to carve out the precious time he wanted to devote to Kurti. It was only natural that Rudi's parents would be welcome on these occasions, and Rudi's mother, Vera, was difficult to ignore.

Countess Vera von Czernin-Chudenitz was an obvious member of European nobility. Her confident bearing somehow added to her dazzling beauty.[78] She had an effortless charm that stimulated curiosity about the mystery of her estrangement from her husband, Count Leopold Fugger-Babbenhausen.[79] The count remained abroad and seldom came to Austria. Their marriage had been intensely unhappy, but the reasons were kept between the couple. Eventually, the marriage was annulled.

She and Schuschnigg were already friends because Vera had been a good friend to Herma.[80] Now, however, she was drawn to him by his need for her support. At some point, she and Schuschnigg awoke to the fact that this friendship, which had put them in each other's company while both were broken people, had lasted long enough to tear him from the grief that consumed him. He began to return to full health, resuming exercise, swimming, and riding daily. Eventually there were also moments of joy; peace became a welcome feature of his gray-blue eyes, and the sun was able to restore a patina to his face. He appeared to have aged markedly, but his white hair took on the glisten of gray during this renewal. He was likewise a source of comfort to Vera, helping her heal the painful emotional scars from her failed marriage. The chancellor and the mysterious countess gradually fell in love, and by late 1937, marriage was on the horizon.

They both realized, however, that a chancellor had to take into account the public and political consequences of such a marriage, and some friends and people of political importance opposed it. Schuschnigg decided that he was going to marry Vera, but he was unwilling to resign in order to do so while Austria was under such intense threat of Anschluss.[81]

· 7 ·

Hitler's Intermediaries with Austria

$\mathcal{H}$itler assigned a frightened, ambitious Westphalian to go to Vienna and work on Schuschnigg. He installed former German chancellor Franz von Papen as ambassador and as his intermediary to galvanize pro-Nazi forces there. The choice of Papen was puzzling, for Hitler had planned to kill Papen on the Night of the Long Knives. Papen, moreover, was not a Nazi and perhaps was chosen so Schuschnigg might trust him more than he should have because the two were Catholics.

The other key intermediary for the Nazis' plan was Austrian German nationalist Arthur Seyss-Inquart. Seyss, as he was known, also had so far refused to become a Nazi, but he was much closer to them than Schuschnigg thought. Some have referred to Seyss as a crypto-Nazi. But Seyss, too, was Catholic. Beyond the linkage of their faith, Seyss was also a lover of classical music, and he established a bond with Schuschnigg discussing in sophisticated depth the music of Anton Bruckner.

Austrians knew that Hitler wanted to annex Austria. Arrayed against the Nazis and some of the Pan-Germans who wanted Anschluss, there were the Christian Socials, Jews, and many others who wanted Austria to remain independent. The wishes of many Austrians, however, remained a mystery.

Hitler had the Nazis working relentlessly to unify the nationalists in Austria under the Nazi umbrella, but beyond the surprise of the 1932 Austrian election results when the Nazis scored big gains, it was a mystery where the majority of Austrians stood. Political leaders did not have modern polling data that could predict the breadth or the fervor of Austrians' willingness to support the Nazis. Outside of Austria, the Stresa signatories wanted Austria to remain independent, but Schuschnigg had seen that all three of them were irresolute. The Stresa alliance promised to assure the independence of Austria against the obvious lust of rearmed Germany. Of course, Britain, France, and Italy had signed the 1935 Stresa alliance and the several 1925 pacts called collectively the Treaty of Locarno for their own self-interests, and their adherence to their guaranty of Austrian independence would be governed by their own interests. Now, Britain was in a deep trough of appeasement, France was on the cliff of governmental collapse, and Italy had completely reversed course. Mussolini had ended Italy's protective posture against Hitler; he had become weakened and reliant on Hitler as a result of his roundly condemned invasion of Abyssinia—so weakened that by 1936 he could no longer do anything displeasing to the Führer.

Hitler, however, could not be absolutely certain in summer 1936 that he could take Austria without provoking a fight with someone. To buy time, Hitler ordered Papen to negotiate an agreement with Schuschnigg to give the Nazis in Austria some relaxation from the suppression Schuschnigg had imposed after the 1934 putsch; Papen had permission to offer one bright light for Austria—Hitler was willing to confirm the independence of Austria.

★ ★ ★

From the moment he took office, Schuschnigg had been walking a tightrope; he suppressed the Austrian Nazis, but because they had the power of the Third Reich behind them, he tried to find steps he could take that might help avoid provoking Hitler himself.[1] Austria was still in survival mode, but at least it had survived fully two years since the Nazi putsch of July 1934. Now in 1936 there was talk of an agreement. In international diplomacy, this would ordinarily signal a coming détente. Austria, however, lacked the hard intelligence to measure Germany's war preparedness; better intelligence would have told Austria that Hitler still needed time to finish building the Nazi war machine and may simply have been buying time with these negotiations.

★ ★ ★

Inside Austria, however, the formerly ragtag Nazis had become the vanguard of rapidly arming Nazi Germany, a gangster government whose leader had launched a week of mass murder and assassination of political and personal enemies. The Nazis of Austria now were able to bark their demands at Schuschnigg with Germany standing right at their elbow. Most domestic political groups and most leaders of the international community recognized that Schuschnigg had to employ gestures, consistent with independence and morality, to address some Nazi demands to keep the Nazis from exploding. Many of their demands were unthinkable, but others that were palatable might buy time. Schuschnigg's effort to walk this shaking tightrope garnered sympathy from many[2] and understanding even from political enemies. Some of them understood the weak position Austria was in as he struggled against the constant pressure from Germany to add Nazis to the government, as well as pressure from Mussolini for Austria to forge a better relationship with Germany.[3] His target audience for the small concessions he made was the German Nationalists—and even the anti-Semites of varying stripes among them—who, despite holding some views in common with the Nazis, had so far refused to join them. Schuschnigg hoped that he could deal productively with those in this group who might be persuaded to refrain from joining the growing herd defecting to the Nazi Party.[4]

★ ★ ★

Most of Schuschnigg's interface on these delicate matters was with Papen. Humbled by Hitler, Papen was now reduced to being the Führer's point man for the Anschluss. Hitler did not take Papen into his confidence; in fact, he still planned to kill him when the time was right. The negotiations also served the interests of the Nazis in Austria who were growing increasingly angry at their suppression and were dissatisfied with Schuschnigg's few steps to appease them. They kept up their demand that he adopt their entire anti-Jewish creed. He continued to refuse.[5] The Austrian Nazis compiled their demands in a several-point list. They demanded freedom for Nazis to spawn racism as they wished, restoration of a Nazi press, an amnesty for jailed Nazis, a plebiscite (confident that they would win), and the adoption by the government of a variety of anti-Semitic actions and policies. They also called for the installation of Nazis in several powerful posts, including vice chancellor, minister of the interior, foreign minister, and minister of justice.[6]

Schuschnigg responded with several small gestures that might keep the Austrian Nazis and Germany from thoroughly erupting against Austria, but he refused the larger Nazi demands; and he declined to allow Nazi captain Joseph Leopold to form a Nazi Party, the Nationalistic Party, in Austria. Instead, he allowed them only to set up a committee of seven Nazis as an opposition group to negotiate with the government. Schuschnigg's olive branch of an opposition committee was insufficient by a wide margin, and it did nothing to stem their charges that he was engaging in reprehensible repression of the Nazis. Nazi agitation, bombings, and disruption simply continued.

★ ★ ★

Papen was an effective messenger of the threats to Schuschnigg to ease up on the Nazis. He had never been a Nazi; indeed, he had been their political opponent. Under a Nazi dictatorship, however, he had become a fearful, insecure, and frustrated man. He was kept worried and off balance by Hitler and the Nazis, and he fell in line. Only a few years earlier Papen had risen to be the chancellor of Germany, yet now he barely clung to the office of ambassador to Austria. Many he knew were not that lucky; another ex-chancellor, Kurt von Schleicher, had simply been murdered by Hitler's killers in the June 1934 "Night of the Long Knives," and Papen's avoidance of the same fate had been exceedingly narrow. The puzzling conduct of Papen after his speechwriter was murdered and his top aide imprisoned on Hitler's orders included toadying up to Hitler and serving his dishonest intrigues. That chapter in Papen's life has earned stern condemnation as "disgraceful" and a "moral low point."[7]

Notwithstanding the callousness with which Papen was being treated by Hitler, Papen played his part and earned his reputation as a gentleman snake. The US ambassador to Germany, William Dodd, knew Papen and described him as devious, capable of betrayal, cowardly, and given to intrigue.[8] Ambassador Alan Rome felt the same, referring to Papen as "Intriguer Number One."[9] Historians have observed that even his "memoirs are frequently dishonest," including his version of a key conversation that is said to be "almost certainly invented."[10]

Schuschnigg very likely trusted Papen more than he should have because of Papen's patina of Catholicism. Papen was from a noble Catholic family, and this credential meant more to Schuschnigg than it should have.[11] And he was not merely a snake; he was also a chameleon. Papen wore the mantle of an independent when no Nazis were near, but he always did their bidding. In Austria, as ambassador, Papen presented a respectable veneer for the Nazi apparatus.[12] He had "wily charms and well-honed diplomatic skills."[13] He deceived Schuschnigg about his own thoughts regarding Austrian independence, and he lied repeatedly to Schuschnigg about Hitler's intentions. The truth was that Papen had urged Hitler back in 1935 to extend National Socialism to Austria.[14] He then did all he could to undermine Austrian independence. He also portrayed Hitler as a charming man of peace even though his own close call made him well aware that Hitler was unspeakably ruthless. Using these soft tools of treachery and habitual dishonesty, Papen repeatedly fed Schuschnigg false assurances of the Nazis' good faith.[15] Papen pretended that he was working with Schuschnigg to improve relations between Austria and Germany, but he had let slip to Ambassador Messersmith "in the clearest and boldest manner of how he was going to destroy the Austrian government."[16]

The relationship of Papen and Schuschnigg was never a friendly one, but Papen's tone worsened as the threat of Anschluss grew. Schuschnigg finally began to see that Papen was seizing every opportunity to exploit Austria's political turmoil for an opportunity to change governments, probably hoping to install Arthur Seyss-Inquart or Edmund Glaise-Horstenau to replace Schuschnigg. These near-Nazis (called crypto-Nazis)—Seyss-Inquart, a lawyer, and Glaise-Horstenau, an army officer and director of the Institute for Military History—were formally merely members of the national opposition, the Nationalbetout, not quite official Nazis, but indistinguishable from them in many respects. They maintained by design a veneer of respectability—essentially a thin Nazi deniability—but both were Nazi Party surrogates. The Austrian Nazi leaders let Seyss-Inquart play this double game because they had confidence that Seyss-Inquart's Sudeten German roots firmly bonded him to Germany and to the Third Reich.[17] Seyss, like a number of Austrian Catholics, appeared tolerant of Jews, and he wore a mantle of legitimacy because of his apparent refusal to join the Nazi Party or participate in its violence.[18] However, his conduct on some occasions did reveal anti-Semitic attitudes.[19] His facade was so effective that Guido Schmidt for one was fooled, and he gullibly assured Schuschnigg that Seyss was in favor of Austrian independence.[20]

Seyss-Inquart briefed aides of Hitler about the concessions Schuschnigg was willing to make. Seyss had access to conversations among the Austrian officials and to the document called the *Punktationen* prepared by Guido Zernatto and Schuschnigg, which reflected that they understood, first, that they would have to concede that some Nazis would be allowed to participate in Austrian affairs and, second, that they were willing to free many of the Nazis still in jail since the July 1934 putsch.[21] Seyss also gave the Nazis an unvarnished description of Schuschnigg's disappointment over the realization that he could expect no support at all from Britain.

★ ★ ★

Few European champions were strong enough to protect Austria from the growing menace of Nazism. By the time of Engelbert Dollfuss's administration, it appeared that the only realistic candidate to help Austria was the vainglorious and unpredictable Benito Mussolini.

Italy enjoyed a unique influence with Austria. Mussolini understood that he had leverage over Austria, and he used it as he saw fit. He aspired to be Europe's great dictator, and he thought it essential that Austria must in these troubled times have a dictatorship as well if it was to preserve its independence.[22] Mussolini had his Black shirts, the Squadristis, and he had an excessive fondness for such militias. Il Duce believed that Austria's government could be strengthened to replicate Italy's fascism if Austria would only use the Austrian version of the private army of the right wing, the Heimwehr, as a central tool in governing.[23] Mussolini failed to convince Dollfuss or Schuschnigg to do so.

Mussolini had been a close friend and a strong supporter, politically and financially, of Prince Ernst von Starhemberg, leader of the Heimwehr and the Fatherland Front. Mussolini would have preferred that Starhemberg be the Austrian chancellor.[24] However, Starhemberg's worrisome history as a former colleague of Hitler in Munich and his intense ambition caused Schuschnigg to harbor concern about Starhemberg.[25] Nevertheless, his position as leader of the Fatherland Front at first gave Starhemberg political stature. It was inevitable with these rivals in high positions that tension would grow between

Schuschnigg and Starhemberg as they shared leadership and tried to navigate the straits of a government with two competitors for that leadership.[26] As Britain and France receded and Austria came to feel more reliant on Italy as their bulwark against Hitler, Starhemberg's friendship with Mussolini was making his star much brighter.

But Mussolini was headstrong and narcissistic; he chafed at the slippage he had suffered, falling from his perch as the top fascist, becoming a receding second to the upstart Hitler. To reclaim his stature, he was about to take risks that would cost him the friendship and the support of both England and France by invading Abyssinia. When he did, the Stresa Front so recently formed in April 1935 disintegrated. Austria was in danger of being left dependent on Benito Mussolini alone.[27]

Britain publicly urged Mussolini not to do it. The British Conservative Party campaigned in the 1935 election based on a platform opposing Italy's threat of aggression in Abyssinia; despite the warning, Mussolini invaded a month after the election. Virtually the entire international community aside from Hitler erupted in criticism of Mussolini, but once the election was behind him, British prime minister Stanley Baldwin took no strong action over Mussolini's aggression.[28] The League of Nations imposed cosmetic economic sanctions but did not expel Italy over this invasion of one of its own small member states. Moreover, the noisy debate in the league, led by Britain, made clear that the Stresa alliance signed in 1935 among Britain, France, and Italy was a dead letter.[29] The unmistakable subtext was that Britain had resolved to avoid confrontation even over aggression committed by the far less threatening Italian army.

France was no better. The French foreign secretary, Pierre Laval, confided, supposedly in secret, to British foreign secretary Samuel Hoare that France would avoid further criticism of Mussolini.[30] When this collusion leaked, Hoare resigned under fire, and Baldwin picked Anthony Eden as foreign secretary. The spectacle of these two bulwark nations sitting on their hands and tolerating aggression by the comparatively weak Italians was a revelation to Hitler and an undoubted tipping point.

The economic crisis caused by Hitler's German tourist blockade had forced Austria to depend heavily on Mussolini. Italy was far stronger than Austria after World War I because Italy, though it had entered into a defensive alliance with Germany and Austria-Hungary early on in the war, did not join the Central Powers, but instead, in 1915, went over to the Allies. Thus, at war's end, Italy had not been required to disarm; it remained free to grow its armament industry.

Moreover, Il Duce was not always viewed as the villain who later emerged. He was initially held in high regard in many quarters. In America, he was virtually revered. Churchill was especially charmed by him.[31] Mussolini burnished his own image with signs of Italy's military strength; he had made an exceptionally bold move when he challenged Hitler over Austrian independence by rushing Italian troops to the border at the Brenner Pass when Nazis assassinated Dollfuss. He also was implying hostility to the Reich by developing friendships with Dollfuss and with Starhemberg. Once Schuschnigg took office, Mussolini also staged friendly meetings with the new chancellor. His support for Austria always sounded resolute coming from his "booming staccato voice."[32]

At Florence in August 1934, Mussolini had pledged to Schuschnigg: "On Italy's support you can count at all times and under any circumstances."[33] He would underscore his pledge by stressing the similarities between Italy and Austria—bonds of Catholicism and histories of monarchy. Mussolini himself had no fondness for either the church or the House of Savoy, but he was well

Schuschnigg and Mussolini, 1936.

Source: Getty Images.

aware that Schuschnigg had nostalgia for monarchy and that he had become friendly with Crown Prince Umberto and Crown Princess Marie and spent time with them during his Italian visits.

Schuschnigg, though, was a well-warned realist on the subject of an Austrian monarchy. He knew that Hitler hated the Habsburgs and that any attempt to restore the Habsburg Empire by placing the pretender, Otto von Habsburg, on the throne would result in swift retribution by Nazi Germany. He had been told exactly that by the German foreign minister, Konstantin von Neurath, who once warned him in no uncertain terms that a restoration of the Habsburgs would be for "Austria to commit suicide";[34] if they were restored, he said, Germany would march right in.[35]

The heavy Catholicism of Italy and Austria was a potentially significant bond, but it was an attenuated one; although Schuschnigg was seriously religious, Mussolini was not. He was an enemy of the Vatican. However, once Mussolini entered into the Lateran Treaty with the Vatican, Italians showed increased enthusiasm for Mussolini and his fascism. Some official statements emanating from the Vatican were supportive of his government.[36] Schuschnigg solidified a bond with the Vatican by his own respectful dealings with Pope Pius XI, as well as Vatican secretary of state Cardinal Eugenio Pacelli, who was to become Pope Pius XII in just a few years.[37] He found Pacelli an astonishing intellect who had a much better understanding of Austria than the "overcautious and timorous hierarchy and clergy" in Austria—where Schuschnigg and Cardinal Innitzer had a cold relationship.[38]

Mussolini, for all his faults, was sometimes quite prescient. He cautioned Schuschnigg that they had only two or three years of breathing space with Germany but that in 1937 "things will begin happening."[39] He repeated, however, "You can count on Italy's unchanged attitude and friendship under any circumstances."[40]

Schuschnigg shared with Mussolini his view that the mistakes at the conclusion of World War I were indeed going to lead to a new conflict and that he was determined that Austria would not be the cause of it.[41] Mussolini was well aware that Schuschnigg was a pacifist;[42] Schuschnigg made no secret of this, but he made clear to Mussolini that he was building up weaponry and increasing Austria's army to seven divisions.[43] As ironic as it would later seem, they discussed the pros and cons and the timing of one interesting demand Hitler had made—an Austrian plebiscite.[44] Schuschnigg told Mussolini that Berlin wanted a plebiscite in August 1934, immediately after the assassination of Dollfuss. Schuschnigg had, of course, refused, but he told Mussolini he was considering holding a plebiscite when he felt the time was right, once the outside pressure from Germany had been neutralized.[45]

For a time, Italy did stand tall with Austria. It provided economic assistance and sold Italian armament, including military planes, to Austria. However, in 1935 Mussolini's position suddenly became vulnerable when his Abyssinian war almost brought him down.

The impulsive Mussolini was all about his image of ferocity and daring, and he undertook the 1935 campaign to conquer Abyssinia primarily to make a mark as a fascist conqueror and show the world he was a power to fear. He offered unpersuasive public justifications for his thirst to take a distant African nation, but his real motives were more tied to brandishing his own glory. His son-in-law, Count Galeazzo Ciano, who had become so close a confidant that some labeled him "*Il Ducellino*" (the little Duce), once lapsed into candor about Il Duce, saying, "He lives in a world of his own . . . on Olympus" and sees all others as "little, little."[46] The justification that Mussolini trumpeted to Italians for attacking Abyssinia was that it was done both to avenge the defeat of an Italian army back in 1896 by Abyssinia at the Battle of Adowa and to eliminate the country of Abyssinia as a bothersome geographic obstacle sitting between two Italian lands on each side of it—Eritrea on the north and Italian Somalia to the southeast. He also saw the campaign as a way to solve severe unemployment and to gain further colonial land rich in minerals in east Africa.[47]

Austrian foreign minister Guido Schmidt, Italian foreign minister Count Galeazzo Ciano, and Chancellor Schuschnigg, November 12, 1936.
Source: Wikimedia, Creative Commons. Bibliothèque Nationale de France. Photographer: Agence de Presse Meurisse.

The start of the slowly originating Italian/Abyssinian war was sparked by an incident at Walwal. There, in the southeast corner of Abyssinia near the Somali border, a dispute arose over which countries owned several valuable wells in the Ogaden desert.[48] Small contingents of hostile troops from Italy and Abyssinia broke into a skirmish, and it turned deadly. Well over 100 were killed. This skirmish on a far continent was to have profound consequences for Austria.

Mussolini demanded an apology and sought retribution against the perpetrators.[49] He sent General Emilio De Bono to enforce his demands, but his actual plan was to use the incident as a justification to conquer Abyssinia. Haile Selassie, however, submitted the dispute to the League of Nations.[50] This move implicated the interests of the Europeans, for Britain was not ready to let Italy thumb its nose at the league Mussolini so detested.

More important was Hitler. He was extremely keen to have Mussolini invade. Europe would criticize Mussolini, and this would distract from the vilification Hitler was receiving for the murders in the Night of the Long Knives and for the assassination of Dollfuss. He egged on Mussolini, assuring him that Germany would not criticize his invasion.[51] Hitler could see what Mussolini could not—that aggression against Abyssinia would drive Mussolini straight into Hitler's arms and alienate Italy from the League of Nations, Britain, and France. And if Mussolini found that he had to align with Hitler, he would no longer be the guardian protecting Austria from Hitler. But to assure there would be actual warfare and not a capitulation by weak Abyssinia, Hitler, with striking duplicity, supplied Haile Selassie with many thousands of rifles to embolden him to defy Mussolini.[52]

The war, however, even with backward Abyssinia, went worse for Mussolini than he hoped; it dragged on, and he suffered even the embarrassment of native victories by tribesmen.[53] Italian losses raised his anxiety that another Adowa was about to humiliate Italy. He fired General De Bono and replaced him with a more vicious commander, General Pietro Badoglio. As the weeks passed, Mussolini became isolated and soon was widely disrespected.[54] Finally, on May 5, 1936, General Badoglio was able to take Addis Ababa. Haile Selassie left for European exile, and Mussolini annexed Abyssinia.[55]

★ ★ ★

Il Duce's great mistake in invading Abyssinia[56] called into question his ability to weather the outrage and remain in power, which, in turn, changed his willingness to honor his pledges to Austria. International condemnation over his assault on Abyssinia poured into Italy from the rest of the world. It did not help that Italy had used mustard gas against the Abyssinians.[57] Britain and France both turned against him.[58] The League of Nations imposed sanctions, and America cut back on trade with Italy.[59] It thoroughly irritated King Victor

Emmanuel III and undermined his confidence in Mussolini. Il Duce became concerned that all this condemnation of Italy might be enough to topple him. Austria worried that the Stresa Front, so crucial to the independence of Austria, might be at an end.[60]

Increasingly desperate, Mussolini came to realize that an alliance with Hitler might be essential to his very survival in office. He had no other way to demonstrate to the king or his political opponents that he could command European support. With the support of Hitler, he could at least regain the king's tolerance and retain his position.

Hitler viewed Mussolini as the only viable obstacle to a nonviolent capture of Austria, and he happily proclaimed neutrality toward Il Duce's Abyssinian adventurism; he then further secured Mussolini as an ally by helping to bail him out of other military fiascos.[61] By this support, Hitler provided Mussolini just the right patter of light applause needed to weather the crisis, but he forced Mussolini to give up any opposition to the annexation of Austria to get that applause. Hitler sweetened the deal by promising Mussolini that Italy would be permitted in the case of a German takeover of Austria to keep the south Tyrol it had gained at the end of World War I.[62]

Hitler had calculated correctly and had manipulated the crisis very effectively. The shaken, vilified Mussolini turned and rushed to the embrace of his only substantial European supporter. Il Duce, only recently Austria's strong protector and one of Hitler's harshest critics, was now firmly in Hitler's camp.

In July 1936, the Spanish Civil War began, and both Germany and Italy rallied to the side of Franco.[63] Mussolini used the war in Spain as a justification for ending arms sales to Austria in order to deploy Italy's armament to the Spanish theater for his own needs.[64] Hitler gratefully accepted this further weakening of Austria's military.

Even as Mussolini's position weakened, he continued to repeat his vow that he would support Austria's independence. Schuschnigg met in Rome with Mussolini and Hungarian prime minister Gyula Gömbös in 1936 to discuss independence, Hitler, and armaments.[65] Mussolini spoke flawless German, which seemed to add clarity to his promises that Austria could depend on him and that he would not waver from supporting Schuschnigg against the German threat. At their final meeting in May 1937, Mussolini once again assured Schuschnigg of Italy's friendship and support, though by then Mussolini had become openly cozy with Hitler.[66]

Austria was abandoned in the wake of this ill-fated alliance. Schuschnigg could see that, unless something changed dramatically, Austrian foreign policy could no longer be based on any level of support from Italy. Nor would Il Duce's volatile persona be available as an unpredictable force to scare away the Nazi regime now leaning hard against Austria's border.[67] Mussolini had made his choice; henceforth he and Italy would have to behave only in ways that would allow him to bask in the favor of the only government that openly applauded him—Hitler's Third Reich.

The final scintilla of hope that Mussolini's siding with Hitler might be a mere momentary expedient due to problems in Abyssinia was dashed on November 1, 1936, when Mussolini announced the Rome–Berlin Axis.[68] In September 1937, Mussolini made a public demonstration of his alliance with Hitler. He made a four-day visit to the Third Reich and was trotted about to witness parades of weaponry and Nazi rallies. He had fully embraced Nazi Germany, and Italy had no remaining need for Austria's cooperation, nor any intention to oppose Hitler on Austria or future undisclosed ambitions. Even the hope that Italy might reverse course if the evidence of Nazi despotism increased was also dashed only one year later when Italy signed the Anti-Comintern Pact with Germany and Japan. Il Duce was now irreversibly committed to the dark side in what was about to become the darkest, most savage decade in history.

★ ★ ★

Mussolini's relationship with the "Mountaineer," the pope's epithet derived from the hiking that was his favorite pastime, had always been a distant one. Pius XI and Mussolini faced off for some sixteen years. Both were difficult personalities, and the two of them had many communications; however, virtually all were through emissaries. The pope only met once with Mussolini, and the pope refused to converse on telephones. Their emissaries worked out major accords between the two, including the 1929 Lateran Treaty, which gave Vatican City sovereign status and restored considerable money to the Vatican. For this, Mussolini acquired a certain valuable respectability among Italian Catholics. For his part, Pius XI achieved peace in dealings with a powerful ruler whom he came to detest.

The détente Mussolini achieved with the Vatican in his early years unraveled over time. For well over their first decade, Pius XI and Mussolini each felt he needed the cooperation of the other, but once Mussolini threw in with Hitler, the pope finally took out after "*Mangiaprete*" (the "priest eater"), Mussolini's sobriquet inspired by his Squadristis' beatings and killings of priests and other conduct showing his hatred of the Catholic Church.[69]

To please Hitler, Mussolini turned against the small Italian Jewish population. There were only some 44,000 Italian Jews, and Mussolini, though anti-Semitic, had been indifferent to them. But Mussolini began flagrant oppression of Jews. He promulgated laws and policies that led to firing of Jews, denying them admission to Italian schools and confiscating business licenses and property. He did not execute Italian Jews (eventually about 8,000 died in concentration camps). Executions only began in 1943 when the Third Reich took over the governing of Italy.

★ ★ ★

Schuschnigg was well aware of the problem Abyssinia had caused among the Stresa Front powers, so he attempted to enlist their support individually, but he simultaneously sought support from others, including Hungary as well as the members of the Little Entente—Czechoslovakia, Yugoslavia, and Romania.[70] Though these efforts produced no help, some modern scholars judge that the foreign policies and security initiatives he pursued while in this isolated plight were "both sound and realistic."[71]

Hungary was vulnerable to German conquest, but Schuschnigg had received occasional modest assurances from Prime Minister Gyula Gömbös. He agreed with Schuschnigg that the interests of Hungary at least coincided with Austria's interests; however, Hungary was at odds with Czechoslovakia and Yugoslavia,[72] and Gömbös became indebted to Germany and Italy. The Treaty of Trianon embodied Hungary's concessions to end World War I; the treaty imposed tough postwar burdens on Hungary, and Gömbös sought support to obtain relief from those burdens. He signed a trade agreement with Hitler and obtained a promise from Mussolini that Italy would support Hungary's plea to amend the treaty.[73] At best, these neighbors would have been sources of faint political support, but even that was not to last. Gömbös died just months after giving Schuschnigg that assurance.

One other offer Schuschnigg had received was hardly a source of hope. At Gömbös's funeral, Schuschnigg had the opportunity to speak with Nazi Reichsmarshall Hermann Göring. They discussed arms, and Göring made the hollow suggestion that instead of Austria depending on Italy for weapons, it should deal directly with Germany, which could, he said, supply whatever Austria needed.[74]

Czechoslovakia was no more helpful than Hungary. In early 1936, Schuschnigg went to Prague to meet with President Edvard Beneš purportedly to explore trade and economic issues, but the looming threat of Germany was at the forefront of the agenda. They discreetly discussed the feasibility of an alliance among the Danubian basin states.[75] Beneš, however, did not appear to foresee that the fall of Austria was sure to mean the end of Czechoslovakia; he offered Austria no meaningful assistance.[76] And the Little Entente as a coalition was little more than a fiction by 1937, due to regional disagreements; by then, its members engaged only in "empty formalities" with each other as Yugoslavia became openly favorable toward Germany and turned away from Czechoslovakia.[77]

★ ★ ★

Who was left? Britain, no one else. It was obvious that Britain, somehow, would have to be awakened. On several occasions, Schuschnigg probed and prodded to determine whether there was any chance of rekindling support from Britain, but each time the door was softly, emphatically closed. Schuschnigg was utterly candid with Britain; he acknowledged to the British after the Rome–Berlin Axis was announced in 1936 that Austria no longer could expect any help from Italy. His pleas, however, did little more than confirm British intelligence's cold assessment that there was no way to prevent Austria from being joined with its "big brother."[78] Even the anti-appeasers in Britain seemed to draw the line against protecting Austria or even encouraging Austria to resist because to do so would raise a false hope that Britain would help. The view of the Foreign Office was summed up by Lord Cadogan as early as 1936. He said the consensus was it would be better just to let Germany have Austria, to get it over with and end all the fuss.[79] But Austria and Britain both had to know that Britain was now in reality Austria's last hope. Neville Chamberlain, however, by 1937 "began to favor the Germans," and his ambassador to Germany, Neville Henderson, became exceptionally friendly to Germany.[80]

It is hard to reconcile the cold shoulder Austria was receiving from Britain and France with any calculus for how to avoid war. Both countries were demonstrating to Hitler that they were willing to tolerate severe insult, even lawless aggression against other nations, in order to avoid provoking Germany to attack them. This was fatalism or self-deception, because many leaders in Britain and France saw Austrian independence as essential to avoiding another war.[81] Some of the Allies of World War I may not have forgiven the Austrian elite of the empire, Franz Joseph and his generals, for starting World War I. That was rarely offered as a justification for their lack of enthusiasm to protect Austria, but it may have influenced popular attitudes in France and elsewhere then, almost a quarter century later.

The lost opportunities to prevent war due to their appeasement policies became clear to almost everyone after the war began, but Ambassador Messersmith foresaw, even before the war, how the squandering of those chances was sure to lead to war:

> England has to make a decision and if she makes it in time a European war can be avoided. If she delays too long, for in my opinion she has to make it eventually, anyway, war will eventually come. If England, France and Italy do not get together, Poland and southeastern Europe, including Austria, will fall definitely into the hands of Germany . . . and Germany will have won the Worlds War.[82]

★ ★ ★

With no help anywhere on the horizon, Schuschnigg redoubled his effort to negotiate peaceful coexistence with Germany. Hitler, after all, had addressed the Reichstag on May 21, 1935, and promised peace, professed his respect for all the territorial provisions of the Treaty of Versailles, claimed he was willing to sign nonaggression pacts with all neighboring countries, and pledged to forego any interference in the affairs of other states.[83] Some European leaders must still have entertained the hope that, with such an archive of Hitler's promises and assurances known to the whole world, any head of state would honor at least his unequivocal pledge of independence for Austria.

Schuschnigg's goal in treating with Germany under these circumstances was reduced to one essential—warding off imminent invasion to buy time. Exactly what benefit the buying of a modest amount of additional time might yield was unknown even to Schuschnigg, and it was surely beyond Austria's control. But if he could somehow delay Anschluss or invasion two years, the rearmament begun in Britain might reverse the current imbalance between Britain and Germany.[84] Schuschnigg could only hope that Europe would enter upon an era of recovery and prosperity. If so, a visible balance of power might develop, and Hitler might back off his acquisitive goals. If that came to pass, he might let Austria remain independent. Papen, however, was conducting a campaign of blending alarming threats and calming assurances in masterfully dishonest fashion; he sometimes pretended diplomacy, but he remained determined to destroy Austria.[85]

When the public terms of the 1936 Austro-German Agreement, the Abkommen, surfaced, those who took the terms seriously were exultant that Germany acknowledged the independence of Austria.[86] Reading the document, it appeared a valuable compromise[87] and a cause for hope. It professed German recognition of the full sovereignty of Austria, and it ended the 1,000 mark tariff.[88] It reaffirmed Hitler's May 21, 1935, speech to the Reichstag proclaiming that Germany had no intention "to interfere in internal Austrian affairs, or to annex or incorporate Austria."[89] Because of these provisions, "a great many observers believed that Schuschnigg had won a victory of tremendous significance."[90] This gave even the coldly practical realist Schuschnigg modest encouragement, but many naive optimists across the world were euphoric. To Schuschnigg, the Abkommen at least bought time to restore Britain's resolve against Germany.

Other terms, however, could be read to undermine the independence clause, particularly the German nation clause in which Austria confirmed it was a German nation—whatever that meant. To most Austrians, this declaration, in context, was comfortable. Schuschnigg took it to mean nothing more than that they were a Germanic people and Austria would not join in opposition to Germany.[91] Numerically, and by heritage, Austrians were indeed German; they spoke German and clung to German culture and tradition. None of that implied an acceptance of Nazism. The German Jews of Austria and Czechoslovakia shared this cultural affinity, and to most of them this clause did not imply an embrace of Anschluss. It seemed merely an expression of pride in their mutual tribal heritage.

But there was a secret protocol, a so-called gentlemen's agreement, that was part of the 1936 pact. That informal pact contained nine additional clauses, all favorable to Germany. One granted amnesty to Nazi prisoners in Austria except for those who were guilty of grave crimes. It also provided that two German nationalists would be admitted to the government soon.[92] The "gentlemen's agreement" later came to be exaggerated by some as "Austria's death-warrant."[93] While the Austro-German Agreement did ultimately serve as background to the events that led to the end of Austria's independence, on its face it reinforced Austrian independence. Hitler viewed the agreement as a setback. He screamed at Papen, claiming that the agreement served as nothing but a trap for Germany.[94] The problem with this agreement, however, was not the terms. It was that the promises by the shamelessly untrustworthy Führer were not genuine and thus were of no real benefit.[95]

Schuschnigg calculated that allowing Edmund Glaise-Horstenau, an Austrian army officer and a Nazi sympathizer (but not a Nazi), into the government merely as a minister without portfolio[96] was a cosmetic gesture; it might slake Hitler's thirst, yet grant no power or influence to Nazis. The other, Guido Schmidt, was even less a danger. Schmidt was no Nazi and was a friend of Schuschnigg.

A joint commission was established to oversee the implementation of the new agreement, and Wilhelm Keppler was named as Germany's appointee. Keppler, with his chicken-beak nose and cold glaring eyes hovering above his mustache, immediately began compiling a dossier of purported Austrian violations, lodging one complaint after another, asserting that Austria was failing to honor the agreement and its secret protocol.[97]

★ ★ ★

Hitler had made his calculation based on the most he could get away with, and he risked exactly that and no more. He believed he could take Austria without provoking war prematurely, but he needed some pretense to convince Chamberlain and Mussolini that their constituents would not erupt with outrage over the conquest. The Nazis, however, had begun to lose financial support in Austria, which drove Hitler to quicken his pace toward Anschluss.[98]

The very best German generals still had a less confident assessment of Germany's readiness for war. Chief among these doubters was Hitler's minister of war, field marshal General Werner von Blomberg, who was also commander in chief of the armed forces. The commander in chief of the army, Colonel General Baron Freiherr Werner von Fritsch, agreed with Blomberg. Hitler's acolytes who believed as he did were the commander in chief of the navy, Grand Admiral Erich Raeder, and the commander in chief of the air force, Hermann Göring. The main provocateur was Göring, who unfailingly encouraged Hitler's premature aggression and always contributed to his overconfidence.

Hitler called these generals and the admiral together on November 5, 1937, three months before the Berchtesgaden meeting with Schuschnigg, and told them what was coming. It was a stunning announcement.[99] The Führer revealed his plan to annex Austria and Czechoslovakia. This was the generals' assignment, and he wanted it done very soon. His goals were to obtain new borders—better strategic frontiers for Germany; to add to the Reich the twelve million Germans in his two targets; to add their manpower for twelve new army divisions; and to obtain their food to feed as many as six million more Germans.[100] The Reich could not wait until 1943 to take the two countries because that would give them time to arm themselves and to defeat his plan to confiscate the *Lebensraum* he wanted. He was confident that internal strife in France was absorbing the French and might soon make the French army incapable of resisting Germany. His generals, he demanded, should prepare to commence the war in 1938.

Most of them were alarmed, but Blomberg was aghast. They were nowhere near ready for the war they were sure would follow the first invasion of another country. Blomberg towered over Hitler; he had previously mustered the temerity to voice his opposition to the Führer's proposals to his face, as well as to question Hitler's assumptions concerning preparedness. The foreign minister, Baron Neurath, and General Fritsch did as well. Neurath was particularly upset at this shame faced reversal of the German foreign policy on which he had staked his own credibility. Days later, General Fritsch took the chief of the general staff, General Beck, into his confidence about the Führer, and Beck found the news extremely disturbing.[101]

In January 1938, Foreign Minister Neurath was able to gain another audience with Hitler at the Berghof. There he remonstrated with Hitler that this would mean starting a war for which they were not prepared. Hitler, however, refused to budge. Neurath paused, and then he told Hitler to find another foreign minister.

Field Marshal Blomberg had somehow remained in the Führer's good graces despite his own resistance in late 1937. When the widowed Blomberg married his secretary just two months later on January 12, 1938, the two men who stood up for him were Hitler and Göring. But a short time later a major revelation was brought to Göring. The bride had a history as a prostitute—an extensive history. Hitler was humiliated and outraged, but Göring was ecstatic—Göring wanted Blomberg's job as minister of war. Now he was sure he would get it. On January 25, Göring barely concealed his glee as he delivered the message to the embarrassed Blomberg that Blomberg had to resign. He did. However, Hitler declined to name Göring to succeed Blomberg as minister of war.

Next came the fall of General Fritsch. The Nazis were well aware that this career officer looked upon them with total disdain, and they hated him for it, so Heinrich Himmler and Reinhard Heydrich concocted a frame-up. They falsely accused Fritsch of a sex scandal. Hitler agreed with them that Fritsch had to go, and even after Hitler learned that the frame-up was based on false evidence, he still sacked Fritsch.

Hitler used these events as the grounds for his February 4, 1938, purge of the military leaders he feared. He fired sixteen other senior generals and foty-four other officers hostile to the Nazis. Hitler himself took Blomberg's place as chief of the armed forces by creating a new chain of command, the OKW (High Command of the Armed Forces), and taking the title of Supreme Commander. He named one of his tested puppets as the OKW's chief of staff—General Wilhelm Keitel—and he named General Walther Brauchitsch to succeed Fritsch as commander in chief of the army.

Days after these events, General Fritsch, General Beck, and others began to talk seriously of a coup against Hitler. For now, however, they were too few and their position too unsure to attempt it.[102]

★ ★ ★

Schuschnigg has asked rhetorically, paraphrasing Churchill: "Was, therefore, Berchtesgaden really the beginning of the end or the end of the beginning."[103] It was only a few days after Hitler dismissed his top generals that he and Papen devised a deceptive plan to meet with Schuschnigg. Hitler hoped the result would be to create the political scenario he needed to make the takeover of

The Guardpost of Hitler's Berghof at Berchtesgaden.
Source: Wikimedia, Creative Commons. Photographer: Heinrich Hoffmann.

Austria tolerable to appeasers. Launching a naked invasion in violation of international law could, he was repeatedly warned, provoke war, and he was being told over and over that Germany was still not ready for war.

By the time of the Berchtesgaden meeting, Hitler already had in place his plans to invade and conquer Austria if necessary. In that sense, Austria's "fate was sealed" before the meeting was ever planned.[104] Schuschnigg knew that, without British, French, and Italian support, "the only option left to him was to play for time."[105] But Hitler's planned sequence, taking Austria, and then Czechoslovakia, then Poland, had already been set in 1934.[106] There is also no doubt now that Hitler expected all along that he may have to take Austria "by force,"[107] and his military plans for doing so—named "Red," "Green," and "Otto"—were ready by June 1937. They described the conquest of Austria long before Berchtesgaden.[108]

But the still-cautious Führer had learned from his meetings with the British lords of appeasement that he could be certain he would escape any British opposition to the takeover of Austria if he could manipulate Austria so it would appear to have agreed to the conquest. The secret to preventing Britain from challenging the Anschluss seemed clear—he had merely to fool much of Britain and avoid a naked military invasion, and Britain would stand down.

Chancellor Schuschnigg in London with (from left) Austrian foreign minister Egon Berger von Waldenegg, the Duchess of York (Princess Helena Victoria), and the Duke of York (King George VI), 1935.
Source: Getty Images.

This had been Hitler's takeaway from meetings with the British, most pointedly from the lengthy meeting he had at Berchtesgaden on November 19, 1937, with Chamberlain's emissary, Lord Halifax. This strong advocate of appeasement that day had his greatest impact on his times. During an oleaginous, several-hour play-up to Hitler, Halifax did his greatest mischief. He lavished praise upon Hitler, gushing over the Führer's record of achievement in Germany and discrediting the occasional signs of displeasure the British public showed at Hitler's treatment of the Jews and religions.[109] The result of this fawning and the assurances that were sprinkled in it was that "Halifax let Hitler see his chance."[110] He made it abundantly clear that there would be no British opposition to Hitler continuing to bully and squeeze Austria and Czechoslovakia into the arms of Germany. On that day, Hitler "heard all he needed to know."[111]

Hours after Halifax rode off down the mountain from the Berghof, Hitler, in an exultant mood, slapping his thighs with excitement over Halifax's message, sat down for a quiet dinner with Eva Braun and other intimates. He revealed to her that "Halifax had assured him that Britain would not stand in Germany's way in respect of its Austrian policy."[112] Good news indeed, since Hitler had already given his generals the timetable for conquering first Austria

Britain's Lord Halifax meets with Hitler, November 19, 1937.
Source: Getty Images. Photographer: Presse-Illustrations Heinrich Hoffmann.

and then Czechoslovakia.[113] Halifax had also demonstrated that Hitler had successfully fooled Britain's leaders. Now he had only to fool them one more time by making the Anschluss plausibly appear voluntary—perhaps grudgingly voluntary, but not an armed invasion.[114] Ideally, it would be orchestrated to look voluntary as to Austria's government; failing that, Hitler could create the needed appearance by rallying into the streets of Austria a clamorous group of Austrian citizens crying for help from Germany—even if that crowd consisted largely of Austrian Nazis. By the time of the Schuschnigg meeting at Berchtesgaden a few months later, Hitler was confident that only a blatant military invasion of Austria presented any risk at all of provoking Britain under the Chamberlain government.

Hermann Göring had gone even further to create the pretense of a welcomed Anschluss. On November 20, 1937, the day after Halifax met with Hitler, Halifax went to Göring's estate at Karinhall outside Berlin. There Göring assured Halifax that "under no circumstances shall we use force."[115] The Nazis were confident that manipulation and propaganda were all they needed to create the illusion of Austrian approval of the Anschluss, at least enough of an illusion that there would be no significant opposition from the British. And without Britain weighing in to support Austria or Czechoslovakia, Germany could proceed to take coercive action and swallow both countries into the Third Reich.

The stronger nations had made a world-changing decision—to distance themselves. But not from Hitler. It was from Hitler's target. They were going to tie the proverbial rope around Schuschnigg's neck, staking him out like a goat being tethered outside a jungle village to test for the presence of lions. Europe was giving in to a pandemic of fear of the Nazis. European leaders decided the one chance they had was to allow him Austria as a sacrifice.

Schuschnigg pleaded with them all. Despite his pleas and warnings, they were unwilling to express even diplomatic resistance to the Nazis. The astounding quiet of Europe virtually shouted to him that a Nazi invasion would be accepted by Britain, France, Italy, and the League of Nations. But, by 1938, Schuschnigg had grown so revolted by Hitler that he could no longer stand seeing the Nazi violence and lawlessness against German Jews. Less still could he accept that the racism that engulfed Germany would be spread beyond the German border into Austria.

On January 5, 1938, Schuschnigg boiled over. He at least, if entirely alone, had to denounce what he was seeing. The audience he chose was the British—and not just the government. Schuschnigg knew the British public approved of Neville Chamberlain, and so he made a direct plea to them.

To assure they heard him, Schuschnigg chose London's *Daily Telegraph and Morning Post*.

Britain's Lord Halifax visits Göring, November 20, 1937.
Source: Wikimedia, Creative Commons. Bundesarchiv Bild 102-17986 2C.Schorfheide.

On January 5, 1938, Schuschnigg preempted any Nazi charade that there could be an agreed Anschluss. He invited respected journalist Kees van Hoek of London's *Daily Telegraph and Morning Post* to the Ballhausplatz for an exclusive interview. He condemned the Nazi treatment of citizens based on "that elusive thing Race." He reaffirmed his refusal to adopt the Nazi creed of intolerance, and he clarified his own beliefs about Germany and Austria. He rejected Anschluss, dictatorship, racial discrimination and persecution, and the very idea of a Thousand Year Reich. The interview was plainly no politician's calculus: "Our children are God's children, not to be abused by the State. . . . Austria has always been a humanitarian State. As a people we are tolerant by disposition." And then he added the jolting rebuke that "an absolute abyss separates Austria from Nazism."[116]

Schuschnigg's interview received favorable press throughout the world, but not in Germany,[117] where Nazis saw it as obstinate support of Jews. His message was replete with terms similar to the pope's German encyclical ten months earlier. Schuschnigg was mindful of the reprisals against clergy that resulted in Germany from the pope's message. As he surely expected, Hitler was seriously angered by the interview.[118] To the top Nazis, Schuschnigg's denouncement of them was a "most disturbing incident."[119] Hitler, however, calculated that he would still succeed with the pretense if he could orchestrate a dramatic scene, a gang-tackle of Schuschnigg at Berchtesgaden. He trotted out the new, less astute, but more compliant generals as props to help him pull off a thuggish browbeating of Schuschnigg. Hitler summoned the generals to create a warlike air at his compound hoping to terrify Schuschnigg with a sudden threat of immediate war. His outbursts were calculated to frighten Schuschnigg into agreeing to the Anschluss.

Widespread fear over Hitler's sudden mass firings of powerful generals just prior to the Berchtesgaden conference spread through the rest of the senior Wehrmacht officers. Most officers who remained were intimidated; most fell in line and did Hitler's bidding. The purge was felt by the diplomatic corps as well. Foreign Minister Neurath had just resigned and had been replaced by a fervent Nazi, Joachim von Ribbentrop. Hitler also had a shock for Ambassador Papen; he fired him.[120] Whether this was a sign intended to raise Schuschnigg's anxiety by a sudden recall of the ambassador, or a dismissal by Hitler of a distrusted former political enemy, Papen was alarmed, and he sprang into action.

★ ★ ★

Papen had great survival skills. He had, after all, dodged execution on the Night of the Long Knives. This time he had the crafty good sense to rush to Berchtesgaden on February 5, 1938, and save himself by calling on Hitler and getting control over arrangements already in the works for Hitler to meet with Schuschnigg to resolve the Austrian question once and for all.[121] Papen convinced Hitler not to fire him; he claimed he was indispensable to Hitler's plan for this meeting and that his dismissal would have the wrong effect upon Schuschnigg.[122] Hitler warmed to the idea, reinstated Papen, and sent him back to Vienna to lay the trap for the meeting.

Papen was in an extremely precarious position even after Hitler gave him a second life, so he did what he needed to do. He told Schuschnigg that he had Hitler's assurance that the time was ripe to amicably resolve their differences. Papen added his own opinion that Hitler's mood was favorable and that the relationship between Austria and the Nazis, both at home and in Germany, could be improved by a discussion of points of friction arising from the Austro-German agreement. Schuschnigg and Papen had spent a year negotiating that agreement, and Schuschnigg had taken the agreement very seriously. To Hitler, however, it was mere paper. He would not hesitate to breach that agreement when he thought the time to take Austria had arrived. In 1938, neither Schuschnigg nor the other leaders of Europe yet understood that Hitler would say whatever he wished and would make agreements with no intention to live up to them and that he would have no shame when he breached them. This event at Berchtesgaden, after all, was going to be Hitler's debut performance in his extravaganza of diplomatic frauds. Other heads of government did not yet comprehend the astonishing extent of his dishonesty as a head of state.[123] Papen readily embraced Hitler's fraud; he portrayed the coming conference to Schuschnigg as an opportunity to meet over a nice lunch in the relaxed setting of the Obersalzberg, and the agenda would be just the July 1936 agreement. Schuschnigg dreaded the meeting but could not decline.[124]

Hitler, however, had in mind a very different scheme. He had no intention of hosting a diplomatic conference. He had grown highly agitated as the start of aggression approached. He warned his high command that Schuschnigg would share Dollfuss's fate if he did not come around.[125] In the days leading up to Berchtesgaden, Foreign Minister Neurath had noticed Hitler's increasing agitation, saying that Austria was an "overheated boiler" about to explode if the pressure found no relief.[126]

Schuschnigg was apprehensive despite Papen's assurances. He insisted upon and received an agreement that the joint communiqué at the meeting's conclusion would announce that both governments reaffirmed the July 1936 agreement. Schuschnigg could, even then, have been justified if he believed the assurances he had received about the meeting. After all, hadn't Hitler announced for the entire world to hear back in 1935 that Germany had no intention to annex Austria?[127]

But Hitler wanted the meeting because he was about to do precisely what he had vowed he would not do, and the meeting was a necessary scene to enable him to mask the flagrancy of his deceit, to disguise an international crime as a rescue, and to pretend that Austria was begging for his help.

In the final analysis, Schuschnigg went to Berchtesgaden because he concluded he simply could not decline the invitation. He could not incur the condemnation of Austrian leaders and European statesmen—condemnation they would quickly deliver if he refused to meet. Moreover, all during 1937, the Austrian Nazis had raked the country with violence as a "new party radicalism set in," with daily bombings, frequent murders, and menacing demonstrations throughout the country producing a state of crisis and fear.[128] This could not go on. Perhaps the meeting could at least be used to stop the violence.

What was actually at hand, however, was Hitler setting the scene for maximum theatrical impact to drive home the brutal reality that Austria "was at Nazi Germany's mercy."[129] Only by striking terror could he hope to get Schuschnigg to agree.

V

CONFRONTATION

· 8 ·

Ambush at Berchtesgaden

"Perhaps you will wake up one morning in Vienna to find us there—just like a spring storm."

—Adolf Hitler

As dawn broke on the bleak, midwinter morning of February 12, 1938, an overnight train screeched to its stop at Salzburg's Hauptbahnhof. An inconspicuous sleeper car concealed a handful of men on a desperate mission. The chancellor of Austria and his small entourage had traveled nearly 200 miles under cover of darkness hoping to save their country from being swallowed whole by Nazi Germany.[1]

Before stepping off the train to head by car toward the German frontier, the Austrian chancellor left ominous instructions with a small cadre of personal staff remaining in Salzburg, a sign that he was well aware what might become of him that day after he crossed the border into Hitler's Germany. Five years of the most ruthless, sometimes violent coexistence with Nazi Germany could come unglued that day. On that morning, Schuschnigg was filled with concern that his beloved nation, barely hanging by a thread and subject to Hitler's mood of the moment, could fall to the mercurial Führer. He shared his own feeling of foreboding by the message he left behind. He warned his contingent in Salzburg that if they did not hear from him by six that evening, they should assume the worst and raise the alarm with Austria's armed forces.[2] The chancellor's directions, more fitting for a hostage negotiation than a meeting of heads of government in the twentieth century, were not alarmist. This "proof of life" contingency acknowledged what the chancellor saw as a very real possibility—that Austria was being lured into a trap, and he may be taken prisoner or, like Dollfuss, shot dead before the day ended.

For more than five years, Hitler's designs had been clear to careful observers, especially those who had read his testament, *Mein Kampf*. They also could have learned from a close reading of his book that he believed there was singular value in striking physical terror in individuals and in the masses.[3]

Schuschnigg had never laid eyes on his German host, but he had a personal taste of the sudden cold-blooded murders Hitler had ordered in Germany and Austria during the last several years. Nothing had occurred to dispel the strong suspicion that Schuschnigg's wife was one of Hitler's victims. He had ample reason not merely to fear and distrust but also to despise Adolf Hitler. Added to the revulsion of having to meet and speak with this killer was the anxiety that Hitler appeared ready to drag many decent Austrians into a living hell as captives of Nazi Germany.

Entering the car that would carry them across the border, Schuschnigg struggled to muzzle the nagging voice in his head about this mission.[4] Despite the years of Nazi duplicity and scores of Nazi murders in Austria and despite all the warning signs, he still could not fully comprehend the Führer. Hitler's twisted plans and motives were foreign to everything about the proper Schuschnigg, a man with a subtle mind; Schuschnigg did not possess the vicious cunning of Adolf Hitler, indeed, Schuschnigg scorned even the politician's willingness for pretense.[5]

Franz von Papen assured Schuschnigg that the Führer's motives were pure. Both were well aware that Hitler had pledged in 1935 that he had no intention to seek European conquests and, in 1936, had approved the Abkommen agreement with Austria acknowledging the independence of Austria, and Papen pretended this meeting was needed merely to resolve some areas of friction that had developed since the agreement and improve relations between the two increasingly unfriendly Germanic states.[6] Schuschnigg wanted very much to believe this was the agenda because the darker scenarios playing out in his head were too grim to contemplate.

Despite the temptation to believe Hitler's earlier assurances that he had no designs to undermine the independence of Austria, Schuschnigg believed that Hitler actually intended war against Austria. He knew in general terms the alarming extent of Germany's recent arms buildup, and he was shocked by the audacious illegality of it. Schuschnigg was also face to face with the awful reality that now, in early 1938, other European powers had not kept up with Germany's rearmament. Little Austria had been forced in 1919 to disarm, and it was no match for the Nazis if left to go it alone—and alone is where Austria was.

The only way forward for Austria was to find ways to forestall Nazi aggression and try to buy time using diplomacy and gestures. Schuschnigg had to believe that, granted time, Austria could be saved.

As the car approached the border, Schuschnigg came to grips with the unsettling fact that he was about to leave the safety of Austria and enter the

Third Reich. With him as they arrived at the border crossing at Freilassing were Foreign Minister Guido Schmidt; his aide, Colonel Georg Bartl; and several police bodyguards. But his bodyguards were refused entry. The Austrians were instructed to send the guards back to Salzburg.[7] An atmosphere of domination was being rolled out by the Führer in advance of the meeting.

Papen was there to greet the Austrians at the border, likely giddy that this gambit of his making was working and might salvage his own falling star in German government and restore the Führer's confidence. As they left the safety of Austria behind them and began the ride along the road to Berchtesgaden, Papen introduced a new ingredient, heightening the tension. Feigning a minor change of plans, Papen casually mentioned that a few German generals[8] "happened" to be present at the Berghof. They had "quite accidentally" joined the Führer there, he said.[9] Hitler had changed the scene and added a new cast for the day's performance. This was no meeting; it was to be a drama to portray Germany's military dominance over virtually powerless Austria.

Papen's rendition of the generals' arrival would have further confused the generals, for they had no clue why they had been summoned; they were mere props Hitler was going to use to stoke maximum fear. Schuschnigg knew it was useless to object. Now on German soil, there would be no turning back. They had not even reached the Berghof, but Schuschnigg could already feel the walls closing in.[10]

★ ★ ★

As they scaled the winding, icy mountain road to the Führer's den on the commanding mountainside above the town of Berchtesgaden, the caravan passed a series of Schutzstaffel (SS) guard barracks. The young faces staring down at the chancellor's entourage were harbingers of the dark days ahead. He would later learn that most of these young SS men, the ultimate Führer loyalists, were Austrian.

The Führer, decked out in the brown jacket of the SA (Sturmabteilung), swastika armband, and black trousers, a classic Storm Trooper outfit,[11] stood at the Berghof entrance flanked by his three generals. He greeted his guests formally. Schuschnigg addressed Hitler as *"Herr Reichskanzler"* (Mr. Reich Chancellor), in accordance with diplomatic protocol. That courtesy would not be reciprocated.

On one of the most stress-filled days of his life, Schuschnigg would need to smoke. Entering the main hall, he flicked open his cigarette case without a second thought and was instantly met with a protest from Hitler, "I do not like smoke!" Lighting a Dunhill, Schuschnigg responded, "That is unfortunate, for I must smoke."[12] He should have savored this small retort—it would be mostly downhill from there.[13]

The Great Room of the Berghof where Schuschnigg and Hitler met.
Source: Wikimedia, Creative Commons. Bundesarchiv, Bild 146-1991-077-31, CC-BY-SA 3.0.

The Führer and Schuschnigg climbed the stairs to the great room on the second floor for their private meeting. There, a stunning Alpine view swept in through huge windows. Schuschnigg attempted to break the ice with a comment on the scenery, but the Führer wasted no time setting the tone for the day: "But we did not gather here to speak of the fine view or the weather!"[14]

What followed bore no resemblance to the friendly negotiation Papen had promised. Hitler immediately chastised Austria and Schuschnigg. He accused Austria of a history of hostility to Germany and condemned Schuschnigg for Austria's failure to resign from the League of Nations when Germany did.[15] Over the course of a nightmarish two hours, the stunned Austrian chancellor was subjected to accusations, personal insults, boasts of Germany's overwhelming military power, taunts about the growing evidence that England and France would not come to the rescue of Austria, and repeated threats of military invasion.[16]

Hitler chastised Schuschnigg's policies as though Austria were already part of Germany but was misbehaving as a lawless province: "The whole history of Austria is just one uninterrupted act of high treason. . . . And I can tell you right now, Herr Schuschnigg, that I am absolutely determined to make an end of all this."[17] The use of the concept of treason plainly meant treason against the German Aryan race. Schuschnigg had committed treason by attacking the ideology of Nazism as unacceptable in Austria.

Schuschnigg had carefully read *Mein Kampf*. He could see past Hitler's airbrushed phrases like *un-German* and his references to Nazi Party practices. He knew this *volkisch* jargon meant the Nuremberg Laws that decreed that Jews were an inferior, corrupting race, a people who were not merely permissible as targets of bigotry but also were to be enslaved and denied the very right to exist. And he knew these were not peripheral thoughts, but that Hitler intended that this would be the "center of life" in his Volkisch state.[18]

Hitler blasted Schuschnigg's refusal but used prosaic-sounding words and classic Nazi idioms and epithets. He condemned Austria's "un-German history" and singled out Schuschnigg's "contemporary Austrian policy in particular," which suppressed "National-Socialism and its practices."[19] Hitler called their differences "'racio-political' [*volkspolitische*],"[20] using Nazism's dog whistles and his own *volkspolitische* jargon.

These were the phrasings he often used for broad public consumption. Hitler early on had learned when to avoid the blunt, hate-filled racial tirades he used with his true believers. With others, he used shrouded politico-speak.[21]

Schuschnigg understood Hitler's racial references. He understood that the Aryanism of the Volkisch state conceived in the pages of Hitler's testament was a monstrous plan. Hitler, for the attentive reader, had sprinkled the ingredients of his Volkisch state in chapters eleven and twelve of *Mein Kampf*. This was the world Hitler demanded that Schuschnigg must embrace. He wanted a public concession that Nazism was compatible with Austrian policy, and he wanted Volkspolitische Offices in Styria and elsewhere to spread his creed. Again, Schuschnigg refused. He responded as calmly as he could stomach: "My opinion on these questions differs basically from yours."

But it was not only Schuschnigg's opinion that infuriated Nazis. His actions were far more offensive to them. Adolf Hitler had likely never taken note of the names Desider Friedmann, Jakob Ehrlich, or Solomon Frankfurter prior to the briefings he received from Papen and some Austrian Nazis he consulted before the Schuschnigg meeting. However, the names of those leaders of Austria's Jewish groups were high on the list of the Austrian Nazis' grievances against Schuschnigg, and they inevitably contributed to the hostility at the Berchtesgaden meeting. The Austrian chancellor had not endeared himself to the Austrian Nazis. Several of them were huddling with Hitler that day. They would surely complain to Hitler of Schuschnigg's appointment of one of the chief spokesmen for Austria's Jews, Desider Friedmann, to Austria's influential Council of State. He had also appointed other Jews, including Jakob Ehrlich, a prominent Jewish councilor, to the Citizens' Council, and Professor Solomon Frankfurter to the Cultural Council. By these and other Jewish appointments, Schuschnigg had done more than announce that the racial policies of the Third Reich were repulsive to him.[22] When he added the exclamation point in his interview before Berchtesgaden denouncing racial discrimination, his rejection of Nazism was unique among European leaders and created the danger that others might follow.[23]

And there was one Schuschnigg appointment of a Jewish professor that had rankled many top Nazis far more than other appointments—Dietrich von Hildebrand. Some even saw Hildebrand as one of the chief obstacles impairing the acceptance of Nazism in Austria.[24] Hildebrand's courageous lectures and articles condemning anti-Semitism in Germany had produced hostility that forced him to flee Germany. He was welcomed in Austria. And there he continued his campaign and drew the hatred of the Nazis. He did not decline to name names of anti-Semites, including some German Catholic clergymen, and he refused to obscure his Jewish ancestry.[25] Although Hildebrand was well aware that there were pockets of anti-Semites in some quarters of the University of Vienna, he wanted to join the faculty. Despite heavy opposition, including a petition signed by Cardinal Innitzer objecting to his appointment, Schuschnigg had gone right ahead and appointed Hildebrand to the faculty.[26] As expected, his first lecture had been quite a scene; students and other protesters loudly sang Nazi songs to disrupt the event.[27] That Schuschnigg had sided so publicly with this most vocal condemner of anti-Semitism was one of the many galling acts that had Hitler in a rage against Schuschnigg. Hitler had no tolerance for any level of comity with Jews; he wrote that any leader who did not attract condemnation by Jews was an enemy of a Volkisch state. Schuschnigg was an implacable enemy of Hitler on race. The one common sentiment the two shared, German pride, in Schuschnigg's case, came without the anti-Semitism Hitler so valued.

Schuschnigg knew that his support of the Jews of Austria was highly offensive to Hitler; yet it was more significant than Schuschnigg realized. At every step prior to the Anschluss, Schuschnigg and the world proceeded unaware that Hitler intended mass murder. Schuschnigg's insistence on full equality for Jews, while in direct opposition to Hitler's Nuremberg Laws, seemed to him a fundamental disagreement on ideology and human rights. To Hitler, however, race was the center of Nazism, and Schuschnigg was a threat to the achievement of the psychotic goal that drove Hitler's life. Despite Hitler's astonishing openness in repressing the Jews of Germany, he had concealed his ultimate plan to exterminate the Jews.

At Berchtesgaden, the Führer had been dramatic from the start, but then he became messianic: "I have a historic mission, and this mission I will fulfill because Providence has destined me to do so . . . I have only to give an order and all your ridiculous defenses will be blown to bits. Perhaps you will wake up one morning in Vienna to find us there—just like a spring storm."[28]

Hitler seemed to relish the opportunity to announce directly to Austria's head of government the hatred he had for their homeland. Long before his adult career as a Nazi, even in his teens, Hitler had come to detest the ruling Habsburgs and to despise all but one of the eleven ethnicities that made up the empire.[29] Only Germans were a worthy race in his view. Vienna occupied a special dungeon in his memory. Initially delighted with its splendor, the capital was the place where he experienced nothing but failure, flophouses, and soup kitchens.[30]

Though shocked by Hitler's abuse, Schuschnigg knew it was counterproductive to engage him in a debate. He felt it was dangerous to allow this to degenerate into an argument when he was all too aware that Austria was overwhelmingly outgunned by the boastfully rearmed Germany. He was distressed by the anger Hitler had mustered on cue, yet he knew there was worse that might come if this man was provoked. The extremely rude dressing down could turn to a burst of hysterical anger and then to violence.[31]

Schuschnigg managed to remain outwardly calm while doing what little he could to fend off the abuse even when Hitler bragged about the armed might of Nazi Germany with his costumed military chorus nearby. Throughout, Schuschnigg remained soft-spoken and undoubtedly sounded ill equipped to combat the dark soul bellowing threats.

★ ★ ★

"I don't believe in bluffing."

—Adolf Hitler

So far, it had all been rhetoric. Nothing specific had been demanded. But Schuschnigg had the feeling he was hearing the overture to war, perhaps in just a few moments.[32] He had endured years of combat in World War I, horrified at the slaughter of the men and the grotesque nature of the wounds produced by the new armaments; he remained a pacifist, committed to finding an end to war.

Only much later would his "host" be revealed to history as a mass murderer utterly devoid of empathy for the gruesome suffering he was to inflict on millions of fellow human beings. On that level, the contrast in their attitudes about sending thousands of young men to their deaths over the independence of Austria could not have been more different as Hitler taunted Schuschnigg: "Don't think for one moment that anybody on earth is going to thwart my decisions. Italy? I see eye to eye with Mussolini, the closest ties of friendship bind me to Italy . . . England? England will not move one finger for Austria . . . And France?"[33]

All of Schuschnigg's attempts to calm the Führer seemed only to make things worse. With each concession, every unchallenged assertion, the Führer smelled blood and increased his tirade. Completely shameless, Hitler even played the victim: "The persecution of National Socialists in Austria must have an end or else I shall put an end to it."[34] In a particularly bizarre turn, he accused Schuschnigg of enlisting a priest to assassinate him. Apparently, a Jesuit, Father P. Frederic Muckerman, a Hitler foe, had been in Vienna briefly in 1938, and this was enough to provoke Hitler to accuse Schuschnigg of plotting against the Reich. (Schuschnigg had not even seen Muckerman since 1933.) Ironically, however, Muckerman was among a group of German patriots, including a few of Germany's own generals, who at that time were plotting the Führer's violent demise. Though Schuschnigg knew nothing about the plot, Hitler apparently did.[35]

Schuschnigg had now been pushed hard enough to venture a disagreement; he could not sit still for Hitler's frivolous complaint that Nazis were still unjustly held in Austrian jails since 1934. He reminded Hitler exactly how he had come to be Austria's chancellor in the first place: "Had it not been for the assassination [by Nazis] of Chancellor Dollfuss, the Austrians would not have a single Nazi in prison today."[36] Challenged for the first time, Hitler feigned innocence; he claimed he had known "nothing of the plot; and had he known of it, certainly would have stopped it."[37]

Quickly resuming control, Hitler abruptly announced a deadline: "Either we find a solution now or events will take their course. And we shall see whether you like these events. Think it over, Herr Schuschnigg, think it over well. I can only wait until this afternoon . . . you will do well to take my words literally. I don't believe in bluffing."[38]

Hitler then began the soliloquy he had planned. After softening Schuschnigg up with crude abuse, he pivoted and attempted to extract the deal he wanted, to convince Schuschnigg that he should be happy to agree to the Anschluss, to see that, if he did so, he would become, alongside Hitler, a fellow hero to Germans for all time.

Hitler attempted to convince Schuschnigg that Anschluss was "a unique and historic opportunity" to have the name "Schuschnigg" "recorded on the roll of great Germans"[39] and applauded by history for making it happen. Or else he would be condemned as a fool if he passed it up.

Nearly stupefied, Schuschnigg quietly refused. He was bewildered by such a clumsy sales pitch, but it stirred him to remind Hitler that, over the course of two hours, he had yet to make any concrete demands. Schuschnigg asked: "Now what exactly are your wishes?"

Hitler demurred. "That we can discuss this afternoon." A ring of the Führer's bell, summoning an aide to open the massive doors, brought a merciful respite.[40]

★ ★ ★

Reeling from the browbeating and the threats, Schuschnigg struggled to maintain his composure as they descended the stairs for lunch. He rejoined the other members of the Austrian delegation; they had been relegated to small talk with the German generals and were eager for news of what had occurred. One look at the chancellor's ghost-white visage told the story.

He took a seat opposite the Führer in the dining hall, and the master race was paraded before them on full display as "tall, remarkably handsome young SS men in snow white steward uniforms" served red cabbage and fruit compote to the vegetarian Führer and cold lobster and asparagus to Schuschnigg and the rest.[41]

The Austrian guests were now called upon to witness the grating spectacle of Adolf Hitler playing gentleman host. Basking in the glow of his exhilarating morning, the Führer held court, bouncing from one topic to another with no apparent pattern—the Autobahn, designs for building the world's tallest skyscraper in Munich, even horse breeding. They sat as a captive audience to his rhapsodizing that he was so beloved by the German people that he had no need of a bodyguard. The common thread between the almost courteous narrator at the head of the luncheon table and the snarling bully Schuschnigg had been forced to endure only minutes earlier was Hitler's casual compulsion to describe his own greatness. When the extraordinary performance was finally finished, the entire party was escorted into the adjoining winter garden room for coffee, and Hitler soon excused himself.

The chancellor at last had a brief respite and unfettered access to his cigarettes. It was also the first opportunity Schuschnigg had to relay to Foreign Minister Schmidt the depressing threats that dominated his "dialogue" with the Führer. Left to sit for more than two hours in an antechamber, the deflated pair had little chance to relax. In the room with them were Otto Dietrich (chief of the German press) and the German generals. Hitler had also arranged a visible Austrian Nazi presence, the son of a prominent Vienna surgeon, brazenly wearing the black SS uniform forbidden in Austria, a reminder that Nazi influence inside Austria was stronger than it seemed. Schmidt had learned that other Austrian Nazis were also on hand at the Berghof to brief Hitler. Kajetan Muhlman, a Nazi Party official from Vienna, was also there and was likely meeting with Hitler and Ambassador Papen at that moment. Muhlmann was an art history expert who later became one of the great art thieves of history while in charge of confiscating art for the Third Reich. At Berchtesgaden, he was briefing Hitler on the most pressing demands of the Nazis of Austria and on what he had been able to learn about concessions that might be acceptable to Schuschnigg and the Austrian cabinet.

★ ★ ★

Schuschnigg and Schmidt were at last summoned to a room to meet with Germany's new foreign minister, Joachim von Ribbentrop, and Papen; there they were handed a two-page typewritten draft containing Hitler's demands for Austria. Ribbentrop announced that this document contained "the limit of the concessions the Führer was willing to make."[42]

Any relief Schuschnigg might have felt when he was finally presented with concrete proposals evaporated when he scanned the document and saw that what Hitler wanted in reality was to have the independence of Austria "snuffed out."[43]

The document demanded the appointment of Arthur Seyss-Inquart as minister of the interior in charge of public security, effectively giving him control over the police; Edmund Glaise-Horstenau, already in the cabinet, was to remain there. Hans Fischbock was to be named minister of finance. All imprisoned Nazis, including the Dollfuss murder conspirators, must be freed within three days; all Nazi officials and officers must be reinstated to their former positions in Austria; Austria must agree that Austria and Nazism were compatible; and the Nazis were to be freed to profess the full racist National Socialist creed—anti-Semitism at its worst—using full-blown Nazi propaganda facilitated by empowering *Volkspolitische* Offices. Ribbentrop announced that Hitler insisted that this document be signed immediately and that it bind Austria's government.

Schmidt cleared his throat and reminded Papen of the agreed upon terms of the meeting, which had now been abandoned and replaced with these Nazi dictates. Feigning innocence, Papen tried to convince the Austrians that he was just as surprised as they were by the Führer's demands.[44] Schuschnigg protested, but Ribbentrop cut him off—the draft had to be accepted as written. He delivered the most concrete message of the day: Hitler had warned that if Schuschnigg refused, "I shall march this very moment."[45]

Schuschnigg paused. Despite the warning that nothing could be changed, one major demand was intolerable even under threat of invasion. Schuschnigg refused to endorse Nazism. He refused the demand that he acknowledge compatibility between Nazism and Austria.[46] Compatibility, another benign-sounding choice of words, implied in backhanded language that Schuschnigg agreed with Nazism at some level. The compatibility provision was Hitler's demand that Schuschnigg abandon his recent public denunciation of Nazi racism—essentially recanting his January 5 interview—and announce that Austria could tolerate Nazism. Hitler was demanding that Schuschnigg, who had announced on a number of occasions in ways calculated to convey the firmness of his detestation for Nazism to Hitler, that he should now reverse himself and give his approval to the ideology of the Nuremberg Laws.[47] The Austrians were told it was a "vital" provision. But Schuschnigg rejected the compatibility provision out of hand.[48] He also refused to name Fischbock as minister of finance.

Papen and Ribbentrop were now in a dilemma but had little choice except to inform Hitler. They sent the Austrians to the anteroom to await Hitler's reaction.[49]

Schuschnigg could only wonder what might happen next. He knew that this racism was the center of Nazism and the foundation of Hitler's Volkisch state.

After some delay, however, Schuschnigg was given the message that Hitler would not insist on the compatibility provision. He would also modify his demand that Fischbock, suspected to be a Nazi, be named minister of finance. Nevertheless, the document as a whole still was a very poor harbinger of continued independence for Austria.[50]

After another long wait, Schuschnigg alone was summoned to the Führer's study. Now, he found Hitler highly agitated, pacing back and forth like an angered beast. The thread of hope to avoid an immediate coup now seemed very thin. Desperate for some breathing room, Schuschnigg watched the angry Hitler and knew he must buy time, escape from this worse-than-imagined day, and get out of Germany with the chance to consult his government about what Austria should do in the face of the central message of the meeting—Hitler was threatening to invade Austria.

Schuschnigg reminded Hitler of the limit of his authority as chancellor; he simply did not have authority to bind the government to such a momentous agreement. "I could not possibly," he said. He insisted that, even after he signed, he would need to bring such an agreement to the Austrian president and the cabinet. Hitler knew the reality of the Austrian hierarchy, and he pretended to grudgingly accept Schuschnigg's plea.[51] He also pretended to regain his composure, but it turned out that the temporary calm was merely preparation for his climactic scene.

Schuschnigg insisted that the time limits stipulated in the document were, in any event, unworkable, but at his mere mention of this obvious constraint, the Führer erupted: "You will either sign it as it is and fulfill my demands within three days, or I will order the march into Austria!" Casting off all restraint, he "seemed to lose all self-control." Throwing open the doors, he yelled for General Wilhelm Keitel, shouting so loudly he could be heard in the winter garden room.[52] Hitler did not hold back. He delivered the ultimate threat—another war—and he gave Schuschnigg what has been termed "the bum's rush,"[53] trying his utmost to panic Schuschnigg into agreeing to Anschluss. The shaken chancellor feared Hitler's explosion marked the launch of his invasion of Austria.[54]

General Keitel scrambled up to the Führer's study to find out what crisis had suddenly arisen. Hitler demanded: "How many divisions are mustered at the border, Keitel?" He asked Keitel to recite for Schuschnigg the German intelligence assessment of Austria's military: "Not worth mentioning, my Führer."[55] Schuschnigg and Schmidt were dismissed; they stood rigid outside the Führer's private chamber, unaware that the tantrum had been staged. Schmidt was in a state of near panic; they both believed they were about to be arrested and that Austria was about to be invaded by Germany.

The deadline Schuschnigg had given to their Salzburg colleagues—to place the Austrian troops on alert if no word was heard from them—was nearly upon them. Just minutes before 6 p.m., he sent word to their "Advance Headquarters" in Salzburg that the talks were continuing.[56]

Schuschnigg was ushered back into the Führer's presence. He felt relieved when Hitler announced he would grant the Austrian government a "concession" and give it three more days to agree. This was, he claimed, the only time in his life he had ever changed his mind.

Hitler's tantrums had an undeniable impact. The Führer had gone into the highest dudgeon and succeeded in creating an atmosphere of crisis—exactly what he thought he needed to set the scene for his final thrust to take Austria without encountering armed resistance or unleashing international condemnation.

Schuschnigg was surprised at this point merely to escape and live to fight another day. They would have three days for the president and cabinet to confer and decide whether Austria could live with Hitler's demands, or whether to call him on his threat to invade. Most pointed was the question whether they could tolerate a cabinet with a second Nazi sympathizer, another Anschluss supporter, and this one in the crucial ministry in charge of the police. Schuschnigg hastily put his own signature on the revised document.

Then Hitler, once again the host, invited them to stay for supper, but Schuschnigg declined. He quickly summoned the car and rode off, descending the mountain into a "gray and foggy winter night."[57]

★ ★ ★

The staged drama that had begun at Hitler's Berghof in the mountains above Berchtesgaden gave rise to an aftermath that was one of Europe's most tumultuous. What followed the meeting was not the product of diplomacy but one of Europe's most momentous election campaigns ending in a sudden resort to militarism. The two chancellors—Hitler and Schuschnigg—squared off directly against each other in a fight for the soul of Austria. Hitler started it with a speech to the Reichstag, expecting he would simply pave the way for "Case Otto," the plans for the invasion of Austria he had issued to his generals almost four months earlier. At Berchtesgaden, Schuschnigg could see that Hitler was ready to begin conquering some parts of Europe. Realists had known that a war was coming and that Hitler would soon begin it. Only the gullible thought he was merely intimidating Austria; realists could see that he had his sights set on France, Britain, and other nations as well, and at Berchtesgaden, he behaved as if he and they all knew they were powerless to stop him. However, he also continued to lie about his intentions because deceiving the gullible made it easier for him, and it had been so easy to dupe so many European leaders for the last five years.

Schuschnigg was aware of the Nazis' plans for Austria. In January, just weeks before the meeting, Austrian police had discovered the Nazis' Tavs Plan and their Action Programme 1938, which showed the Nazis' strong reaction against Schuschnigg's London *Daily Telegraph* interview, and reflected the Nazis' confidence that Britain, France, and Italy would do nothing to interfere with a takeover of Austria and that "preparations for violent upheaval were afoot."[58] The Nazis concluded that "the German Reich has freedom of action."[59] The most Schuschnigg could have achieved at Berchtesgaden was the refusal to agree to Anschluss or Nazism and to state those positions without triggering an immediate invasion.[60] Whether he had done so would be seen in just a matter of weeks.

Mussolini sensed what was coming at Berchtesgaden; he became alarmed that he only learned of the meeting of Schuschnigg and Hitler from an Italian foreign office official. Mussolini was sufficiently unnerved that he reached out to Britain looking for any sign that Britain planned to weigh in to save Austria. Chamberlain, however, provided no such sign.[61]

Nothing Schuschnigg said or did at the meeting had provoked the ultimatum or Hitler's aggression. The drama of a choreographed gang of generals, and Hitler "spitting with rage," was all planned to enhance the threat and underscore the demands.[62] Those demands had been delivered with barked warnings and shouted abuses to make convincing Hitler's threat of "immediate invasion if Schuschnigg refused to sign."[63] The posturing, however, was not an empty bluff. Evidence that emerged later leaves little room to doubt that Hitler was itching to use his army and was likely on the verge of abruptly changing course and invading that day.[64] Hitler's intensity can be seen in Schuschnigg's description of Hitler to a diplomat: "Is this a madman who thinks he is a God?"[65]

Papen that day had assured Schuschnigg that if he signed Hitler's demands, that would permanently solve the crisis and there would be no further difficulties for Austria.[66] Schuschnigg had ample reason even by then to doubt Papen, and he was no dupe, yet he may still have harbored hope that Papen was sincere.[67] However, before the month was gone, Hitler had made it clear by his speech to the Reichstag that this was mere prelude to further conquest.

When the shaken chancellor returned to Vienna and regained his equilibrium, he reported the meeting to the president and the cabinet. He told them that he had informed Hitler that he was not willing to agree to Anschluss or to compatibility with Nazism.[68] He reported that he could accept the addition of Seyss-Inquart to the cabinet, but he had insisted that only the president had power[69] under the constitution to commit to Hitler's demands,[70] and, when pushed to make a binding agreement on his own, he said, "I could not possibly."[71] Austria had been given three days to deliver the agreement of the Austrian president and cabinet.[72]

German troops and tanks began noisily conducting military maneuvers close to the Austrian border,[73] and rumors spread that invasion was about to occur. The president and the government ministers quickly approved the agreement. The language Schuschnigg employed to portray the meeting with Hitler to the Austrian public and to Europe was euphemistic, understated in tone, and calibrated to avoid provoking an attack by the volatile Hitler he had just encountered. Some envoys were told a milder version of the roughing-up Hitler had dished out at Berchtesgaden, though at least one had been given the raw description.[74]

Most points in the agreement could be seen as ordinary peacemaking gestures, the kind that reduce tensions between border rivals. The most alarming news of the meeting was that Austria would appoint a well-known Nazi sympathizer, Arthur Seyss-Inquart, to the powerful position of minister of the interior, in charge of the national police. Even this significant concession was far from a capitulation, and it was not without its ray of hope. Schuschnigg could take modest comfort that Hitler had not held fast to his demand that Fischbock, a Nazi, be named to the cabinet. Schuschnigg thought Seyss was civilized and might prove bearable as a minister. However, the position Hitler demanded for Seyss was potentially crucial. The chronic Nazi violence in Austria would no longer be certain to be challenged by the police if Seyss turned out to be a traitor. The trusted Michael Skubl remained the official directly in charge of the security forces, but the security forces were now answerable to a Nazi designate. Schuschnigg could, of course, countermand Seyss's orders, but it might then be up to the chancellor himself to keep peace by calling out the army instead of the police to quell Austrian Nazi disturbances.

Hitler's presumptuousness in selecting Seyss-Inquart for Austria's cabinet raised suspicions in the minds of some that Seyss was more sinister than they thought, perhaps a Trojan horse. Schuschnigg, however, was no doubt aware that Dollfuss had trusted Seyss enough that in 1934 Dollfuss had discussed with Seyss the possibility of naming him to the cabinet. Schuschnigg had come to view Seyss as someone who was not a radical Nazi or a Hitler disciple but, instead, an Austrian who wanted some sort of satellite relationship with Germany. Seyss had, after all, steadfastly declined to become a member of the Nazi Party. He described himself as a liaison between the Fatherland Front and the Austrian Nazis, and indeed, that function was well known. Seyss could, however, plan and plot with Nazis in private but keep his fingerprints off the Nazi violence and thereby retain some level of trust from others. He was very much a front for the Nazis from 1931, according to evidence at the Nuremberg trials. But the alliance Seyss had advocated was a peaceful, politically obtained relationship.

Schuschnigg had, in an effort to find ways to calm the violent Nazis, proposed to Seyss in June 1937 that Seyss accept an appointment to the Council of State.[75] By February 1938, Schuschnigg felt they had no choice but to accede to Hitler's demand that Seyss be appointed to the cabinet itself, but he had his own experiences with Seyss and had reason to harbor the hope that this appointment was not that of a thoroughgoing Nazi who would corruptly betray Austria. Schuschnigg and Seyss had long been acquaintances and had a level of respect for each other. They were quiet intellectuals and had long conversations over classical music discussing their shared love of the symphonies of Anton Bruckner.[76] Whether this fed optimism or just hope, Schuschnigg seemed to believe that perhaps he knew the real Seyss better than Hitler did. Schuschnigg spoke of Seyss as a loyal Austrian; he also took comfort that the beliefs of his own Catholicism were completely at odds with Hitler's beliefs, and Seyss appeared to be a devout Catholic.

But Seyss, though not violent or radical, did embrace National Socialism. Schuschnigg's cautious hopes since Hitler had not demanded an official Nazi Party member in his cabinet were in vain. Seyss, though he seemed an honest man-in-the-middle, at bottom, had thrown in with the Nazis. He had since 1918 pinned his hopes for Austria's recovery on some form of relationship with Germany. The American consul general in Vienna, John C. Wiley, ambivalent about Seyss's appointment to the cabinet, said that even if Seyss is loyal, his appointment is not a solution, but if he is disloyal, it is a catastrophe.[77]

Shortly after Seyss was added to the cabinet, he met with Hitler for two hours on February 17, with Schuschnigg's approval, to deliver the message that Schuschnigg insisted that, first, Seyss must adhere to the independence of Austria and was not to function as a Trojan horse and, second, that Nazi ideology was not to be imposed on anyone in Austria by force. According to Seyss, Hitler agreed.[78]

Hitler plainly saw Berchtesgaden as a success, for there was still no sign of resistance from Britain, France, or Italy. He expected none from Austria. His speeches in the days after the meeting revealed his naked intention to force an Anschluss. The clear signal what was next came in his announcement that it was his goal to rescue the ten million Germans outside Germany's borders. The number he used left no real room for doubt that he intended to take Austria.[79]

Nevertheless, he was still bent on using veiled threats of invasion, like his "spring storm" allusion, because he believed that what he needed in order to be certain he would keep the international community at bay was a smooth-looking Anschluss with Austria, after the ugly fiasco in 1934 when Dollfuss was murdered during the failed putsch.[80] He was also in a less-than-ideal posture to invade anywhere just weeks after firing so many of his generals. He had become aware of plots[81] against him; fear of a coup had his attention, and a smooth Anschluss would leave the plotters with no rallying point. To enhance the threat and intimidate President Miklas and the cabinet, Hitler ordered his generals to conduct sham maneuvers rehearsing an invasion near the Austrian border for the next two weeks.[82]

The last chance for the League of Nations, the Stresa Front, or others to offer a show of opposition was fast approaching. After his dreadful day with Hitler, Schuschnigg tried a new series of contacts. One by one, he contacted Mussolini, Chamberlain, and Daladier, making the rounds like the lonely sheriff in an old movie seeking help for a looming showdown, and one after another they turned him down. Not a single call by Schuschnigg or his ministers and ambassadors elicited the slightest sign of encouragement. America, too, remained in isolation.

At this crucial moment, France had only worsened; its government was in a free fall by early 1938. Radicals and conservatives were at odds over the same fundamentals as warring factions in other governments. And on the most crucial date, France had no premier—Camille Chautemps had "jumped"; he resigned, and Leon Blum had not yet succeeded him.[83] Confusion, grudges, dysfunction, despair, and incompetence riddled the French government and military. Those in Europe, even the realists in France who predicted that an Anschluss made war inevitable, nevertheless knew that France could not and would not challenge Hitler over Austria by itself; they also knew that the best they could hope for was that a strong diplomatic effort by France might rally Britain to oppose the Anschluss and might bring these two powers together in some way that would stop the Führer before another European war was unleashed.

Britain, however, was not about to be rallied by France or anyone; it was even more resolute in its policy of appeasement by February 1938. Churchill was a critic of appeasement, but he was not in Chamberlain's government; he was still only a controversial voice in the wilderness, and one viewed as discredited by many British at the time. Only Anthony Eden and his small contingent of young Conservative members of Parliament offered any hope against the iron will of the reigning prophet of appeasement—Neville Chamberlain.[84] These younger Tories in Britain had been in earnest in making their attacks on Chamberlain's appeasement policy. But just as the little remaining hope had focused upon Anthony Eden, he announced that he and his undersecretary, Robert "Bobbety" Cranborne, were resigning, and he left the cabinet in frustration.

The triggering event of Eden's resignation was Chamberlain's decision to open direct negotiations with Mussolini.[85] Chamberlain had in mind the notion that he might at least achieve a separate peace with Italy if he offered that Britain would recognize Italy's conquest of Abyssinia. However, Chamberlain took diplomatically unorthodox steps to bring about a meeting with

Mussolini knowing that Eden opposed such a meeting. Chamberlain's unilateral overtures ignored and insulted Eden. On February 18, 1938, shortly after Schuschnigg's trip to Berchtesgaden, Chamberlain hosted a visit to Downing Street by an Italian delegation headed by Ambassador Dino Grandi. During the meeting, Chamberlain showed, quite rudely, right in front of Eden, that he did not support Eden's diplomacy.[86] Chamberlain also rejected President Roosevelt's offer to assist as a mediator of the looming crisis, inexplicably passing up the valuable opportunity to demonstrate to Hitler that America might yet weigh in; and Eden disagreed with that action as well.[87]

Even then, a full week after Hitler's meeting with Schuschnigg, British public opinion was still so pro-appeasement that Eden and other opponents of Chamberlain were vilified.[88] Lord Halifax was quickly named to replace Eden as foreign minister. Halifax's appeasement views—and his reputed anti-Semitism—were a comfort to Hitler, and the Führer's language concerning the fate of Austria became more shrill. Halifax had already met with Hitler in November 1937, in his capacity as an emissary of Chamberlain, as leader of the House of Lords and lord president of the council, and conveyed his assurance of friendship from Chamberlain; Halifax's visit had left Hitler so reinforced in his belief that Britain would not fight him over Austria that he taunted Schuschnigg with the claim that he had the agreement of Lord Halifax and the British.[89]

One voice in Great Britain was entirely out of step with Chamberlain, Halifax, and Neville Henderson—the oratory of Winston Churchill; Churchill was a Tory like Chamberlain, but he was a very independent thinker opposed to appeasement. Churchill urged Britain to insist that the Anschluss question be brought before the League of Nations, but Chamberlain was a staunch critic of the league, and the proposal went nowhere.[90]

Churchill and Eden both favored an additional step that was also opposed by Chamberlain—the proposal of President Roosevelt that the European leaders come to the United States for a meeting and allow him to resolve the mushrooming disputes. But this proposal was anathema to Chamberlain because he had only contempt for Roosevelt.[91]

★ ★ ★

Schuschnigg, however, had ideas of his own. He spent the days after Berchtesgaden holding meetings with various constituencies, assessing their support for a risky announcement. He had to find out who these Austrians were—anti-Semites who quietly yearned for the racial policies of the Nazis, or a far better people than the worst of them seemed. On February 24, Schuschnigg met with Desider Friedmann, head of the Jewish community, the Kultusgemeinde, and with Hermann Oppenheim, president of the Union of Austrian Jews. Both promised support and expressed gratitude for what Schuschnigg was about to do.[92] He was going to address the Austrian nation announcing his response to all that had happened.

The narrative Hitler envisioned was about to be changed in dramatic fashion by a speech in the Diet in Vienna. Hitler's control of the narrative and domination of the pulpit in Europe was about to be challenged. It was about to become a debate. Within days, it would be seen as an election campaign going on in parallel with the Führer of Germany campaigning there for support from Austrians and Germans alike, while the chancellor of Austria rose to campaign against him in Austria. Schuschnigg scheduled an address four days after Hitler delivered his ominous speech in the Reichstag in which he abandoned past assurances and made his real intentions clear. Three years earlier in a speech in the Reichstag Hitler had assured Europe that "Germany neither intends nor wishes to interfere in the internal affairs of Austria, to annex Austria, or to conclude an Anschluss."[93] His words back then had been "lapped up" by Europeans who "desperately yearned" for peace "on almost any basis."[94] But now he had slickly shed the pretense that had lulled Europe and provided talking points for the use of appeasers. On February 20, 1938, Hitler again appeared before his Reichstag and delivered a three-hour harangue. It contained not a word suggesting that Austria's independence would be respected. Instead, Hitler loudly renewed his pledge to obtain *Lebensraum*. He announced he was about to rescue millions of Germans across the border. His longtime aim, Anschluss, could now be heard brushing its feet at Austria's doorstep.[95]

★ ★ ★

Austria's response to Hitler came suddenly, twelve days after Berchtesgaden and four days after Hitler's Reichstag speech. Schuschnigg appeared in the Diet on a night when the streets of Vienna were resplendent with banners and flags of red, white, and red, the colors of Austria. It was as though a premonition had swept through Austria that the time had come. Austrians were glued to radios from Vienna to the Tyrol, and thousands gathered in squares before loudspeakers, sensing that this was the turning point of Austria's history.

The chronically reserved chancellor suddenly swelled to life. Even as he approached the podium, shouts began ringing out from the benches: "Schuschnigg! Schuschnigg!"[96] He spoke with a startling passion and a newfound tone of resolve. He addressed the Austrian people, but spoke to the world, and for all the Nazis to hear. He declared that Austria should remain free and independent. He had never, ever spoken this fervently.[97] He finished with a full-throated call to Austrians: "Until Death! Red–White–Red! Austria!"[98]

The Diet shook with the shouts of the members repeating his ending; the hall thundered with applause as they became a single, unified "roaring chorus."[99] His speech "electrified both Austria and the outside world"; it had a "magical effect."[100] Crowds in the streets listening to loudspeakers erupted

Schuschnigg delivering "Red White Red" speech in the Diet, February 1938.
Source: Alamy, Everett Collection.

with cheers. In the Ringstrasse, they began singing the song of the Tyrol, "Andreas Hofer," and the Austrian Imperial anthem, "Gott Erhalte" ("God preserve").[101] This was the Austria for which he had hoped. Hitler's march to Anschluss had been turned into a public fight, and Schuschnigg's summons to the Austrian people had awakened the resistance.

* * *

Nazis, however, also began to demonstrate and push their agenda. In the heavily Germanic enclave of Graz in Styria, Nazis destroyed the loudspeakers broadcasting Schuschnigg's speech, and they unfolded swastikas on nearby buildings. They took steps to add Nazi dogma to the policies of the Volkspolitische Offices. Shuschnigg quickly condemned that and called it treason; he saw it was a brazen attempt to undo his rejection of the compatibility clause. They announced a huge Nazi rally against Schuschnigg that weekend. Schuschnigg now had to face the choice whether to call out the military against the Austrian Nazis. He decided to do it. He sent three army battalions and a squadron of light bombers to Graz to break up the rally, and the Nazis canceled it.[102]

The widespread euphoria gave Schuschnigg immense encouragement; he decided to reach out to the workers, the Social Democrats, the implacable enemies of the government. On March 3, Schuschnigg met with several of the workers' spokesmen. The meeting went on for four hours, and at long last, the workers set aside their pledge to resist the government. Their common enemy was Adolf Hitler, and he was bringing the workers and the government together as never before.[103] The radicals who had led the socialist revolt, Otto Bauer, Julius Deutsch, and Richard Bernaschek, were gone; those socialists who were leading the workers were moderate socialists, and in this crisis, they now were willing to support Schuschnigg.[104] Both sides agreed to take steps to resolve old labor grievances. Schuschnigg, for his part, assured that their demands for political freedom and improved social laws would all be revisited with a new spirit of reconciliation. While this was not a broad embrace of Schuschnigg's platform, it was a dramatic change; the previously entrenched opposition would join his struggle to preserve Austria's independence.[105]

Schuschnigg had become the leader Austrians other than Nazis had longed for. The hours he endured being bullied by Hitler on the mountain at Berchtesgaden seemed that night to have been erased by the energy that flowed from his speech. Seeing crowds in the street praising his name seems to have touched even the shy Schuschnigg. In the following days, he took his message to the countryside.

Hitler found he had to give speeches to counter Schuschnigg's. Suddenly he realized he had become Schuschnigg's opponent in an unprecedented campaign challenging the creed of Nazism and his own fitness to be the leader of Austria. On March 9, at a public meeting in Innsbruck Schuschnigg defied Hitler again. He announced a plebiscite to let the world hear definitively from the people of Austria. They would make their own decision about independence. There, in his home province, dressed in an alpine green waistcoat, before 20,000 Tyroleans in the Innsbruck town square, Schuschnigg once again

"Ja mitt Schuschnigg" ("Yes, with Schuschnigg for a free Austria") plebiscite campaign poster.
Source: Bundesarchiv Plak 003-005-029.

delivered an impassioned plea: "Tyroleans and Austrians say 'Yes' to Tyrol. Say 'Yes' to Austria." Once again he was an orator, not a scholar. He ended with the words Andreas Hofer had once used for his call to arms against Napoleon's army: "*Mannder, es isch Zeit!*" ("Men, the time has come!")[106] Hitler was at first more astounded than enraged that Schuschnigg would dare to call for a vote. But he soon realized it was a vote on him.

Schuschnigg's decision to call the plebiscite was every bit his own. Papen speculated in his memoirs that Minister Gabriel Paux of France suggested the plebiscite, but Schuschnigg refuted that.[107] Indeed, he had long ago revealed to Mussolini he would one day call one when the time was right.[108] And that time had come. It now seemed ironic that Hitler had taunted Schuschnigg about just such a referendum.[109] Schuschnigg had announced the very plebiscite Hitler had once dared him to hold—the vote would be on Sunday, March 13.[110]

Austrians were about to exercise a true shout of democracy. No longer would their political fate be dictated by an emperor or a political apparatus. Their exhilaration at this prospect could be heard in the streets, and that sound was not a welcoming greeting for Adolf Hitler.

★ ★ ★

The Jews of Vienna, who had perennially seen any Christian Social government as suspect, had fully awakened to the realization that Schuschnigg was different. Even under the threats of violence, assassination, and invasion, he was unwilling to adopt Hitler's repression of Jews. Virtually the entire Jewish

Street banner supporting Schuschnigg in the plebiscite.
Source: Getty Images.

community rallied to his support. "In early March [1938], Jews of all political shades rallied around Schuschnigg, collecting money and actively campaigning on behalf of the plebiscite, in favor of continued Austrian independence."[111]

A full-blown political campaign erupted and immediately became a contest between the two contenders. It was Schuschnigg against Hitler. The Nazis' central campaign theme was anti-Semitism. Schuschnigg had long been criticized by anti-Semitic Austrians as overly supportive of the Jews, and the Nazis trumpeted that theme. Nazis plastered posters on every available space with a cartoon of Schuschnigg running alongside caricatures of frightened Jews carrying money boxes.

When the rest of Europe first heard the announcement of an Austrian plebiscite, they could only guess at the outcome. The belief was that the Nazis constituted 20 percent of the Austrian population and that an overwhelming majority of Austrians "if permitted freely to do so," would vote for independence.[112]

It took only a few days for it to become obvious to Hitler that Schuschnigg was going to win.[113] Some commentators estimated that the Austrian plebiscite would have yielded a two-thirds "yes" vote.[114] The professionals of the foreign press corps were astute observers of the political climate, and many of them were convinced that Schuschnigg would win the referendum. The Austrian Nazis certainly sensed defeat. The chief *New York Times* reporter,

Anne O'Hare McCormick, interviewed Nazi leaders in Vienna a few days before the scheduled date, and they conceded that in Vienna the Nazis could expect to win no more than 20 percent of the vote.[115]

As privately humiliating as it was for Hitler to behave as though there was a possibility that he could lose, let alone admit it even to his close henchmen, the fact that he would lose became obvious.[116] German intelligence recorded by General Alfred Jodl concluded that Schuschnigg was going to win a "strong majority."[117] Hitler at last exploded. He demanded that the election be canceled or he would invade. Hitler had awakened to the drastic consequences a public rejection in Austria would bring. He feared that the loss would effectively stop his plan for *Lebensraum* in the east and put his very tenure as Führer at risk.[118] Hitler confided to Glaise-Horstenau that he was convinced that the plebiscite would result in a victory for Schuschnigg and therefore must be stopped.[119]

Most devastating would be the bursting of that bubble of fantasy stoked by Nazi propaganda that Hitler was beloved by the public. If the Germanic people of Austria resoundingly slapped his face and rejected him, the people of Germany might be next. This, it appeared, was about to end his cult of personality and empower his enemies.

When Schuschnigg returned to Vienna on the morning of March 10, the streets that had often brayed Nazi slogans now echoed with shouts and cries of "Hail Schuschnigg!" "Hail Liberty!" The name *Schuschnigg* was posted on signs and written on sidewalks. Some shouted "We vote 'Yes,'" and many simply roared "Austria" over and over.[120] An early spring storm seemed to have swept over Vienna, but on this morning, the storm was Schuschnigg's.

Many anti-Nazi groups and others were now emboldened to come out in support of holding the plebiscite. Schuschnigg was particularly encouraged by his exchange that day with Seyss-Inquart. The new minister had initially voiced objections to the plebiscite, but Schuschnigg told Seyss: "I am neither capable nor desirous of playing a puppet's role." To Schuschnigg's relief, Seyss said he would go on the radio the next day and urge his followers to vote "Yes."[121] Comforted by Seyss's support, seeing real hope for the first time since Berchtesgaden, Schuschnigg retired for the night.

VI

INVASION

· 9 ·

"Leo Is Ready to Travel"

In Berlin at the Reich chancellery, Hitler had made his own decision. According to Edmund Glaise-Horstenau, who was there, the Führer was in a "furious and excited mood" and was giving off an atmosphere "laden with danger."[1] Franz von Papen, also there, said Hitler was in a state bordering on hysteria.[2] And this time it was no act.

The Führer issued instructions to the military that the plebiscite was to be stopped or the invasion would be launched, and any resistance would be "mercilessly crushed by force of arms."[3] General Beck was ordered to get two corps and the Second Panzer Division, as many as 200,000 men, ready to occupy Austria on March 12.[4]

To validate the invasion, they planned to draft a phony telegram. Hermann Göring prepared it. He addressed it to himself, but listed Arthur Seyss-Inquart as the author. Göring was going to pretend that Seyss-Inquart was pleading with Göring to send German troops into Austria "to restore order."[5] This was a clumsy reprise of the scam he had scripted with the Reichstag fire. Göring gave the draft to Glaise-Horstenau to take back to Austria, but Glaise was offended by the ruse, and perhaps by the naked treachery to Austria, and he refused to take it.[6]

Black Friday in Vienna was March 11. Schuschnigg had gone to sleep comforted by Seyss-Inquart's cooperation, but he was jarred awake at 5:30 a.m. by news that the Germans had closed the border at Salzburg and had withdrawn all customs officials. Massive troop movements were evident, and the Austrian consul general in Munich had sent him a coded warning during the night: "Leo is ready to travel."[7] It meant that German divisions in Munich had been mobilized.[8] The invasion could come at any moment.

Was this a bluff? Of all the exultant Austrians shouting for independence last night, Schuschnigg was one of the very few who had ever been face to face with the Führer. Hitler had used a bluff at Berchtesgaden, but only the imme-diacy had been bluff. Hitler's determination to take or invade Austria soon was never a bluff. The Führer's march into the Rhineland a full year ago had been no bluff. And his massive increase of Germany's military was as real as can be.

A small nation going into battle totally alone against an overwhelming tyrant would seem a gripping tale, but in March 1938, that did not fit with the reality that 200,000 Austrians might have to die to make that theatrical gesture, and they would have to die in vain. The Austrian armed forces compared to the German were bluntly labeled "worthless."[9] The clash of their armies has been imaged as a rabbit trying to take on a python.[10]

Schuschnigg pushed to get further information, but he was told Papen had gone to Berlin and that Seyss-Inquart also could not be found. But at 9:30 a.m., Schuschnigg heard the quiet shuffle, the sound that was about to bring Austria to its end; it was the soft patter of approaching steps of the compro-mised Austrian government minister, Arthur Seyss-Inquart, walking into the chancellor's office. As quiet and simple as his visit looked, he virtually whis-pered a stunning order—Schuschnigg must call off the plebiscite.

Seyss delivered Hitler's ultimatum to postpone the plebiscite for two weeks ostensibly to allow time for some type of poll. Seyss was shaken him-self, and he threatened to resign if Schuschnigg refused; he implied that this would result in an eruption of Nazi violence and an invasion. Schuschnigg, however, did refuse.[11]

Instead, Schuschnigg ordered a call up of reserves and put security forces on alert. The reserves boarded trucks and rode off toward the German border, likely anticipating a slaughter.[12] Schuschnigg gathered his inner cabinet, his top advi-sors, in the early afternoon, and together they weighed the alternatives: reject Hitler and appeal to world opinion; resign and accept the ultimatum; or attempt a middle course proposing technical changes to the plebiscite plan.[13] The group chose the middle course, but when Seyss returned, he summarily rejected it.

Schuschnigg made repeated calls to London and Paris and was told there would be no help or support for Austria.[14] London had already signaled Hitler directly in recent days that Britain would pose no problem. Britain's ambas-sador to Germany, Sir Neville Henderson, had contacted the German Foreign Office on March 3 with the message that Britain was willing to confer with Germany on all issues—a clear signal that appeasement, not resistance, was still the British plan.[15] Perhaps Henderson's real message was even worse, for he got word to Hitler that he himself was in favor of the Anschluss.[16]

Other significant leaders of the British had a different view. Churchill's trusted biographer, William Manchester, spent many hours speaking with Churchill discussing the historical background of the period, and Manchester refers to Schuschnigg as "a born leader," "a man of action" and "not a man to be intimidated." Such strength may not have been easy to see since, Manchester says, he possessed "impeccable old-world Viennese manners."[17] Based on his analysis of history, seen through the perspective of Churchill rather than Chamberlain, Manchester called Schuschnigg's "Rot-Weiss-Rot!" speech in the Bundestag ("Rot-Weiss-Rot bis in der Tod" ["Red-White-Red until we're dead"]) "an act of desperate courage."[18] He called the decision to hold a plebiscite a wise and proper move, and he recounts that British member of Parliament Harold Nicolson, one of Churchill's allies, commended Schuschnigg's bravery in standing up to Hitler when Chamberlain and Britain abandoned him.[19]

Schuschnigg called the one last leader with whom he might have a chance—Benito Mussolini—but Il Duce would not take or return his calls.[20] The last remote chance for help was gone, and the beleaguered chancellor was staring directly at the beginning of the dreaded new European war now on his doorstep. He could not let Austrians suffer that carnage again—uselessly.

He went to President Miklas and said he was calling off the plebiscite. Otherwise, war was about to erupt, a war between German peoples. Despite his resolve of the last few days, he could not let such a thing happen. At that moment, he believed that canceling the plebiscite would end the immediate crisis and avoid the horror of Germans killing other Germans. The other leaders of his government were surprised at the news of his abrupt reversal, but they too thought that, with the cancellation of the plebiscite, the crisis would now pass.[21]

But Göring had taken charge. He sent word that calling off the plebiscite was not enough.[22] He decided this was Nazi Germany's great opportunity, and he should take full advantage of the sudden drama. Instead of letting the crisis end, Göring, whose constantly angry eyes seemed to intimidate most other Nazi decision makers, escalated the conflict and converted the moment of instability into Germany's breakout attack.[23] Now it was Göring who was the man driving the Third Reich to force the Anschluss of Austria. He determined it would be done that day. Checking with Hitler for approval each step of the way, Göring called Seyss and dictated to him the instructions for the death blow to Austria.

Schuschnigg must resign, Göring ordered. The reason given was that he had broken the agreement. Seyss-Inquart must be chosen by President Miklas to form a new government. If not, the troops would march in.[24] Göring's phony telegram requesting the invasion would complete the charade and provide a facade of legitimacy to paralyze the abstentionist world of 1938.[25] The cover stories the Nazis contrived, saying that they were saving Austria from the chaos occurring in the streets of Vienna, were all lies; no such thing had occurred.[26]

Schuschnigg had come full circle since the Great War. He now faced the decision to spill vast amounts of Austrian blood in a doomed gesture. He would not and, instead, decided he must resign to prevent it.[27] At 3:30 p.m., he went again to President Miklas.[28] Mussolini still refused to return his calls or the calls of his foreign office aide. Schuschnigg broke the news of Hitler's ultimatum to Miklas and said that he was resigning as demanded.[29] Miklas attempted to dissuade him, but, in view of the "silence of the outside world," Schuschnigg bowed to "the futility of going to war against Germany."[30] Miklas could not change his mind. Miklas, however, remained defiant. He refused to name Seyss chancellor as Göring demanded. Instead, he asked the chief of police, Michael Skubl, then Otto Ender, then General Schilhawsky to accept the post, but each refused.[31]

Göring was alerted at 5:26 p.m. that things were not falling into place. Miklas had not relented; he refused to appoint Seyss as chancellor. Göring exploded; he directed that they inform Miklas that 200,000 German troops would invade Austria if Göring was not promptly informed that Seyss was chancellor, but Miklas still refused to budge.[32]

As Britain and France were fed the reports that the Austrian government was being threatened with invasion and bullied into surrendering its independence, they both were politely rebuffed by Ribbentrop and other Nazi contacts when they protested. Britain's protests were intentionally timid and lifeless; France's were little better. British ambassador Henderson took any spark of life out of Britain's objection; he took it upon himself to criticize Schuschnigg's actions when he presented the British objection to the Berlin Foreign Ministry.[33] In response, Henderson's own colleague, the British minister to Austria, criticized Henderson for his "ill-placed criticism" of Schuschnigg.[34] Eventually, the most charitable description of Britain's diplomacy in the matter of the Anschluss was "indignant acquiescence."[35]

Both Britain and France sought audiences with Mussolini more to determine his plans than to influence them, believing that only a joint effort by the Stresa Front nations—with Italy, not them, at the fore—could stop Hitler. Mussolini, however, refused even to receive their emissaries or speak to them. Mussolini's son-in-law, Count Ciano, brusquely declined their requests to meet. France, at that crucial moment, had no leadership; Chautemps had resigned and Leon Blum would not become premier until days later.

Abandoned by the entire continent and by Britain, and faced with an overwhelming German mobilization, Miklas and Schuschnigg were still being urged by some in their cabinet to fight, even though Austria had only a two-day supply of ammunition and would need to husband what bullets remained if there were to be a longer fight against the 200,000 Wehrmacht just over the border from the 5,000 Austrians who were mobilized—with only 25,000 more available within days and a maximum of 80,000 who could eventually be mobilized in the future. That was it.

The Treaty of St. Germain had limited Austria's maximum military strength to 30,000 men. However, disputes between the Left and Right over the mission of the Bundesheer (the Austrian army) and pressure from the Social Democrats, plus the financial crisis crippling Austria's economy, limited the army's actual strength to 20,000. Though increased by this time to 30,000, this small army was a purely defensive force arrayed largely along the border.[36] Since March 1935, Germany had been building by universal military conscription and was now heavily rearmed.[37] William Shirer, who covered the rise of Hitler, had attempted to learn just how large an army was being assembled in Germany; however, he found it difficult to obtain that information, and he learned that seeking it may get a reporter expelled from Germany.[38] Aside from Germany's army, there were also as many as 80,000 violent Nazi activists already living in Austria.[39] When Josef Göbbels first announced the beginning of conscription in March 1935, he promised there would soon be twelve army corps, but he had refused to provide numbers of troops.[40] Other sources, however, reveal how massively outnumbered the Austrian Bundesheer was in 1938. The Wehrmacht alone had thirty-six infantry divisions of 600,000 men.[41] Some estimated the full strength of the German military in 1939 in the millions, most of them in the army.[42] Schuschnigg gave in on March 11, 1938, not from cowardice but because his tiny Austrian army of barely 30,000 was confronted by an assembled invasion force at the border of between 100,000 and 200,000 Wehrmacht and a total German armed force in the millions that was by then "the greatest military power in the world."[43] The massive Sturmabteilung (SA) had numbered in the millions when it was added to the Wehrmacht.[44] Moreover, the German military was an offensive force trained for blitzkrieg.[45]

The Austrians had artillery, albeit World War I artillery, but virtually no tanks, no air force, and no anti-aircraft weapons.[46] Schuschnigg, therefore, pushed back against Miklas. Guido Zernatto, Guido Schmidt, and others agreed with Schuschnigg that a two-day battle of resistance would be a useless sacrifice of soldiers' lives, and the many lives of the civilians who would die in the aerial bombing of the nearly undefended heaviest population center, Vienna. Without air defenses, the losses would be catastrophic when Vienna was bombed.[47] A mere show of resistance provoking a German attack was to him simply not justified. It was not worth the slaughter of thousands of Austrians, which would surely be the price for such a gesture.

Schuschnigg could not prevent the takeover of Austria by fighting. Less still could he prevent the war.[48] Chamberlain said as much to the British Parliament days later when he confessed the significance of the Stresa Front's refusal to help: "The hard fact is that nothing could have arrested this action by Germany unless we, and others with us, had been prepared to use force against it."[49] It is reasonable to claim that the Nazi threat would then and there, if Austria had opened fire, have lost all ambiguity, if any lingered. The Anschluss was outrageous, but it may have been seen in even more startling relief if Schuschnigg had ordered Austrian troops to resist and fire upon the invading German troops. Additional emphasis, however, would not have jolted Britain, France, or anyone else out of their nearly catatonic states to take up arms to challenge Hitler at this moment. Isolationism and appeasement had crippled not just Europeans but also Americans, and they, too, were unprepared to begin a war at that moment.

One tantalizing question that will never be answerable is whether, if Britain and Austria had incurred the loss of lives and resisted invasion, might that have spurred the lurking German generals who were patriots and opponents of the Nazis, the remaining generals whom Hitler had not dismissed, to spring into action and succeed in taking Hitler down. Churchill had urged British resistance to the Anschluss. Many today still feel exquisite agony when they read the numerous opinions that, had Chamberlain resisted, it "would almost certainly have led to a military coup in Berlin, toppling the Nazi regime."[50] Even after the Anschluss, Britain resisted Churchill's cries for a program of rearmament and bonding of all allies. Churchill also urged that the smaller countries like Czechoslovakia, Hungary, Romania, and Yugoslavia renew efforts to form alliances by which they could combine forces and become a serious opposition.[51]

★ ★ ★

Austrian Nazis were given the word to pour into the streets to march and shout. Soon a Nazi mob surrounded the chancellery, and many pushed their way inside. Austrian soldiers and sentries kept them out of the chancellor's office, but their shouts drowned out all other sounds in Vienna. The Nazi crowd at the Ballhausplatz was chanting "Kill the Jews. Hang Schuschnigg."[52] Göring was still intent on seizing the broadcast facilities and using the phony telegram claiming riots in the streets to justify the Anschluss and sell the invasion to the world as a rescue of Austria. Nazi propaganda techniques were put to work supporting that story. The Berlin press office sent Britain a communication flagrantly lying about these events, denying any ultimatum had been given Austria to call off the plebiscite or that any force was being threatened.[53]

At 7:50 p.m., Schuschnigg realized that the broadcast equipment was soon going to be in Nazi hands. He was mindful of the Nazis' attempt to capture the radio station in their 1934 putsch, and he was acutely aware they were going to lie to the world. He remembered Hitler's plea at Berchtesgaden trying to tempt Schuschnigg to agree to Anschluss and thereby become an immortal German, and he was certain that Hitler wanted very much to camouflage the invasion to prevent opposition and to keep plotters from rising against him. Schuschnigg decided he had to try to go on the air before the Nazis blocked the transmitter. He set up the broadcast equipment in the room where the Nazis had murdered Dollfuss and was elated to find the airwaves were still open. He acted quickly knowing they could pull the plug at any moment. His broadcast to the nation was spontaneous. First came his order that there should be no resistance to the German troops.[54] The Nazis were still telling every European government that would listen that reports that

Austria had been given an ultimatum to call off the plebiscite were "foolish gossip" and that no threats had been made; instead, they insisted, communists were taking up arms in Austria.[55] But Schuschnigg's next sentences destroyed Hitler's camouflage. He announced that this was an invasion. The Nazis were not coming by invitation and were not welcome. He announced that Austria had "yielded to force."[56]

William Shirer, who spoke fluent German, was beside his radio in Vienna, listening as Schuschnigg delivered the address.[57] Shirer realized what this was—that Schuschnigg was destroying the Nazis' attempt to repeat their Reichstag fire fraud; he was exposing Hitler and Göring in one jarring, well-timed announcement. He did it while a Nazi mob stood just outside in the corridors and in the Ballhausplatz screaming for his head. With surprising control, ignoring their chants, Schuschnigg was standing at ground zero telling the world that the claims being made by the Nazi propaganda were "lies from A to Z."[58] With that, the so-called Anschluss was revealed to be the first invasion of what was to become a new war.

Shirer felt the pulse of Schuschnigg's denunciation of the Anschluss: "Towards the end you feel his voice will break; that there will be sobbing. But he controls it to the last. There is a second silence. And then the national anthem played from an old record."[59] "God protect Austria,"[60] was Schuschnigg's final plea.[61] What he had done was make a "heroic gesture to call the world's attention to Austria."[62] Moments later, the Nazis blocked the broadcast facilities.

★ ★ ★

Like many Europeans, Georg and Maria von Trapp hoped that another war was only a temporary fear. They had been clinging to the comfort of Hitler's assurances that Austria would remain independent. Thus, they were struck with disbelief when they heard Schuschnigg's broadcast.

The Trapps, however, knew the futility of armed resistance. Maria later said: "[W]hen the big brother, eighty million strong, falls upon the little one, with only six million, what good does it do to fire a few guns?"[63] At their home, as they listened to Schuschnigg's broadcast, Baron von Trapp rose; he walked over to the telephone and sent Schuschnigg a consoling telegram offering his blessing.[64]

Seyss-Inquart phoned Göring and explained that the government had essentially stood down but not resigned. This was enough. At about 8:15 p.m., Hitler slapped his thigh and barked *"Jetzt gehts los"* ("Off we go").[65] Hitler signed Operational Instruction No. 2 ordering the invasion, using as a pretense that Austria had not fulfilled Germany's demands.[66] Göring instructed General Georg Keppler to get Seyss to send the telegram claiming Germany must invade to put down violence in the streets. Keppler naively told Göring that there was no such violence. Göring persisted. He also told Keppler that Seyss did not actually have to send the telegram; he merely had to say that he had sent it. Sometime later, someone among the Nazi leaders in Austria sent Göring a version of his telegram inviting the Nazis to invade.[67] Thereafter, the Nazis insisted that they had made no threat or invasion and they had only moved on Austria after Seyss became chancellor.[68] Acting as though no one would notice or remember Schuschnigg's announcement that this was a hostile armed invasion, the Third Reich wrote Britain that it had received a telegram from Seyss inviting German troops to come to Austria to quell chaos in the streets.[69] *Time* soon made clear that Schuschnigg had put up heroic opposition.

The new cabinet under Seyss-Inquart was installed just after midnight on March 12. Schuschnigg watched as a string of Nazi torches gathered into a triumphal parade, and Vienna filled with Nazi yells and songs. Forty black-clad Schutzstaffel (SS) men arrived in the anteroom of his offices.

★ ★ ★

Many Austrian citizens promptly fled Austria, Guido Zernatto among them. Others like Prince Ernst von Starhemberg who was abroad, decided not to return. Seyss-Inquart told Schuschnigg that he had a plane ready and would get him to safety in London or the Hungarian embassy, but Schuschnigg refused. He would not leave Austria or seek protection.[70] Shirer, reporting on this, used one word to describe Schuschnigg's refusal to leave on the waiting plane: "Guts."[71] Another historian later added: "This was courage."[72]

As the long night wore on, it at last came time for Schuschnigg to take his leave of the chancellery. As he stepped out into the corridor, the sharp clack of boot heels of Austrian sentries rang loudly in the dark of early morning. A tall sentry could be seen weeping as Schuschnigg shook his hand for the last time. The stairs were already lined with Nazi civilians wearing swastikas. Schuschnigg, as if in a trance, ignored them as he descended the stairs for the drive home.[73]

★ ★ ★

There was considerable debate among the Nazi high command whether, after Schuschnigg's resignation, there now was any need at all for the military actually to invade, or whether that would be an entirely unnecessary provocation. Hitler briefly told his generals to call off the invasion; however, Göring went to work on him, and Hitler renewed the order for the invasion to go forward.[74] Seyss and Papen's military aide, General Wolfgang Muff, asked to have Hitler awakened with a last request that a military invasion should now be called off. General Wilhelm Keitel, however, told them that Hitler said it was now too late.[75] Keitel later admitted he had not even passed the request on to Hitler.[76]

Hitler had once again accurately assessed how well he had done in fooling Europe that, even after this naked invasion of an independent European nation, there would be no retaliation. The fact that some European nations endorsed the Anschluss facilitated the restraint of the others. Hungary expressed approval in private ministerial meetings with German officials.[77] Mussolini sent a message to the Führer in advance of the Anschluss that he approved it, and he thereby gained Hitler's fervent support.

★ ★ ★

Hitler's Wehrmacht marched into Austria on the morning of March 12, 1938, with no opposition and virtually without noticeable protest.[78] The troops sent into Austria were led by the tanks and the armored cavalry of General Heinz Guderian's Second Panzer Division—a force trained for blitzkrieg.[79] It was immediately apparent that resistance, even for a day or two, would have brought far greater death than historically predictable. Astute correspondents of the day called it a turning point of history.[80] Despite the continued efforts of the Nazis to give it the euphemism of Anschluss to help characterize it as an agreed merger or a rescue, it is commonly described simply as a "bloodless invasion."[81]

Later in the day, Hitler himself arrived for celebratory speeches in Braunau am Inn, his birthplace; he then went on to Linz and then Vienna.[82] Loud welcoming crowds cheered him at each location. The enthusiasm may seem mystifying in many ways, but historians have concluded that it did not reflect a pent-up, preexisting, near nationwide support for Anschluss that old footage appears to signify. One historian suggests that many were shouting side by side with fervent Anschluss supporters because they yearned for relief from the crisis and were giving voice to their anxiety-driven hope that somehow this would bring relief.[83] It was not joy emanating from a desire for Nazi rule but, instead, it was fear, acceptance, and total resignation that the Nazis were now in obvious command of Austria.[84] Swastika banners were draped on public buildings everywhere the army progressed.[85] Yet, the appearance of enthusiasm of these mixed crowds of Austrians was undeniable.[86]

Some correspondents who were on the scene as the troop trucks rolled into Austria sharply dispute the impression created by the loud Nazi rallies staged to cheer the invading Wehrmacht with shouts of "Heil Hitler" in Linz and Vienna. Some insist that these joyful scenes actually show a mere minority of Austrians participating in Nazi-organized demonstrations. The impression conveyed by films, even the photos run in *The Times* in London, of an enthusiastic welcome are called a "shocking distortion," and the correspondents and foreigners who were there "give it the lie," in the words of William Manchester.[87] The Nazis by then had perfected control of the implements of propaganda and knew exactly how to stage loud Nazi rallies to welcome the invasion. Churchill judged that the more valid evidence was that, a few days earlier, before the propaganda and invasion force, some two-thirds of the Austrians had supported Schuschnigg's independence referendum.[88]

That is not to say that the crowds were 100 percent Nazis. They were not. Some Austrians, when they learned Germany had taken control of their lives, made the pragmatic decision that they had better show themselves cheering the new regime. Many chose to focus on the sharp contrast between Austria's stubborn recession and the booming economy in Germany. Few had to be told that any jobs were going to go to Nazis. Some even bought Hitler's promise that their economy would instantly share in Germany's prosperity. Others were merely shocked and apprehensive as they were treated to their first glimpse of intimidating weapons and troops parading down their streets, and they were quick to decide that the wise move was to applaud rather than curse the invaders. Some Austrians were seduced by the burst of enthusiasm stoked by the flashy propaganda—the sudden appearance of striking Nazi banners and flags nearly everywhere. Some just joined the very loud bandwagon, and they rallied to the triumphant blare of martial music from Wehrmacht troop trucks entering Austria, some of which were filled with musicians playing familiar marches followed by trucks filled with friendly waving soldiers.

Hitler entering Wildenau, Upper Austria, March 1938.
Source: Bundesarchiv.

German tanks in the Heldenplatz, March 1938.
Source: Alamy.

Many Austrians did not yet realize this was an invasion. Not everyone had the prescience to catch Schuschnigg's sudden broadcast exposing the lies surrounding the phony telegram by which the Reich invited itself to come to Austria's rescue.

German troops entering Austria, March 1938.

Source: Alamy.

Many Catholics poured into the streets and welcomed the Nazis upon the order of Austria's Cardinal Theodor Innitzer, who took it upon himself to call all Catholics to come out in full support of Hitler—an inexplicable announcement for which he was brutally chastised by the pope and Cardinal Pacelli and consigned to disgrace.

By the time the extravaganza reached Vienna, after three days of Nazi rallies in Braunau, Wildenau, and Linz, Hitler orchestrated a grand assembly in the Heldenplatz. By the time of his arrival in Vienna on March 14, thousands more had been primed to an intense curiosity and gave in to the irresistible itch to come out and see this greatest showman.

The scenes captured on film at the Heldenplatz show a pep-rally spirit, but one that was fueled by falsehood and gullibility. A true-believer celebration is white hot. Such fervor was seen in Nazi-dominated Linz. The Heldenplatz crowd in Vienna was very large, and most there did not pulse with the mania of the Nuremberg rallies. Many who turned out looked resigned to the overwhelming power lavishly paraded to elicit fear and demand a show of approval. Economic blackmail was also in the air, for it was always clear that prosperity would only be available to Nazis.[89] Any uncommitted Austrian could see the necessity to cease forthwith all signs of opposition. Nevertheless, in a space of four days, these carefully filmed scenes were made to look very different from the Austria that, days earlier, as both sides had predicted, was about to vote to support Schuschnigg's independence referendum.[90]

For his triumphal appearance, a speech at Vienna's Heldenplatz, Hitler directed Heinrich Himmler to pack the crowd and unleash the full Göbbels toolbox. Himmler bussed thousands of activist supporters from heavily Nazi areas in upper Austria to Vienna to make certain there was a loud, disciplined audience to greet Hitler's choreographed entrance. Tanks, troops, and field artillery poured into the broad boulevards. A wave of arrests of Viennese Jews and Nazi opponents had muzzled even the slightest show of protest. By then, Hitler and the Nazi propaganda apparatus had accumulated many years of experience perfecting such public presentations, mustering massive throngs of Nazi supporters and carefully rehearsing them how to show wild enthusiasm at Zeppelin Field in Nuremberg. Nothing about such events was spontaneous; every photo at the Heldenplatz was well planned.

That sudden about-face has been extensively analyzed in postwar reflections. Some historians call attention to national personality traits attributed to Austrians. Some of them contend that most prewar Austrians were better people than appears from their role in the war.[91] Others are more accusatory, pointing at Austria's history of anti-Semitism. Another view is that these Nazi era Austrians were a people prone to drift whichever way the wind blew. The word used is *Schlamperei*, a genial passivity born of a lazy, muddleheaded approach to such events. How many were responding to which motives and traits is unknowable.

Whatever the motives, it was an overwhelming throng that jammed Vienna's spacious Heldenplatz outside the Hofburg Palace. They came to cheer

Hitler entering the Heldenplatz in Vienna, March 1938.
Source: Alamy

Hitler as he rode into the center of the Vienna he so hated. Had those in the crowd read his venom about Vienna in *Mein Kampf*, or heard his contempt for Austria spouted at Berchtesgaden, the wildly applauding Austrians would have realized that Hitler's beaming at them was not the glow of love but the glare of a vengeful conqueror.

Göring and Hitler decided to capitalize on the appearance of widespread enthusiasm. They escalated the conquest and directly subsumed Austria into Germany. Their prior plans to treat Austria as a self-governed satellite named Ostmark were abruptly jettisoned in favor of complete rule by the Third Reich, and they enacted statutes in both countries for their "Reunification."[92] Ostmark would be a province of Germany itself. The Nuremberg Laws were now in place, and they stripped from Austrian Jews their human rights and citizenship.

Seyss-Inquart, Hitler, and Reinhard Heydrich in Austria, March 1938.
Source: Bundesarchiv.

Seyss-Inquart met with Hitler on March 13 and, with apparent relief, suggested that his position as chancellor was now through since Austria was a part of Germany. He, nevertheless, rode triumphantly with Hitler in Vienna on March 15, and in the presence of the many Nazi officers who joined the celebration, Seyss virtually wore out his arm with abundant Nazi salutes. He asked for permission to return to private life, and the Führer agreed. Another post would, of course, be found in due course for this key player in the Anschluss.

After the invasion, Göring sought out the Czechoslovak minister, Voytech Masny, and assured him that Czechoslovakia had nothing to fear from Germany. ("I give you my word of honor.")[93]

★ ★ ★

Josef Bürckel, a notorious Nazi leader from the Saar, was brought in to take charge of reorganizing the unruly Austrian Nazi Party.[94] In the immediate

Hitler with Rudolf Hess greeting Arthur Seyss-Inquart after the Anschluss, March 1938.
Source: Alamy.

aftermath, 70,000 Austrians tried to flee. Some made it, but most failed and were sent back to Austria for insufficient visas and passports. Almost all who made the attempt were identified and sent to concentration camps. Many were killed by SS firing squads.[95] In short order, some 76,000 Austrians identified as Nazi opponents or affiliated with opposition groups were caught and jailed. While some others were released and allowed to pack quickly and leave Austria, most of those arrested wound up in concentration camps.

The festering anti-Semitism of Austrian Nazis and other radicals, so hopefully held in check in recent days, was unleashed. The ugliness that Schuschnigg's insistence on equality for Jews had restrained was immediately visible. Gangs of storm troopers took to the streets and beat and murdered Jews. They abused many others as well, but the Jews bore the brunt of street violence. They ordered people to clean Nazi toilets. They forced Jews to paint identifying signs on their shops and homes; they made them get on their knees in public places and scrub "Ja Schuschnigg" off the pavement.[96] Churchill's friends wrote to him from Austria about the abuses. One wrote that he saw "two well-dressed women forced to their knees to scrub 'Heil Schuschnigg!'" from the pavement.[97] It was not only the Brownshirt types who humiliated and assaulted Jews throughout Austria but also many citizens gleefully fell on them as well. Jews were grabbed,

Austrians and German soldiers forcing Jews to scrub "Ja Schuschnigg" off the sidewalk.
Source: Alamy.

abused, and tormented at random on many streets.[98] A Viennese-born student of this phenomenon describes it:

> The Viennese showed a hatred accumulated over centuries. Men and women could harbor spite and anger and manifest it in many ways, but before this date they couldn't actually notoriously kill or plunder. Now, finally they could open their heart and do what they wanted to do: humiliate, rob, and persecute. The state wasn't in it before, endorsing, encouraging. Now there was official sanction. Almost every house suddenly had swastika flags. So great was the transformation from one day to the next, that it was like being transferred to the moon. People were like hyenas.[99]

Was this, after all, the real Austria? Was this level of barbarity lurking beneath the moderate anti-Semitism all along? Thousands of Jews were arrested in the immediate aftermath of the arrival of the Wehrmacht and the Gestapo.[100] It quickly became clear to them that an Austrian Jew faced a grim choice—flee or die.[101]

Austrian Nazis were well able to identify the Austrian generals, office-holders, and other leaders who were anti-Nazi. They were rounded up; some were reported by the Nazi Gauleiter Bürckel to have committed suicide while in custody. The US ambassador suspiciously observed, "The 'suicides' while under 'preventative arrest' appear to have been numerous and it is curious that so many people while under 'preventative arrest' should have had access to revolvers wherewith to shoot themselves."[102]

Others, however, were already so terrified of what the Anschluss had in store for them that they did choose suicide. Emil Fey may have fixated on concern that his role as a Heimwehr leader might make him a Nazi target, or that his failure to join the Nazi putsch against Dollfuss might be viewed by Hitler as a double-cross; but on March 16, Fey shot and killed his wife and son, and then himself.[103]

Many Jews began committing suicide within days after the Anschluss, and this telltale sign of what was to come gave Vienna a sudden, extremely high rate of Jewish suicides.[104] Edward R. Murrow saw one Jewish man standing at a bar in Karnerstrasse; after a while, he just pulled a razor from his pocket and slit his own throat.[105] One Austrian wrote Churchill that his neighbors, a family of six Jews, had all just shot themselves.[106] Another Jewish man's suicide hit close to home. Kurti often spent time at the Munich home of his friend Peter Schlessinger, and he knew the family well. Peter's father was Jewish, and he was becoming daily more fearful, an anxiety enhanced by living across the street from the Munich apartment of Adolf Hitler. Vera used her Munich contacts to help Schlessinger obtain exit papers. However, the grip of fear had already become too great. On the day Schlessinger arrived at the Munich train station to flee, he overreacted to two soldiers nearing him on the platform, pulled out his pistol, and killed himself. The soldiers were dumbfounded. They had not even noticed him.[107]

Scores of Jews, including Sigmund Freud,[108] began to flee. The morning after the Anschluss, there was a flight from Aspern Airport to London. William Shirer had to get to London to report on the Anschluss, but the flight was booked. He was able to offer "fantastic sums" to several passengers for a seat, but they were Jews and all turned him down.[109]

This people who had been Austrians for a millennium were soon being herded through a processing center the Nazis set up in a confiscated Rothschild mansion, robbed of everything they owned, and then given permission to cross the border provided they left that day.[110] And as costly as it was for them, it was fortunate for 125,000 of them that they were able to escape what lay ahead. Far less fortunate were those who could not manage the escape—the elderly, the ill, and many Jewish women—some 66,000 who, beginning in October 1939, were deported to the East. Ultimately most of them would be imprisoned at Theresienstadt and die at Auschwitz.[111]

★ ★ ★

Hitler staged his own plebiscite. With no organized opposition left to rally votes against him, and with Jews prohibited from voting, the Nazis used propaganda, military parades, and crude voter intimidation; and their campaign was bolstered by a very public call by Cardinal Innitzer that Catholics should vote for the Nazis. Those who did go to the polls found the polling sites awash with uniformed SS and SA glaring at them; with these assists, Hitler's Anschluss referendum received more than 99 percent approval.[112]

For the vote on Hitler's plebiscite, the Nazis made it clear to all that they were conducting surveillance of the Austrian voters. They opened wide slits in the voting booths, and voters saw they were being watched to assure they all had resigned themselves to Nazi rule; all realized it was now a *fait accompli*, and all had the good sense to realize they had better vote "*Ja*" for Hitler.[113] Cardinal Innitzer's nationally publicized endorsement of Hitler undoubtedly added heavily to the Catholic vote for the Anschluss. Schuschnigg was always circumspect about relations with the church, and he held his tongue about the cardinal, but he apparently had little respect for Innitzer's judgment.[114] Former Social Democrat chancellor Karl Renner, an opponent of Schuschnigg, also added his encouragement for Austrians to vote to approve the Anschluss.[115]

The isolationist US government was, as events unfolded, almost irrelevant to the Anschluss. When German ambassador Hans-Heinrich Dieckhoff met with Secretary of State Cordell Hull on March 12 to present the official German version of those events, there were few questions and no protest.

However, public reaction in the United States quickly turned against Germany, and when Ambassador Dieckhoff met with Under Secretary of State Sumner Welles only three days later, he was met with stony silence. Still later, in an informal setting, Welles finally became more blunt with Dieckhoff and revealed the government's bitterness over the crude invasion.[116] Secretary of State Hull began speaking with equal condemnation, reportedly on orders from President Roosevelt.[117]

Perhaps the rapid unfolding of the Anschluss caught the US government off guard, and the Americans had merely been suffering from a delayed reaction, but the American public seemed to experience a notable change in attitude due to the Anschluss. America's press coverage of the events of the previous year and the growing crisis over Austria had seemed to Schuschnigg favorable to Germany. That largely ended with the Anschluss.[118] The *St. Louis Globe-Democrat* reported on March 12, 1938: "Austria has capitulated to Hitler this night; under the pressure of the German war machine the Austrian government has given up its five-year struggle against Hitler's tyranny."[119] On March 21, *Time* published resounding praise of Schuschnigg.

The invasion itself may have been a wholly unnecessary mistake in Hitler's larger plan to take as much as he could without war. Once the Schuschnigg government resigned, with Seyss-Inquart now in charge, occupation would seem quite unnecessary. Erich Kort is among those who branded it foolish, calling the invasion "incredible folly" because it provided clear evidence for the whole world that the Anschluss was not voluntary.[120] When the occupation was followed with the sudden orgy of beatings and humiliation of Jews in Austria, none but the most mindless of the anti-Semites in America could any longer voice acceptance of the Nazi regime.[121]

Neville Chamberlain was not ready to do anything more hostile than to grumble weakly at Ribbentrop over the Anschluss. France also declined to voice demands for withdrawal and register threats against any more such invasions. But other than some complaints, the brazen Anschluss, now obvious as a naked invasion with transparent pretense, proceeded unopposed by foreign governments. The arc of revulsion over the Great War had swung back so powerfully upon its victims that it was now on the way to the most unintended consequence—setting the stage for another, an even worse war.

Only the press and some individual statesmen of Europe and the world condemned the takeover of Austria unequivocally. Hitler was ecstatic over the success[122] of his audacity; he could now enjoy complete confidence that he would face no real opposition when he threatened his next attack. It was clear that many countries did not comprehend the lesson this astounding invasion presented about Hitler's real intentions, for even after Austria, they still lacked the resolve needed to take action to prevent his next confiscation—Czechoslovakia.

VII

THE JAWS OF THE NAZIS

• *10* •

Swallowed by the Beast

*S*everal months after the Anschluss, twenty-seven Jews were murdered and more than a hundred synagogues throughout Austria were destroyed in the rampage that became known as Kristallnacht.[1] The excuse offered was that a provocation had occurred in Paris. On November 10, 1938, a seventeen-year-old German Jew, enraged that his father had been arrested by the Nazis and shipped off to Poland, had shot and killed an official of the German embassy in Paris.

Reinhard Heydrich issued reprisal orders. Nazis were ordered to burn synagogues, destroy Jewish homes and shops, and arrest Jews in droves for shipment to concentration camps.[2] The Nazi government oversaw the ensuing riots and rampages and kept the police from stopping them. In Germany, hundreds of Jews were murdered; rape and looting was rampant.[3] Austria received the same treatment. It was not just one night; it was better described as the "Week of Broken Glass."[4] Within days, thousands were sent to Dachau; and in very short order, 700 Austrian Jews committed suicide.[5]

Trucks and trains had begun taking hundreds of Austrian Jews and so-called undesirables to unfamiliar sites named Mauthausen, Theresienstadt, and Dachau. Then Jews started disappearing in ever larger numbers. Some were seen being taken away by grim soldiers. Others who had gone to bed one night were strangely absent in the morning.

Even before the Anschluss, some clergymen had begun to speak from pulpits in opposition to persecution of Jews, and when they did, they found themselves and their churches targeted. In 1935, the Protestant churches throughout Germany had read a protest from their pulpits against Nazi persecution, and the Nazis arrested several hundred of the pastors who had done so. Pope Pius XI issued a 1937 encyclical plainly aimed at the Nazis, and the Nazis confiscated the copies all over Germany. Catholic monsignor Bernard Lichtenberg called on the congregation of the Berlin Cathedral simply to pray for Jews and people in concentration camps. Even for this, he was arrested, and he was reported to have died very suddenly en route to Dachau.[6]

The Nazis were cunning opportunists, well aware that it would be political suicide to attack religions openly while they struggled to gain power at the polls, but once they acquired power, they became more brazen. They summarily arrested many anti-Nazi priests, so many that Dachau had a priests' barracks, and some of its priests were executed.[7]

As the persecution became visible, the basic decency of many ordinary people surfaced. Many Catholics, Quakers, and Protestants in Austria and in Germany began to display hostility to this more virulent Nazi form of anti-Semitism. They then became targets of the Nazis themselves. Once the full Nazi campaign of extermination began, ordinary people saw that saving Jews from arrest would require taking extremely brave action and accepting awful risks themselves. Many Austrians and Germans did muster that courage despite the knowledge that they were volunteering themselves and their families to become targets of Nazi retribution. Many Aryans hid Jews, even in Berlin, knowing that discovery would cost them their own lives.[8]

Eventually, any open opposition to Nazi persecution of Jews risked death, but some went public anyway. Notable among Germans who dared to become vocal public opponents of Hitler and the Nazis in Germany was Lutheran theologian and pastor Dietrich Bonhoeffer. He and many others were executed for their opposition to the persecution of the Jews.[9]

Little was known of the numberless sacrifices of courageous people when the events occurred. Most tales of those days are stories of savage cruelty that prove humans are capable of unthinkable evil; but in the years following the Holocaust, stories began to emerge of astounding bravery, sacrifice, and kindness—thousands of such stories—tales that prove that the most ordinary people will sacrifice themselves sometimes to save complete strangers.

Yad Vashem undertook to investigate these stories and identify the people who had helped Jews and others against the Nazi terror. They compiled well over 20,000 stories of non-Jews who helped Jews and others at the risk of their own lives and the lives of their children. Frequently, it was at the actual cost of those lives. They are honored by the State of Israel as "Righteous among the nations," an ancient Hebrew honor. Undoubtedly, many thousands more whose stories were never found also took such risks.[10]

• 11 •

The Clutches of the Gestapo

𝒰nlike other European leaders faced with expulsion by the Third Reich, Schuschnigg continued to refuse offers to flee.[1] He was not oblivious to the danger to his life, though he likely underestimated what lay in store. That night when he resigned, with raucous Nazis and their assembled sympathizers screaming for his head in the Ballhausplatz, the thought crossed his mind that the best solution for him personally would likely be to walk out and surrender to the mob with its gruesome, quick consequence.[2] Instead, he went home.

The Nazis dealt with him quickly. He was first placed under house arrest in the gardener's house at the Belvedere Palace on Prinz Eugenstrasse.[3] However, the Nazi command became concerned when public admiration for Schuschnigg began to appear, culminating in his picture on the cover of *Time* with glowing tributes. Hitler could not so soon forget the outpouring after Schuschnigg's speech to the Diet, and he feared the formation of a resistance movement focused on Schuschnigg. He wanted Schuschnigg publicly vilified, and Nazis spent considerable effort publishing baseless propaganda against the former chancellor, then they set out to dig into his files to try to find some evidence to support it. They told Schuschnigg that he would be put on trial for treason and could expect the death penalty.[4] He languished in anxious uncertainty all during April.

It had been some time since he had the leisure to walk and talk in the garden with his father. He and the elderly General Schuschnigg recalled their earlier captivity together as prisoners after the Great War, and now here they were again. They reminisced about their family and their country and speculated about what lay ahead. Those were pleasant if bittersweet times together and added to the deep relationship with his father. They could only wonder how many such days were left.

His personal life, however, added to the complexity and provided hope in these dark hours. He had recovered from his depression over Herma's death. He was now deeply in love with Vera, and they planned to marry.

In May, however, the Gestapo came. They brought him to a jail, to a small room at the Gestapo's Vienna headquarters in the Metropolitan Hotel.[5] He was now in the clutches of some of the Austrian Nazis who hated him, and they began vicious abuse. For a year and a half he was subjected to the worst treatment he endured during the war, brutal abuse he later said he did not think he would ever get over.[6]

The Gestapo circulated the news that Schuschnigg was about to be charged with treason. They flooded their press and radio with outlandish accusations to extinguish the last resistant strain of public support for him. They rifled through his records, certain they would find graft and corruption. After all, the Nazis' own atrocities were bathed in a shower of corruption. The opulent excess Hitler, Hermann Göring, and other Nazis lavished on themselves was astounding, and they seemed to assume that Schuschnigg must have pillaged Austria as they had Germany. The Nazis felt free to spend flamboyantly to construct Hitler's Eagles Nest chalet just above the Berghof and to make it accessible by blasting an incredibly costly new road up the steep mountain. Göring's Karinhall pleasure palace of 100,000 acres was filled with gadgets and pillaged priceless art.[7] Surely Schuschnigg had done the same. What they learned, however, was that he was squeaky clean. He had no assets to speak of. Even the lake house at St. Gilgen had merely been rented, and he paid the rent out of his own pocket.[8]

★ ★ ★

One day his son, Kurti, received a message summoning him to a Gestapo office where he was to appear before Reichsführer Heinrich Himmler. Kurti hurried to the address but arrived so early he had to kill time nearby, and so he dropped in to a shop where a Jewish collector sold stamps. The shopkeeper recognized the boy and refused to let him pay for a stamp that had caught his eye; instead he offered some badly needed consolation: "Your father is a wonderful man. He did everything he could to help us Jews."[9]

Refreshed by this exchange, Kurti proceeded to Himmler's office; he was sent in and was confronted by the dreaded Reichsführer. Himmler curtly gave him the disquieting message that he and the Führer had decided that it would be good if Kurti were to join the Hitler Youth. There was nothing else of substance behind the summons that had terrified Vera and her household.[10] Kurti went home. He ignored Himmler's order.

★ ★ ★

Vera knew how much Schuschnigg needed her. During eight-minute weekly visits, she was outraged to see that he was nearly hopelessly broken in mind and body. He lost more than fifty pounds. She was frightened at how badly he had deteriorated in the face of the unrelenting night and day Gestapo abuse. He would frequently be subjected to sleep deprivation, and his captors screamed threats with a pistol aimed at his head. They seemed to particularly enjoy making him clean the Gestapo bathrooms, forcing him to scrub the freshly fouled toilets with his toothbrush, and then ordering him to brush his teeth.[11]

★ ★ ★

On October 21, Vera arrived looking much sadder, bearing the grim news that General Schuschnigg had died. He had passed away suddenly the previous night from heart failure. Their requests that Schuschnigg be allowed to attend the funeral were denied; nor was he permitted a consoling visit from his brother.[12]

Despite the cruel treatment, Vera remained dangerously unintimidated by the Nazis; she protested their treatment of Schuschnigg. Vera, it seems, was not easily intimidated. She met in person with Himmler, and it became clear that she was not going to be silenced.[13] She was a strong-willed woman, used to being listened to, and she began pestering the Nazis—sending letters not only to Himmler but also to Hitler as well, and voicing complaints to the wife of Hermann Göring. One peculiar discomfort these Nazi confrontations caused her was that she found it difficult to avoid staring at what appeared to be Himmler's glass eye.[14]

Himmler visited Schuschnigg in his cell. He began ominously making brief mention of their plans to try Schuschnigg for treason. Prompted more by an entirely clear conscience than confidence in Nazi due process, Schuschnigg called for a prompt trial, but the occupying Gestapo authorities found no evidence and were never willing to attempt even a show trial. Himmler, however, must have privately recoiled at the conditions a former chancellor was enduring, for after the visit, guards brought Schuschnigg a small radio.

★ ★ ★

In October 1939, the Nazi command ordered Schuschnigg transferred. At some point, Hitler realized the value of high-ranking prisoners and ordered that none of them be killed without his order. Whether or not this was the catalyst, they let up on Schuschnigg. He was told that his troubles were now over, but at the end of a long drive, he found he was at the Munich Gestapo facility at the Wittelsbach Palace and set for solitary confinement.[15] Although his confinement in Munich was in a Gestapo jail, it turned out to be far better than the brutality in Vienna. The Munich guards there were quite humane in their behavior.[16] Gone were the daily threats of a bullet to the brain, sleep deprivation, and screams of seemingly deranged Gestapo thugs. Imprisonment, deprivation, tedium, and malaise were substituted for the terror and abuse he had received for more than a year from the Gestapo in Vienna.

He was also allowed to marry by proxy; Schuschnigg's brother stood in for him at the small ceremony, and Schuschnigg only learned afterward that his marriage to Vera had taken place.[17] The Nazis granted Schuschnigg conjugal visits, initially one hour each week, and soon twice a week. During the two-year period when he was jailed in the Munich Gestapo facility, Vera lived nearby in a rooming house with friends, and there she gave birth to a daughter. Maria von Schuschnigg was born in a hospital nearby.[18]

From Munich, Schuschnigg was taken, together with Vera and Maria, to a small town near Berlin—Oranienburg.[19] There the Sachsenhausen concentration camp would be their home for most of the rest of the war. Sachsenhausen was originally the Oranienburg concentration camp for political prisoners. It changed to house many others, particularly Soviet prisoners. While not a mass extermination camp (there were only six of those), nor a slave labor variant such as Auschwitz I, where the goal was to work prisoners to death, still, more than 100,000 would die at Sachsenhausen.

On arrival, they were greeted by the cruel hoax of the Third Reich, "*Arbeit Macht Frei*" (Work Sets You Free), forged in metal letters on the camp gate. However, the reality of Nazi evil was plainly visible to the left beyond the gate—a huge smokestack over the crematorium, a monstrous tube looming over the camp behind whose walls "reigns gray, nameless misery."[20] This towering cylinder was to be the only portal out of the camp for many prisoners who were herded inside the gate to endure the horrors of Sachsenhausen and then murdered.

Schuschnigg was not bundled into the barracks with the prisoners. He and Vera and the baby were housed in a blockhouse at the wall of the camp—one of four such small quarters called the Special Prisoners Colony. Kurti was sent to live at the home of friends and attend school in Munich.[21] Occasionally, Schuschnigg caught sight of one of the other special prisoners. He recognized Prince Philip of Hesse from a distance, but he was forbidden to talk to anyone in the camp except guards.

As the Russian front took its toll, Sachsenhausen's mass murders would increase; the smokestacks of even these camps eventually became such a constant spout of human ashes that camp commandants expressed concern for the health of the baby. One Nazi camp commandant at another camp cautioned Schuschnigg that crematorium odors became especially awful once the wind began to blow in their direction.

For the inmates living on the other side of the wall, the Schuschniggs could only hear the sounds of brutalization and killing—frequent outbursts, a warning shouted by a guard, then floodlights followed by machine gun and rifle fire, screams of a prisoner, and then silence.[22]

The citizens of Oranienburg lived just over the walls of the camp, and they, too, were treated to the unmistakable evidence that their village was an involuntary host to great atrocities. The smell from the crematorium reached them as well. Work crews of camp prisoners went each day to work for local businesses in Oranienburg for the entire war, and their cryptic comments and sad gestures were undoubtedly enough to spread the secret of the executions that surrounded the town.

The threat of his own execution dulled with the passage of time, and life for Schuschnigg became much better than the terror practiced on him in Vienna.[23] Nazi precision listed Schuschnigg himself as a special prisoner using a pseudonym for him, but Vera and Maria, whom they called Sissi, were simply inmates of some undefined sort. Vera was free to leave the camp and go to Berlin where Schuschnigg's brother Artur and his wife lived.[24]

Sachsenhausen's Obersturmbannführer Anton Kaindl treated Schuschnigg and his family rather decently. His lenity did not go unnoticed by the guards who followed his example; they often checked Vera only perfunctorily, enabling her to smuggle the occasional treat back into the blockhouse. Kurti was also able to visit on several occasions and once spent a week in Sachsenhausen with his family, learning the horror endured by the prisoners inside.[25]

Schuschnigg also began to write again. As the months went on, he committed to paper candid comments about the Nazi experience. He concealed his notes sufficiently that the pages he drafted successfully eluded the searches conducted of their quarters. He seemed to have foreseen some fate that made him willing to risk death, for if his manuscript were discovered and it gave rise to a serious complaint to the Gestapo, the consequences would be swift and grim. He seems to have kept his diary as some symbol of hope, as proof to himself that he would live and tell what had happened. Why he would take such a risk and persist through one dangerous encounter after another has never been clear, but he continued periodically to write, and he kept these writings through the war.[26]

Teenager Kurti Schuschnigg was left to face the demands being placed on all young men who fell under the rule of the Third Reich. Many like Kurti were pushed and prodded to join the Hitler Youth. Kurti continued to ignore that order.[27]

★ ★ ★

Inside Germany, the reactions to the Anschluss were not universally the heartfelt approvals displayed by the Nazis. In certain circles, the reactions were very mixed. Although most Germans were euphoric, a powerful group of generals, alarmed at Hitler's daredevil lawlessness, were gathering together in clandestine meetings; soon they had begun planning to take the Führer down before he dragged their country into another catastrophic war.

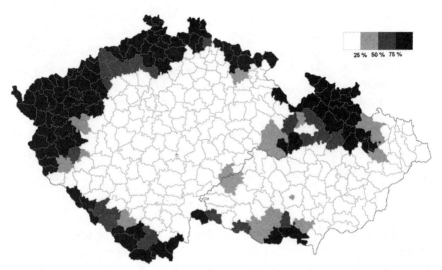

25 % 50 % 75 %

The German-speaking areas of the Czechoslovakian Sudetenland.
Source: Wikimedia, Creative Commons. Author: Fest.

Several of the top German officers understood the reality of Hitler's megalomania, and this small group foresaw tragic consequences for Germany. They believed that a war commenced by Germany against the great powers was a fool's adventure and, ultimately, a doomed one. They saw Hitler's unshakeable belief in his ability to conquer all in his path for what it was, the manic fantasy of an unstable narcissist hyped by a propaganda apparatus of extraordinary dishonesty.

As Hitler zeroed in on his next target, the Sudetenland of Czechoslovakia, a group of Wehrmacht generals held several surreptitious meetings at the Berlin apartment of a top Abwehr official, General Hans Oster, a German patriot and a friend of General Kurt von Schleicher whom Hitler had killed in July 1934.[28] Oster hated Hitler, and he had a special hatred of the Schutzstaffel (SS).[29] The group numbered major Wehrmacht figures, including former army chief of staff General Ludwig Beck and General Franz Halder, among Oster's coconspirators.[30] Also included were Hjalmar Schacht, the head of the Reichsbank; Hans Gisevius; and Carl Fredrick Goerdeler.[31] Some conspirators preferred to kill Hitler; others felt arrest and trial would be preferable. But one way or another they were planning to put an end to Hitler. General Halder had come close to doing it on his own; on several occasions, he had carried a pistol into meetings with Hitler, torn over whether to use it on the spot.

Once it became evident that another conquest was at hand, these conspirators planned to execute a coup in September 1938 as soon as Britain awoke from slumber and declared war over Hitler's threat to Czechoslovakia. Their plans were hashed out on September 15; everything depended, however, on Britain declaring war.[32] The conspirators met again on September 20 at Oster's Berlin apartment to finalize their plan[33] and pass it along to British intelligence before Prime Minister Chamberlain's Munich Conference. Oster's emissary, Ewald von Kleist, told the British that if Britain and France stood up to Hitler over the Nazi demand to annex the Sudetenland, the German generals would overthrow Hitler.[34]

General Beck supported kidnapping Hitler and putting him on trial; but Beck viewed assassination as murder. Hans Oster argued that Hitler must be killed because he had so many fanatical followers that a jailed Hitler would still be stronger than his opponents.[35] Oster became the center of the conspiracy, facilitating the many highly secret contacts necessary to bring like-minded Germans together without risk of discovery.[36]

Jacob Beam, a young American diplomat assigned to Berlin, had a German contact who was opposed to Hitler. This man, a source of sorts, Erwin Respondek, was a little known economist and a Catholic, and he despised the Nazi movement.[37] Respondek was eager to feed information about the Nazis to the United States.[38]

One evening in the second week of September 1938 at the height of the Sudetenland crisis, Respondek invited Beam to his home for dinner. There, Beam was joined by the Jesuit priest Professor P. Friederich Muckerman who so rattled Hitler that he complained about Muckerman and his disloyalty during the Berchtesgaden meeting.[39] Another guest was a Luftwaffe colonel hostile to Hitler.

The conversation at the dinner was surprisingly unguarded. Respondek and his German guests discussed a contingency plan they attributed to chief of staff General Halder and other senior officers. Their plan was to launch a coup against Hitler if he were to provoke a war over Czechoslovakia. Beam filed a report that night with the US State Department, describing the conversation. Beam later rose to become the US ambassador to Czechoslovakia as well as to Poland and the Soviet Union, and that night he wrote that the plan of the senior officers, as understood by Respondek and the Luftwaffe colonel, was to assassinate Hitler if his Sudetenland aggression caused war.[40]

★ ★ ★

Most Czechoslovakians other than the Sudeten Germans were horrified to learn that their nation, the one democratic nation east of the Rhineland, was about to become the next victim and that it might be sacrificed to the Nazis as Austria had been in a futile effort by France and Britain to save themselves. But the nations of Europe still did not see that Hitler's plans included many more victims. As Schuschnigg later wrote, this was a serial conquest with more pieces yet to be taken: "The invasion of Austria started a chain reaction."[41] It led to the Munich Agreement and the invasions of Czechoslovakia, Poland, Denmark, Norway, Belgium, Holland, and the rest.[42]

Hitler greeting British prime minister Neville Chamberlain at the Berghof, September 15, 1938.
Source: Wikipedia, Creative Commons. Bundesarchiv_Bild_183-H12478.

When confronted by the Nazi demands for the Sudetenland only months after the Anschluss of Austria, Britain's "splendid isolation" was for a third time more than matched by France's ugly chaos.[43] Leaders of both nations were ready to grant Hitler's demands in the desperate hope that he would then cease growling and lapse into a friendly purr.[44]

The taking of Czechoslovakia started in earnest on September 14; there were sporadic revolts by Sudeten Germans prodded by Germany with weapons supplied by Germany. The revolts were quickly put down by the police. It was far from the bloodshed depicted in the lies that filled the headlines of German newspapers; there were no atrocities being committed against Germans by Czechs as the propaganda claimed.[45] Hitler, as planned, used these Nazi-provoked events to exaggerate the mistreatment of Germans in Czechoslovakia.

On September 26, 1938, Hitler delivered an alarming speech at the Sportpalast. He was unusually excited, shrieking that he would have the Sudetenland by October 1, but he promised that this was his last territorial demand in Europe.[46] By the time of the final meeting at Munich at which the Sudetenland agreement was signed, Chamberlain had already signaled his capitulation on the Sudetenland to Hitler. Chamberlain told Hitler on

September 15, 1938, when the two met at Berchtesgaden, that he, and likely Britain's government, would agree to Germany taking Czechoslovakia's Sudetenland.[47] Williams Shirer learned that the capitulation was so obvious to others that "the Hungarians and the Poles had been down to Berchtesgaden [on September 20, 1938] to demand, like jackals, their share of the Czech spoils."[48] Hungary received some Czechoslovakian territory, and Poland did as well.

By then, there remained little chance that Britain would do what only Britain was able to do. One respected British official who was not on board with Chamberlain's program was Colonel Frank Mason-MacFarlane, the British military attaché to Berlin. Mason-Mac, as he was affectionately known, was against appeasement, and he harbored no illusions about the perfidy of Hitler. Mason-Mac's robust personality and captivating earnestness lent his outranked opinions greater force than his station demanded. His blunt views were startling but persuasive, though at complete odds with the appeasement orthodoxy of his bosses. He famously quipped before the Munich Conference that he had been musing that he should simply shoot Hitler himself for the sake of world peace.[49]

Another, Lord Cadogan, delivered a strong dose of the anti-appeasement reasoning of Churchill and Leo Amery to Lord Halifax on the very eve of Munich. Surprisingly, it was not without effect; Cadogan's fervent spiel produced a sudden conversion of Halifax. The foreign secretary confessed the next morning to Cadogan that he had spent a sleepless night over those views, and at last he agreed with them.[50] This conversion, however, was tragically late; and it seems to have been without lasting effect. Chamberlain was still in charge, and he had foolishly decided that he could trust Hitler. More astonishing, he convinced himself that he had established some level of control over Hitler.[51]

Hitler and Chamberlain also met on September 22, at Bad Godesberg, and this encounter fairly proclaimed the imminent end of Czechoslovakia—Chamberlain agreed that he would personally deliver to Czechoslovakian president Edvard Beneš Hitler's demand that he must hand over the Sudetenland by October 1.[52] After that, the giveaway at the historic Munich Conference seemed quite predictable, even anticlimactic.

By the end of the Munich Conference, after the announcement was made on September 30, Édouard Daladier appeared to be a broken man.[53] Hitler had now firmed up his assessment of the weakness of the British and French leaders; privately, he called them "worms."[54]

Chamberlain saw his work as a great political victory, and he would tolerate no interference that might mar his triumphant return to London. He imperiously informed Beneš that if he refused to approve the Munich Agreement allowing Germany to annex the Sudetenland, Britain and France would not come to his assistance upon a German invasion.[55] As high-handed as it was, forcing Czechoslovakia to forfeit the Sudetenland, roughly two-thirds of its border area, quickly proved to be terribly counterproductive.

The day after they met at Munich and agreed that Hitler could have the Sudetenland, Chamberlain and Hitler issued an additional joint communiqué about their separate so-called nonaggression pact. Chamberlain sighed with vast relief and puffed the worthless signature as a triumph; yet, he had obtained Hitler's signature on a paper saying nothing more substantial than that their peoples desired never to go to war against each other.[56] That was the document Chamberlain so famously brandished before the British public as he landed at Heston and, again, that night waved to a relieved crowd outside 10 Downing Street. This meant, he crowed, "peace for our time."[57] With far greater realism, Churchill condemned the Munich sellout ("We have sustained a total, unmitigated defeat").[58]

Churchill also foresaw what else this capitulation meant. On August 13, 1938, he wrote to David Lloyd George:[59] "England has been offered a choice between war and shame. She has chosen shame, and will get war."[60]

★ ★ ★

When the plotting German generals and their fellow conspirators saw that spectacle of appeasement, they had no place to go. Everything had depended on Britain taking a stand. Without Britain, no one among them was willing to take action against Hitler, and there was no conspiracy left.[61]

Sometime later, after the Munich appeasement, Jacob Beam cautiously raised the subject of the coup plans he had observed with Respondek; he asked what had become of the plot. Respondek said it was abandoned when Britain and France tamely accepted Hitler's demand.[62] After the war, General Halder and other senior generals told the story of the planned coup just as Respondek had reported it to Beam.[63] Historians can only speculate what might have happened if Chamberlain and Daladier had resisted Hitler. Skeptical historians argue that the plotters were unlikely to have dared to attack him, that none did revolt until July 1944, and only a few even then. Moreover, Hitler had bribed many career officers and surely felt he had nothing to fear from that group.

After the Munich Agreement, President Edvard Beneš feared assassination, and when Hitler demanded he resign, he promptly complied. On October 5, Beneš fled to London. For the next few weeks, Beneš was succeeded temporarily by General Jan Syrový, but Syrový was then succeeded by the chief justice of the Supreme Court, Emil Hácha, a man who was glaringly inexperienced. Though an intellectual and a highly distinguished lawyer, Hácha was chosen as president because he had played no role in the Munich appeasement catastrophe. He also, however, had a very bad heart and, by 1939, less than robust mental faculties.

President Emil Hácha of Czechoslovakia.
Source: Public Domain. Wikipedia, Creative Commons.

To finish Czechoslovakia completely, Hitler dusted off the dramatic script he had used on Schuschnigg, and he summoned President Hácha to Berlin. On March 14, 1939, Hácha traveled by train to meet with Hitler. The Führer made him wait for several hours while he finished watching a movie, but as soon as Hitler chose to receive him, he subjected Hácha to a Berchtesgaden-style manic tirade. Unlike the shaken but stoic Schuschnigg, under Hitler's browbeating Hácha suddenly collapsed to the floor. To the startled Nazis, he appeared to have died on the spot.

Joachim von Ribbentrop and Göring were alarmed, and they called for first aid. Hitler's physicians rushed in and injected Hácha with vitamins, and he revived. No sympathy was generated by Hácha's apparent heart attack, however. Göring and Ribbentrop coldly propped him up and ordered him to phone Prague to deliver instructions that the Czechoslovakian troops should not resist the Nazi invasion. With the way cleared, the Nazis invaded Czechoslovakia—what they called the "rump" of Czechoslovakia—on March 15, 1939; they met no resistance or any welcoming crowd.

Hitler entered Prague with great fanfare. He proceeded to Hradcany Castle, strode into Beneš's office, settled himself into Beneš's chair, and signed a proclamation that Czechoslovakia had ceased to exist. Shortly, Slovakia gave in also, and it, too, ceased to exist.[64]

★ ★ ★

To Americans, the calculus was that the Atlantic was so wide that, absent an American expedition to Europe, the United States could avoid the looming war. Yet America also had unstated premises underlying this belief, which many Americans poorly understood. American isolationism was grounded in confidence in the strength of the French army and the British navy. These beliefs were objectively justified, for France was well armed and the Royal Navy unequaled. Moreover, the American public seemed to appreciate how ill equipped and undermanned was the entire US military.

Despite the American attitude prior to Munich, when Britain and France sold out Czechoslovakia, American sentiment broke sharply against both countries, only adding to America's isolationism. Anthony Eden was troubled by America's reaction. When he visited the United States, he became aware that, behind their isolationism, Americans had also concluded that mighty Britain must have lost its nerve.[65]

★ ★ ★

The unimpressive, clumsy man at the next table in the Munich restaurant erupted with a very loud laugh and boorishly slapped his thigh at something one of his uniformed Nazi tablemates said. His laugh made him wobble, and he nearly tumbled out of his seat; but he was able to wrestle his chair to keep from falling foolishly to the floor. Maria von Trapp and Georg, sitting a few feet away, then saw the thin wisp of hair flip across his forehead above his odd, familiar moustache. They both recognized him—it was the Führer himself.[66]

There, in a restaurant inside an art gallery at the English Garden in Munich, the tyrant appeared as innocuous as men can be when stripped of the pomp of a Göbbels extravaganza. Inconceivable, she thought, that this drab individual was the heart and soul of the dreaded Nazis. Yet there he was, unrefined, eating an ordinary lunch with six of his military, and by happenstance sitting right beside the table she and her husband had chosen. Stunned that the Hitler they saw off guard lacked any hint of charisma and seemed pedestrian and awkward, they watched for some forty minutes the antics of his gaggle of uniformed street types.

Was this the real Adolf Hitler? And was the formidable menace who threatened Schuschnigg at Berchtesgaden a mere actor delivering a performance? Since the war, some observers have reported that Hitler in private was quite a surprise. He spoke with a strong Austrian accent.[67] He was a man who, during conversation, would not look at you steadily but only glance your way on occasion as he spoke. He could, moreover, be entirely colorless.[68] Even earlier, a correspondent who had spent time interviewing Hitler in 1931 described him in similar terms: "He is formless, almost faceless, a man whose framework seems cartilaginous, without bones. He is inconsequential and voluble; ill poised and insecure. He is the very prototype of the little man."[69]

The von Trapps were in Munich that day in 1938 performing, trying to earn enough from their newfound career of singing to support their still growing family as they struggled to come to grips with the loss of their beloved Austria. Only a few days later, the von Trapps' hopes for a peaceful future in their captured homeland suddenly disappeared. Officials of the Reich contacted the family and simultaneously summoned them into three Nazi entanglements they could not in good conscience endure. First, as a naval commander, Georg was called by the Reich to assume command of a new Nazi submarine, and he smelled that this signaled war. To the proud Austrian, fighting on behalf of the detested Nazis was utterly unthinkable.[70] Next, his son, Rupert, a newly graduated physician, was told to accept a posting to a hospital that was now understaffed because of the sudden thinning of Austria's skilled Jewish doctors.[71] Third, however, was a booking any ambitious entertainers would ordinarily die for—an invitation to sing at the birthday celebration for Hitler.[72] They had received two prior invitations from the Nazi Party to perform but had politely begged off. This would, if accepted, launch the von Trapp Family Singers to new fame and secure an unending flood of lucrative engagements. They would be set for life. But that life would be a Nazi existence of some sort. A rejection, the third in a row, was never going to be viewed as polite.

Maria and Georg discussed all this with the children, and they all cast their votes for the family's future path—they decided unanimously to try to flee. An escape from Austria, now a part of Nazi Germany, and from the naval and hospital directives awaiting their response, would be dangerous and difficult. At best, the family would have to abandon their home and all they owned and forfeit a lifetime of family and friends. If caught, well, they had seen enough brutality against Austrian Jews and Nazi enemies to fear the worst, but they hatched a plan of escape. They would pretend they were off to a day of hiking in Tyrol—but in the south Tyrol that lay in northern Italy, just a short distance over the border.

Maria, Georg, and the children showed up at the Salzburg train station in Tyrolean hiking garb, carrying nothing that would hint of an extended stay. Though the crackling drama of Nazi border officials squinting suspiciously at the children one after another never occurred, a gut-wrenching anxiety surely accompanied the now broke and unemployed fugitive von Trapp Family Singers. The tension and stress was especially worrisome for Maria. She was pregnant. The train they boarded slowly clattered away from the station and took them safely toward the border, and as it crossed into Italy, the family von Trapp left the Third Reich behind.[73] It was just in time. The border was closed the next day; thereafter, no one was permitted to leave Ostmark without full Nazi processing.

The family had one promising contact. An American impresario had recently encouraged them to seek bookings in America, and once settled in Italy, they made contact with him and asked for an advance that would pay for ocean passage to America. The agent came through for his new act. Maria, Georg, and their many children sailed away from the rumbling war clouds of Europe toward an entirely new life and a thrilling greeting by the Statue of Liberty. Within months, Europe was engulfed in the worst war in history.

★ ★ ★

Once the war began in earnest, and quickly consumed more and more manpower, many Hitler Youth became soldiers and sailors, and Kurti found that military service was not optional; he was conscripted, at age 17 in 1943, into the German navy and sent for training to a naval academy.[74] Soon he was serving as a cadet engineer on a German heavy cruiser out of Hamburg, the *Prinz Eugen*.[75] The ill-fated ship was under way at sea when it was spotted by an Allied aircraft and bombed. Its steam turbine exploded, and Kurti was badly injured. He suffered a torn lung and burns. The ship made it to port, and Kurti was hospitalized. But the *Prinz Eugen* was out of commission for months, in need of time-consuming repairs.[76]

When Kurti regained his health, he learned that the *Prinz Eugen* was still undergoing repairs, and he discovered certain weaknesses in the navy's procedures for reassignment. He was able to slip into an odyssey, moving around, eluding a new assignment. He showed up at one military installation after another pretending to seek assistance getting back to his ship. Helped along by inefficiencies in German military administration, the navy never succeeded in reassigning him to a duty station. He made what looked like efforts to return to his ship, but he repeatedly never quite made it.[77] Gradually, he converted these efforts into a determined search for a way to escape Germany.

· 12 ·

The "Dirty Business": Execution

"Shoot them all!"

—Adolf Hitler

$\mathscr{T}$hroughout the war, the Gestapo imprisoned many deposed heads of conquered governments, as well as European nobles and political opponents. The Nazis' precise plans for such special prisoners as Schuschnigg and others are difficult to determine. The one order that was abundantly clear to the Schutzstaffel (SS) was that the fate of these prisoners was entirely up to the Führer—only Hitler could decide how and when to dispose of them.

The Gestapo sent several of these former heads of government to Sachsenhausen. Schuschnigg was one of the most prominent, but he was not the only major figure sent there. Unbeknown to Schuschnigg, very close to his blockhouse, the Gestapo imprisoned Paul Reynaud, the former premier of France, who was arrested by order of Philippe Pétain and turned over to the Gestapo, then held at Sachsenhausen from November 1942 to May 1943. The special prisoners were kept in separate quarters and isolated from each other. Conversation with others was forbidden at Sachsenhausen, and Schuschnigg and Reynaud apparently never saw each other despite five months in the same camp. Reynaud, like Schuschnigg, was Catholic, but no clergy or Masses were available. Moreover, Reynaud had not risen to high office until more than a year after Schuschnigg was arrested, so Schuschnigg may not have recognized him.

Another prominent French figure, Georges Mandel, was there also. Mandel was a former deputy and minister of the interior in France, as well as an outspoken critic of the Nazis. Other French special prisoners were held in various other locations and were moved from time to time. They included former premiers Édouard Daladier and Leon Blum and generals Maurice

Gamelin and Maxime Weygand, leaders of France during its final days; several of them had engaged in bitter clashes with each other, heaping blame upon each other as France crumbled under the German blitzkrieg.

In May 1943, Paul Reynaud was taken to Schloss Itter—a paradise, in his view, compared to Sachsenhausen.[1] Mandel was treated very differently, more like a pawn, and he was moved elsewhere in 1944.

Blum had been elected French premier in 1936, and he appointed Daladier minister of national defense and war.[2] Blum was succeeded by Daladier, who served as premier three times.[3] As he took office after Blum on April 10, 1938, Daladier did not believe France was up to strength to oppose Germany.[4]

Daladier would be most remembered for sacrificing Czechoslovakia's Sudetenland to Hitler at the September 1938 Munich Conference. While Chamberlain believed that sellout had appeased Hitler, Daladier harbored no such illusion. His performance in that doomed effort was coldly realistic. He needed to buy time, and he felt this sacrifice of a portion of an ally's country would buy him time to rearm and better defend his own.[5] Although much of Britain hailed Chamberlain, Daladier's role in the Sudetenland crisis was seen in France as a terrible show of weakness, and he resigned as premier in March 1940. His successor was a bitter enemy, Paul Reynaud.[6] Reynaud cynically or pragmatically appointed Daladier to his government despite their roiling personal and political differences. Daladier became Reynaud's minister of national defense and war. Despite detesting each other, Premier Reynaud appreciated that Daladier possessed military logistical skills. Yet, they disagreed in their evaluation of the most impactful decision they had to make—the choice for army chief of staff.

Daladier was a fan of the aged incumbent, General Maurice Gamelin, and it was a point of personal pride with Daladier that his view of Gamelin must be respected. Gamelin remained chief of staff until the German invasion showed he had completely miscalculated. Hitler's invasion chose the same route that had so surprised the French army in 1914, and the embarrassment of France being fooled twice by the same trick destroyed Gamelin's chances to retain command even amid the ongoing blitzkrieg.[7] Gamelin was woefully slow in comprehending the German plan.[8] He blamed his subordinates and dismissed some of them. Reynaud fired Gamelin himself a week later.[9]

Daladier smarted; he treated the firing of Gamelin as a humiliating affront. He railed against Reynaud and intensified the bitterness of their mutual hatred.[10] Reynaud then made a poor choice of his own; he appointed as Gamelin's emergency successor General Maxime Weygand, even older than and as feckless and slow as Gamelin. Few generals have urged surrender quite as readily as General Weygand. The collapse and surrender of France was only weeks away.[11]

Daladier and others decided to escape or relocate to French Morocco, but they were soon constrained and detained by the Vichy government run by Marshal Philippe Pétain and former premier Pierre Laval. The Vichy French officials sent Daladier and his cohorts back to be prosecuted by the Vichy government. They were charged with treason and put on trial in France; however, their trial was suspended, and they were incarcerated by the French administration. After the Allies invaded North Africa in late 1942, Daladier and the others who had been charged with him were transferred to the custody of the Reich and held at Buchenwald. Several other French special prisoners joined them, including former premier Leon Blum. Several other deposed European leaders were also held at various camps.[12]

The quarters allotted to these French special prisoners at Buchenwald were separate from the grim confines in which camp victims were brutalized, worked to death, and murdered. The French were housed in separate rooms and were allowed after dinner to gather together and drink and smoke.[13] But their prospects began to seem ominous in spring 1943 as the war in the east turned badly against Germany.

In April 1943, the Nazis decided to gather up the captured high-ranking French officials and generals and relocate them to Schloss Itter in Bavaria, very near Berchtesgaden. Blum was kept behind to be sent to a place of special detention. This treatment of Blum and Georges Mandel was a very troubling sign.[14]

When Reynaud arrived at Schloss Itter, after enduring bleak isolation in the curtilage of the Sachsenhausen crematorium, he was very relieved to be in such far better conditions. The presence of old French colleagues, however, was not a plus. Reynaud's bitter enemy Daladier was a prisoner at Schloss Itter; they were granted the dubious privilege of being allowed to fraternize, so Reynaud could not avoid the daily hostility Daladier exuded in his presence.

The group at Schloss Itter now included General Weygand as well. Weygand had joined the Vichy government after the French surrender and remained free until Hitler ordered his arrest after the Allied invasion of North Africa. Generals Gamelin and Weygand, once colleagues who worked well together, had fallen to clashing repeatedly; they were now housed together but were implacable enemies.[15]

Leon Blum was singled out for different treatment. He was detained at Buchenwald until the approach of the Allies; then he was moved to Dachau and then to Tyrol, joining the group of special prisoners taken there. The moves added to the awful feeling that the Germans were not intending to spare any prisoners.

★ ★ ★

Kurti's odyssey, meanwhile, had become a cleverly evasive quest to find some way out of Germany. Finally, he was told of a dangerous escape route in the mountains, one that was heavily patrolled by SS but sprinkled with partisans who could show the way, and at long last, with the help of those partisans, he made it through a wooded mountain pass to the safety of Switzerland.[16]

* * *

Schuschnigg and Vera spent several long years in captivity, lurching from depression to hope. They had been given a radio by the Sachsenhausen camp commandant, and Schuschnigg found "unspeakable solace in music" listening to Mozart, Schubert, and Beethoven. Their hopes were growing as the course of the war slowly ground Germany toward defeat. Schuschnigg's diary entry for June 6, 1944, terse as it was, still shouted with enough transparent joy that it might have gotten him executed if discovered: "*Invasion!* The Allies have landed in Normandy."[17] And by 1945, they knew that it was just a matter of time for the Third Reich as they listened surreptitiously to the forbidden BBC broadcasts, thrilled at news of the Allied advances toward Germany from west and from east.[18]

They also listened to the increasingly rare and far more subdued speeches of Hitler.[19] Having seen and heard Hitler in highest provocation, Schuschnigg was fascinated that, by 1943, Hitler's speeches were bland; Hitler was speaking without the stimulus of an audience, and the speeches fell flat.[20] Although the war was being lost in Russia, Hitler made no mention whatever of Russia.[21]

The end of the war was coming closer. Schuschnigg and Vera began hearing the sound of distant bombs and could see the far-off night sky aglow, and they knew the Allies were pulverizing Berlin itself.[22] But just when the glimmer of hope had begun, Commandant Kaindl informed Schuschnigg that he and Vera and the baby were to be moved away from Sachsenhausen. Every such change struck a note of terror that something awful was in the works.

Throughout the war, prisoners like Schuschnigg, Daladier, and others of exceptionally high rank could cling to the hope that the Nazis' intention might be to use them for prisoner swaps for high-ranking Nazis captured by the Allies. But as the defeat of Germany became clear, such exchanges became moot. In their place, revenge executions began.[23]

Schuschnigg asked if they could be spared this move, but Anton Kaindl wistfully replied that he himself wished that he could leave this doomed location. Sachsenhausen had been a camp in which many thousands of Russian prisoners of war were brutally executed. It was clear that the German soldiers in the Berlin sector knew that they were virtually certain to be overrun sometime soon by the Red Army, a soldiery already notorious for vicious reprisals, torture, and rape. None of this was explained to Schuschnigg; he was left entirely in the dark concerning their destination or the fate that awaited them at their final place.[24]

They were taken with other special prisoners to nearby Berlin, where they spent a night in the Gestapo prison on Prinz Albrecht-Strasse, just blocks from the underground bunker in which Hitler now cowered awaiting what would soon be the utter destruction of much of Berlin. The next day, they and twenty-five other prisoners of some note were taken to the dreaded Flossenbürg camp. They were still strictly forbidden to talk en route, but Schuschnigg recognized some of those in his group.

One fellow prisoner he did not recognize was the deposed head of German intelligence, former Abwehr chief Admiral Wilhelm Canaris, who had insisted on basic standards of civilized conduct and, as a result, became a hated enemy of Reinhard Heydrich and Heinrich Himmler. He was now a target of allegations of treason. Whether Canaris recognized Schuschnigg is not known.

Schuschnigg, however, did recognize the former head of the central bank, Hjalmar Schacht, and must have wondered just what Schacht, a banker and once a financier of Hitler's revival of the collapsed German economy during the mid-1930s, had done to upset the Führer. He could not have known Schacht's role in the conspirators' meetings where a coup was once planned to topple or kill the Führer.

★ ★ ★

Upon their arrival at Flossenbürg, a terrifying announcement greeted Schuschnigg. The Gestapo called for an overnight search. Their meager bags were confiscated. His contained the hidden wartime diary, and the Gestapo was certain to find provocative notes he had written that could cause them all to be executed. The next morning, sleepless, he winced as the footsteps came unmistakably directly to their cell. He cursed himself for the fate his writings were about to inflict on his wife and daughter: "I thought that was the end."[25] Gestapo agents opened the cell, pushed the bags inside, glanced at Schuschnigg, and then turned and left.

Vera's bag was a mess from being rifled. His was neat and undisturbed. The Gestapo search had somehow simply overlooked his bag and missed the notes. Schuschnigg realized, however, that he now had no way to discard the diary, and further searches might be conducted at any stop.[26]

The prisoners were packed on vehicles and, on April 8, 1945, were sent off to Dachau. They were unnerved that the size of their party of prisoners had decreased. Hjalmar Schacht was still with the group; Admiral Canaris, however, was not. The day after Schuschnigg and the group left Flossenbürg, Canaris and several others were summarily executed. The sudden, unexplained drop in numbers at such a murderous camp as Flossenbürg may have dampened the relief Schuschnigg had just experienced over his diary. The mingling of these varied special prisoners with each other was also to give rise to some confusion in later reports about their fates.

★ ★ ★

On April 10, 1945, Schuschnigg and the prisoners arrived at Dachau, by then a dreaded name. Hjalmar Schacht told Schuschnigg and the others that he was sure the end had come for most of them.[27] The former German generals among them were now speaking more freely about Hitler with "bottomless hatred and contempt."[28] At Dachau, they were held for two weeks during which they could hear distant explosions as the front closed in.

Suddenly the special prisoners, once again, were ordered to move. As they were being taken away, they walked near 35,000 emaciated prisoners, all wearing the blue and white striped prison garb, suddenly being evacuated to begin their death march. A number were Austrians, and they recognized Schuschnigg. Some smiled and waved to him. As recognition of him spread, many turned toward him and gave silent respectful gestures. Thousands of hands slowly began to rise in quiet salute, a gesture of understanding or farewell, as they were taken away from Dachau on a march few were going to survive. Whatever this gesture was, to Schuschnigg their greeting was "the most impressive moment of all these years."[29]

★ ★ ★

The end would not be easy for any of the 140 South Tyrol special prisoners with whom Schuschnigg, Vera, and their daughter Sissi were sharing their fate. Theirs was to be a harrowing, dramatic climax to history's bloodiest war. These prisoners and other special prisoners—the French leaders held in Bavaria at Schloss Itter, Konrad Adenauer held in Germany—were all glowing remnants of the people who had opposed the Nazis, and they were the few remaining feasible targets on whom Hitler still had the power to take out his irrational hatred.

The special prisoners in Schuschnigg's group were a treasure trove of revenge for Hitler and the SS. They included three former prime ministers, two Russian generals, and a tempting lineup of officers from the armed forces of the Nazis' combat enemies. Prince Philip of Hesse was one of them. He had been dismissed from the Nazi Party largely due to his father-in-law, King Victor Emmanuel III, turning on Mussolini, and Il Duce remained a Hitler favorite after helping smooth the way for the Anschluss. Some of them, including Schuschnigg, were named in the most urgent Nazi execution list.[30]

These special prisoners, called *Prominenten*, moreover, were still in the clutches of the SS. In May, they were transported to Niederdorf in Italy's south Tyrol by an SS escort "armed to the teeth." It was surely no comfort to learn that the SS officer in charge of them was a former Buchenwald SS Untersturmführer who was "the commander of special liquidation squads for undesirable prisoners."[31] When at last they arrived at Niederdorf, the weary, terrified prisoners saw every indication that their extermination was at hand by SS guards who would not be likely to pass up their final chance to feast on such a tempting array of scores with whose blood they could mark their sensational final kills.[32] Perhaps most concerned were Schuschnigg, former Wehrmacht general Franz Halder, and Leon Blum, former prime minister of France.

★ ★ ★

Back in Berlin, the officer responsible for disposing of these prisoners, SS Obergruppenführer Gottlob Berger, hurried down the dusty steps into the claustrophobic underground Führerbunker to meet with the increasingly deranged Führer on the night of April 22, 1945. Hitler could feel the ground under him rumbling from Russian shells inexorably destroying the capital and his Thousand Year Reich. Berger could see that Hitler had badly deteriorated, and his shock was beyond anything he had expected. Hitler seemed a "broken man," seeing plots all around him as his own doom crept toward him.[33] Berger's SS was in overall charge of the two groups of special prisoners—Schuschnigg and the Tyrol prisoners and Daladier and the top echelon of France in Bavaria at Schloss Itter.

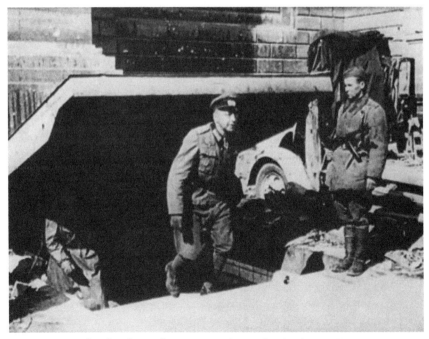

General Helmuth Weidling exiting Hitler's Führerbunker in May 1945.
Source: Alamy.

General Berger was about to travel that very night to deal with the special prisoners in the Tyrol. Concealing his discomfort at Hitler's deterioration, Berger tried to brief Hitler on the outbreaks of separatism that were occurring in Austria and Bavaria where these two special prisoner groups were held. He briefed Hitler on uprisings. Now, at this most desperate hour, a revolt may be under way in Hitler's own native Austria. Hitler could not forget how Schuschnigg had stirred Austrians against him with his "Red, White, Red" oration in 1938. But now, Schuschnigg had survived, and he was right there in Austria and could become a rallying point for a separatist coup.

Hitler nearly came unglued as Berger spoke to him; he virtually had a convulsion, then gave Berger the order to execute Schuschnigg and the prisoners: "His hand was shaking, his leg was shaking and his head was shaking; and all that he kept saying was: 'Shoot them all! Shoot them all!'"[34]

By then, it had been an incredible seven years since Schuschnigg and Hitler had clashed at the Berghof in Berchtesgaden. Hitler, however, obviously had not forgotten how Schuschnigg had gone back to Vienna and defied him, exposing the pretense that Austrians welcomed him and rallying them to vote for independence. Time had evidently not dimmed the Führer's hatred.

General Halder was another who had incurred Hitler's lasting contempt. Hitler often spoke of Halder as one of those who had failed him and betrayed him. More accurate was the view of some in the military that Halder was a symbol of Hitler's ineptitude as a military tactician. Halder had urgently advised that Wehrmacht armored cavalry and troops attack the British and French trapped at Dunkirk, but Hitler had rejected Halder's professional military advice and accepted Göring's empty boast that he could wipe out the 300,000 British and French from the air. The escape of so many troops was still being cited as one of the Führer's historic blunders by which he had brought upon himself the humiliating destruction he was now facing. Halder had surely never been a fan of the Nazis, but in fact, he was a worse enemy than Hitler knew; he contemplated relatively early in the war assassinating Hitler all by himself.

Former French prime minister Leon Blum had perhaps the most uncomfortable profile of all the prisoners. Blum was not only a three-time prime minister of hated France; Blum was a Jew. He had been held at Buchenwald for special detention when Daladier and others were sent to Schloss Itter, and now Blum was in the South Tyrol side by side with Schuschnigg.

A number of the other South Tyrol prisoners were special targets, too. A few were linked to the earlier attempts to assassinate the Führer. Among them were members of the family of Claus von Stauffenberg, the executed leader of the July 1944 Valkyrie plot that culminated in setting off a bomb in Hitler's Wolf's Lair headquarters in Rastenburg, East Prussia.

Vera herself had been given a blunt prediction from a Nazi guard. She had succeeded in hiding her jewelry and a painting throughout the war. The jewelry was discovered and taken from her days earlier by a Nazi guard at Dachau who told her, "Where you are going you won't need this anymore."[35]

Schuschnigg was exceedingly on edge; he had seen his life upended several times by the approach of Nazi boots. This could be the very worst of all. Chaos was not confined to Hitler's bunker. At Niederdorf, the prisoners could see that many of the SS, feeling the end at hand, were drunk and increasingly menacing. The fact that a number of the prisoners had their children with them did nothing to temper the menace exuded by the SS. With an enlarged group of prisoners, the SS had essentially given up trying to keep them from speaking to each other, and information now spread quickly. The warnings, sudden threats, the rumors, and the worried frowns of Blum and the others heightened the fear and intensified the sharp tightening of Schuschnigg's visceral core whenever footsteps approached.

★ ★ ★

En route from Dachau to Niederdorf, the prisoners had heard their next stop described ominously as their "Final Halt." Several prisoners reported that they had overheard enough to conclude that the SS was now all set to conduct the "dirty business"—to massacre them.[36]

The prisoners were briefly quartered in a hotel in the Niederdorf village square. The former Wehrmacht officers among the prisoners were permitted to stretch their legs outside the hotel, and one of them walked to the nearby SS headquarters in the town square.[37] He somehow succeeded in making a phone call from the SS office to a Wehrmacht friend in Bolzano and convinced him to send a small company of Wehrmacht to Niederdorf to confront and perhaps calm Friedrich Bader and his hard-drinking SS killers. Confusion and anxiety reached a peak when those Wehrmacht troops arrived and brandished machine guns in the town square of Niederdorf.

Before long, the prisoners were taken to a nearby hotel, a picturesque lodge on a lake. The Pragser-Wildsee had served as headquarters for several German generals. The generals were gone, and the unheated rooms had become very cold up in the mountains. As they waited in their rooms, the prisoners spent what the understating Schuschnigg conceded was "an anxious night."[38] Many of the prisoners still were nurturing hope, but it began to look more and more like self-delusion. With some, anxiety was turning to bouts of cold fear as more prisoners found it hard to deny that execution rumors might very well be true. Some of the former German officers had learned from one of the SS escorts that Berlin SS headquarters had issued the execution order that they had all feared.[39] They were unsure, however, whether they were all going to die. The written order would have the list of those slated for execution.[40]

Some of the prisoners saw a spark of hope when they heard that partisans in the area were seeking to help them escape in very small groups if any of them were willing to hazard a trek into the mountain wilderness. But many of the special prisoners were women and children, the families of the Valkyrie and other prisoners whose relatives were deemed traitors by affiliation. Even though one of the prisoners was an expert in escape, RAF group captain Harry Day, one of the leaders of "the Great Escape," those with families saw the demands of such an escape impossible for all but the toughest prisoners. Many of those prisoners were Germans, and they feared that the partisans were their natural enemies. How they could escape was in no way clear, and this dangerous option seemed impossible for Schuschnigg with a wife and a four-year-old daughter.

★ ★ ★

At the same time, the other group of special prisoners, the French dignitaries, was being held in the Bavarian Obersalzberg in the Castle Hotel Schloss Itter above the Brixental Valley. Those prisoners included not only Daladier, Reynaud, Gamelin, and Weygand but also Michel Clemenceau, the son of former premier Georges Clemenceau, and Charles de Gaulle's sister Marie-Agnès Cailliau. There, at Schloss Itter, the French prisoners were facing the same fate as the Tyrol special prisoners at Niederdorf. But unlike Schuschnigg and his fellow Tyrol prisoners, the Schloss Itter French prisoners were being guarded by a less fanatical company of Wehrmacht, soldiers who had lost their stomach for these final wasteful deaths.

Hitler's decision to execute Schuschnigg and the other special prisoners could have been carried out very quickly earlier in the war; however, by April 1945, communications lines and facilities from Berlin to South Tyrol had been bombed out, and many lines were compromised or distrusted.[41] Execution orders were being sent by hand delivery, and Hitler's peremptory order to kill the special prisoners had been delayed.

At last, the order reached a Gestapo command in Sillian, Austria, on May 1.[42] There, Gestapo chief Hans Philipp received the order, and it directed him to go immediately to Pragser-Wildsee, seize the prisoners, and take them back to a site in Austria to execute them. But Philipp stalled. His stalling most certainly was not out of mercy, but out of fear. He knew that the South Tyrol was highly dangerous and that he would have to fight for some distance to reach Pragser-Wildsee. The partisans had exploded into a general insurrection, and no one was safe. Not the prisoners, not even Philipp's armed company of hardened killers. They were executioners, not a skilled combat force.

SS chief Karl Wolff, on the other hand, believed he could gain fame by killing these luminaries, and he formulated his own plan to capture them.

Heinrich Müller, another SS leader, also had a shot at the special prisoners. He had earlier received a cryptic order to deal with the prisoners, but he had explicit orders to execute only one of them, a participant in a conspiracy to kill Hitler.[43]

Among the several death squads roaming Bavaria and the South Tyrol near Pragser-Wildsee and Schloss Itter were some of the Waffen SS, exceptionally brutal, loyal-to-the-end killers. Schloss Itter and the French leaders were more accessible to them. One small company of Waffen SS headed toward Schloss Itter, while others from Austria were headed to the Brenner Pass in the direction of Pragser-Wildsee. In the first days of May, a company of Waffen SS received the order to attack Schloss Itter and execute the French prisoners. To do the killing, a platoon of SS gunmen was chosen. The SS, however, in this final stage of the lost war, anticipated they would encounter resistance from their Wehrmacht colleagues over such senseless slaughter. Fanatical to the end, the SS began the climb through the woods up toward Schloss Itter to ambush the site and kill the French premiers and generals.

The Wehrmacht soldiers at Schloss Itter concluded that for them the war was over. They decided to turn for help to the Allies, to take advantage of the Allied advance, and to try to enlist Allied troops against the SS. They succeeded in making contact with the vanguard of the Allies pouring into Bavaria; they sent word to a small US Army tank platoon, which had reached the village of Kufstein near the mountain Schloss.[44]

The Wehrmacht soldiers asked the American tank platoon to help them. The Americans were highly suspicious, but the commander of the Wehrmacht troops at Schloss Itter succeeded in convincing the American tank platoon captain that he and his Wehrmacht soldiers were indeed going to fight the SS with or without the help of the Americans. They appeared determined, to salvage their own dignity, to save Daladier and the other French dignitaries. Once the American officer was told the names of the prisoners at Schloss Itter, he could see that the SS was about to commence a killing spree that would eliminate most of the leaders of prewar France. The Allied armies had by then uncovered the horror in the death camps, and they had learned that, even now, with defeat certain, the SS was forcing untold thousands of the prisoners into final death marches. The Reich was not just collapsing; it was calling down *Götterdämmerung* upon Europe.

The American soldiers quickly obtained approval and went to Schloss Itter to join forces with the Wermacht soldiers; together they fought a unique battle against the SS.[45] This previously unimaginable team of German and American soldiers opened fire and fought off the Waffen SS and saved all the

Schloss Itter special prisoners. There was one casualty of this final battle of the war in Europe—a Wehrmacht officer shot and killed by an SS sniper.[46]

★ ★ ★

The Tyrol prisoners were in a worse predicament—they were prisoners of the SS as they awaited death.[47] These final spasms of the war in Europe had raised Schuschnigg's own anxiety, but it had made his young son's alarm sky-rocket. He had no word of his father. Perhaps even more than the French, Schuschnigg was one of Hitler's most hated and most celebrated prisoners.[48] Seven years previously the political competition for Austria had come down to a choice of Schuschnigg or Hitler, and Hitler hated it that so many knew he would lose to Schuschnigg. That still fueled his hatred of Schuschnigg. And now, seven years later, the competition could resume. Soon Tyrol might be rallying to a cry to restore Schuschnigg to power.

Young Kurti was safe in Switzerland when a grim-faced Swiss diplomat came up to him, put his hand on his shoulder, and handed him a newspaper with a headline reading: "Schuschnigg assassinated."[49] The crushed young boy sat there in shock. Then he forced himself through his tears to read the details of the discovery of the charred corpse; he came to a line explaining how the body had been identified. The word "dentures" leapt off the page, and he jumped to his feet. He shouted, "It's not Father." Schuschnigg had all his teeth.

★ ★ ★

Although still alive, the chancellor and Vera remained in a precarious state. Having been driven for days in silence, thrown into one concentration camp, then whisked away only to be thrown into another, then guarded by Gestapo agents who joined the prisoners' caravan after Dachau; rescue seemed a pipe dream. They were 5,000 feet up in the south Tyrollean Alps, where the dark, foreboding crags of the dramatic gray Dolomites blocked the vista. The peaks were a symbol of hopeless captivity. They were so close to the war's end, so very near the freedom of the sky, yet still captives beneath rocky peaks that soared to the heavens and glared down on them like Neolithic avengers.[50] And the awful irony was that, to Schuschnigg, the Tyrol was home; this was the place he loved most. How exquisitely depressing that he and his family were about to be murdered in the beauty of the Puster Valley just as Tyrol was on the verge of liberation.

Despite their predicament, Schuschnigg clung to an unshakeable sense that the end of the war was very near. But the memory was still fresh that a similar hope had been dashed years earlier for the Russian czar, Nicholas II, and his wife and children when they were executed just before they could be rescued. Schuschnigg still had a small flicker of hope. He could permit himself to think this way—against all realism—for he had no idea that Hitler had ordered the special prisoners to be executed, as Lenin had ordered the executions of the Romanovs. However, before Schuschnigg's chronic optimism could award him even a single night of untroubled sleep, he received the grimmest confirmation. The Gestapo could be gratuitously vicious, often adding their own cruel twists to murders. They may have resented Schuschnigg's hopeful look. The SS man who could execute all the prisoners held in the South Tyrol without delay, Obersturmführer Friedrich Bader, was a ruthless killer.[51] Bader intended to execute the prisoners when circumstances called for it, believing that was within the authority he already possessed, and he expected that their mass execution would soon be called for. Bader singled out Schuschnigg and told him that he had an order, and he slowly unfolded Himmler's personal execution list in front of Schuschnigg. There, neatly printed, was his name and Vera's name. Thereafter, sleep was not easy. Now, he could only pray.

Some prisoners listened closely when they were near their captors. One prisoner heard Bader himself tell a guard that he would kill all the prisoners if Hitler was killed. Another prisoner overheard Bader confide to Edgar Stiller, Bader's adjutant, that he already had an order to kill them when the moment was right.[52] Any random air raid might provide cover for an abrupt mass murder.

Any basis to doubt their fate would soon be gone. One hopeful prisoner had found a stash of wine and shared it with an SS guard who engaged him in a loose-lipped debate. The prisoner said he doubted that the SS would really kill them with only days of combat remaining, but the drunk guard pulled out his trump card to end the debate—an order with an execution list. Schuschnigg was on that list. The drunk guard added his own assurance that the ruthless Bader of the SS was still in charge and would have no stomach to let them live.[53]

Another prisoner sat down to rest in a bus when a heavy-drinking SS guard plopped down next to him and passed out. The prisoner could see a document in the guard's disheveled tunic, and he nimbly extracted the paper from the guard's pocket. It was an execution list.[54]

The rumors were now hard evidence, and prisoners were too emotional to conceal what they were hearing. Learning that the word had spread, Stiller was worried they would attempt an escape. Bader, too, felt sure the prisoners would now try to escape, so he had Stiller announce that the SS was turning them over to the jurisdiction of the more restrained Wehrmacht.[55] However, eleven SS killers remained near the prisoners, and they were not hesitant to brandish their lethal threat. The risk of an abrupt execution remained high even as the Germans tried to lull the prisoners. Most prisoners knew the risk; indeed, they expected, despite the efforts to calm them, that the quieter Wehrmacht would, in the end, murder them as well.[56]

There were also many less-disciplined stragglers in the area who were likely to kill almost anyone they encountered. Some marauders in South Tyrol were near-crazed Nazi deserters. They were desperate to get rid of their uniforms and steal the clothes of a group like this to elude capture.[57] They would happily kill for life-saving costumes.

The SS, moreover, were becoming even more murderous as things deteriorated. Most dangerous of all were the eleven SS from Bader's company. They were hardened to killing, and they were openly seething with hatred of Schuschnigg and the prisoners, cursing them as traitors who had undermined Hitler.[58] These eleven were the best situated to kill the Schuschniggs since some were still quartered in Niederdorf and some others were at Pragser-Wildsee itself.

The threat from those SS was palpable; however, the prisoners knew there were also many partisans roaming the South Tyrol in lawless bands, and the various resistance groups were all wild cards. Groups of partisan gunmen repeatedly arrived at Pragser-Wildsee, and some went stomping into prisoners' rooms at random with guns drawn, terrifying the prisoners.[59] Some partisans were vengeful to some of the prisoners they found there, but they were sympathetic toward others. A number of partisans were communists who would love to find and kill the notorious anticommunist Schuschnigg, but so far only one partisan had visited him. That partisan leader offered to help Schuschnigg escape, but he rejected the suggestion due to the risk of capture and the likelihood of reprisals against the others. At least so far, hostile partisans had not yet come storming into their room.

A few of the prisoners viewed an escape or a miraculous rescue as their only hope, and they hatched escape plans. Several of the hardiest prisoners decided to slip away and climb down the mountain slopes through the cover of the forests to try to make contact with Allied forces near Bolzano. But Bolzano was sixty miles away. Worse, the escapees would have to make it through German lines to reach any Allied troops. But there was still bitter fighting in many zones, and the Allied progress had been slowed; they had not reached Bolzano as the prisoners hoped.[60]

Still, the execution order from the now-dead hand of Adolf Hitler had not yet claimed its first victim. But Schuschnigg had no doubt who that would be.

Just a few hours before the war in Europe thundered to its end, the alarming sound of heavy boots was suddenly echoing in the halls. Tall soldiers stood face to face with Schuschnigg. At their front was an officer, someone he had not seen before. He wore an unusual uniform. The rattled former chancellor could see that this officer was not SS; not Gestapo; not Wehrmacht. The young man said he was an officer in the United States Fifth Army, and he was here to tell Schuschnigg that he was free. Yes, free. Yes, for him the war was over. He and Vera and Sissi were going to live after all.[61]

★ ★ ★

Schuschnigg's exultation was breathlessly recorded in his hastily scribbled diary entry. He seemed, however, unsure just how close to death they had come. William Manchester and others concluded that the American troops arrived just as the Gestapo was about to execute Schuschnigg.[62] Others confirmed that the American advance had reached them just as guards were "on the point of executing the whole lot."[63] Schuschnigg's own recital of May 4, 1945, read: "At two o'clock this afternoon, alarm. The Americans! An American detachment takes over the hotel. We are free."[64] The war in Europe was over. He and Vera and Sissi, after years in the belly of the world's most notable beast, had survived Adolf Hitler and his Third Reich.[65]

★ ★ ★

It seems that the former Wermacht officers among the prisoners had injected just enough delay to save them.[66] The Wehrmacht, or the South Tyrolese Resistance Movement fighters,[67] had been successful in convincing the SS guards to cede control of the prisoners to the Wehrmacht when the Americans were almost there; that was just the added time needed for the Allies to make it to the hotel. When they arrived, the Wehrmacht were actually relieved, and they laid down their arms. Schuschnigg and his fellow prisoners were freed without bloodshed and without a shot being fired.[68]

Almost all the SS troops who had been guarding them vanished. They had the good luck to be, at war's end, in "Nazi Bolt Hole Number One," as the South Tyrol came to be called. This heavily German area gained a reputation for facilitating Nazi escapes. Surrounded by a helpful local population at Niederdorf, the SS guards decided not to wait. They knew the clock was ticking and that the Allies could appear at any moment, and they decided they had better not push their luck against their angered Wehrmacht colleagues. If they took the time to regain full control over the prisoners and murder them, they would risk capture by the Allies. In the process, they reluctantly abandoned the Reich's plans to execute the famous enemy heads of government on their final death list.

All special prisoners of the Tyrol group were rescued from the SS; exactly how it came about or who achieved it for them has been hard to determine. Schuschnigg later wrote that "contradictory stories about our liberation" were circulated.[69] It may have been the confluence of forces—the Allied advance in the Tyrol, the daring effort of some of the prisoners to escape and contact the Allies, decisions of some saner men who made up the officer corps of the Wermacht, and the efforts of the friendly cadres among the South Tyrol resistance fighters.

★ ★ ★

The mistaken story in the Swiss newspaper Kurti read turned out to be about the death and the remains of someone else—a top German officer. Much later, the corpse was identified as that of Admiral Canaris. Schuschnigg and Canaris had been in the same group of special prisoners transported together to Flossenbürg. After Schuschnigg and others were taken away to Niederdorf in Tyrol, the Nazis had executed Canaris, the former head of their Abwehr intelligence service.[70]

Young Kurti was soon bound for Italy to be reunited with his father, Vera, and Sissi.

★ ★ ★

Upon their liberation, the French and Russian special prisoners in the Tyrol group, as members of the Allied Powers, were free to leave for their homes. Axis Powers prisoners, which in the shambles of the war included Schuschnigg, were not. His history was, of course, well known to the American forces who freed him, and he was accordingly treated very well, but the many predicaments the Allies faced in the aftermath of Europe's greatest chaos made repatriation of Schuschnigg to his native Austria, and the repatriation of thousands of others, quite complicated. As a prisoner with a wife and small child, Schuschnigg was shuttled from Verona to Naples, then out temporarily to the Tyrrhenian Sea onto the beautiful Isle of Capri.

Schuschnigg wanted to return to Austria immediately, but postwar Vienna was not a comfortable place for an avowed anti-Marxist. Austria was carved up much like Germany for multiparty administration, with Tyrol largely under American administration. Vienna, however, was carved into several zones with a rotating control over central Vienna,[71] and the Soviet Union had its own plans for Austria. Josef Stalin personally selected a Marxist to serve as acting chancellor, and the man he picked was the bitter foe of the Christian Social era of Austrian government, Karl Renner.[72] One-third of Renner's cabinet members were Austrian communists. The United States and Britain were also not pleased; they protested Renner's appointment and refused his government recognition.[73]

The grateful family settled for a time in Rome where Schuschnigg contemplated their options, searching about as a famous but impoverished war refugee. He received encouragement to return to Austria from Leopold Figl, a former protégé of Engelbert Dollfuss. Figl became chancellor of Austria and later foreign minister. Figl's message encouraged Schuschnigg not to leave Europe out of despair or impatience, and he suggested that a comfortable return to life in Austria was nearing feasibility.[74] However, other information revealed that the Russian occupation of Vienna had made life in the capital very difficult. Renner, and the heavy hands of Stalin's Soviet administrators repressing the civilian population, plus startling waves of violence committed by Russian soldiers occupying Vienna, made it clear that under Soviet administration his homeland might not be a friendly place. Faced with this unsettling status in postwar Austria, he turned to thoughts of emigrating. America was an obvious first choice.

Schuschnigg and family arriving in New York, 1947.
Source: Austrian National Library: Interfoto/Alamy.

★ ★ ★

The Austrian Jews who had survived were similarly leery of Vienna. Before the war, Austria had been home to a thriving Jewish community, and it was one of the most lively, talented, and creative in Europe. After the war, fewer than 10,000 Jews reestablished residence in Austria.[75] Among the many who could not return were Desider Friedmann and his wife, Ella. They had succeeded in saving their children by sending them away, eventually to Israel, but Desider and Ella, notable Jewish leaders, had been sent to Theresienstadt. On October 28, 1944, there was one last train from Theresienstadt to Auschwitz-Birkenau and a special order that they were to be aboard that train and to be murdered, as they both were, immediately upon arrival at Birkenau.

· 13 ·

The Best Days

$\mathscr{K}$urt von Schuschnigg spent the next chapter of his life far from the Tyrol; he found himself living in the American Midwest, in St. Louis, Missouri. An Austrian dental professor, Dr. Wilhelm Bauer of Innsbruck, a Jew who had been helped by the young Schuschnigg when he was minister of education, took the initiative. In 1938, Dr. Bauer had fled Austria for America and had joined the dental faculty at Saint Louis University. With Dr. Bauer's help, Schuschnigg came to the United States. He began lecturing at universities in California until he, too, joined the faculty at Saint Louis University.

The oldest university west of the Mississippi, Saint Louis University proved a nearly perfect fit for Schuschnigg. It was a Jesuit university. The St. Louis population had grown as the result of European immigration, initially through its early French Catholic settlers, and it had attracted other Catholic immigrant groups who came in the mid-nineteenth-century waves fleeing revolutions, famine, poverty, and repression in countries with large Catholic populations, including Germany, Ireland, Poland, and Italy.

In St. Louis, Schuschnigg settled into a classic academic career. The still youthful fifty-year-old intellectual found academic life refreshing and satisfying. He would remain there and live in St. Louis longer than in any other city in his life.

At the university, he was an undeniable world celebrity, but his natural personal reserve let him wear fame as well and humbly as it can be worn. He taught government and international law both in the College of Arts and Sciences and in the School of Law. Within a few years, Sissi enrolled there, and she graduated from the university in 1964. She had grown to be as beautiful as her mother. Eventually, the baby from the Nazi concentration camp returned to Europe to marry a French nobleman. Like Vera, Sissi became a countess.

Maria (Sissi) von Schuschnigg and her father in St. Louis, Missouri, 1957.
Source: Getty Images.

Schuschnigg did not make his return visit to Austria until summer 1957. By then, trusted journalists and others had assured him that Austria had changed and that he would feel no discomfort. He had also, however, become surprisingly bonded to America. During these years in America, studying and teaching about its law and political process, he was genuinely moved by the American principles of government, and he greatly admired the quality of the American system of justice. It was not democracy's philosophical garb alone that so appealed to him; it was also the unbridled joy it gave him to be a free man. He would attend symphonies at the beautiful Kiel Opera House where the splendid St. Louis Symphony Orchestra performed. One spring night, returning from the symphony, Schuschnigg gushed that a night like this, ordinary to most others there, was to him one of the happiest of his life, for he was free to walk out at night, to hear beautiful music, and to look at the stars. He would tell anyone how terribly happy he was living in St. Louis. Though once chancellor of the Austria he loved so much, he chose to become an American citizen.

After some twenty years at the university—and by then a beloved figure, who in turn had grown to love the university, calling his days there "the best time in my life"[1]—Schuschnigg began to think about the final chapter of his life. Vera had died. Sissi was married and living in Paris. As the years went on, he began making plans to return to his roots, to go home again, to try after all this time to recapture the memories of his parents buried in Mutters.

★ ★ ★

As faculty, former students, and many friends assembled for his final address at the university's library in 1967, he gave them a warm and dignified farewell. Many of them had read about—but very few had ever actually heard—his "Red White Red" speech in defiance of Adolf Hitler. Such high drama, barely imaginable to most in attendance, was now in the distant past, and he was far more subdued on this bittersweet occasion. Hitler, once the most feared person on the planet, was not around to storm in on him. Schuschnigg's retirement speech was a gentle close to the public life of that other chancellor at the Berchtesgaden drama.

His place in history was not the browbeating at Berchtesgaden; instead, his legacy had become the story of the first and loneliest resistance to Nazi Germany. His denunciation of Nazism, and his defiance—calling on Austria to choose freedom—was the zenith of the days preceding the war, but it was his quiet insistence on equality for Jews in even greater defiance of a monstrous power that could murder him at will for doing so that warranted a tribute few historic figures have earned. The spotlight had become focused on his speeches in Vienna and Innsbruck. When Hitler had shut down free speech and intimidated the voices the world should have heard from during his stealthy advance, when courageous words were needed most desperately, it was Schuschnigg who had provided them. He retired carrying the mystique of the very first head of government to speak out and dare to defy the Thousand Year Reich and the first to refuse to go along with the Nazi propaganda and their pretense that the Anschluss was voluntary. He had done it alone, utterly without support.

And he had provided a memorable crescendo—he would not flee. Many others rushed off to safe places. He remained to face the first Nazi invaders and the clutches of the Gestapo.

Without elaborate fanfare, but with tears glistening in his eyes, Schuschnigg thanked the assembly of Americans whose soldiers had brought about his deliverance, and he expressed his appreciation to the professors who had welcomed him after he emerged ravaged, penniless, and bludgeoned from the shipwreck of Nazi Europe. As he had at Berchtesgaden, he spoke softly as he bade his colleagues—his fellow Americans—farewell.

★ ★ ★

His decision was to go home to Mutters. Neither Vienna nor central Innsbruck seemed quite right. Political tension there might be less pleasant. As an elder statesman returning nearly a quarter century after the war, he wanted to spend his last years in his beloved Austria and was ready to risk whatever cacophony might be found there. Instead, he was met with exceptional kindness and shown great respect. What he had endured was known far more accurately than it had been during the fantasy surrounding Hitler's entry. The tragic error so many Austrians had made embracing Hitler was now so clear.

Schuschnigg became a friend of Mutters, a quiet villager who attended fairs and public events, but he was quite unobtrusive. The people of Mutters showed their immense fondness for Schuschnigg with outpourings of grief at his death in 1977. "He took part in village events, we saw him at church on Sunday, and we experienced his open friendliness. We thank him and count it a great honor that he wanted to be buried among us."[2] A Vienna paper said: "In prison and after his liberation Schuschnigg showed his true greatness."[3]

A reporter who had covered the Anschluss wrote: "A man of the highest intellectuality was placed where in human judgment even the hardest man could not have changed fate. . . . To him the resurrection of Austria may have been the first triumph—history will bring his vindication."[4]

Another wrote that he was "a man who had to bear a double burden: his honesty, which was out of step with a time in which braggarts and weak reeds made history; and the titanic role that fate measured out for him, which even stronger men could not have been strong enough to bear."[5]

★ ★ ★

Years after the war, a reporter researching the speeches of that era listened to a collection of notable radio broadcasts. Most, of course, had been carefully composed and edited. From among all those he heard, his selection for the best was Schuschnigg's spontaneous final broadcast while surrounded by Nazis screaming for his head: "The absolute highlight: Schuschnigg's farewell speech of March 1938, an address that suddenly departs from the cultivated pathos of the rhetorician to remain utterly brave, human, and stirring."[6]

William Shirer agreed: "It was the most moving broadcast I have ever heard."[7]

Epilogue

Arthur Seyss-Inquart, former cabinet minister designated by Hitler, and later Nazi official in The Netherlands, was convicted at Nuremberg and hanged for atrocities committed as a minister of the Third Reich during the war, particularly atrocities he supervised in The Netherlands as well as his role in the Anschluss.

Arthur Seyss-Inquart's Nuremberg Detention Report, 1945.
Source: Public Domain. Nuremberg IMT.

Edmund Glaise-Horstenau, former cabinet minister in Austria, committed suicide while in Allied custody after the war.

Franz von Papen, former chancellor of Germany, and German ambassador to Austria was prosecuted at Nuremberg but was acquitted. One judge dissented and wrote that Papen should have been convicted. Papen survived and wrote his memoirs.

Wilhelm Keitel, a German field marshal, was convicted at Nuremberg and executed.

Heinrich Himmler, Reichsführer of the Schutzstaffel (SS), was caught in 1945 while attempting to escape; he committed suicide by biting a cyanide pill.

Reinhard Heydrich, a high-ranking SS official, was assassinated in Prague in 1943 by two Czech commandos helped by the underground.

Rudolf Hess, deputy Führer, was convicted at Nuremberg and sentenced to life in prison; he died at Spandau prison.

Joachim von Ribbentrop, foreign minister of Nazi Germany, was convicted at Nuremberg and executed.

Alfred Rosenberg, a Nazi Party official, was convicted at Nuremberg and executed.

Josef Bürckel, a Nazi Gauleiter and Party official, died of natural causes in 1944.

Martin Bormann, a Nazi Party official, is believed to have been killed in Berlin on May 2, 1945, while attempting to flee the Red Army.

Josef Göbbels, minister of propaganda for Nazi Germany, committed suicide at war's end in the Vorbunker adjacent to the Führerbunker; he died along with his wife, after they murdered their six children.

Hermann Göring, one of the most powerful figures in the Nazi Party, was sentenced to death at Nuremberg, but he committed suicide on the morning he was to be hanged.

Anton Kaindl, the Sachsenhausen commandant, was captured and tried by the Red Army and sent to a Soviet gulag where he died in 1948.

Benito Mussolini, the Italian dictator, was captured by Italian partisans and executed along with his mistress, Clara Petacci, on April 28, 1945, at Dongo near Lake Como.

Ernst von Starhemberg, the Heimwehr leader, spent much of the war in Argentina and returned to Austria after the war; he died there in 1956.

Kurt (Kurti) von Schuschnigg, Kurt von Schuschnigg's son, died on October 26, 2018, age 92, in New York City; he is survived by his wife, Janet.

Maria (Sissi) von Schuschnigg, Kurt von Schuschnigg's daughter, died in 1989, like her father and mother, of lung cancer.

Vera von Schuschnigg, Kurt von Schuschnigg's second wife, died in 1959 of lung cancer.

Notes

INTRODUCTION

1. Dorothy Thompson, foreword to *My Austria*, by Kurt von Schuschnigg (New York: Knopf, 1938), xxii.

2. John Toland, *Adolf Hitler* (New York: Anchor, 1976), 456.

3. Declaration of Moscow Conference, Joint Four-Nation Declaration of Allies, US, UK, USSR, and China, October 18–November 11, 1943. Declaration on Austria 3–8, United Nations Documents 1941–1945 (Oxford: Oxford University Press for the Royal Institute of International Affairs, 1946). In addition, Churchill also named Austria the "first victim" of Nazi aggression. Steven Beller, *A Concise History of Austria* (Cambridge: Cambridge University Press, 2006), 245.

4. *Daily Express*, September 17, 1936. Lloyd George proclaimed that Hitler was a man of peace and had no plan to march across any frontiers. He called him the George Washington of Germany.

5. *Boston Globe*, November 10, 1940.

6. David Nasaw, *The Patriarch: The Remarkable Life and Turbulent Times of Joseph P. Kennedy* (New York: Penguin, 2012), 200–202, 294, 295.

7. Lynne Olson, *Those Angry Days* (New York: Random House, 2013), 103, 312.

8. Foreign Relations of the United States (FRUS), US Department of State 1:791–92, October 5, 1938, cable from Under secretary Sumner Welles to Ambassador Joseph P. Kennedy.

9. In Germany, Hitler's popularity was widespread, enthusiastic, and shared by many eminent people and groups. Julia Boyd, *Travelers in the Third Reich: The Rise of Fascism: 1919–1945* (New York: Pegasus, 2018), 262.

10. Erik Vuillard, *The Order of the Day*, trans. Mark Polizzotti (New York: Other Press, 2017), 39.

11. *Time*, March 21, 1938, 20, 21.

CHAPTER 1

1. William L. Shirer, *The Rise and Fall of the Third Reich* (New York: Simon & Schuster, 1960), 280.

2. Shirer, *Rise/Fall*, 279.

3. Kurt von Schuschnigg, interview by Gerhard Jagschitz, 1972–1974, Saint Louis University Archives, DOC MSS 69.6.2, 159.

4. Shirer, *Rise/Fall*, 280.

5. Schuschnigg, interview by Jagschitz, 134–37; William L. Shirer, *Berlin Diary: The Journal of a Foreign Correspondent 1934–1941* (New York: Knopf, 1941), 10; George S. Messersmith, report on presenting his credentials, n.d., University of Delaware Collection, Messersmith Papers, 19716/7939; Ibid., (MSS 0109) identifier 2015–00.

6. The Nazis engaged in a week of violent attacks from June 12 to 19, 1933, and Dollfuss banned the party and all Nazi activity immediately afterward. Gordon Brook-Shepherd, *Prelude to Infamy: The Story of Chancellor Dollfuss of Austria* (New York: Ivan Obolensky, 1961), 194, 195.

7. Shirer, *Rise/Fall*, 280.

8. Schuschnigg, interview by Jagschitz, 159.

9. Brook-Shepherd, *Prelude to Infamy*, 254, 255.

10. Kurt von Schuschnigg, *My Austria* (New York: Knopf, 1938), 232.

11. Schuschnigg, *My Austria*, 233 (quoting Griefeneder).

12. Schuschnigg, *My Austria*, 235.

13. Schuschnigg, *My Austria*, 233. Once the news broke that Dollfuss had died, Schuschnigg and the other members of the cabinet rescinded the amnesty for the killers. Shirer, *Rise/Fall*, 280.

14. John Toland, *Adolf Hitler* (New York: Anchor, 1976), 353.

15. Schuschnigg, interview by Jagschitz, 164.

16. Schuschnigg, *My Austria*, 229.

17. Schuschnigg, interview by Jagschitz, 161. Other officials who joined in the discussions included Minister Odo Neustädter-Stürmer and General Wilhelm von Zehner.

18. Schuschnigg, interview by Jagschitz, 161.

19. Shirer, *Berlin Diary*, 13.

20. Schuschnigg, interview by Jagschitz, 161.

21. Brook-Shepherd, *Prelude to Infamy*, 264.

22. Schuschnigg, *My Austria*, 238, 239.

23. Schuschnigg, *My Austria*, 238, 239.

24. Messersmith, report on the assassination of Dollfuss, n.d., University of Delaware Collection, Messersmith Papers (MSS 0109, identifier 2015–00).

25. Brook-Shepherd, *Prelude to Infamy*, 263.

26. Schuschnigg, *My Austria*, 240.

27. Schuschnigg, interview by Jagschitz, 49, 164–70.

28. Schuschnigg, interview by Jagschitz, 164–170; Schuschnigg, *My Austria*, 243.

29. Schuschnigg, interview by Jagschitz, 164; Schuschnigg, *My Austria*, 243.

30. Schuschnigg, interview by Jagschitz, 49, 161.

31. Schuschnigg, interview by Jagschitz, 164.

32. Schuschnigg, interview by Jagschitz, 53.

33. Schuschnigg, interview by Jagschitz, 56.

34. Shirer, *Rise/Fall*, 49, 50; Charles A. Gulick, *Austria from Habsburg to Hitler*, vol. 2, *Fascism's Subversion of Democracy* (Oakland: University of California Press, 1948), 999.

35. Messersmith, report to the secretary of state, March 19, 1935, University of Delaware 19716/6466.

36. Shirer, *Rise/Fall*, 280. The Berlin propaganda office tried to retrieve all copies, but US ambassador William Dodd obtained a copy and saw the Nazi dissembling for what it was. IMT, vol. 2, November 28, 1945, 356, 357.

37. Toland, *Adolf Hitler*, 354, 355. It was reliably reported by the wife of Baron Werner von Alvensleben that Hitler had directly asked the baron if he would murder Dollfuss. Messersmith, letter to William Phillips, August 18, 1934, University of Delaware 19716/6377.

38. Brook-Shepherd, *Prelude to Infamy*, 256, 257.

39. Kurt von Schuschnigg, *The Brutal Takeover* (New York: Atheneum, 1971), 165; The evidence acquired from the Third Reich by the time of the Nuremberg War Crimes Trials reveals many instances of Hitler's control of the Austrian Nazis, including the side-by-side evidence of Hitler's military ultimatum on March 11, 1938, contrasted with Berlin's effort to sell to Britain its pretense that independent Nazis inside Austria were the spontaneous driving force for the Anschluss. IMT, Nuremberg Trial Proceedings, vol. 2, Thursday, November 29, 1945, 399–409, 423.

40. Schuschnigg, interview by Jagschitz, 55.

41. Schuschnigg, interview by Jagschitz, 172.

42. Jamie Bullock, *Karl Renner, Austria; Makers of the Modern World* (London: Haus Histories, 2009), 134; Shirer, *Rise/Fall*, 280.

43. Schuschnigg, *My Austria*, 109, 110, 235.

44. Schuschnigg, interview by Jagschitz, 52, 55.

45. Schuschnigg, interview by Jagschitz, 52, 55.

46. Schuschnigg, *My Austria*, 218, 219.

47. M. W. Fodor, memorandum to Messersmith, August 6, 1938, University of Delaware 19716/6980.

48. Messersmith, letter to Under secretary of State William I. Phillips, July 19, 1935, University of Delaware 19716/6504.

49. Messersmith, report on the Dollfuss assassination, n.d. University of Delaware, identifier 2015–00.

50. Kurt von Schuschnigg, with Janet von Schuschnigg, *When Hitler Took Austria* (San Francisco, CA: Ignatius, 2012), 35.

51. Steven Beller, *A Concise History of Austria* (Cambridge: Cambridge University Press, 2006), 225.

52. Schuschnigg, interview by Jagschitz, 1.

53. To Messersmith, Dollfuss was a very admirable person. Messersmith, report on the assassination of Dollfuss, n.d., University of Delaware (MSS 0109), identifier 2015–00. Dollfuss is "remembered by all those who came into personal contact with him as the kindest and gentlest of mortals." Not a "single anecdote survives which points to viciousness or brutality in his private character." Ibid. See also Brook-Shepherd, *Prelude to Infamy*, 181, 182. Some others hated him, especially Nazis and Marxists and some socialists.

54. Schuschnigg, interview by Jagschitz, 134–37.

55. Messersmith, letter to Sir Walford Selby (former British ambassador to Austria), February 26, 1938, University of Delaware 19716/6932; Messersmith, report to William I. Phillips, October 26, 1934, University of Delaware 19716/6406.

56. Dietrich von Hildebrand, *My Battle against Hitler: Faith, Truth, and Defiance in the Shadow of the Third Reich* (New York: Image, 2014), 184.

57. Hildebrand, *My Battle*, 97, 170, 182. Dietrich von Hildebrand offered such high praise despite his sharp disagreement with Schuschnigg's political moves, particularly the entry into the Abkommen agreement. Hildebrand was a determined monarchist/legitimist who believed Schuschnigg was clueless in refusing to seek restoration of the Habsburgs.

58. Schuschnigg, *My Austria*, 80.

59. David Clay Large, *Between Two Fires: Europe's Path in the 1930s* (New York: Norton, 1990), 97.

60. Schuschnigg, *My Austria*, 80.

61. Zara Steiner, *The Triumph of the Dark: European International History 1933–1939* (Oxford: Oxford University Press, 2013), 155, 156; Large, *Between Two Fires*, 97.

62. Messersmith, report to William I. Phillips, October 26, 1934, University of Delaware 19716/6406. Knowing the men Schuschnigg chose, Messersmith confirmed that Schuschnigg was "getting the best men into these corporative positions." Ibid.

63. Schuschnigg, interview by Jagschitz, 1.

64. Schuschnigg, interview by Jagschitz, 6.

65. Schuschnigg, interview by Jagschitz, 6.

66. Schuschnigg, *My Austria*, 27.

67. Schuschnigg, interview by Jagschitz, 3, 5. A *gymnasium* is a school that prepared German and Austrian students to enter universities. Beller, *Concise History*, 49.

68. Schuschnigg, *My Austria*, 27.

69. Schuschnigg, interview by Jagschitz, 4.

70. Schuschnigg, interview by Jagschitz, 3, 4.

71. Schuschnigg, interview by Jagschitz, 5.

72. Schuschnigg, interview by Jagschitz, 6.

73. Schuschnigg, interview by Jagschitz, 6.

74. Luise Muhlbach, *Andreas Hofer. Erscheinungsjahr* (1871), chapter 44. Hofer himself shouted the order, "Fire!" to the firing squad. Schuschnigg, interview by Jagschitz, 6.

75. Schuschnigg, interview by Jagschitz, 6, 7.

76. Schuschnigg, interview by Jagschitz, 7.

77. Schuschnigg, interview by Jagschitz, 8.

78. Schuschnigg, *My Austria*, 35, 36.

79. "La Leggenda del Piave," by E. A. Mario. The lyrics contain the fighting mantra, "Il Piave mormorò, 'Non passa lo straniero.'" ("The Piave whispered, 'The foreigner shall not pass'"). The casualties of the Isonzo front were in the hundreds of thousands for the Austrians and for the Italians. G. J. Meyer, *A World Undone: The Story of the Great War, 1914 to 1918* (New York: Delacorte, 2006), 459, 463, 465, 466, 583–85.

80. Kurt von Schuschnigg, *Austrian Requiem* (New York: Putnam, 1946), 113; Schuschnigg, interview by Jagschitz, 7, 8.

81. Schuschnigg, interview by Jagschitz, 10, 11.

82. Schuschnigg, interview by Jagschitz, 9, 11, 12.

83. Schuschnigg, interview by Jagschitz, 11, 12.

84. Shirer, *Rise/Fall*, 11; Adolf Hitler, *Mein Kampf*, trans. James Murphy, 2nd ed. (1925–1926; repr., Stockholm: White Wolf, 2014), 14, 15.

85. Toland, *Adolf Hitler*, 7, 9, 12.

86. Toland, *Adolf Hitler*, 7, 8.

87. Toland, *Adolf Hitler*, 9.

88. Toland, *Adolf Hitler*, 9, 13.

89. Shirer, *Rise/Fall*, 15.

90. Hitler, *Mein Kampf*, 18; Shirer, *Rise/Fall*, 27.

91. Hitler, *Mein Kampf*, 15.

92. Toland, *Adolf Hitler*, 14, 17–19.

93. Toland, *Adolf Hitler*, 15, 22, 37–39.

94. Toland, *Adolf Hitler*, 38, 47.

95. Hitler, *Mein Kampf*, 15, 20.

96. Toland, *Adolf Hitler*, 45.

97. Toland, *Adolf Hitler*, 44. The sources of Hitler's ideas are sometimes difficult to locate. His belief that interest is a trait of slavery seemed to come from Gottfried Feder. Shirer, *Rise/Fall*, 35.

98. Toland, *Adolf Hitler*, 49.

99. Hitler, *Mein Kampf*, 43, 47.

100. Hitler, *Mein Kampf*, 49.

101. Hitler, *Mein Kampf*, 53.

102. Hitler, *Mein Kampf*, 23, 25, 27.

103. Hitler, *Mein Kampf*, 27, 28.

104. Toland, *Adolf Hitler*, 32–35, 39, 41, 43.

105. Hitler, *Mein Kampf*, 23.

106. Toland, *Adolf Hitler*, 41, 42.

107. Shirer, *Rise/Fall*, 27, 28. Benjamin Carter Hett, *The Death of Democracy* (New York: Henry Holt, 2018), 47.

108. Toland, *Adolf Hitler*, 50, 51.

109. Hitler, *Mein Kampf*, 63.

110. Toland, *Adolf Hitler*, 52, 53.

111. Toland, *Adolf Hitler*, 54.

112. Toland, *Adolf Hitler*, 55, 56.

113. Toland, *Adolf Hitler*, 57, 58.

114. Toland, *Adolf Hitler,* 60–64.

115. Toland, *Adolf Hitler*, 65.

116. Shirer, *Rise/Fall*, 30, 31. Confusion abounds concerning the origin and validity of President Hindenburg's references to Hitler as the "Austrian corporal" (Shirer, *Rise/Fall*, 4) and the "Bohemian corporal" (Shirer, *Rise/Fall*, 153). He was not Bohemian; he served in a Bavarian regiment. Moreover, his promotion while serving as a private may only have been to private first class, not corporal. Hett, *Death of Democracy*, 45. He was denied further promotion because he lacked leadership, or Führer, qualities. Hett, *Death of Democracy*, 46.

117. Toland, *Adolf Hitler*, 71; Shirer, *Rise/Fall*, 29, 30.

118. Toland, *Adolf Hitler*, xix.

119. Toland, *Adolf Hitler*, xix.

120. Toland, *Adolf Hitler*, 73–78.

121. Toland, *Adolf Hitler*, 73–75.

122. Shirer, *Rise/Fall*, 32, 33.

123. Hett, *Death of Democracy*, 142.

124. Hett, *Death of Democracy*, 21.

125. Hett, *Death of Democracy*, 135.

126. Meyer, *World Undone*, 693; Shirer, *Rise/Fall*, 31.

127. Dennis E. Showalter and William J. Astore, *Hindenburg, Icon of German Militarism* (Lincoln, NE: Potomac, 2005), 80, 81.

128. Toland, *Adolf Hitler*, 82.

129. Toland, *Adolf Hitler*, 78–81.

130. Toland, *Adolf Hitler*, 81.

131. Toland, *Adolf Hitler*, 82; Shirer, *Rise/Fall*, 35, 37, 38, 39. Eckart was Hitler's earliest mentor; he was accompanied in the beginning days of Hitler and the Nazis by Alfred Rosenberg and Rudolf Hess. Shirer, *Rise/Fall*, 110.

132. Adolf Hitler, letter to Adolf Gemlich, September 16, 1919, Simon Wiesenthal Center, Los Angeles Museum of Tolerance; see article, Jack Ewing, "Letter of Hitler's First Anti-Semitic Writing May Be the Original," *New York Times*, June 3, 2011. That original letter bearing Hitler's signature is in the Wiesenthal Center. An unsigned copy is in the Bavarian State Archives in Munich.

133. Toland, *Adolf Hitler*, 82.

134. Toland, *Adolf Hitler*, 87.

135. Toland, *Adolf Hitler*, 87, 88.

136. Shirer, *Rise/Fall*, 37, 38.

137. Hett, *Death of Democracy*, 53.

138. Shirer, *Rise/Fall*, 43.

139. Schuschnigg, interview by Jagschitz, 12.

140. Schuschnigg, *Brutal Takeover*, 338n14.

141. Stefan Zweig, *The Post-Office Girl*, trans. Joel Rottenberg, *New York Review of Books* Classics, 1982, 24–26.

142. Schuschnigg, interview by Jagschitz, 12.

143. Schuschnigg, interview by Jagschitz, 12.

144. Schuschnigg, interview by Jagschitz, 12, 14.

145. Schuschnigg, interview by Jagschitz, 15.

146. Schuschnigg, interview by Jagschitz, 15.

147. Schuschnigg, *When Hitler Took Austria*, 10.

148. Schuschnigg, *When Hitler Took Austria*, 20, 228, facing pages photos.

149. Schuschnigg, interview by Jagschitz, 32.

150. Schuschnigg, *My Austria*, 62.

151. Schuschnigg, *When Hitler Took Austria*, 10.

152. Schuschnigg, interview by Jagschitz, 43, 44; Schuschnigg, *My Austria*, 105.

153. Schuschnigg, *My Austria*, 94, 95.

154. Schuschnigg, *My Austria*, 93, 94.

155. Schuschnigg, *Austrian Requiem*, 188.

156. Lisa Silverman, *Becoming Austrians: Jews and Culture between the World Wars* (Oxford: Oxford University Press, 2012), 198n106.

157. Schuschnigg, *Brutal Takeover*, 28.

158. Harriet Pass Freidenreich, *Jewish Politics in Vienna, 1918 to 1938* (Bloomington and Indianapolis: Indiana University Press, 1991), 7; Gordon Brook-Shepherd, *The Anschluss* (Philadelphia and New York: Lippincott, 1963), xvi.

159. Beller, *Concise History*, 17.

160. Schuschnigg, *Brutal Takeover*, 85.

161. Schuschnigg, *My Austria*, 93–95.

162. Schuschnigg, *My Austria*, 78, 97.

163. Large, *Between Two Fires*, 85, 92.

164. Schuschnigg, *My Austria*, 79.

165. Schuschnigg, *My Austria*, 94.

166. Schuschnigg, *My Austria*, 89.

167. Schuschnigg, *My Austria*, 94.

168. Schuschnigg, *My Austria*, 90, 91.

169. Schuschnigg, *My Austria*, 93, 96.

170. Schuschnigg, *My Austria*, 95, 96.

CHAPTER 2

1. Michael Mann, *Fascists* (Cambridge: Cambridge University Press, 2003), 214.

2. Mann, *Fascists*, 214.

3. John Toland, *Adolf Hitler* (New York: Anchor, 1976), 459, 460, 479, 514, 519.

4. Kurt von Schuschnigg, *My Austria* (New York: Knopf, 1938), 70.

5. Adolf Hitler, *Mein Kampf*, trans. James Murphy, 2nd ed. (1925–1926; repr., Stockholm: White Wolf, 2014), 63. Hitler was by no means the first to raise his severe form of these Germanic aspirations. Georg von Schönerer, who served in the Austrian Parliament in the late nineteenth century, was a much earlier leader of the Austrian Pan-German Nationalists with similar ideas. Harriet Pass Freidenreich, *Jewish Politics in Vienna, 1918 to 1938* (Bloomington and Indianapolis: Indiana University Press, 1991), 6. In 1882, Schönerer and other upper Austrians in Linz—Viktor Adler and Karl Lueger—drafted a program for Austria's German Nationalist movement. It was aimed at establishing a new and better German Reich, gathering all adjacent German areas in Europe into a socialist democracy. The heart of their program, however, was racial purity, which was even then already translating to open and angry polemics against Jews. Schönerer has been described as a "fanatical Jew-baiter." Hilde Spiel, *Vienna's Golden Autumn, 1866–1938* (London: Weidendfeld and Nicolson, 1987), 49. To him, Judaism—and Catholicism as well—were incompatible with German heritage and religion; his Pan-German agenda soon became "violent opposition to the dynasty and the Catholic Church," and he proclaimed "racial anti-Semitism as a national imperative." Kurt von Schuschnigg, *The Brutal Takeover* (New York: Atheneum, 1971), 26. This party had given voice to the ideas that attracted Hitler. William L. Shirer, *The Rise and Fall of the Third Reich* (New York: Simon & Schuster, 1960), 23. The German Workers' Party, the initial nucleus of what became the Nazis, was a separate movement from Schönerer's; it arose in Austria and Moravia in 1903, and in May 1918, led in Austria by Rudolph Jung, it became the Austrian NSDAP, with a handful of founding members. Schuschnigg, *Brutal Takeover*, 26.

6. Hitler, *Mein Kampf*, 63.

7. Schuschnigg, *Brutal Takeover*, 62.

8. Kurt von Schuschnigg, interview by Gerhard Jagschitz, 1972–1974, Saint Louis University Archives, DOC MSS 69.6.2, 33.

9. Gordon Brook-Shepherd, *The Anschluss* (Philadelphia and New York: Lippincott, 1963), xvi.

10. Schuschnigg, *My Austria*, 74, 75.

11. Schuschnigg, *My Austria*, 35, 36.

12. Schuschnigg, *My Austria*, 35.

13. Schuschnigg, *My Austria*, 66.

14. Schuschnigg, interview by Jagschitz, 22.

15. Schuschnigg, *Brutal Takeover*, 70 (quoting the *Volkzeitung* newspaper).

16. Schuschnigg, *Brutal Takeover*, 55.

17. Schuschnigg, interview by Jagschitz, 22. A vacuum in leadership was created by the death of Emperor Franz Joseph and the disestablishment of the Habsburg Dynasty. Schuschnigg, interview by Jagschitz, 16–28. Both the Left and the Right searched for new leaders and often wound up with bombastic orators, clerics, and demagogues of varying stripes. Fear of the Schutzbund enabled Heimwehr leaders to pull the political platform of the Christian Social Party hard to the Right, as the Schutzbund pulled the Social Democrats hard to the Left. Fear grew in Austria over Marxism as the communist movement seemed poised to destabilize every society in Europe, and that fear helped fuel the rise of the anti-Marxist demagogues—with awful consequences in Germany and Austria. Schuschnigg, interview by Jagschitz, 18–22.

18. David Clay Large, *Between Two Fires: Europe's Path in the 1930s* (New York: Norton, 1990), 64.

19. Schuschnigg, *My Austria*, 130; Steven Beller, *A Concise History of Austria* (Cambridge: Cambridge University Press, 2006), 219, 220.

20. Schuschnigg, *My Austria*, 132.

21. Hugh Seton-Watson, "Fascism, Right and Left," *Journal of Contemporary History* 1, no. 1 (1966): 133; Beller, *Concise History*, 209, 225.

22. Schuschnigg, *My Austria*, 141; Mann, *Fascists*, 210, 211.

23. Mann, *Fascists*, 210, 211.

24. R. John Rath, "The Dollfuss Ministry: The Intensification of Animosities and the Drift toward Authoritarianism," in *Austrian History Yearbook* (Minneapolis: Center for Austrian Studies, University of Minnesota, 1999), 30:376.

25. Charles A. Gulick, *Austria from Habsburg to Hitler*, vol. 2, *Fascism's Subversion of Democracy* (Oakland: University of California Press, 1948), 999, 894.

26. Seton-Watson, "Fascism, Right and Left," 133; Gulick, *Austria from Habsburg to Hitler*, 2:818, 2:907.

27. Seton-Watson, "Fascism, Right and Left," 130.

28. Gordon Brook-Shepherd, *Prelude to Infamy: The Story of Chancellor Dollfuss of Austria* (New York: Ivan Obolensky, 1961), 122–24, 127, 148–50, 214.

29. Brook-Shepherd, *Prelude to Infamy*, 214; Gulick, *Austria from Habsburg to Hitler*, 2:1205.

30. Schuschnigg, *My Austria*, 144.

31. Schuschnigg, *My Austria*, 141.

32. Schuschnigg, *My Austria*, 129.

33. Schuschnigg, interview by Jagschitz, 22, 24.

34. Schuschnigg, *My Austria*, 138. Schuschnigg described himself as a "godfather" to the birth of the Ostmarkisch Sturmscharen and described it as a Catholic youth group and a Young Austria movement. Schuschnigg, *My Austria*, 138. Schuschnigg eventually soured on this group, and it became one of the many that were folded into the Fatherland Front and the army when conscription was introduced. Schuschnigg, *My Austria*, 138fn, 142, 143.

35. Schuschnigg, interview by Jagschitz, 22–24, 146. Schuschnigg, *My Austria*, 280.

36. Schuschnigg, interview by Jagschitz, 27; Brook-Shepherd, *The Anschluss*, 111.

37. Hitler, *Mein Kampf*, 63.

38. Kurt von Schuschnigg, *Austrian Requiem* (New York: Putnam, 1946), 110.

39. Mann, *Fascists*, 211.

40. Mann, *Fascists*, 223–25. The Austrian Nazis recruited riding the coattails of every new sign of prosperity in Germany. Mann, *Fascists*, 220–25.

41. Mann, *Fascists*, 207.

42. Messersmith, report to Secretary of State Cordell Hull on the situation of the Jews in Austria, October 24, 1934, University of Delaware 19716/6405.

43. Messersmith, report to Secretary of State Cordell Hull on the situation of the Jews in Austria, October 24, 1934, University of Delaware 19716/6405.

44. Mann, *Fascists*, 140–44, 209.

45. Mann, *Fascists*, 219.

46. Mann, *Fascists*, 220.

47. Mann, *Fascists*, 140–44, 209.

48. Schuschnigg, *Brutal Takeover*, 86; Kurt von Schuschnigg, with Janet von Schuschnigg, *When Hitler Took Austria* (San Francisco, CA: Ignatius, 2012), 17.

49. Mann, *Fascists*, 207. The fact that both Nazism and anti-Semitism were strongest in the provinces where few Jews lived suggests that the underlying racial and religious hostility was stronger at a distance. Mann, *Fascists*, 226.

50. M. W. Fodor, memorandum to Ambassador Messersmith, August 6, 1938, University of Delaware 19716/6980.

51. Mann, *Fascists*, 207.

52. Mann, *Fascists*, 212, 215, 218–21, 226.

53. Mann, *Fascists*, 212–14, 218–21, 226.

54. Mann, *Fascists*, 213, 214, 223–25.

55. Schuschnigg, *Brutal Takeover*, 45, 46.

56. Margaret MacMillan, *Paris 1919: Six Months That Changed the World* (New York: Random House, 2003), 247.

57. Beller, *Concise History*, 210.

58. Brook-Shepherd, *The Anschluss*, 12.

59. Brook-Shepherd, *The Anschluss*, 13; Toland, *Adolf Hitler*, 454.

60. Brook-Shepherd, *The Anschluss*, 12.

61. Schuschnigg, *Austrian Requiem*, 189.

62. Schuschnigg, *Brutal Takeover*, 70. There appeared a serious chance that the largest party, the Social Democrats, might gain the votes necessary to elect a majority in the Diet, form a lasting government, and move Austria toward socialism; however, they failed to achieve a majority, and the failure reinforced their vow to fight the second-largest party, the conservative Christian Socials. Schuschnigg, *Brutal Takeover*, 71. After Chancellor Renner's Social Democratic–led coalitions with the Christian Socials collapsed in 1920, Renner was succeeded briefly by Chancellor Michael Mayr. But when a referendum in Styria called for Austria to merge with Germany, Mayr and his cabinet resigned, and he was replaced by Johannes Schöber, an independent. Schuschnigg, *Brutal Takeover*, 71.

63. Lisa Silverman, *Becoming Austrians: Jews and Culture between the World Wars* (Oxford: Oxford University Press, 2012), 198n106. "After 1920, the conservative Christian Socials controlled the national scene, in conjunction with the various German Nationalist groups who held the balance of power." Freidenreich, *Jewish Politics in Vienna*, 7.

64. Schuschnigg, interview by Jagschitz, 92.

65. Schuschnigg, interview by Jagschitz, 93.

66. Schuschnigg, interview by Jagschitz, 106.

67. Schuschnigg, *My Austria*, 65.

68. Schuschnigg, *My Austria*, 163.

69. Schuschnigg, *My Austria*, 66.

70. Schuschnigg, *My Austria*, 65.

71. Schuschnigg, *My Austria*, 107.

72. It became a common belief that Schuschnigg was a disciple of Seipel because Seipel saw him as a man on whom he could rely. Schuschnigg, *My Austria*, 65, 66. They had, however, only the occasional "passing nod" or "friendly gesture." Schuschnigg, *My Austria*, 66; Schuschnigg, interview by Jagschitz, 106; Eric Solsten and David E. McClave, eds., "Austria: A Country Study," Federal Research Division, vol. 5, series 6 (sponsored by the Department of the Army) (Washington, DC: Library of Congress, December 1993; 2nd ed., 1994), 43. Seipel seemed to have the same kind of complicated relationship with President Wilhelm Miklas. Although they were cordial, and members of the same party, they too had fundamental disagreements. Schuschnigg, interview by Jagschitz, 106. This gave Miklas and Schuschnigg something in common—respectful difficulties with Seipel—which created a bond between them. Some factions, however, were opposed to Seipel because he was friendly with the Heimwehr, a friendliness that Schuschnigg did not share.

73. When Seipel took office, Austria's economy was at its closest to complete collapse, but Seipel succeeded in obtaining a crucial loan from the League of Nations, part of an October 4, 1922, Protocol for the Reconstruction of Austria. The irony was that the socialist leaders in the Diet, Karl Renner and Otto Bauer, the very men who had writhed before the League of Nations over the financial weight of war reparations, now bitterly attacked the Christian Social government's efforts to secure needed financial relief. They called the Christian Socials traitors and pushed for Anschluss. Schuschnigg, *My Austria*, 74, 75.

74. Schuschnigg, *My Austria*, 121, 154, 167.

75. Schuschnigg, *My Austria*, 155, 216; Schuschnigg, interview by Jagschitz, 97.

76. Schuschnigg, interview by Jagschitz, 96.

77. Schuschnigg, *My Austria*, 155.
78. Schuschnigg, interview by Jagschitz, 44, 45.
79. Schuschnigg, interview by Jagschitz, 106.
80. Schuschnigg, interview by Jagschitz, 45.
81. Shirer, *Rise/Fall*, 324.
82. Toland, *Adolf Hitler*, 433.
83. Schuschnigg, interview by Jagschitz, 173.
84. Schuschnigg, *My Austria*, 169.
85. Schuschnigg, *Brutal Takeover*, 87.
86. Schuschnigg, *My Austria*, 167, 169.
87. Schuschnigg, *Brutal Takeover*, 87.
88. Schuschnigg, interview by Jagschitz, 45.
89. Brook-Shepherd, *The Anschluss*, 6, 43.
90. Messersmith, letter to Jay Pierrepont Moffat, September 20, 1934, University of Delaware 19716/6393.
91. Schuschnigg, *My Austria*, 121; Freidenreich, *Jewish Politics in Vienna*, 196, 197, 201–3.
92. Schuschnigg, *My Austria*, 170, 171.
93. Schuschnigg, interview by Jagschitz, 132, 133.
94. Schuschnigg, interview by Jagschitz, 134.
95. Schuschnigg, interview by Jagschitz, 135.
96. William L. Shirer, *Berlin Diary: The Journal of a Foreign Correspondent 1934–1941* (New York: Knopf, 1941), 10.
97. Messersmith, report on the assassination of Dollfuss, n.d., University of Delaware Collection, Messersmith Papers (MSS 0109, identifier 2015–00).
98. Messersmith, report on presenting his credentials, n.d., University of Delaware 19716/7939.
99. Schuschnigg, interview by Jagschitz, 134.
100. Schuschnigg, interview by Jagschitz, 135, 137.
101. Schuschnigg, interview by Jagschitz, 134.
102. Rath, "The Dollfuss Ministry," 73, 74.
103. Rath, "The Dollfuss Ministry," 67, 71.
104. Rath, "The Dollfuss Ministry," 68, 71.
105. Schuschnigg, *My Austria*, 157.
106. Beller, *Concise History*, 221.
107. Schuschnigg, *My Austria*, 177.
108. Schuschnigg, *My Austria*, 161.
109. Brook-Shepherd, *Prelude to Infamy*, 95. Even Austro-Marxist leader Karl Renner despaired of the danger of Otto Bauer's intense revolutionary agenda and tactics, and Renner warned that the inability to restrain him was sure to result in a "blood bath." Brook-Shepherd, *Prelude to Infamy*, 123.
110. Schuschnigg, *My Austria*, 173.
111. Schuschnigg, *My Austria*, 173, 175.
112. Schuschnigg, *My Austria*, 176.
113. Schuschnigg, *My Austria*, 179.
114. Dollfuss was devoutly Catholic and had been surrounded all his life by farmers, countrymen, and other politicians who were the same. The devout shared a set of values, many of which were admirable in anyone's hierarchy of virtues. However, such religious hegemony in government carried with it a cliquish solidarity, and yet, despite the overwhelming numbers, the Christian Socials could not attain a majority in the Diet and, instead, were left to bargain their way into coalitions to govern. Freidenreich, *Jewish Politics in Vienna*, 7.

115. Schuschnigg, *My Austria*, 213. In governing, both Dollfuss and Schuschnigg tried to put the principles of *Quadragesimo Anno* into reality. Schuschnigg, interview by Jagschitz, 145, 146.

116. Schuschnigg, *My Austria*, 133.

CHAPTER 3

1. Andrew Nagorski, *Hitlerland: American Eyewitnesses to the Nazi Rise to Power* (New York: Simon & Schuster, 2012), 42, 43.

2. Nagorski, *Hitlerland*, 239.

3. Nagorski, *Hitlerland*, 45.

4. Nagorski, *Hitlerland*, 46.

5. Otto Strasser, *Hitler and I*, trans. Gwenda David and Eric Mosbacher (London: Jonathan Cape, 1940).

6. Adolf Hitler, *Mein Kampf*, trans. James Murphy, 2nd ed. (1925–26; repr., Stockholm: White Wolf, 2014), 226.

7. Benjamin Carter Hett, *The Death of Democracy* (New York: Henry Holt, 2018), 233.

8. Hett, *Death of Democracy*, 54, 56, 57. He began the administration in Germany of the Dawes Plan and, by 1929, lowered Germany's reparations payments through the Young Plan. With the Treaty of Locarno, Stresemann brought Germany into the League of Nations. Hett, *Death of Democracy*, 57.

9. Hett, *Death of Democracy*, 54. Particular credit for the crucial stabilization of the currency is due to Hjalmar Schacht. William L. Shirer, *The Rise and Fall of the Third Reich* (New York: Simon & Schuster, 1960), 112. Chancellor Heinrich Brüning deserves credit for the efforts to convince Britain and France to end reparation payments; for the Hoover Moratorium of June 20, 1931, on reparations payments; and for a very effective jobs creation program. Hett, *Death of Democracy*, 122, 123.

10. Hett, *Death of Democracy*, 80.

11. John A. Lukacs, *The Great Powers and Eastern Europe* (New York: American Book Company, 1953), 29.

12. Hett, *Death of Democracy*, 106, 107. A central piece of what the Nazis wanted to end was the gold standard.

13. Hett, *Death of Democracy*, 101.

14. Shirer, *Rise/Fall*, 168.

15. Hett, *Death of Democracy*, 118. Despite the many decrees, Brüning's time as chancellor was more democratic in practice than in appearance. Hett, *Death of Democracy*, 147.

16. John Toland, *Adolf Hitler* (New York: Anchor, 1976), 259.

17. Shirer, *Rise/Fall*, 4, 132, 169; Andreas Dorpalen, *Hindenburg and the Weimar Republic* (Princeton, NJ: Princeton University Press, 1964), 257. Hitler's low opinion of Hindenburg contrasted with the reverential way in which he dealt with the president in public.

18. Toland, *Adolf Hitler*, 259; Hett, *Death of Democracy*, 156.

19. Toland, *Adolf Hitler*, 259, 260.

20. Toland, *Adolf Hitler*, 261.

21. Toland, *Adolf Hitler*, 262.

22. Toland, *Adolf Hitler,* 262.

23. Toland, *Adolf Hitler*, 263.

24. Shirer, *Rise/Fall*, 159.

25. Shirer, *Rise/Fall*, 159.

26. Toland, *Adolf Hitler*, 265.

27. Toland, *Adolf Hitler*, 261, 262.

28. Shirer, *Rise/Fall*, 159–61.

29. Toland, *Adolf Hitler*, 265.

30. Hett, *Death of Democracy*, 81, 229.

31. Hett, *Death of Democracy*, 152. One charge the Nazis planned to assert against Hindenburg was that his actions in the so-called Prussian coup, when he replaced Prussian ministers with Papen, were illegal and grounds to impeach. Hett, *Death of Democracy*, 149, 150, 152.

32. Toland, *Adolf Hitler*, 265, 266.

33. Hett, *Death of Democracy*, 146, 152.

34. Hett, *Death of Democracy*, 215. One colleague described him in crude language.

35. Toland, *Adolf Hitler*, 265, 266.

36. Toland, *Adolf Hitler*, 266.

37. Hett, *Death of Democracy*, 150.

38. Toland, *Adolf Hitler*, 269, 270.

39. Shirer, *Rise/Fall*, 168.

40. Toland, *Adolf Hitler*, 270.

41. Hett, *Death of Democracy*, 150.

42. Toland, *Adolf Hitler*, 270.

43. Shirer, *Rise/Fall*, 168; Toland, *Adolf Hitler*, 271, 272.

44. Toland, *Adolf Hitler*, 271.

45. Toland, *Adolf Hitler*, 277.

46. Toland, *Adolf Hitler*, 277.

47. Hett, *Death of Democracy*, 172.

48. The *Führerprinzip*, a philosophical tenet attributed to Russian/Estonian philosopher Hermann Graf Keyserling, was advanced by Hitler, *Mein Kampf*, 449–50. Hitler embraced that philosophy as early as 1921 when he wrested control of the Nazi Party from Anton Drexler and insisted he must have dictatorial power over it. Shirer, *Rise/Fall*, 45. The chief tenet of this principle was that certain individuals are born to lead and should do so, and all others should follow them without challenge. This central flaw of Nazism and of the Third Reich explains at least a part of the mechanism behind the willingness to commit the atrocities so abundant in the Third Reich. Keyserling's premise was taken by Nazis to a ridiculous second proposition that because Hitler had such a messianic skill, all must obey even insane and inhuman commands. How that tragic leap of logic prevailed is still not understood. Shirer, *Rise/Fall*, 90.

49. Toland, *Adolf Hitler*, 278.

50. Toland, *Adolf Hitler*, 278, 279.

51. Shirer, *Rise/Fall*, 175.

52. Shirer, *Rise/Fall*, 176.

53. Shirer, *Rise/Fall*, 176.

54. Toland, *Adolf Hitler*, 279, 280.

55. Toland, *Adolf Hitler*, 279, 280.

56. Kurt von Schuschnigg, *Farewell Austria* (New York: Cassell, 1938), 165–67.

57. Kurt von Schuschnigg, interview by Gerhard Jagschitz, 1972–1974, Saint Louis University Archives, DOC MSS 69.6.2, 46; Kurt von Schuschnigg, *My Austria* (New York: Knopf, 1938), 112, 189–91.

58. Schuschnigg, *My Austria*, 189–91.

59. Toland, *Adolf Hitler*, 283, 284.

60. Toland, *Adolf Hitler*, 284.

61. Toland, *Adolf Hitler*, 284.

62. Toland, *Adolf Hitler*, 281.

63. Toland, *Adolf Hitler*, 285.

64. Hett, *Death of Democracy*, 156, 174.

65. Shirer, *Rise/Fall*, 181.

66. Dorpalen, *Hindenburg*, 424. Hindenburg was also fearful of other possible accusations that might support indictment or impeachment. Hett, *Death of Democracy*, 178, 179.

67. Hett, *Death of Democracy*, 234.

68. Shirer, *Rise/Fall*, 180.

69. Toland, *Adolf Hitler*, 287.

70. Toland, *Adolf Hitler*, 287.

71. Hett, *Death of Democracy*, 153.

72. Shirer, *Rise/Fall*, 23, 24.

73. Hett, *Death of Democracy*, 182.

74. Shirer, *Rise/Fall*, 181.

75. Oskar Hindenburg was viewed as neither very strong nor very bright. Hett, *Death of Democracy*, 137. Hitler referred to Hindenburg as "the personification of stupidity." Hett, *Death of Democracy*, 175. In their private meeting, it is suspected that Hitler not only charmed him but also bribed him and threatened revelation of harmful information about the tax and financial scandal. Shirer, *Rise/Fall*, 181; Hett, *Death of Democracy*, 173, 178. At the same time, industrial and agrarian interests, some of which had become heavily infiltrated by Nazis, were strongly urging Hindenburg to name Hitler as chancellor. Mary Fulbrook, *A Concise History of Germany*, 2nd ed. (Cambridge: Cambridge University Press, 1991), 177.

76. Toland, *Adolf Hitler*, 285, 286; Shirer, *Rise/Fall*, 181, 227. Hitler concluded that Hindenburg was "senile" and that his "weary, wandering mind" was being steered by those around him. Shirer, *Rise/Fall*, 163.

77. Toland, *Adolf Hitler*, 319.

78. Hett, *Death of Democracy*, 113.

79. Shirer, *Rise/Fall*, 192–93. At the Nuremberg trials and elsewhere, evidence was presented that Göring, whose Berlin town mansion was connected to the Reichstag by a tunnel, had Karl Ernst and others use the tunnel to seed the building with gasoline and kindling, and that the Nazis had in recent days encouraged van der Lubbe to set fire to the building. Shirer, *Rise/Fall*, 191–95.

80. Toland, *Adolf Hitler*, 301.

81. Toland, *Adolf Hitler*, 300–302.

82. Hett, *Death of Democracy*, 183.

83. Toland, *Adolf Hitler*, 270; Hett, *Death of Democracy*, 201.

84. Shirer, *Rise/Fall*, 196. When supported by German Nationalist votes, the Nazis could enact legislation by March 5, 1933. Steven Beller, *A Concise History of Austria* (Cambridge: Cambridge University Press, 2006), 222.

85. Toland, *Adolf Hitler*, 305, 306. By this time, Hindenburg's former comrade, General Ludendorff, had soured on Hitler and on Hindenburg as well. He wrote to Hindenburg: "Future generations will damn you in your grave for what you have done." Dennis E. Showalter and William J. Astore, *Hindenburg, Icon of German Militarism* (Lincoln, NE: Potomac, 2005), 95.

86. Hett, *Death of Democracy*, 234, 235.

87. Hett, *Death of Democracy*, 205.

88. Schuschnigg, interview by Jagschitz, 49.

89. Toland, *Adolf Hitler*, 310.

90. Toland, *Adolf Hitler*, 303, 304, 308.

91. Toland, *Adolf Hitler*, 345, 346, 352.

92. Hett, *Death of Democracy*, 228.

93. Toland, *Adolf Hitler*, 331.

94. Toland, *Adolf Hitler*, 329.

95. Toland, *Adolf Hitler*, 334, 336.
96. Toland, *Adolf Hitler*, 331, 332.
97. Toland, *Adolf Hitler*, 337.
98. Toland, *Adolf Hitler*, 334.
99. Shirer, *Rise/Fall*, 223.
100. Toland, *Adolf Hitler*, 346. A later effort to learn the total concluded that 401 had been killed, only 116 of whom could be identified; but at a Munich court proceeding in 1957, it was proposed that more than 1,000 were killed in the Night of the Long Knives. Shirer, *Rise/Fall*, 223.
101. Shirer, *Rise/Fall*, 221–22; Toland, *Adolf Hitler*, 341.
102. Toland, *Adolf Hitler*, 342, 343.
103. Toland, *Adolf Hitler*, 342, 343. One of the most transparent of the revenge killings was the murder of Gustav von Kahr. This former minister president of Bavaria had been out of politics for many years and living quietly in his Munich apartment. Hitler, however, had a major grudge dating back more than ten years. Kahr had been the man who sabotaged Hitler's first revolution, the 1923 Beer Hall Putsch. Moreover, Kahr was hacked to pieces with axes rather than merely executed. Toland, *Adolf Hitler*, 77–78, 347; Shirer, *Rise/Fall*, 223.
104. Toland, *Adolf Hitler*, 343, 345.
105. Toland, *Adolf Hitler*, 347. Some historians have speculated that the Hindenburg telegram may have been a forgery, but they cite no evidence. Showalter and Astore, *Hindenburg*, 99, 119fn40. Others state categorically, given the circumstances and the ample opportunity to disavow it, that Hindenburg sent it. Anna Von der Golt, *Hindenburg: Power, Myth and the Rise of the Nazis* (Oxford: Oxford University Press, 2009), 180; Hett, *Death of Democracy*, 229. Though it was apparently drafted by the Nazis, Hindenburg signed it according to Toland, *Adolf Hitler*, 347.
106. Kurt von Schuschnigg, *Austrian Requiem* (New York: Putnam, 1946), 180.
107. Toland, *Adolf Hitler*, 355.
108. Toland, *Adolf Hitler*, 350.
109. Hett, *Death of Democracy*, 230.
110. The office of president was essentially abolished. Hett, *Death of Democracy*, 231.
111. Toland, *Adolf Hitler*, 358.
112. Toland, *Adolf Hitler*, 277fn.
113. Toland, *Adolf Hitler*, 277fn.
114. Shirer, *Rise/Fall*, 867.
115. Schuschnigg, *My Austria*, 204; Kurt von Schuschnigg, *The Brutal Takeover* (New York: Atheneum, 1971), 92, 93.
116. Schuschnigg, *My Austria*, 204.
117. Toland, *Adolf Hitler*, 330.
118. Schuschnigg, interview by Jagschitz, 211.
119. Schuschnigg, interview by Jagschitz, 132.
120. Schuschnigg, *My Austria*, 182.
121. Lynne Olson, *Troublesome Young Men* (New York: Farrar, Straus and Giroux, 2007), 72.
122. Schuschnigg, *Brutal Takeover*, 92, 339n35.
123. Schuschnigg, *Brutal Takeover*, 95.
124. Schuschnigg, *Brutal Takeover*, 95.
125. Schuschnigg, *My Austria*, 222, 223.
126. Schuschnigg, *My Austria*, 223.
127. Schuschnigg, *Brutal Takeover*, 95, 96; Schuschnigg, *My Austria*, 223, 227.
128. Schuschnigg, *Brutal Takeover*, 96–97.
129. Schuschnigg, *Brutal Takeover*, 98.
130. Schuschnigg, *Austrian Requiem*, 198.

131. Lisa Silverman, *Becoming Austrians: Jews and Culture between the World Wars* (Oxford: Oxford University Press, 2012), 86–87, 180n4, 232n62.

132. Schuschnigg, interview by Jagschitz, 147, 176, 177; Schuschnigg, *Brutal Takeover*, 100.

133. Schuschnigg, interview by Jagschitz, 146, 176.

134. Schuschnigg, *Austrian Requiem*, 110.

CHAPTER 4

1. Kurt von Schuschnigg, *My Austria* (New York: Knopf, 1938), 133. Dollfuss's one-vote majority was at some moments a one-to-three-vote majority when he was able to juggle certain German Nationals' votes. R. John Rath, "The Dollfuss Ministry: The Intensification of Animosities and the Drift toward Authoritarianism," in *Austrian History Yearbook* (Minneapolis: Center for Austrian Studies, University of Minnesota, 1999), 30:66, 30:99. The dispute that led to the resignations of the three presidents was quite prosaic—disciplinary proceedings for striking railway workers. Gordon Brook-Shepherd, *Prelude to Infamy: The Story of Chancellor Dollfuss of Austria* (New York: Ivan Obolensky, 1961), 97, 98.

2. Rath, "The Dollfuss Ministry," 76.

3. Kurt von Schuschnigg, *The Brutal Takeover* (New York: Atheneum, 1971), 90.

4. Charles A. Gulick, *Austria from Habsburg to Hitler*, vol. 2, *Fascism's Subversion of Democracy* (Oakland: University of California Press, 1948), 1021.

5. Rudolf Ramek, a Christian Social, resigned to vote to offset Renner's vote; then a third vice president, a German National, did the same. Brook-Shepherd, *Prelude to Infamy*, 95.

6. Gulick, *Austria from Habsburg to Hitler*, 2:1022.

7. Schuschnigg, *Brutal Takeover*, 91. Prince Metternich ruled without a diet from 1811 to 1825. Steven Beller, *A Concise History of Austria* (Cambridge: Cambridge University Press, 2006), 120, 121. In 1848 after the "Spring" rebellions and the departure of Metternich, an Imperial Parliament was elected by universal male suffrage during the period of renewal. Beller, *Concise History*, 128. In 1860, in the midst of an economic crisis, a new and expanded Reichsrat was established to serve the empire. Beller, *A Concise History*, 135.

8. Rath, "The Dollfuss Ministry," 101; Gulick, *Austria from Habsburg to Hitler*, 2:1022.

9. Tim Kirk, "Fascism and Austrofascism," in *The Dollfuss/Schuschnigg Era in Austria: A Reassessment*, ed. Günter Bischof, Anton Pelinka, and Alexander Lassner, Contemporary Austrian Studies 11 (Abington on Thames: Routledge, 2003), 20.

10. Helmut Wohnout, "A Chancellorial Dictatorship with a 'Corporative' Pretext: The Austrian Constitution between 1934 and 1938," in Bischof, Pelinka, and Lassner, *The Dollfuss/Schuschnigg Era in Austria*, 151.

11. Brook-Shepherd, *Prelude to Infamy*, 98, 99. There was no shortage of outcry against the parliament. This author ranked the parliament during the 1920s as an "active despot." Ibid.

12. Brook-Shepherd, *Prelude to Infamy*, 102.

13. Brook-Shepherd, *Prelude to Infamy*, 103.

14. Brook-Shepherd, *Prelude to Infamy*, 158.

15. Kirk, "Fascism and Austrofascism," 21.

16. Gulick, *Austria from Habsburg to Hitler*, 2:1074, 2:1075.

17. Schuschnigg, *My Austria*, 209.

18. Brook-Shepherd, *Prelude to Infamy*, 100; Elizabeth Barker, *Austria 1918–1972* (Miami, FL: University of Miami Press, 1973), 110. After widespread arrests, the camp at Anhaltelager Wollersdorf was crowded but was never, prior to the Nazi takeover, anything like a brutal slave labor camp. Ibid. Schuschnigg, *Brutal Takeover*, 105. These coercion measures were much like

the measures so widely used in Britain, the United States, and elsewhere in times of war or civil war. Brook-Shepherd, *Prelude to Infamy*, 100.

19. Dollfuss explained the origin of the concept of the Ständestaat in speeches he gave about its roots in the papal encyclicals, *Rerum Novarum* and *Quadragesimo Anno*. John Warren, "Cultural Decline in Vienna in the 1930s," in *Interwar Vienna: Culture between Tradition and Modernity*, ed. Deborah Holmes and Lisa Silverman (Rochester, NY: Camden House, 2009), 40; James Shedel, *Art and Society: The New Art Movement in Vienna, 1897–1914* (Vienna: Sposs, 1981), 98.

20. Brook-Shepherd, *Prelude to Infamy*, 163.

21. Beller, *Concise History*, 186.

22. Eric Solsten and David E. McClave, eds., "Austria, a Country Study," Federal Research Division, vol. 5, series 6 (sponsored by the Department of the Army) (Washington, DC: Library of Congress, December 1993; 2nd ed., 1994), 42.

23. Harriet Pass Freidenreich, *Jewish Politics in Vienna, 1918 to 1938* (Bloomington and Indianapolis: Indiana University Press, 1991), 193.

24. Wohnout, "A Chancellorial Dictatorship," 150.

25. Wohnout, "A Chancellorial Dictatorship," 149.

26. Wohnout, "A Chancellorial Dictatorship," 149.

27. Beller, *Concise History*, 222; Brook-Shepherd, *Prelude to Infamy*, 163.

28. Schuschnigg, *My Austria*, 228. Odo Neustädter-Stürmer was a central contributor to the content of the new constitution. Wohnout, "A Chancellorial Dictatorship," 155.

29. Gulick, *Austria from Habsburg to Hitler*, 2:1413.

30. Schuschnigg, *My Austria*, 228.

31. Brook-Shepherd, *Prelude to Infamy*, 159.

32. Wohnout, "A Chancellorial Dictatorship," 148.

33. Brook-Shepherd, *Prelude to Infamy*, 158.

34. Wohnout, "A Chancellorial Dictatorship," 156.

35. Beller, *Concise History*, 130, 131. The Habsburgs summoned diets and parliaments and dismissed them when they wished, all to still "the hankerings of the populace for a say in government." Beller, *Concise History*, 131. Prince Metternich ruled without the Diet for fourteen years from 1811 to 1825. Beller, *Concise History,* 120, 121.

36. Beller, *Concise History*, 117, 126–29.

37. David Clay Large, *Between Two Fires: Europe's Path in the 1930s* (New York: Norton, 1990), 92.

38. Large, *Between Two Fires*, 81.

39. John A. Lukacs, *The Great Powers and Eastern Europe* (New York: American Book Company, 1953), 23, 24.

40. Large, *Between Two Fires*, 81.

41. Rath, "The Dollfuss Ministry," 65, 75, 83, 100; Dollfuss told Mussolini he would not use Italian fascism by using the Heimwehr as Mussolini used his Brownshirts. Schuschnigg, *Brutal Takeover*, 107.

42. Beller, *Concise History*, 227.

43. Michael Mann, *Fascists* (Cambridge: Cambridge University Press, 2003), 211 ("rather than the real thing"); Brook-Shepherd, *Prelude to Infamy*, 100 ("never . . . an all-out dictatorship"). Other writers have been critical of Dollfuss, Schuschnigg, and many other leaders of the era calling them dictators, often without describing the facts or the action they took that supposedly matched the conduct of a dictator, and often with no citation to any facts to provide context or support for such free-standing conclusions. See, for example, Erik Vuillard, *The Order of the Day*, trans. Mark Polizzotti (New York: Other Press, 2017). The Vuillard book is not presented as a traditional history but, instead, as a heavily fictionalized recit; it is recognized as an imaginative work speculating on what Schuschnigg and others were thinking. It thus "resorts inevitably

to fiction." Robert O. Paxton, "The Reich in Medias Res," review of *The Order of the Day*, by Erik Vuillard, *New York Review*, December 6, 2018, 49, at 50. See also Eileen Battersby's review of *The Order of the Day* in the *Financial Times*, January 12/13, 2019 ("*The Order of the Day* is not history—it is fact mixed with opinionated bombast"). Schuschnigg himself acknowledged the accusations that the government was authoritarian were made with some apparent justification. Schuschnigg, *Brutal Takeover*, 66.

44. Lukacs, *The Great Powers*, 24, 25. The government under Dollfuss was not set up to be guided by the arbitrary decisions of a dictator but, instead, was planned as an orderly administration for the benefit of all classes, one endeavoring to eliminate class divisions by selflessness, and to restore human dignity to laborers. James Shedel, "The Legacy of Empire: History and Austrian Identity in the *Ständestaat*," in *Austria: Forschung under Wissenschaft*, Geschichte, Band 13. Andrassy University, Budapest. Lit Verlag GmbH & Co. KG. (Wien: 2015), 93–109, at 99.

45. Solsten and McClave, "Austria, A Country Study," 42.

46. Solsten and McClave, "Austria, a Country Study," 42. Under Schuschnigg, the Fatherland Front became a bureaucratic entity of no great significance. Wohnout, "A Chancellorial Dictatorship," 156.

47. Gulick, *Austria from Habsburg to Hitler*, 2:1174.

48. Large, *Between Two Fires*, 90.

49. Large, *Between Two Fires*, 83–87.

50. Mann, *Fascists*, 229–31; Large, *Between Two Fires*, 62, 83, 92. The killing of a policeman in the 1927 uprising, found with his throat slit, and the killing of a plant director at a munitions factory in Steyr convinced some that Austria's socialists were capable of Marxist/Leninist reprisals. Large, *Between Two Fires*, 62, 83, 85. Even allowing for this level of provocation, however, the Dollfuss government's 1934 blunt force shelling of the Vienna housing complex and the executions even of the most culpable in the uprising led to heavy condemnation from many sources. Large, *Between Two Fires*, 62, 83, 85. Another inflammatory action among the most often cited was the use of concentration camps to house prisoners charged with crimes during battles arising out of the political standoff. These were never Nazi slave labor camps, but the incarcerations raised due process issues and often came from courts-martial and mass arrests during the fighting in 1934; they followed the pattern used by prior chancellors during the rising of 1927 in which the Schutzbund burned the Palace of Justice. Large, *Between Two Fires*, 65, 66, 83–85.

51. Gulick, *Austria from Habsburg to Hitler*, 2:1147–53.

52. Gulick, *Austria from Habsburg to Hitler*, 2:1047, 2:1148, 2:1149, 2:1151; F. L. Carsten, *The First Austrian Republic 1918–1938* (Middlesex, UK: Tower/Maurice Temple Smith, 1986), 225.

53. Gulick, *Austria from Habsburg to Hitler*, 2:1149–53. Censorship in America during the war was imposed under the later discredited espionage laws pushed by President Woodrow Wilson. The US postmaster general had nearly complete authority over the foreign press, and the Sedition Act of 1918 allowed the government to punish expressions of opinions that were "profane, scurrilous or abusive." There were 1,500 arrests in the United States under these laws, and only ten were for actual sabotage. John Morton Blum, *Woodrow Wilson and the Politics of Morality* (Boston: Little, Brown, 1956), 143, 144.

54. Gulick, *Austria from Habsburg to Hitler*, 2:1047–51.

55. Mann, *Fascists*, 211.

56. Large, *Between Two Fires*, 99.

57. Brook-Shepherd, *Prelude to Infamy*, 163.

58. Kurt von Schuschnigg, *Austrian Requiem* (New York: Putnam, 1946), 198.

59. Dietrich von Hildebrand, *My Battle against Hitler: Faith, Truth, and Defiance in the Shadow of the Third Reich* (New York: Image, 2014), 139.

60. Beller, *Concise History*, 222.

61. Rath, "The Dollfuss Ministry," 75.

62. Schuschnigg, *Brutal Takeover*, 93.

63. One rough measure of the success of Hitler's economy was that the German unemployed totaled six million in 1933 and one million in 1937. Shirer, *Rise/Fall*, 231fn. As for the credit due Hitler, many have noted, first, that he cared little for economics and knew little about it and, second, that the credit for such successes as stabilizing the currency was due years earlier to the sophisticated skills of Hjalmar Schacht and Gustav Stresemann and the job creation bill of Kurt von Schleicher. Shirer, *Rise/Fall*, 112; Benjamin Carter Hett, *The Death of Democracy* (New York: Henry Holt, 2018), 180. Schleicher's last initiative was a large jobs program that, within six months, had provided employment to two million of the six million unemployed. Hett, *Death of Democracy*, 180.

64. Hett, *Death of Democracy*, 54, 56, 57, 180.

65. Gerhard Senft, "Economic Development and Economic Policies in the *Ständestaat* Era," in Bischof, Pelinka, and Lassner, *The Dollfuss/Schuschnigg Era in Austria*, 35, 36.

66. Rath, "The Dollfuss Ministry," 65, 100.

67. Kurt von Schuschnigg, interview by Gerhard Jagschitz, 1972–1974, Saint Louis University Archives, DOC MSS 69.6.2, 77.

68. Schuschnigg, interview by Jagschitz, 32.

69. Schuschnigg, *Brutal Takeover*, 107.

70. Schuschnigg, interview by Jagschitz, 41.

71. *Radio e Televisao de Portugal* poll completed March 25, 2007. For a thorough analysis of the lengthy Salazar governance of Portugal, see David L. Raby, *Fascism and Resistance in Portugal: Communists, Liberals, and Military Dissidents in the Opposition to Salazar 1941–1974* (Manchester, UK: Manchester University Press, 1988).

72. Janek Wasserman, *Black Vienna: The Radical Right in the Red City, 1918–1938* (Ithaca, NY: Cornell University Press, 2013), 211. The debate between the Austrian Left and the Austrian Right over the Dollfuss and Schuschnigg Ständestaat continues in political and academic circles. "[T]hose employing the words '*Ständestaat*' and 'Austrofascism' have sought, too often, to defend or accuse the Dollfuss and Schuschnigg governments, rather than to uncover and consider evidence in as objective a manner as possible. While those on the Right have tended to portray the Dollfuss/Schuschnigg governments strictly as a defense bastion against Nazi Germany, those on the Left have indicted these governments as decisive contributors to the successful Anschluss through their rejection of parliamentary democracy." Alexander Lassner and Günter Bischof, introduction to Bischof, Pelinka, and Lassner, *The Dollfuss/Schuschnigg Era in Austria*, 1. A verdict has been offered by Alexander Lassner. He concluded that Schuschnigg's policies were both "sound and realistic" and that Schuschnigg "correctly understood that the only way to prevent armed aggression against Austria by the Third Reich was through a politico-military guarantee to be obtained from Britain, France and Italy. Unfortunately, for reasons that had nothing to do with Austria's form of government, such a guarantee was not forthcoming—with disastrous results." Lassner and Bischof, introduction to Bischof, Pelinka, and Lassner, *The Dollfuss/Schuschnigg Era in Austria*, 5. See also Senft, "Economic Development and Economic Policies in the *Ständestaat* Era," 35, 36.

73. William L. Shirer, *Berlin Diary: The Journal of a Foreign Correspondent 1934–1941* (New York: Knopf, 1941), 9; Schuschnigg, *Brutal Takeover*, 56.

74. Schuschnigg, *Brutal Takeover*, 55, 56; Shirer, *Berlin Diary*, 9.

75. Gordon Brook-Shepherd, *The Anschluss* (Philadelphia and New York: Lippincott, 1963), 110.

76. Schuschnigg, interview by Jagschitz, 128.

77. Schuschnigg, interview by Jagschitz, 128.

78. John Toland, *Adolf Hitler* (New York: Anchor, 1976), 433; Rath, "The Dollfuss Ministry," 75.

79. Robert M. Spector, *World without Civilization: Mass Murder and the Holocaust, History and Analysis* (Lanham, MD: University Press of America, 2004), 1:264.

80. Brook-Shepherd, *Prelude to Infamy*, 163, 164. Other historians emphasize that the definitions used to call some governments fascist are "vague or inconsistent" and, as applied to the Ständestaat, the issue of what it was like "cannot be resolved." Kirk, "Fascism and Austrofascism," 26. Another observes that the diagnosis has never been made in valid fashion: "As yet, no attempt has been made to draw a comprehensive map of the Austrian government system between 1934 and 1938 on the basis of historical, judicial and political analysis." Wohnout, "A Chancellorial Dictatorship," 144.

81. James Q. Whiteman, "Of Corporatism, Fascism and the First New Deal," *American Journal of Comparative Law* 39, no. 4 (1991): 747–78; Richard Moe, *Roosevelt's Second Act* (New York: Oxford University Press, 2013), 254.

82. Michael Fullilove, *Rendezvous with Destiny* (New York: Penguin, 2013), 324.

83. Whiteman, "Of Corporatism, Fascism and the First New Deal," 218. Concentration camps had been used for large-group confinement by Britain in the Boer War and by America under, among others, presidents Lincoln, Wilson, and Roosevelt to hold uncharged large groups of Native Americans, Japanese Americans, and strikers.

84. Kendrick A. Clements, *Woodrow Wilson, World Statesman* (Chicago: Ivan R. Dee, 1999), 167, 174–76.

85. Brook-Shepherd, *Prelude to Infamy*, 130, 131.

86. Schuschnigg, interview by Jagschitz, 93.

87. Schuschnigg, interview by Jagschitz, 93.

88. Large, *Between Two Fires*, 83–85.

89. Large, *Between Two Fires*, 66.

90. Large, *Between Two Fires*, 72.

91. Large, *Between Two Fires*, 65, 66.

92. Schuschnigg, interview by Jagschitz, 112; Large, *Between Two Fires*, 63, 82.

93. Brook-Shepherd, *Prelude to Infamy*, 123.

94. Rath, "The Dollfuss Ministry," 77.

95. Beller, *Concise History*, 210.

96. Rath, "The Dollfuss Ministry," 83.

97. Kurt von Schuschnigg, with Janet von Schuschnigg, *When Hitler Took Austria* (San Francisco, CA: Ignatius, 2012), 15.

98. Large, *Between Two Fires*, 62.

99. Large, *Between Two Fires*, 92.

100. Rath, "The Dollfuss Ministry," 81.

101. Gulick, *Austria from Habsburg to Hitler*, 2:1048, 2:1049.

102. Rath, "The Dollfuss Ministry," 79.

103. Brook-Shepherd, *Prelude to Infamy*, 132.

104. Brook-Shepherd, *Prelude to Infamy*, 122, 127, 128.

105. Large, *Between Two Fires*, 76.

106. Large, *Between Two Fires*, 74, 75.

107. Rath, "The Dollfuss Ministry," 73.

108. Large, *Between Two Fires*, 62.

109. Brook-Shepherd, *Prelude to Infamy*, 123.

110. Large, *Between Two Fires*, 61, 62.

111. Large, *Between Two Fires*, 61, 62.

112. Lukacs, *The Great Powers*, 57.

113. Brook-Shepherd, *Prelude to Infamy*, 122.

114. Rath, "The Dollfuss Ministry," 76.

115. Rath, "The Dollfuss Ministry," 71.

116. Mann, *Fascists*, 231, 232; Large, *Between Two Fires*, 83.

117. Rath, "The Dollfuss Ministry," 77.

118. Mann, *Fascists*, 231.

119. Schuschnigg, *Brutal Takeover*, 343n28.

120. Brook-Shepherd, *Prelude to Infamy*, 195.

121. Large, *Between Two Fires*, 79.

122. Rath, "The Dollfuss Ministry," 78.

123. Large, *Between Two Fires*, 83, 96; Brook-Shepherd, *Prelude to Infamy*, 124, 129, 130.

124. Gulick, *Austria from Habsburg to Hitler*, 2:1319, 2:1320.

125. Mann, *Fascists*, 231, 232. Large, *Between Two Fires*, 83; Most of the workers refused to strike. In this sense, they left Bauer and Deutsch in the lurch and instead rode the trams to their jobs the next morning. Brook-Shepherd, *Prelude to Infamy*, 136.

126. Schuschnigg, *Brutal Takeover*, 102.

127. Large, *Between Two Fires*, 83, 85.

128. Brook-Shepherd, *Prelude to Infamy*, 13–32.

129. Gulick, *Austria from Habsburg to Hitler*, 2:1319, 2:1320. Cited as support for the absence of leadership's approval is that there was no mention of such approval in the newspapers. Gulick, *Austria from Habsburg to Hitler*, 2:1319, 2:1320. Documents were found, however, that showed systematic plans for socialist military headquarters, tribunals, and black lists. Schuschnigg, *My Austria*, 219, 220.

130. Brook-Shepherd, *Prelude to Infamy*, 122. Schuschnigg himself agrees with that conclusion; he wrote later that "it would be unjust to blame one of the parties exclusively." Schuschnigg, *Austrian Requiem*, 187, 188.

131. Brook-Shepherd, *Prelude to Infamy*, 127.

132. Brook-Shepherd, *Prelude to Infamy*, 123, 125, 127, 129, 149. Mussolini had a hand in pushing Fey and Starhemberg to use force to disable the Social Democrats. Brook-Shepherd, *Prelude to Infamy*, 127.

133. Brook-Shepherd, *Prelude to Infamy*, 122–25.

134. Brook-Shepherd, *Prelude to Infamy*, 148. See also Brook-Shepherd, *Prelude to Infamy*, 122, 124, 129, 149.

135. Brook-Shepherd, *Prelude to Infamy*, 149.

136. Rath, "The Dollfuss Ministry," 97.

137. Rath, "The Dollfuss Ministry," 87–96.

138. Brook-Shepherd, *Prelude to Infamy*, 128, 129.

139. Schuschnigg, *My Austria*, 219.

140. George S. Messersmith, telegram to Secretary of State Cordell Hull, June 12, 1934, US State Department Archive 863.00/Telegrams.

141. Messersmith, telegram to Hull, June 12, 1934, US State Department Archive 863.00/Telegrams.

142. Brook-Shepherd, *Prelude to Infamy*, 133, 134. Searches conducted prior to this by the government had seized many thousands of rifles, 710 machine guns, and hordes of ammunition from Schutzbund arsenals. Brook-Shepherd, *Prelude to Infamy*, 134. They had quickly replenished what had been seized. Brook-Shepherd, *Prelude to Infamy*, 134.

143. Large, *Between Two Fires*, 85, 89.

144. Brook-Shepherd, *Prelude to Infamy*, 137–40.

145. Large, *Between Two Fires*, 83.

146. Large, *Between Two Fires*, 83, 87.

147. Hildebrand, *My Battle against Hitler*, 134–36. Dollfuss begged the workers to stop; he eschewed the demagoguery that sometimes is shown rebels. Hildebrand, *My Battle against Hitler*, 135.

148. Brook-Shepherd, *Prelude to Infamy*, 138–43.

149. Large, *Between Two Fires*, 94.

150. Large, *Between Two Fires*, 85, 89.

151. Mann, *Fascists*, 233. Some suggest that the government, instead of the crackdown, "might have sought a grand democratic alliance with the socialists." Mann, *Fascists*, 233.

152. Shirer, *Berlin Diary*, 12; See also Large, *Between Two Fires*, 90, 93.

153. Brook-Shepherd, *Prelude to Infamy*, 138.

154. Schuschnigg, *Austrian Requiem*, 189.

155. Large, *Between Two Fires*, 86.

156. Large, *Between Two Fires*, 93, 99.

157. Brook-Shepherd, *Prelude to Infamy*, 143. Some assert that Dollfuss's actions somehow paved the way for Hitler, but some historians reject that claim as entirely without historical support since Hitler ultimately invaded Austria pursuant to a long-standing plan. It has been said that this particular claim is merely "propaganda" and has to "ignore the plain facts." Brook-Shepherd, *Prelude to Infamy*, 146.

158. Schuschnigg, *Austrian Requiem*, 190; Schuschnigg, *Brutal Takeover*, 104; Schuschnigg, interview by Jagschitz, 52; Gulick, *Austria from Habsburg to Hitler*, 2:1858.

159. Jamie Bullock, *Karl Renner, Austria; Makers of the Modern World* (London: Haus Histories, 2009), 134. The morality of capital punishment was permissive at the time. The Vatican pronouncements did not forbid it. It was not until 1997 that capital punishment was branded immoral, but even then flexible language was employed to endorse it in some subjective circumstances. It was not until 2018 that the Vatican clearly announced that capital punishment is immoral. *New York Times*, August 4, 2018, A1.

160. Large, *Between Two Fires*, 89.

161. Gulick, *Austria from Habsburg to Hitler*, 2:1321.

162. Large, *Between Two Fires*, 93.

163. Brook-Shepherd, *Prelude to Infamy*, 122–24, 130–32, 135.

164. Large, *Between Two Fires*, 88.

165. Mann, *Fascists*, 229–31.

166. Large, *Between Two Fires*, 74; See also Large, *Between Two Fires*, 63.

167. Large, *Between Two Fires*, 92.

168. Michael John, "We Do Not Even Possess Ourselves: On Identity and Ethnicity in Austria, 1880–1937," in *Austrian History Yearbook* (Minneapolis: Center for Austrian Studies, University of Minnesota, 1999), 30:53.

169. Large, *Between Two Fires*, 96. Bernaschek had once proposed that the socialists and the Nazis unite to bring down the Dollfuss government. John, "We Do Not Even Possess Ourselves," 54.

170. Mann, *Fascists*, 219. To jail these large numbers, the government opened a concentration camp facility at the Anhaltelager Wollersdorf industrial site near Wiener-Neustadt. Gulick, *Austria from Habsburg to Hitler*, 2:1188. The periods of incarceration were generally short for the internees, often a few months, and camp conditions were civilized. Austrian jails had become overcrowded in summer 1933 with the eruption of Nazi violence. Paul Moore, "And What Concentration Camps Those Were!: Foreign Concentration Camps in Nazi Propaganda, 1933–9," *Journal of Contemporary History* 45, no. 3 (2010): 649–656.. Wollersdorf was one of several large facilities that had to be opened to house the many Nazis arrested, but soon it and other Anhaltelager facilities housed Marxists and others arrested in the course of Schutzbund violence and during the Socialists Revolt. Moore, "And What Concentration Camps Those Were," 651–53. Photos of the camps were widely available, and the health and ordinary confinement conditions of prisoners was readily apparent. However, Nazi propaganda condemned the camps, claiming mistreatment of Nazis compared to Marxists who they said were quickly released. Nazi

propaganda did not claim torture, food deprivation, or executions but condemned restricting the newspapers available to Nazi prisoners to only publications supportive of the government. Moore, "And What Concentration Camps Those Were," 652. They also claimed far greater numbers of prisoners than there were and asserted arbitrary arrests for trivial charges. Marxist publications criticized the camps as well. Moore, "And What Concentration Camps Those Were," 653. Hitler, Hess, and the entire propaganda team gave speeches about the camps, but modern analyses report that claims of "their alleged mistreatment were greatly exaggerated." Moore, "And What Concentration Camps Those Were," 654. The Nazis also undertook to smear the British by launching propaganda at the same time exaggerating the mistreatment of their prisoners in their concentration camps operated in the Transvaal during the Boer War. Moore, "And What Concentration Camps Those Were," 655.

171. Toland, *Adolf Hitler*, 307.

172. Messersmith, letter to William Phillips, August 9, 1934, University of Delaware 19716/6370.

173. Messersmith, letter to Phillips, August 9, 1934, Delaware 19716/6370. Ambassador Messersmith reported that the high opinion he had developed of the previously little-known Schuschnigg "is without exception the opinion of my colleagues with whom I have discussed the matter." Messersmith, letter to Jay Pierrepont Moffat, September 24, 1934, University of Delaware 19716/6393.

174. Schuschnigg, interview by Jagschitz, 138–41. A telltale sign that this was no dictatorship was Schuschnigg's restraint; he made no significant changes in the structure or the political direction of the government in his four years as chancellor. Wohnout, "A Chancellorial Dictatorship," 156.

175. Messersmith, letter to Phillips, August 31, 1934, University of Delaware 19716/6382.

CHAPTER 5

1. Adolf Hitler, *Mein Kampf*, trans. James Murphy, 2nd ed. (1925–1926; repr., Stockholm: White Wolf, 2014), 263, 268–72.

2. Hitler, *Mein Kampf*, 65.

3. Hitler, *Mein Kampf*, 63.

4. William L. Shirer, *The Rise and Fall of the Third Reich* (New York: Simon & Schuster, 1960), 348fn; IMT, Nuremberg Trial Proceedings, vol. 14, May 24, 1946, testimony of Baldur von Schirach, 429.

5. For the development of Hitler's anti-Semitism, see Shirer, *Rise/Fall*, 25–27; see also Hitler's hopelessly vague statements trying to justify the war at its conclusion by blaming unspecified Jewish financiers for unspecified conduct that, in some unspecified way, caused the war he started. Ian Kershaw, *Fateful Choices* (New York: Penguin, 2007), 431, 432.

6. Shirer, *Rise/Fall*, 26, 27, 236; Martin Luther, *Von den Juden und iren Lügen* [On the Jews and their lies] (Wittenberg, 1543); Hitler, *Mein Kampf*, 20, 34, 35, 63.

7. August Kubizek, *The Young Hitler I Knew* (Boston: Houghton Mifflin, 1955), 79.

8. Shirer, *Rise/Fall*, 236.

9. Austria as a nation has been said to have long had a "humane and cultured spirit." James Shedel, *Art and Society, The New Art Movement in Vienna, 1897–1914* (Vienna: Sposs, 1981), 104. See also Shirer, *Rise/Fall*, 28; Kurt von Schuschnigg, *My Austria* (New York: Knopf, 1938), 204–8.

10. Andrew Wheatcroft, *The Habsburgs, Embodying Empire* (New York: Penguin, 1996), 328n49 (Maria Theresa "hated unconverted Jews"); Hilde Spiel, *Vienna's Golden Autumn, 1866–1938* (London: Weidenfeld and Nicolson, 1987), 9.

11. Steven Beller, *A Concise History of Austria* (Cambridge: Cambridge University Press, 2006), 120.

12. Beller, *Concise History*, 130, 131. During Franz Joseph's "purely absolutist regime," some say he ruled "without any Baroque niceties." Beller, *Concise History*, 131.

13. Beller, *Concise History*, 135.

14. Lisa Silverman, *Becoming Austrians: Jews and Culture Between the World Wars*. Oxford: Oxford University Press, 2012), 15; Spiel, *Vienna's Golden Autumn*, 9, 24.

15. Silverman, *Becoming Austrians*, 14. Poland and Russia to the east were both home to much greater populations of Jews.

16. Harriet Pass Freidenreich, *Jewish Politics in Vienna, 1918 to 1938* (Bloomington and Indianapolis: Indiana University Press, 1991), 20.

17. Freidenreich, *Jewish Politics in Vienna*, 2, 15; Kurt von Schuschnigg, *The Brutal Takeover* (New York: Atheneum, 1971), 62, 63.

18. The majority of those in the liberal professions and the ranks of academia were generally more open and less discriminatory, but even there, success was more difficult for Jews. Rejection by social peers was painful and a hindrance to professional fulfillment. Beller, *Concise History*, 189–94. Moreover, the prevalence of Nazis among students and some faculty certainly assured that faculties would have a minority of openly hostile individual anti-Semites. Michael Mann, *Fascists* (Cambridge: Cambridge University Press, 2003), 218–20.

19. Beller, *Concise History*, 212. Freud was appointed to professorial status in 1902, and to a more elevated status in 1920.

20. Freidenreich, *Jewish Politics in Vienna*, 12.

21. Beller, *Concise History*, 185–87.

22. Mann, *Fascists*, 225, 226. Some Jews chose to keep to themselves, but many engaged fully in society and confronted the often hostile world around them. Many Jews lived in Jewish communities, but quite a few lived in other areas. The greatest concentration of Jews was in Leopoldstaadt near the Danube on Mazzesinsel ("Matzo Island"). Freidenreich, *Jewish Politics in Vienna*, 13. Briggitenau and the Inner City were also large Jewish neighborhoods. John Toland, *Adolf Hitler* (New York: Anchor, 1976), 42. Many of the Viennese Jews tended to socialize among themselves, but many assimilated into the wider Viennese society. Freidenreich, *Jewish Politics in Vienna*, 13. They joined the political organizations of the day, but they also formed their own ethnic, religious, and political organizations, some of which pursued special goals. The Jewish Ex-Servicemen's League formed in July 1932, for example, helped remind Austrians of the patriotism and military service of Jews. Schuschnigg, *Brutal Takeover*, 61.

23. Freidenreich, *Jewish Politics in Vienna*, 2; Schuschnigg, *Brutal Takeover*, 62.

24. Freidenreich, *Jewish Politics in Vienna*, 4, 5.

25. Mann, *Fascists*, 184, 185. Jewish cohesion was neither ideal nor strong enough to bond them together as a single, powerful voting bloc. East kept its distance from west. Rarely did eastern immigrant Jews in Austria align politically with western Jews. Some native Austrian Jews trying to escape bigotry kept their distance from the Galician and Bukovina Jewish immigrants wearing long beards and caftans. Beller, *Concise History*, 218; Freidenreich, *Jewish Politics in Vienna*, 7, 88. Virtually all parties revealed informal anti-Semitism of their members. Beller, *Concise History*, 244. Some secular and some assimilated Jews also, at times, kept their distance from observant Jews. Silverman, *Becoming Austrians*, 18. As a result, although the Jewish population was large enough to exert influence, had it spoken and voted as a bloc, its impact on pre-Anschluss government policy and electoral politics was less than the total number promised because Austrian Jews rarely behaved at the polls as a politically homogeneous group. Indeed, they were "extremely" heterogenous. Freidenreich, *Jewish Politics in Vienna*, 2; Silverman, *Becoming Austrians*, 1. Many Jewish voters cast their votes based on their differing socioeconomic interests, not on ethnic or religious interests. Even when guided by Jewish

interests, they sometimes split over Jewish nationalism and along religious orthodoxy lines. Freidenreich, *Jewish Politics in Vienna*, 1, 5.

26. Freidenreich, *Jewish Politics in Vienna*, 186.

27. Schuschnigg, *My Austria*, 27.

28. Freidenreich, *Jewish Politics in Vienna*, 186.

29. Schuschnigg, *Brutal Takeover*, 62. Widespread anti-Semitism in Austrian society was evidenced by demands in the 1920s for quotas limiting acceptance of Jewish students in Austrian schools. However, discrimination in education was prohibited by law, and those prohibitions even then were enforced by the courts and the government; thus, quotas had been declared illegal by the Constitutional Court. Freidenreich, *Jewish Politics in Vienna*, 184. Yet anti-Semitism in schools remained, and it was rampant among the German Student Federation at the University of Vienna from 1919 to 1933. Riots aimed at Jewish students erupted often, but the university rector did nothing to stop them. Freidenreich, *Jewish Politics in Vienna*, 183.

30. Freidenreich, *Jewish Politics in Vienna*, 84–91, 209.

31. Silverman, *Becoming Austrians*, 16.

32. Freidenreich, *Jewish Politics in Vienna*, 84, 86, 87–91.

33. Freidenreich, *Jewish Politics in Vienna*, 9, 84–91.

34. Mann, *Fascists*, 215.

35. Mann, *Fascists*, 233.

36. Freidenreich, *Jewish Politics in Vienna*, 20. Before the Great War, Catholics had also been a dominant force in the multireligious Habsburg Empire in which thirty-one million of the empire's population of forty-six million were Catholic, and most Austrians could be confident that uniquely Catholic interests would always be secure. Silverman, *Becoming Austrians*, 12.

37. Mann, *Fascists*, 219; Freidenreich, *Jewish Politics in Vienna*, 88.

38. Silverman, *Becoming Austrians*, 216n106.

39. F. L. Carsten, *The First Austrian Republic 1918–1938* (Middlesex, UK: Tower/Maurice Temple Smith, 1986), 201, 202.

40. Freidenreich, *Jewish Politics in Vienna*, 7.

41. Freidenreich, *Jewish Politics in Vienna*, 88; Beller, *Concise History*, 218.

42. Mann, *Fascists*, 219.

43. Beller, *Concise History*, 218. It has been noted that "even the Liberals and the Socialists were not entirely immune." Freidenreich, *Jewish Politics in Vienna*, 7, 88. What the Social Democrats did better than the Christian Socials, however, is accept the Jews as equals. Beller, *Concise History*, 218. Even though Jews were allowed to join the Fatherland Front, there was still "informal anti-Semitism." Beller, *Concise History*, 224.

44. Beller, *Concise History*, 218, 224.

45. Mann, *Fascists*, 219.

46. Freidenreich, *Jewish Politics in Vienna*, 88, 89.

47. David Clay Large, *Between Two Fires: Europe's Path in the 1930s* (New York: Norton, 1990), 88.

48. Freidenreich, *Jewish Politics in Vienna*, 89.

49. Freidenreich, *Jewish Politics in Vienna*, 89.

50. The Social Democrats at times used anti-Semitic rhetoric. Beller, *Concise History*, 218. It has been noted that "even the Liberals and the Socialists were not entirely immune." Freidenreich, *Jewish Politics in Vienna*, 7, 88.

51. Freidenreich, *Jewish Politics in Vienna*, 9. Years earlier it had been a Social Democratic governor, Albert Sever, who issued the Sever decree in 1919 aimed at deporting 25,000 Galician Jews. Michael John, "We Do Not Even Possess Ourselves: On Identity and Ethnicity in Austria, 1880–1937," *Austrian History Yearbook* (Minneapolis: Center for Austrian Studies, University of Minnesota, 1999), 30:46.

52. Freidenreich, *Jewish Politics in Vienna*, 9, 88. Zionists (Mizrachists) often had different political preferences in Austrian elections than anti-Zionists. Likewise, orthodox and ultraorthodox (Agudists) groups voted differently from other Jewish groups. Secular Jews were especially hard to predict. All of these groups had their own conceptions of an ideal Jewish community and what their relationship should be to the overwhelmingly Catholic population. Freidenreich, *Jewish Politics in Vienna*, 209.

53. Mann, *Fascists*, 222–25. Fascist attitudes also grew during recessions.

54. Freidenreich, *Jewish Politics in Vienna*, 16.

55. Freidenreich, *Jewish Politics in Vienna*, 16.

56. Freidenreich, *Jewish Politics in Vienna*, 17.

57. Carsten, *The First Austrian Republic*, 201.

58. Charles A. Gulick, *Austria from Habsburg to Hitler*, vol. 2, *Fascism's Subversion of Democracy* (Oakland: University of California Press, 1948), 1189.

59. Kurt von Schuschnigg, interview by Gerhard Jagschitz, 1972–1974, Saint Louis University Archives, DOC MSS 69.6.2, 131, 146.

60. Freidenreich, *Jewish Politics in Vienna*, 196.

61. Schuschnigg, interview by Jagschitz, 146.

62. George S. Messersmith, "Some Observations on the Situation of the Jews in Austria," report for Secretary of State Cordell Hull, October 24, 1934, University of Delaware 19716/6405.

63. Messersmith, "Some Observations on the Situation of the Jews in Austria." In Tyrol, cultural anti-Semitism, viewing Jews as foreigners, was widespread. Silverman, *Becoming Austrians*, 35. Likewise, such provincial-style anti-Semitism was a "given" in the Salzburg region and widespread in the Zillertal region. Silverman, *Becoming Austrians*, 35. Schuschnigg had been too young to participate in the government of the early 1920s during the severe financial crisis that fueled the heights of open anti-Semitism. Freidenreich, *Jewish Politics in Vienna*, 180, 181. He had relatively minor dealings with the most notable anti-Semites of the Christian Social Party of the 1920s. He had little relation at all with Karl Luegger, who was said to have been a strange combination, sometimes referred to as a raucous anti-Semite and a moderate anti-Semite, yet one whom the Jewish community saw as an otherwise rather decent mayor and chancellor. Beller, *Concise History*, 195; Shirer, *Rise/Fall*, 24. His political acceptance has been attributed in part to his "milking the ambiguities of Viennese anti-Semitism for all they were worth." Beller, *Concise History*, 195. It has also been referred to as hypocrisy and double talk. Ibid. Likewise, the priest and chancellor Ignaz Seipel, who had been a cabinet minister during the Habsburg Empire, then a formative leader of the Christian Social Party under the early Republic, was older and out of office before Schuschnigg entered the cabinet. Seipel is described as a restrained and ambiguous anti-Semite. Silverman, *Becoming Austrians*, 216fn106. As for Seipel, he did not display an openly racial anti-Semitism but rather openly disagreed on religious grounds with Jews and was an outspoken opponent of socialism and communism. Freidenreich, *Jewish Politics in Vienna*, 7, 8. Schuschnigg had been a junior member of the Diet when Seipel was chancellor, and he respected Seipel; however, Schuschnigg had only a handful of substantive conversations with Seipel, and Seipel did nothing to encourage a relationship. Schuschnigg found Seipel difficult to approach and hard to know. Schuschnigg, *My Austria*, 65, 66.

64. Messersmith, "Some Observations on the Situation of the Jews in Austria."

65. Messersmith, letter to Jay Pierrepont Moffat, September 20, 1934, University of Delaware 19716/6393.

66. Schuschnigg, *My Austria*, 213.

67. Schuschnigg, interview by Jagschitz, 145, 146.

68. Carsten, *The First Austrian Republic*, 242, 243.

69. Carsten, *The First Austrian Republic*, 242, 243.

70. Schuschnigg remained firm that there was to be no anti-Semitism of any sort in his government, and he insisted that no Jews be harmed. Schuschnigg, *Brutal Takeover*, 62. At the same time, Schuschnigg was blunt in his assessments of others in his party; he agreed with Oskar Karbach, the prominent Jewish writer and a critic of the Christian Socials, that many in his party were "moderate anti-Semites" as Dr. Karbach had labeled them. Schuschnigg, *Brutal Takeover*, 62, 63. Karbach, however, also applauded the fact that both Dollfuss and Schuschnigg resisted following the intensified Nazi anti-Jewish campaign. Schuschnigg, *Brutal Takeover*, 66. Karbach confirmed that "under the corporate state the position of the Jews in political and legal matters was unaffected." Schuschnigg, *Brutal Takeover*, 66.

71. Freidenreich, *Jewish Politics in Vienna*, 180, 186.

72. Freidenreich, *Jewish Politics in Vienna*, 191.

73. Carsten, *The First Austrian Republic*, 241.

74. Carsten, *The First Austrian Republic*, 241. Viewed from the perspective of the anti-Semites, Dollfuss and Schuschnigg were criticized as having sold out to Jewry. Carsten, *The First Austrian Republic*, 201.

75. Freidenreich, *Jewish Politics in Vienna*, 186, 187, 188.

76. Gulick, *Austria from Habsburg to Hitler*, 2:1735.

77. Gulick, *Austria from Habsburg to Hitler*, 2:1694.

78. Gulick, *Austria from Habsburg to Hitler*, 2:1697.

79. Carsten, *The First Austrian Republic*, 201.

80. Freidenreich, *Jewish Politics in Vienna*, 181; Dorothy Thompson, foreword to Schuschnigg, *My Austria*, xiv. The pragmatists among the Jewish leaders saw at a minimum that Schuschnigg was the strongest Austrian enemy of Hitler and, if only for that reason, he was their friend. Freidenreich, *Jewish Politics in Vienna*, 194. With fewer of those old Austrian politicians who had been more prone than the younger to anti-Semitic talk, Jews came to accept more readily the reins of government in the hands of the Christian Social Party than they had in the 1920s. Many Jews under Schuschnigg appreciated that, at the very least, they could live in Austria with confidence that they would be free, as long as he lasted, from any state-tolerated anti-Semitic actions. Freidenreich, *Jewish Politics in Vienna*, 180. They could see a marked contrast between his morally sound, high-minded speeches and writings and the open anti-Semitism of old. Likewise, he showed no signs in his public or private statements of hostility to other religions or races, including Islam or Protestantism. His criticisms of socialists and Marxists were strong, but those criticisms were about their use of violence for political change. Freidenreich, *Jewish Politics in Vienna*, 180.

81. In heavily Catholic Austria, Jews could see that Catholics accepted the guidance of the Vatican. Jewish leaders kept an eye on the Vatican in part because many viewed the Catholic Church in Austria as a wall of protection against the Lutheran influence in Germany. They had concern about German Protestants because of the anti-Semitism in the writings of Martin Luther. His writings were used by the Nazis to validate their positions and to stoke anti-Semitism. Silverman, *Becoming Austrians*, 13. Accordingly, Jews who integrated into Austria's broader population found it somewhat easier to integrate mostly into the Catholic population. Silverman, *Becoming Austrians*, 189fn52. Nevertheless, even though anti-Semitism is contrary to Catholic teaching—indeed to all Christian doctrine—many Catholics were also anti-Semitic, and the legacy of the horrid madness of the Inquisition into which prior popes had taken the church still called into question their modern attitudes. In the Austrian Catholic Church, some clergy openly condemned the anti-Semitism all around them, but some participated in it, seemingly oblivious to the paradox they were living. Jewish leaders were anxious to learn where this new chancellor actually fit in that varied spectrum of Catholic views.

82. Jewish perceptions of degrees of toleration or embrace of anti-Semitism by Catholics were not helped by the fact that Hitler had once been Catholic. But Jewish leaders were well aware

that it was an affiliation Hitler had by now solidly rejected. They knew that Jews and the Vatican now had an enemy in common in Adolf Hitler. The difference, however, was that he hated every Jew, not every Catholic; his hostility toward the Christian establishment was against the organized churches and their teachings. Hitler was not hesitant to tell Schuschnigg about his contempt for the Catholic Church in private during the Berchtesgaden encounter. Schuschnigg, *My Austria,* 14. That hatred may have begun in school, for he despised his teachers, some of whom were Benedictines. Shirer, *Rise/Fall*, 11–14. As a youth, Hitler blamed his Catholic teachers for much of his misery, particularly his failures in school. H. R. Trevor-Roper, *Hitler's Secret Conversations, 1941–1944* (New York: Signet, 1953), 346, 547, 566–67; Shirer, *Rise/Fall*, 11, 12. Hitler and his religion-hating zealots particularly emphasized the Semitic origins of Catholicism, making Catholicism all the more antithetical to German tradition. His political calculus, however, guided him to keep his hatred of the Catholic Church less obvious in public. In this, Hitler was merely being pragmatic; he decided early in his rise to power that no political movement could win the minds of the public if it tried to engage in an open conflict against a large, well-established church. Shirer, *Rise/Fall*, 23; Mann, *Fascists*, 215. On one occasion when Papen warned Hitler that his achievements could come undone if he abused the Catholic Church, Hitler cut him short, boasting that he knew that better than anyone. Toland, *Adolf Hitler*, 455. What place in the spectrum Schuschnigg, a devout Catholic, occupied remained to be seen and to be tested.

83. Silverman, *Becoming Austrians,* 13; David Josef Bach,"Politik der Schuljungen," *Arbeiter-Zeitung,* January 3, 1905.

84. Employing masterful deceit, Hitler's real plan was to end the churches; that decision was already made, but in 1933, he did not believe he was powerful enough to take dispositive action. That year, he confided to Winifred Wagner, the composer's daughter-in-law, that when he amassed full power, he was going to dissolve monasteries and confiscate church properties. Toland, *Adolf Hitler*, 316. His hatred of the church was eventually made sufficiently clear that Jewish and Catholic leaders came to appreciate the common plight they shared. Toland, *Adolf Hitler*, 455.

Eventually, when Hitler became confident in his dictatorial power, he revealed his hatred of all churches, and he subjected all Christian churches in Germany to a campaign to eradicate religion and churches.

The term *Kirkenkampf* has been used to signify the struggle the Christian churches endured during their persecution by the Reich and to signify the various struggles against each other during this era. Erwin L. Lueker, Luther Poellet, and Paul Jackson, "Kirkenkampf," *Christian Cyclopedia* (St. Louis: Concordia, October 17, 2009); Ian Kershaw, *Hitler: A Biography* (New York: Norton, 2008), 382; Shirer, *Rise/Fall*, 234–40; National Catholic Welfare Conference, *The Nazi War against the Catholic Church* (Washington, DC: 1942), 27, 28.

Nazi thought leaders, including Martin Bormann, Alfred Rosenberg, and Josef Göbbels, plotted the steps to eliminate the churches and religions, planning eventually that they would create a pagan church, the National Reich Church of Germany, to replace all religions. Bibles were to be eliminated, and swastikas were to replace crosses in the churches. Their thesis was that "National Socialism and Christianity are irreconcilable." Martin Bormann speech, in Shirer, *Rise/Fall*, 234, 240; Richard J. Evans, *The Third Reich at War: How the Nazis Led Germany from Conquest to Disaster* (New York: Penguin, 2008), 253. Hitler made it clear to his closest people that the conflict with religion was a fundamental one—the church purported to answer only to God, and he would not tolerate anything superior to the Reich: "No matter what it is, not even the Church." Toland, *Adolf Hitler*, 412. To free Hitler's government from religion, Alfred Rosenberg prepared a detailed thirty-point plan with which the Third Reich would simply eliminate religions.

As brazenly totalitarian as this plan was, Hitler did nothing with Catholics or Protestants remotely of the enormity of his attempt to exterminate the Jews, but once secure in his power, he revealed the hatred he had developed for the Catholic Church. Despite the Concordat guaranteeing the Vatican freedom of religion in Germany, Hitler set about breaching it once he had reaped the benefits he sought from this early gesture. Shirer, *Rise/Fall*, 234. In the ensuing years, many German Catholics of all stations were rounded up, and Catholic publications were suppressed. Shirer, *Rise/Fall*, 234, 235. The Catholic Youth League was dissolved. Erich Klaussner, the leader of Catholic Action, was murdered. When Pope Pius XI published an encyclical accusing the Nazi government of fundamental hostility to Catholicism, and of a plan to exterminate the church, reprisals against the church sharply increased. Shirer, *Rise/Fall*, 235; Peter Bartley, *Catholics Confronting Hitler: The Catholic Church and the Nazis* (San Francisco, CA: Ignatius, 2016), 52–54.

The Nazi goal was to substitute the Nazi pagan regime using a National Reich church. Shirer, *Rise/Fall*, 240. Hitler's *Mein Kampf* would be placed on all altars instead of scripture. Shirer, *Rise/Fall*, 240. Himmler was central to this plan. Though a Catholic, he relentlessly attacked the church; he did, however, claim to have used the discipline of the Jesuits as a formative program for building the Schutzstaffel (SS). Toland, *Adolf Hitler*, 764.

Hitler wound up persecuting not just the Catholic Church but all Christian churches. Shirer, *Rise/Fall*, 234. Large numbers of Germans were Protestants, and most of those were Lutheran and members of the Prussian Union of Churches and the Evangelical Church of the old Prussian Union. They, too, had welcomed the Nazis, and some had formed organizations supporting the Third Reich. Some other Protestant organizations, however, had opposed the Nazi racial policies. Shirer, *Rise/Fall*, 235, 236. Moreover, though Martin Luther had been an anti-Semite, many Lutherans even then were not. The Lutheran Church in 1994 totally denounced Martin Luther's anti-Semitism and expressed its "deep and abiding sorrow at its tragic effects on later generations of Jews." See Declaration of the Evangelical Lutheran Church in America to the Jewish Community, April 18, 1944.

When at last Hitler's astonishing evil grew more apparent, some individual church leaders who had at first supported Hitler saw through him. The 1933 autobiography of Reverend Martin Niemöller, an anti-Semitic Lutheran pastor in Germany, celebrated the rise of the Nazis to power, but Niemöller later came to understand what they intended and finally saw Hitler's true colors and began leading a new faction, the Confessing Church, in open resistance to him. Shirer, *Rise/Fall*, 235–39. Indeed, it was this former sympathizer who came to pen the famous lament that ended: "Then they came for me—and there was no one left to speak for me."

The Nazis did indeed come for him. In 1937, Niemöller was arrested and spent most of the war in the Gestapo's Moabite detention center and in Sachsenhausen. Shirer, *Rise/Fall*, 239.

Not all, however, came to grips with the enormity of the Nazis. Many Protestant clergy were called upon by Bishop August Marahrens of the Evangelical Lutheran Church (and a leader of the Confessing Church) to swear an oath of allegiance to Hitler, and they did so in large numbers. Shirer, *Rise/Fall*, 239.

85. A succession of three popes in the turbulent sixteenth century promulgated anti-Semitic policies and practices: Pope Paul IV issued a Papal Bull, *Cum Nimis Absurdum*, containing anti-Jewish regulations that confined the Jews of Rome to the Ghetto, made them wear yellow hats and distinctive garb, and began the Roman Inquisition modeled on the madness into which the church descended in the Spanish Inquisition. John Julius Norwich, *Absolute Monarchs: A History of the Papacy* (New York: Random House, 2011), 316, 416fn16. Pope Pius IV continued all that. He also imposed the death penalty on relatives of his predecessor whom he feared, and he published a new index of forbidden books. Pope Pius V had been an Inquisitor and, as pope, regularly attended the sessions of the Inquisition. Norwich, *Absolute Monarchs*, 319. He kept in place Paul IV's regulations imposed on Jews. Norwich, *Absolute Monarchs*, 319. He banished Jews from all ecclesiastical lands other than Rome and Ancona. John G. Cornwell, *Hitler's Pope: The Secret History of Pius XII* (New York: Penguin, 2008), 26; David Kertzer, *The Pope and Mussolini: The Secret History of Pius XI and the Rise of Fascism in Europe* (New York: Random House, 2014),

12, 13. Pius V did not restrict the harshness of his papacy to Jews. He employed "undue severity against heretics" and has been described as "no respecter of persons." Norwich, *Absolute Monarchs*, 295, 296. As for Protestants, he is the pope who finally excommunicated Queen Elizabeth I. Norwich, *Absolute Monarchs*, 297. As for Muslims, he was behind the assembly of the fleet of Spanish and Venetian ships that challenged the Turkish fleet and destroyed it in 1571 at the Battle of Lepanto. Norwich, *Absolute Monarchs*, 297. The modern controversy over whether Pius XI's successor, Pope Pius XII (Cardinal Eugenio Pacelli) was anti-Semitic, based on his failure to speak out against Nazism or Italian anti-Jewish laws or to call for a halt to the deportation of Italian Jews to concentration camps, continues today. See Norwich, *Absolute Monarchs*, 447.

86. See, for example, Pius XI's September 6, 1938, speech to Belgian pilgrims. La Documentation Catholique (1938), 1459–1460, reprinted in Johannes G. M. Willebrands, *Church and Jewish People: New Considerations* (Mahwah, NJ: Paulist, 1999), 60. Also, in July 1938, the day after Mussolini authorized the Aryan Manifesto, the pope gave a speech condemning the measures. He continued his public attack in several speeches that same month. Bartley, *Catholics Confronting Hitler*, 69. For other acts by Pius XI in opposition to anti-Semitism, see Bartley, *Catholics Confronting Hitler*, 62–75. One contemporary cardinal who spoke out forcefully against anti-Semitism and infuriated the Mussolini government was the Vatican envoy to Turkey, Angelo Roncalli. He would later become Pope John XXIII. Bartley, *Catholics Confronting Hitler*, 74, 75.

87. Pius XI, Vatican City speech, September 6, 1938. Pius XI expressed his rejection of anti-Semitism to Mussolini in their only meeting. He called hostility to Jews "anti-Christian." Kertzer, *The Pope and Mussolini*, 186.

88. Peter Eisner, *The Pope's Last Crusade: How an American Jesuit Helped Pope Pius XI's Campaign to Stop Hitler* (New York: William Morrow, 2014), 72.

89. John A. Lukacs, *The Great Powers and Eastern Europe* (New York: American Book Company, 1953), 93. The anti-Nazi encyclical's "meaning was clear enough." Norwich, *Absolute Monarchs*, 435. Its reference to the value of the Old Testament was seen as the emphatic point that the treatment of Jews was now being called out by the papacy's most formal medium. Norwich, *Absolute Monarchs*, 435. Hitler's rage and Nazi arrests over the encyclical are recounted in Anton Gill, *An Honourable Defeat: A History of the German Resistance to Hitler* (Westport, CT: Heinemann, 1994), 58. See also Anthony Rhodes, *The Vatican in the Age of Dictators, 1922–1945* (Austin, TX: Holt, Rinehart and Winston, 1974), 204–5. Other historians also perceived the encyclical as a warning to the faithful against following a mad prophet of repulsive arrogance. See also Thomas Bokenkotter, *A Concise History of the Catholic Church* (New York: Doubleday, 2004), 389–92.

90. Kertzer, *The Pope and Mussolini*, 186, 259, 355, 356, 358. Among his later increasingly outspoken statements in proximity to Mussolini was the pope's September 6, 1938, speech at the Vatican.

91. Dietrich von Hildebrand, *My Battle against Hitler: Faith, Truth, and Defiance in the Shadow of the Third Reich* (New York: Image, 2014), 81.

92. Guided by that pragmatic restraint, though he was determined to bring an end to the church in his own good time, Hitler was happy to have Papen discuss a concordat with the Vatican in 1933, giving the church the entirely false assurance that he would leave it in peace and free to practice its religion if the church in turn avoided engaging in politics detrimental to the Reich. Toland, *Adolf Hitler*, 315. The Vatican agreed in the concordat to cease any political activity—and it was clear that was expansively defined—and to disband the Catholic Centre Party. Toland, *Adolf Hitler*, 315. The Nazis, however, prohibited not only traditional political activity but also public expressions of Catholicism. Hitler's Brownshirts attacked a march of some 25,000 Catholic apprentices in Munich in June 1933 and severely beat hundreds of them. The Vatican got the message and signed the concordat the following month. Cornwell, *Hitler's Pope*, 146, 149–51.

93. Schuschnigg, *My Austria*, 213. One major Austrian voice that should have taken leadership on the treatment of Jews was that of the senior Catholic prelate in Austria, Cardinal Theodor Innitzer. However, the cardinal was far less vocal than the pope. Nevertheless, Innitzer was viewed by some Jewish leaders as friendly to Jewish interests as a result of some limited moves he made in opposition to anti-Semitism by university students. Freidenreich, *Jewish Politics in Vienna*, 187. Later, however, when Innitzer saw German troops pouring into Austria, he urged Catholics to support Hitler. He ordered Catholic churches to hang swastikas, and he greeted Hitler with a raised arm and a "Heil Hitler." Lukacs, *The Great Powers*, 122. For this, Innitzer was almost fired. The pope summoned him to Rome and berated him for two hours but eventually declined to fire him. Eisner, *The Pope's Last Crusade*, 13; Bartley, *Catholics Confronting Hitler*, 58, 59. The pope concluded that Innitzer was simply weak and cowardly. After that, when the evil of the Nazis became apparent to him, Innitzer did speak out against them, and his residence was sacked by the Nazis when he did. Eisner, *The Pope's Last Crusade*, 13. Another contemporary who saw Innitzer as a weak, easily swayed person was Dietrich Hildebrand.

94. The speech was written at the ailing pope's request by an American Jesuit, Father John La Farge, SJ, in collaboration with a German Jesuit, Father Gustav Gundlach SJ. La Farge also prepared an encyclical against anti-Semitism at the pope's request, *Humanis Generis Unitas*. It was found with the speech. Eisner, *The Pope's Last Crusade*, 189, 225. Less confrontational leadership that succeeded Pius XI reverted to attempts to achieve diplomatic peace with Mussolini. The Duce welcomed this; his contempt for Pius XI had become well known; he ranted about the confrontational pontiff to his mistress, Clara Petacci, and others. Eisner, *The Pope's Last Crusade*, 199, 225, 226.

95. Freidenreich, *Jewish Politics in Vienna*, 187. One of Europe's most outspoken and relentless critics of even mild anti-Semitism, Dietrich Hildebrand, regularly called out priests, bishops, public officials, seminaries, and prominent Catholics for any signs of anti-Semitism as utterly immoral and against all Catholic belief. Hildebrand, *My Battle against Hitler*, 49, 77, 78, 217, illustration 15 following page 184. Though a political foe of Schuschnigg, Hildebrand describes Schuschnigg's character, morality, and decency in the most glowing terms. The fact that Schuschnigg appointed Hildebrand to the faculty of the University of Vienna is relevant not only as a possible diluent to Hildebrand's political hostility but also as evidence of a courageous move by Schuschnigg to strike against anti-Semitism. Hildebrand, *My Battle against Hitler*, 97, 182, 184.

96. Hildebrand, *My Battle against Hitler*, 155.

97. Freidenreich, *Jewish Politics in Vienna*, 187.

98. Freidenreich, *Jewish Politics in Vienna*, 189n50.

99. Silverman, *Becoming Austrians*, 184n18.

100. One of Cardinal Innitzer's counterparts in Germany was Cardinal Michael von Faulhaber of Munich, who decried the persecution of Jews and, notably, helped the pope write the "anti-Nazi" (Lukacs, *The Great Powers*, 93) encyclical *Mit brennender Sorge*. Eisner, *The Pope's Last Crusade*, 72. Nazis confiscated copies of the encyclical throughout the country, but not before it had been thoroughly disseminated. Even that provocative document was crafted in the language of diplomacy; it did not expressly mention Nazism or Jews, but it condemned a society that chose to extol and elevate but a single race. Faulhaber's personal efforts inside Germany against anti-Semitism were also noteworthy given his vulnerability. His main focus, however, was Nazi repression of the Catholic Church, and on several occasions, his attempts to appease Hitler with slight praise for some signs of leniency created a rather half-hearted public image of Faulhaber's opposition to the Nazis. Cornwell, *Hitler's Pope*, 137, 140. Faulhaber did, nevertheless, earn praise for opposing repression of Jews. Eisner, *The Pope's Last Crusade*, 199, 225, 226.

101. Freidenreich, *Jewish Politics in Vienna*, 186.

102. Kertzer, *The Pope and Mussolini*, 369. The prelude to this missed opportunity was replete with Vatican intrigue, for several top Vatican officials opposed, indeed feared, open attacks on

Mussolini or Hitler. They constantly shrouded Pius XI's speeches, writings, and encyclicals in muted diplomatic and topical language rather than emphatic words calling Nazism out by name. In fact, his encyclical *Mit brennender Sorge* did not mention Nazism by name or the Jews as the affected group. It condemned selecting a "single race" as unacceptable. Kertzer, *The Pope and Mussolini*, 259. Its effect was dramatic; it was seen as anti-Nazi, and Hitler exploded over it and seized all copies. Kertzer, *The Pope and Mussolini*, 259. On another occasion, the Vatican opponents of confrontation revised what the pope had approved because it was seen as too inflammatory as a public statement. When he learned what they had done, he exploded at Cardinal Pacelli and others. Kertzer, *The Pope and Mussolini*, 349, 350. The efforts expended by the more timid Vatican officials to restrain the church's public pronouncements met with some resistance. One was a speech delivered from the pulpit in Milan by Cardinal Ildefonso Schuster. He denounced Italy's racial laws. Kertzer, *The Pope and Mussolini*, 350, 351. And in mid-December, Pius XI delivered a speech that infuriated Mussolini. Kertzer, *The Pope and Mussolini*, 355, 356. Shortly, the *London Daily Mail* ran a story leaking the fact that the pope was planning to issue a "ringing denunciation of racism." Kertzer, *The Pope and Mussolini*, 358. Indeed, he was, but he suffered another heart attack, and the speech and encyclical demanding an end to persecution of the Jews was on his desk on February 10, 1939, when he died. Kertzer, *The Pope and Mussolini*, 369.

103. Eisner, *The Pope's Last Crusade*, 194, quoting Rabbi Edward L. Israel of Baltimore, Maryland.

104. When the Creditanstalt failed, many Jews employed there and in affected businesses lost work. Freidenreich, *Jewish Politics in Vienna*, 16. The government's crackdown on the violence of the February 1934 Schutzbund uprising had been antisocialist; however, in the aftermath of the Schutzbund uprising, a third of the arrested socialist leaders were Jewish, and many other Jewish socialists fled into hiding to avoid arrest. The outlawing of the Social Democrats directly reduced Jewish employment. Silverman, *Becoming Austrians*, 172; Freidenreich, *Jewish Politics in Vienna*, 189. There was little direct harm to any Jews, and few have characterized any of the punishments issued afterward as anti-Semitic. Freidenreich, *Jewish Politics in Vienna*, 189. One notable exception, however, was the post–civil war treatment of Jewish doctors. It was expected that many socialists would be penalized by the loss of their employment, and this number would include many Jewish doctors who were socialists. In fact, however, relatively few non-Jewish socialist doctors lost employment. Freidenreich, *Jewish Politics in Vienna*, 189.

105. Gulick, *Austria from Habsburg to Hitler*, 2:1554.

106. Julie Thorpe, *Education and the Austrofascist State: Das Dollfuss/Schuschnigg-Regime 1933–1938* (Vienna: Bohlau Verlag Wien, 2013), 387.

107. The orthodox community wanted the separation. Freidenreich, *Jewish Politics in Vienna*, 199. Other communities wanted Jewish students to be able to attend any school. Thorpe, *Education and the Austrofascist State*, 387. Public disagreement broke out over the issue with considerable argument among Zionists, Nationalists, and Liberals. Freidenreich, *Jewish Politics in Vienna*, 199–201. A delegation of the American Jewish Congress (AJC) presented a petition to Austria's ambassador to the United States, Edgar Prochnik, asserting that there had been episodes of anti-Semitism in Austrian schools and elsewhere. The Jewish delegation called on the ambassador to bring these complaints to the attention of the chancellor. Many of the complaints had to do with unfair hiring practices and the lack of affirmative action in employment. Petition of the AJC quoted in the *New York Times*, December 4, 1934. The protest alleged that "Jewish children are being segregated in the schools." The class separation regulation had been promulgated at the urging of Protestant and other non-Catholic parents of schoolchildren. Non-Catholics objected to recitation of Catholic prayers and Catholic religion lessons. The Ministry of Education refused to eliminate the Catholic teachings, but the new regulation provided that there should be a separation of Catholic students from non-Catholic students when two classes were necessary. The separation of the non-Catholic students from the Catholic would, they said, give these

non-Catholics, including the Jewish students, de facto relief from Catholic prayers and Catholic religion classes in this limited situation. Gulick, *Austria from Habsburg to Hitler*, 2:1553, 2:1554.

However, the presidium of the Jewish Council, the Israelitische Kultusgemeinde Wien, insisted that this separation had the effect in heavily Jewish neighborhoods in Vienna of making Jewish students feel like second-class citizens; therefore, in September 1934, the presidium generated the petition, and Ambassador Prochnik agreed to present it to the new government now headed by Schuschnigg. The AJC petition acknowledged that Schuschnigg had, two months earlier on September 20, rejected Nazi demands that he adopt their anti-Jewish creed and, instead, reaffirmed that in Austria "[t]here is equality for all according to their outward and inward attitude toward the State and society." Quoted in the AJC Petition, December 4, 1934. The AJC also acknowledged Schuschnigg's resistance to Hitler's demands: it applauded Schuschnigg's "valiant and noble stand . . . in defense of Austrian sovereignty and independence against the assault of Hitlerized Germany . . . [and acknowledged] the courage and nobility of the government." See Gulick, *Austria from Habsburg to Hitler*, 2:1553, 2:1554.

108. Messersmith, "Some Observations on the Situation of the Jews in Austria." Messersmith had earlier correctly predicted that Schuschnigg was a man who will "take a correct and understanding attitude with respect to the Jewish problem in Austria." Messersmith, letter to Jay Pierrepont Moffat, September 20, 1934, University of Delaware 19716/6393. He reported that the Jews in turn give Schuschnigg their "loyal support." Ibid.

109. Messersmith, letter to Jay Pierrepont Moffat, September 20, 1934, University of Delaware 19716/6393.

110. Thereafter, Jewish leaders from most points on the spectrum supported Schuschnigg. No elections were being held during this reorganization of the state, but popular support of the government was still very important. Data about how the Jewish population would have voted in this unprecedented government status is lacking. The leaders of the communities do appear to have reflected the political sentiments of their members, and the president of Israelitische Kultusgemeinde Wien, Desider Friedmann, became an important spokesman for Schuschnigg with the Jewish community. He expressed praise for Schuschnigg and supported him in office. Schuschnigg, *Brutal Takeover*, 65. Friedmann had also supported Dollfuss, and he delivered a eulogy at Dollfuss's funeral. Freidenreich, *Jewish Politics in Vienna*, 200.

There continued, nevertheless, to be disagreements among segments of the community, including a split within the Jewish community over the desirability of separation of religions in parallel overflow classes. The orthodox community wanted the separation. Others did not. Freidenreich, *Jewish Politics in Vienna*, 199, 201. The conditions that had proved uncomfortable to Jewish students ended, and Jewish symbols were allowed in the classrooms of the eleven separated classes that remained. Freidenreich, *Jewish Politics in Vienna*, 199–201.

111. Freidenreich, *Jewish Politics in Vienna*, 196; Schuschnigg, *Brutal Takeover*, 4.

112. Freidenreich, *Jewish Politics in Vienna*, 196.

113. Freidenreich, *Jewish Politics in Vienna*, 195–97.

114. Freidenreich, *Jewish Politics in Vienna*, 195.

115. Freidenreich, *Jewish Politics in Vienna*, 193, 195. Not all segments of the Jewish population agreed. Some members, particularly the leftist anti-Zionists, like the Jewish leader Lenni Brenner, opposed Schuschnigg's plebiscite while most Jews supported it. Not all Jews opposed the separation of students in the overcrowded classes; many Jews supported that separation while others protested it. Freidenreich, *Jewish Politics in Vienna*, 201. Some critics say, first, that the Jews would have been better to continue backing the Social Democratic Party and, second, that their decision to back Schuschnigg was merely opportunism or pragmatism since the enemy of their enemy, Hitler, had to be their friend. Freidenreich, *Jewish Politics in Vienna*, 195. "The vast majority of Viennese Jews had voted Social Democratic before 1933, and while many might have

preferred a viable Liberal or Jewish Nationalist Party, very few, except for some wealthy industrialists and perhaps some of the Orthodox, had ever backed the Christian Social Party, which was widely known to be anti-Semitic." Freidenreich, *Jewish Politics in Vienna*, 195.

116. Freidenreich, *Jewish Politics in Vienna*, 193.

117. Freidenreich, *Jewish Politics in Vienna*, 194, 202.

118. Freidenreich, *Jewish Politics in Vienna*, 200, 201.

119. Freidenreich, *Jewish Politics in Vienna*, 200.

120. Schuschnigg, *Brutal Takeover*, 68.

121. Oskar Karbach is quoted by Schuschnigg. Schuschnigg, *Brutal Takeover*, 68.

122. Mann, *Fascists*, 140–44. Many other precepts of Nazism were borderline incomprehensible and inconsistent, amounting to what has been called a ragbag of slogans. Anti-Semitism was clear as a bell.

123. Horthy was a leader whose own conversation, even with foreign diplomats, flowed with hostile anti-Semitism. He embraced the idea of a policy committed to violence against the Judeo-Bolshevik enemy. Mann, *Fascists*, 241. Horthy's messages to Hitler included an assurance that he was a "fellow racist" and a promise that he would install totalitarianism. Mann, *Fascists*, 241, 243. He appointed as chancellor Gyula Gömbös, who was, at the time, a noted anti-Semite (though he later recanted his anti-Jewish rhetoric). Mann, *Fascists*, 244. Hungary enacted laws discriminating against Jews in 1938 and even worse laws in 1940. Mann, *Fascists*, 241–44; Hitler, *Mein Kampf*, 19, 20, 50.

124. Schuschnigg, *Brutal Takeover*, 158.

125. Schuschnigg, *Brutal Takeover*, 156, 157.

126. Schuschnigg, *Brutal Takeover*, 163.

127. Papen, letter to Hitler, July 27, 1935, introduced in evidence at the Nuremberg Trial. Drexel A. Sprecher, *Inside the Nuremberg Trial: A Prosecutor's Comprehensive Account* (Lanham, MD: University Press of America, 1999), 2:215.

128. Kees van Hoek, *London Daily Telegraph and Morning Post*, January 5, 1938; Schuschnigg, *Brutal Takeover*, 156.

CHAPTER 6

1. Shirer, *Rise/Fall*, 324.

2. Kurt von Schuschnigg, *Austrian Requiem* (New York: Putnam, 1946), 23.

3. Schuschnigg, *Brutal Takeover*, 165.

4. Schuschnigg, *Brutal Takeover*, 67.

5. Schuschnigg, *My Austria*, 299; Helmut Wohnout, "A Chancellorial Dictatorship with a 'Corporative' Pretext: The Austrian Constitution between 1934 and 1938," in *The Dollfuss/Schuschnigg Era in Austria: A Reassessment*, ed. Günter Bischof, Anton Pelinka, and Alexander Lassner, Contemporary Austrian Studies 11 (Abington on Thames: Routledge, 2003), 156.

6. Wohnout, "A Chancellorial Dictatorship," 156, 157; Gulick, *Austria from Habsburg to Hitler*, 2:1812.

7. Schuschnigg, *Brutal Takeover*, 67.

8. Schuschnigg, *Brutal Takeover*, 67.

9. Wohnout, "A Chancellorial Dictatorship," 157.

10. Wohnout, "A Chancellorial Dictatorship," 157; More overt opposition is also available. One noted historian characterizes his work as offering a "case against Schuschnigg." Gulick, *Austria from Habsburg to Hitler*, 2:1857fn276.

11. Schuschnigg, *Brutal Takeover*, 68, 69.

12. Schuschnigg, *Brutal Takeover*, 68, 69.

13. Schuschnigg, *Brutal Takeover*, 66.

14. Schuschnigg, *Brutal Takeover*, 66.

15. Gulick, *Austria from Habsburg to Hitler*, 2:1074, 2:1075.

16. Constitution Act, 1867, Austro-Hungarian Compromise of 1867.

17. Gulick, *Austria from Habsburg to Hitler*, 2:1857.

18. Messersmith, report to the Secretary of State, University of Delaware 19716/6466.

19. Beller, *Concise History*, 227.

20. Lukacs, *The Great Powers*, 57. As the Great Depression reached its ninth year, the Austrian economy was still not robust, but, under Schuschnigg, economic reconstruction was under way. Schuschnigg, *My Austria*, 295. Austria was still weighed down by the unemployment that was the signature of the Great Depression, but his government had made considerable progress in battling its way toward a modest recovery. Unemployed on relief had averaged 310,000 in 1932, but by fall 1937, the number was down to 176,000. Schuschnigg, *My Austria*, 295, 296. While Schuschnigg's efforts to improve all industrial and economic segments had not, by 1938, ripped Austria entirely free from the myriad shackles of the worldwide Great Depression, many improvements occurred under his administration. Exports improved; heavy industry showed recovery; and pig iron, crude steel, and textiles all benefited from his rearmament. Gerhard Senft, "Economic Development and Economic Policies in the *Ständestaat* Era," in Bischof, Pelinka, and Lassner, *The Dollfuss/Schuschnigg Era in Austria*, 36.

21. Schuschnigg, *My Austria*, 296–98.

22. Beller, *Concise History*, 228. Nevertheless, because of Hitler's planned conquest and the armaments and troops to achieve it, Schuschnigg was in a desperate position. Ibid.

23. Lukacs, *The Great Powers*, 25.

24. Messersmith, letter to Under secretary of State William I. Phillips, July 19, 1935, University of Delaware 19716/6504.

25. Kurt von Schuschnigg, with Janet von Schuschnigg, *When Hitler Took Austria* (San Francisco, CA: Ignatius, 2012), 50.

26. Schuschnigg, *When Hitler Took Austria*, 41.

27. Messersmith, letter to Phillips, July 19, 1935, University of Delaware 19716/6504.

28. Schuschnigg, *When Hitler Took Austria*, 41.

29. Schuschnigg, *When Hitler Took Austria*, 41.

30. Messersmith, letter to Phillips, July 19, 1935, University of Delaware 19716/6504.

31. Schuschnigg, *When Hitler Took Austria*, 45–48.

32. Schuschnigg, *When Hitler Took Austria*, 45–48.

33. Thompson, foreword to Schuschnigg, *My Austria*, xxxi.

34. Messersmith, letter to Phillips, July 19, 1935, University of Delaware 19716/6504.

35. Messersmith, letter to Phillips, July 19, 1935, University of Delaware 19716/6504.

36. Maria Augusta Trapp, *The Story of the Trapp Family Singers* (Philadelphia: Lippincott, 1949), 104.

37. Trapp, *The Story of the Trapp Family Singers*, 105.

38. Trapp, *The Story of the Trapp Family Singers*, 105.

39. Trapp, *The Story of the Trapp Family Singers*, 106.

40. Trapp, *The Story of the Trapp Family Singers*, 107.

41. Trapp, *The Story of the Trapp Family Singers*, 108.

42. Trapp, *The Story of the Trapp Family Singers*, 109.

43. Trapp, *The Story of the Trapp Family Singers*, 98.

44. Trapp, *The Story of the Trapp Family Singers*, 111.

45. Shirer, *Rise/Fall*, 281.

46. Shirer, *Rise/Fall*, 293.

47. Toland, *Adolf Hitler*, 383.

48. Robert M. Spector, *World without Civilization: Mass Murder and the Holocaust, History and Analysis* (Lanham, MD: University Press of America, 2004), 1:158.

49. Spector, *World without Civilization*, 1:158.

50. Shirer, *Rise/Fall*, 280, 283.

51. Spector, *World without Civilization*, 1:158.

52. Spector, *World without Civilization*, 1:293.

53. Spector, *World without Civilization*, 1:293.

54. Spector, *World without Civilization*, 1:293.

55. Lukacs, *The Great Powers*, 70.

56. Robert Alden, "The Life of Edward—as Prince, King and Duke," *New York Times*, May 29, 1972.

57. Shirer, *Rise/Fall*, 294.

58. Lynne Olson, *Troublesome Young Men* (New York: Farrar, Straus and Giroux, 2007), 217.

59. "Churchill," *New York Times*, January 21, 1940 (report of a BBC broadcast of the speech on January 20, 1940).

60. Shirer, *Rise/Fall*, 295.

61. Lukacs, *The Great Powers*, 29.

62. Shirer, *Rise/Fall*, 295.

63. Margaret MacMillan, *Paris 1919, Six Months That Changed the World* (New York: Random House, 2003), 492, 493.

64. Gulick, *Austria from Habsburg to Hitler*, 2:1693.

65. Gulick, *Austria from Habsburg to Hitler*, 2:1693.

66. Wohnout, "A Chancellorial Dictatorship," 156.

67. Wohnout, "A Chancellorial Dictatorship," 156.

68. Wohnout, "A Chancellorial Dictatorship," 156, 157.

69. Gulick, *Austria from Habsburg to Hitler*, 2:1694. Schuschnigg also dissolved the Ostmarkische Sturmscharen, the Catholic youth militia that had been conceived as a counterweight to the Heimwehr. Gulick, *Austria from Habsburg to Hitler*, 2:1694.

70. Starhemberg's pro-fascist sentiments were a last straw leading to his dismissal by Schuschnigg. Beller, *Concise History*, 227.

71. Beller, *Concise History*, 227.

72. Gulick, *Austria from Habsburg to Hitler*, 2:1695; Lukacs, *The Great Powers*, 61; Wohnout, "A Chancellorial Dictatorship," 156, 157.

73. Wohnout, "A Chancellorial Dictatorship," 157.

74. Wohnout, "A Chancellorial Dictatorship," 156, 157.

75. Wohnout, "A Chancellorial Dictatorship," 156. See also Tim Kirk, "Fascism and Austrofascism," in Bischof, Pelinka, and Lassner, *The Dollfuss/Schuschnigg Era in Austria*, 26.

76. Schuschnigg, interview by Jagschitz, 176.

77. Kees van Hoek, *Daily Telegraph and Morning Post*, January 5, 1938, 12; *Time*, March 21, 1938, 20, 21; Thompson, foreword to Schuschnigg, *My Austria*, xxii.

78. Schuschnigg, *When Hitler Took Austria*, 19.

79. Schuschnigg, *When Hitler Took Austria*, 19.

80. Schuschnigg, *Austrian Requiem*, 68–74.

81. Schuschnigg, *Austrian Requiem*, 68–74.

CHAPTER 7

1. William L. Shirer, *The Rise and Fall of the Third Reich* (New York: Simon & Schuster, 1960), 296.

2. Shirer, *Rise/Fall*, 296.

3. Zara Steiner, *The Triumph of the Dark: European International History 1933–1939* (Oxford: Oxford University Press, 2013), 156.

4. Steiner, *Triumph of the Dark*, 155, 156.

5. See American Jewish Committee Petition quoted in the *New York Times*, December 4, 1934.

6. Kurt von Schuschnigg, *The Brutal Takeover* (New York: Atheneum, 1971), 182, 187.

7. Benjamin Carter Hett, *The Death of Democracy* (New York: Henry Holt, 2018), 230.

8. Andrew Nagorski, *Hitlerland: American Eyewitnesses to the Nazi Rise to Power* (New York: Simon & Schuster, 2012), 159.

9. Alan S. Rome, letter to George S. Messersmith, April 1, 1938, University of Delaware 19716/6948.

10. Hett, *Death of Democracy*, 225.

11. Jamie Bullock, *Karl Renner, Austria; Makers of the Modern World* (London: Haus Histories, 2009), 135.

12. Bullock, *Karl Renner*, 135.

13. Bullock, *Karl Renner*, 135.

14. Bullock, *Karl Renner*, 296. Evidence presented at the Nuremberg Trial showed that Papen wrote Hitler on July 27, 1935, about Schuschnigg's ideological resistance to Nazism in Austria. He said, "National Socialism must and will over power the new Austrian ideology. . . . National Socialism must win." Drexel A. Sprecher, *Inside the Nuremberg Trial: A Prosecutor's Comprehensive Account* (Lanham, MD: University Press of America, 1999), 2:215.

15. Bullock, *Karl Renner*, 296.

16. George S. Messersmith, report on the assassination of Dollfuss, University of Delaware Collection (MSS 0109), identifier 2015–00. Some historians rank Papen as one of the "pathological liars" of the Nazi apparatus. Alexander Lassner and Günter Bischof, introduction to *The Dollfuss/Schuschnigg Era in Austria: A Reassessment*, ed. Günter Bischof, Anton Pelinka, and Alexander Lassner, Contemporary Austrian Studies 11 (Abington on Thames: Routledge, 2003), 3.

17. David Faber, *Munich: The 1938 Appeasement Crisis* (London: Pocket Books, 2009), 117.

18. Faber, *Munich*, 117.

19. He appeared anti-Semitic in connection with the Phoenix Insurance Company matter. Schuschnigg, *Brutal Takeover*, 201.

20. Faber, *Munich*, 117.

21. Schuschnigg, *Brutal Takeover*, 182.

22. Robert M. Spector, *World without Civilization: Mass Murder and the Holocaust, History and Analysis* (Lanham, MD: University Press of America, 2004), 1:264.

23. Steiner, *Triumph of the Dark*, 156; Schuschnigg, *Brutal Takeover*, 107.

24. Messersmith, report to William I. Phillips, October 26, 1934, University of Delaware 19716/6406.

25. Messersmith, letter to J. Pierrepont Moffat, June 6, 1934, University of Delaware 19716/6348. But the Heimwehr remained strong, and Schuschnigg needed to show Starhemberg respect, despite Starhemberg's pro-German statements and impulsive nature. Kurt von Schuschnigg, *My Austria* (New York: Knopf, 1938), 144.

26. Charles A. Gulick, *Austria from Habsburg to Hitler*, vol. 2, *Fascism's Subversion of Democracy* (Oakland: University of California Press, 1948), 1694.

27. Kurt von Schuschnigg, interview by Gerhard Jagschitz, 1972–1974, Saint Louis University Archives, DOC MSS 69.6.2, 177.

28. Lynne Olson, *Troublesome Young Men* (New York: Farrar, Straus and Giroux, 2007), 72.

29. John Toland, *Adolf Hitler* (New York: Anchor, 1976), 379.

30. Olson, *Troublesome Young Men*, 73.

31. David Clay Large, *Between Two Fires: Europe's Path in the 1930s* (New York: Norton, 1990), 142.

32. David Kertzer, *The Pope and Mussolini: The Secret History of Pius XI and the Rise of Fascism in Europe* (New York: Random House, 2014), 244.

33. Kurt von Schuschnigg, *Austrian Requiem* (New York: Putnam, 1946), 110.

34. John A. Lukacs, *The Great Powers and Eastern Europe* (New York: American Book Company, 1953), 66.

35. Gulick, *Austria from Habsburg to Hitler*, 2:1748; Schuschnigg, *Austrian Requiem*, 99; Shirer, *Rise/Fall*, 12.

36. Kertzer, *The Pope and Mussolini*, 217, 218.

37. Schuschnigg, *Austrian Requiem*, 107.

38. Schuschnigg, *Austrian Requiem*, 107.

39. Schuschnigg, *Austrian Requiem*, 114.

40. Schuschnigg, *Austrian Requiem*, 115.

41. Schuschnigg, *Austrian Requiem*, 114.

42. Schuschnigg, *Austrian Requiem*, 113.

43. Schuschnigg, *Austrian Requiem*, 114.

44. Schuschnigg, *Austrian Requiem*, 110.

45. Schuschnigg, *Austrian Requiem*, 110.

46. Kertzer, *The Pope and Mussolini*, 244, 246.

47. Large, *Between Two Fires*, 138, 144.

48. Large, *Between Two Fires*, 149–52.

49. Large, *Between Two Fires*, 152, 153.

50. Large, *Between Two Fires*, 153.

51. Kertzer, *The Pope and Mussolini*, 219; Large, *Between Two Fires*, 157, 158.

52. Large, *Between Two Fires*, 157, 158.

53. Large, *Between Two Fires*, 162–70.

54. Kertzer, *The Pope and Mussolini*, 248; Large, *Between Two Fires*, 141.

55. Large, *Between Two Fires*, 172, 173.

56. Haile Selassie had served as regent for Empress Zauditu, daughter of Menelik II. He earned stature in his own right by leading the successful fight to defeat her rival, Lin Yasu, and enhanced his international acceptance by an impressive visit to European capitals. Though very small in stature, Selassie exuded confidence, strength, and dignity. In 1928, Haile Selassie had himself crowned king (Negu) and, at Zauditu's death in 1930, elevated himself further as imperial majesty and king of kings. Large, *Between Two Fires*, 146, 147.

Mussolini was determined to go to war against Haile Selassie and to take Abyssinia. His troops began to muster in Italian Somaliland near the Abyssinian border, and Mussolini was hoping that this would cause Abyssinia to flinch and commit some provocation that would give him justification for invading. But when none came, on October 3, 1935, Mussolini ordered General De Bono to invade anyway. Italian forces crossed the Mareb River into Abyssinia, and the war Hitler wanted was under way. Large, *Between Two Fires*, 152, 162.

57. Large, *Between Two Fires*, 170, 173; Kertzer, *The Pope and Mussolini*, 217, 219, 223–24, 248, 456fn21.

58. Schuschnigg, *Austrian Requiem*, 119.

59. Kertzer, *The Pope and Mussolini*, 217, 219; Large, *Between Two Fires*, 166, 170.

60. Schuschnigg, *Austrian Requiem*, 119.

61. Steiner, *Triumph of the Dark*, 156.

62. Steven Beller, *A Concise History of Austria* (Cambridge: Cambridge University Press, 2006), 227.

63. Schuschnigg, *Austrian Requiem*, 123.

64. Schuschnigg, *Austrian Requiem*, 123.

65. Schuschnigg, *Austrian Requiem*, 100.

66. Schuschnigg, *Austrian Requiem*, 123.

67. Gulick, *Austria from Habsburg to Hitler*, 2:1687, 2:1688.

68. Spector, *World without Civilization*, 1:157.

69. Kertzer, *The Pope and Mussolini*, 10, 52, 82, 190, 191.

70. Lukacs, *The Great Powers*, 59.

71. Lassner and Bischof, introduction to Bischof, Pelinka, and Lassner, *The Dollfuss/ Schuschnigg Era*, 5.

72. Schuschnigg, *Austrian Requiem*, 98, 99. Yugoslavia was led by its Germanophile Serbian premier, Milan Stoyadinovic, who expressed his view to Count Ciano that Anschluss was simply inevitable. Lukacs, *The Great Powers*, 46, 76, 710fn18.

73. Lukacs, *The Great Powers*, 58.

74. Schuschnigg, *Austrian Requiem*, 101.

75. Lukacs, *The Great Powers*, 59.

76. Gulick, *Austria from Habsburg to Hitler*, 2:1687, 2:1688.

77. Lukacs, *The Great Powers*, 46, 76, 710fn18.

78. Maria Augusta Trapp, *The Story of the Trapp Family Singers* (Philadelphia: Lippincott, 1949), 113; Hansard, March 14, 1938; Documents on British Foreign Policy, 3rd ser., 1, no. 79, ed. by E.L. Woodward and Rohan Butler, 1968.

79. Faber, *Munich*, 117.

80. Lukacs, *The Great Powers*, 74.

81. Messersmith, letter to Sir Walford Selby, February 26, 1938, University of Delaware 19716/6932.

82. Messersmith, letter to J. Pierrepont Moffat of the office of the Secretary of State, June 6, 1934, University of Delaware 19716/6348.

83. William L. Shirer, *Berlin Diary: The Journal of a Foreign Correspondent 1934–1941* (New York: Knopf, 1941), 38, 39.

84. Gordon Brook-Shepherd, *The Anschluss* (Philadelphia and New York: Lippincott, 1963), 22.

85. Messersmith, report on the assassination of Dollfuss, n.d., University of Delaware 19716/7983.

86. Gulick, *Austria from Habsburg to Hitler*, 2:1725.

87. Beller, *Concise History*, 236. Germany not only recognized Austria's sovereignty but also lifted the 1,000 mark tariff. Austria in exchange granted amnesty to 17,000 Nazis. Ibid. These were substantial achievements for Austria considering that all historians agree that it had very little alternative but to placate Germany. Ibid., 237.

88. Schuschnigg, *Brutal Takeover*, 5.

89. Schuschnigg, *Brutal Takeover*, 5.

90. Gulick, *Austria from Habsburg to Hitler*, 2:1725.

91. Schuschnigg, *Brutal Takeover*, 163.

92. Bullock, *Karl Renner*, 135, 136. The German people in Austria, Czechoslovakia, and elsewhere in Europe bonded together and considered themselves different from, for example, the Czech peasants who surrounded them in Bohemia and Moravia. Beller, *Concise History*, 144.

93. Bullock, *Karl Renner*, 136.

94. Shirer, *Rise/Fall*, 296.

95. Spector, *World without Civilization*, 1:157.

96. Schuschnigg, *Brutal Takeover*, 334n2.

97. Spector, *World without Civilization*, 1:157.

98. Dorothy Thompson, foreword to Schuschnigg, *My Austria*, xv.

99. Shirer, *Rise/Fall*, 305.

100. Shirer, *Rise/Fall*, 307.

101. Shirer, *Rise/Fall*, 309.

102. Shirer, *Rise/Fall*, 317.

103. Schuschnigg, *Brutal Takeover*, 203.

104. Lukacs, *The Great Powers*, 66. The Nuremberg evidence confirmed that Hitler's plan was set as early as June 1937. General Blomberg issued a directive to his troops to prepare for war against Austria, calling the plan "Case Otto." IMT, Nuremberg Trial Proceedings, vol. 2, Thursday, November 29, 1945, 399–402.

105. Helmut Wohnout, "A Chancellorial Dictatorship with a 'Corporative' Pretext: The Austrian Constitution between 1934 and 1938," in Bischof, Pelinka, and Lassner, *The Dollfuss/Schuschnigg Era in Austria*, 157.

106. Lukacs, *The Great Powers*, 101.

107. Lukacs, *The Great Powers*, 69. IMT Nuremberg Trial Proceedings, Vol. 19 530-557, July 29, 1946 (189th day).

108. Lukacs, *The Great Powers*, 69.

109. Faber, *Munich*, 36.

110. Andrew Roberts, *The Holy Fox: A Biography of Lord Halifax* (London: Weidenfeld & Nicholson, 1991), 75; Faber, *Munich*, 45.

111. Faber, *Munich*, 38.

112. Henrik Eberle and Matthias Uhl, eds., *The Hitler Book: The Secret Dossier Prepared for Stalin*, trans. G. MacDonagh (London: John Murray, 2005), 25.

113. Faber, *Munich*, 41.

114. Faber, *Munich*, 44, 45.

115. Paul Schmidt, *Hitler's Interpreter*, ed. R. Steed (London: William Heinemann, 1951), 78; Faber, *Munich*, 42.

116. Kees van Hoek, *London Daily Telegraph and Morning Post*, January 5, 1938, 12. In the interview, Schuschnigg made clear that neither he, nor the government under him, had any taste for dictatorship, either Austrian or German. Ibid., 12. See also Dorothy Thompson, foreword to Schuschnigg, *My Austria*, xxii. Schuschnigg derived obvious satisfaction from the fact that the Jewish organizations in Austria reported that they had few difficulties with his government. Schuschnigg, *Brutal Takeover*, 64.

117. Gulick, *Austria from Habsburg to Hitler*, 2:1775, 2:1776.

118. Schuschnigg, *Brutal Takeover*, 156.

119. Schuschnigg, *Brutal Takeover*, 156.

120. Brook-Shepherd, *The Anschluss*, 30. Guido Schmidt testified at Nuremberg that he spoke to Papen on February 5, and Papen was astonished and angry at being recalled. He concluded he was dismissed as part of the removal of Neurath and the generals. IMT, vol. 16, June 13, 1946, 157.

121. Schuschnigg, *Brutal Takeover*, 172, 173.

122. Brook-Shepherd, *The Anschluss*, 18, 19; Toland, *Adolf Hitler*, 432.

123. Brook-Shepherd, *The Anschluss*, 33.

124. Schuschnigg, *Brutal Takeover*, 174, 187, 188.

125. Brook-Shepherd, *The Anschluss*, 15.

126. Brook-Shepherd, *The Anschluss*, 23.

127. Shirer, *Rise/Fall*, 296.

128. IMT, Nuremberg Trial Proceedings, vol. 15, Monday, June 10, 1946, testimony of Arthur Seyss-Inquart, 619; Shirer, *Rise/Fall*, 323.

129. Beller, *Concise History*, 228.

CHAPTER 8

1. Kurt von Schuschnigg, *Austrian Requiem* (New York: Putnam, 1946), 11.

2. Gordon Brook-Shepherd, *The Anschluss* (Philadelphia and New York: Lippincott, 1963), 59.

3. Brook-Shepherd, *The Anschluss*, 58, 59; Steven Beller, *Concise History of Austria* (Cambridge: Cambridge University Press, 2006), 228; Adolf Hitler, *Mein Kampf*, trans. James Murphy, 2nd ed. (1925–1926; Stockholm: White Wolf, 2014), 94. Hitler understood the value of stoking fear because of the effect it had on him. He, too, was repeatedly rattled and panicked. Based on those experiences, he was prone to intimidate others by threats, fake ploys, and by demonstrating real brutality such as the murders of his enemies during the "Night of the Long Knives." John Toland, *Adolf Hitler* (New York: Anchor, 1976), 338–45.

4. Brook-Shepherd, *The Anschluss*, 40.

5. Dorothy Thompson, foreword to *My Austria*, by Kurt von Schuschnigg (New York: Knopf, 1938), vi.

6. William L. Shirer, *The Rise and Fall of the Third Reich* (New York: Simon & Schuster, 1960), 296; Robert M. Spector, *World without Civilization: Mass Murder and the Holocaust, History and Analysis* (Lanham, MD: University Press of America, 2004), 1:157.

7. Thompson, foreword to Schuschnigg, *My Austria*, xviii.

8. Wilhelm Keitel, Walter von Reichenau, and Hugo Sperrle.

9. Schuschnigg, *Austrian Requiem*, 11.

10. Brook-Shepherd, *The Anschluss*, 40.

11. Schuschnigg, *Austrian Requiem*, 12.

12. Kurt von Schuschnigg, with Janet von Schuschnigg, *When Hitler Took Austria* (San Francisco, CA: Ignatius, 2012), 89.

13. Schuschnigg, *When Hitler Took Austria*, 89. Another version of the beginning of this meeting is that Schuschnigg had been alerted to Hitler's aversion and saved his smoking for later and that they were first permitted to smoke when Hitler left the winter garden room at 2 p.m. Schuschnigg, *Austrian Requiem*, 21.

14. Schuschnigg, *Austrian Requiem*, 12.

15. Schuschnigg, *Austrian Requiem*, 1.

16. Schuschnigg, *Austrian Requiem*, 16, 17, 19.

17. Schuschnigg, *Austrian Requiem*, 13.

18. Hitler, *Mein Kampf*, 175. The astounding implications of Hitler's racism—the stripping of all rights from Jews, the allusions to the appropriateness of slavery for such people, the plan to banish them, their alleged intrinsic evil—all were actually articulated as early as *Mein Kampf*. See part 1, chapters 11 and 12, 125, 126, 129; part 2, 175. Schuschnigg had read and understood *Mein Kampf*. Kurt von Schuschnigg, *The Brutal Takeover* (New York: Atheneum, 1971), 157.

19. Schuschnigg, *Brutal Takeover*, 193.

20. Schuschnigg, *Brutal Takeover*, 6.

21. Harriet Pass Freidenreich, *Jewish Politics in Vienna, 1918 to 1938* (Bloomington and Indianapolis: Indiana University Press, 1991), 193. Toland, *Adolf Hitler*, 227. Shirer, *Rise/Fall*, 88–90. Hitler, *Mein Kampf*, 383, 384. Hitler would test the words he could use to make his racist goals sound palatable, "avoiding the usual terminology and working with new words and new conceptions." Toland, *Adolf Hitler*, 227. His preferred word to encapsulate the racist plan

less shockingly was *Volkspolitische*. At other times, he referred to it as nationalist ideology. IMT, vol. 16, 1946, 168. He found that when he used such vague labels, they were better received, and "[n]o longer was he the *volkisch* fanatic. . . . His 'basic values and aims' were as reassuring as they were acceptable. His listeners could not possibly know that the 'reasonable' words were a mask for one of the most radical programs in the history of mankind." Ibid., 227. Hitler planned to free the Volkspolitische Offices in Styria and elsewhere to trumpet Nazi propaganda. Schuschnigg, *Brutal Takeover*, 196.

22. Freidenreich, *Jewish Politics in Vienna*, 193.

23. Kees van Hoek, *London Daily Telegraph and Morning Post*, January 5, 1938; Thompson, foreword to Schuschnigg, *My Austria*, xxii; Schuschnigg, *Brutal Takeover*, 156.

24. Dietrich von Hildebrand, *My Battle against Hitler: Faith, Truth, and Defiance in the Shadow of the Third Reich* (New York: Image, 2014), 232.

25. Hildebrand, *My Battle against Hitler*, 174.

26. Hildebrand, *My Battle against Hitler*, 176.

27. Hildebrand, *My Battle against Hitler*, 179.

28. Schuschnigg, *Austrian Requiem*, 16.

29. Shirer, *Rise/Fall*, 15.

30. Shirer, *Rise/Fall*, 15–19.

31. August Kubizek, *The Young Hitler I Knew* (Boston: Houghton Mifflin, 1955), 59. The 400 or so murders ordered by Hitler in the Night of the Long Knives were adequate precedent that murder was to be one of his weapons.

32. Schuschnigg, *Austrian Requiem*, 24.

33. Schuschnigg, *Austrian Requiem*, 17.

34. Schuschnigg, *Austrian Requiem*, 17.

35. Schuschnigg, *Brutal Takeover*, 351n31; Andrew Nagorski, *Hitlerland: American Eyewitnesses to the Nazi Rise to Power* (New York: Simon & Schuster, 2012), 238.

36. Schuschnigg, *Brutal Takeover*, 351n31; Nagorski, *Hitlerland*, 238.

37. Schuschnigg, *Austrian Requiem*, 18.

38. Schuschnigg, *Austrian Requiem*, 19.

39. Schuschnigg, *Brutal Takeover*, 193.

40. Schuschnigg, *Austrian Requiem*, 19.

41. Schuschnigg, *Austrian Requiem*, 19.

42. Schuschnigg, *Austrian Requiem*, 21; Brook-Shepherd, *The Anschluss*, 53.

43. Brook-Shepherd, *The Anschluss*, 62.

44. Schuschnigg, *Austrian Requiem*, 22; Brook-Shepherd, *The Anschluss*, 55.

45. Schuschnigg, *Brutal Takeover*, 195.

46. Schuschnigg, *Brutal Takeover*, 198. Guido Schmidt testified at Nuremberg that Hitler's demand was that Schuschnigg agree to incorporate the "Austrian Nationalist ideology." IMT, vol. 16, June 13, 1946, 168.

47. Schuschnigg, *Brutal Takeover*, 195; Well before his *London Daily Telegraph* interview, Schuschnigg had taken the step of writing a lengthy letter to Edmund Glaise-Horstenau, condemning the central elements espoused in *Mein Kampf*. Schuschnigg, *Brutal Takeover*, 156, 157.

48. Schuschnigg, *Brutal Takeover*, 197.

49. Schuschnigg, *Austrian Requiem*, 23.

50. Schuschnigg, *Brutal Takeover*, 198, 199. The belief was that neither Seyss nor Glaise-Horstenau was a Nazi but, instead, that Hans Fischbock was. He would not be named to the cabinet as minister of finance but would be given a lesser position in government.

51. Schuschnigg, *Austrian Requiem*, 23, 24.

52. Schuschnigg, *Austrian Requiem*, 14–27; Toland, *Adolf Hitler*, 435. Hitler's retelling of Keitel's dash up the stairs differs from Keitel's recollection. See Henrik Eberle and Matthias Uhl,

eds., *The Hitler Book: The Secret Dossier Prepared for Stalin*, trans. G. MacDonagh (London: John Murray, 2005), 25, 26.

53. Beller, *Concise History*, 228.

54. Schuschnigg, *Austrian Requiem*, 24, 25.

55. Eberle and Uhl, *The Hitler Book*, 26.

56. Brook-Shepherd, *The Anschluss*, 59. Guido Schmidt testified later that they were afraid "we might not get away." IMT, vol. 16, June 13, 1946, 169.

57. Schuschnigg, *Austrian Requiem*, 21; Brook-Shepherd, *The Anschluss*, 62.

58. Schuschnigg, *Brutal Takeover*, 165, 166. The Action Programme referred to the same interview reported in the *London Daily Telegraph and Morning Post*.

59. Schuschnigg, *Brutal Takeover*, 165, 166.

60. Kurt von Schuschnigg, *My Austria* (New York: Knopf, 1938), 10–12.

61. Thompson, foreword to Schuschnigg, *My Austria*, xviii.

62. Jamie Bullock, *Karl Renner, Austria; Makers of the Modern World* (London: Haus Histories, 2009), 136.

63. Bullock, *Karl Renner*, 137.

64. Schuschnigg, *Brutal Takeover*, 195.

65. Brook-Shepherd, *The Anschluss*, 80; David Faber, *Munich: The 1938 Appeasement Crisis* (London: Pocket Books, 2009), 118.

66. Shirer, *Rise/Fall*, 329; N.C. 2995–PS (Nuremberg Document 2995–PS).

67. Shirer, *Rise/Fall*, 324. Some terms of the formal agreement did read like those of two countries bent on a future cooperative policy toward each other. They agreed to exchange views on future policies that impacted each other and to increase commerce between the two countries; they also agreed to some steps usually seen as military cooperation, including exchange of some fifty military officers. Schuschnigg, *Brutal Takeover*, 199.

68. Hitler "dropped" the compatibility provision despite having warned that it was vital. Schuschnigg, *Brutal Takeover*, 198. This demand seems to have been a challenge to Schuschnigg's constancy concerning his letter of May 31, 1937, in which he stated to Glaise-Horstenau that Nazism was "incompatible" with Austria's constitution. See Schuschnigg, *Brutal Takeover*, 156–58. But, he remained constant. At the Nuremberg trials, Seyss's counsel asserted that, at the Berchtesgaden meeting, Schuschnigg had rebuffed successfully some of Hitler's important demands; Schmidt did not disagree. IMT, vol. 16, June 13, 1946, 158. Schmidt testified that Hitler demanded that they embrace Nazi ideology. IMT, vol. 16, 1946, 168. This, however, was one of the "irreconcilable differences" between Austria and the Reich. Ibid., 156. Hitler's use of oblique language when referring to his racial laws was calculated to make these stunning outrages sound benign, even reasonable. He had early on tested the words he could use to make his anti-Jewish principles sound palatable. Toland, *Adolf Hitler*, 227.

69. Schuschnigg, *Austrian Requiem*, 24.

70. Toland, *Adolf Hitler*, 435.

71. Schuschnigg, *Austrian Requiem*, 24; Toland, *Adolf Hitler*, 435.

72. Shirer, *Rise/Fall*, 329.

73. General Keitel was supervising the sham maneuvers, and Admiral Canaris was busy spreading false intelligence about an imminent invasion. IMT, Nuremberg Trial Proceedings, Thursday, November 29, 1945, 405.

74. Upon confirmation of the agreement, Schuschnigg carried out the few specific changes called for. He granted amnesty for political crimes, and he did so not only for Nazis but also for socialists and communists as well. Schuschnigg, *Brutal Takeover*, 204. The violent Austrian Nazis who followed Tavs and Leopold remained illegal, but certain less radical Nazis were admitted into the Fatherland Front under agreed conditions. Schuschnigg, *Brutal Takeover*, 198, 237.

75. Schuschnigg, *Brutal Takeover*, 159, 163.

76. Brook-Shepherd, *The Anschluss*, 27. Seyss was on good terms with many in the Fatherland Front, including Dollfuss and Zernatto. How far the discussion of adding Seyss to the Dollfuss cabinet might have progressed remains an interesting speculation. IMT, Nuremberg Trial Proceedings, vol. 15, testimony of Arthur Seyss-Inquart, 615.

77. Schuschnigg, *Brutal Takeover*, 222.

78. Shirer, *Rise/Fall*, 332. The prosecutors at Nuremberg charged Seyss with playing a "double game." IMT, Nuremberg Trial Proceedings, vol. 15, 616, 617, 634. Skubl testified that once Seyss took office, they had no rifts but, instead, a "harmonious relationship." IMT, vol. 16, June 13, 1946, 177. Seyss himself disputed the "double game" accusation and testified that his meetings and discussions with each side were known to both. He had proposed to Zernatto and Schuschnigg prior to the Berchtesgaden meeting that they appoint Nazis to non-cabinet positions. He also discussed the idea of formation of a coalition government before Berchtesgaden with Papen in a meeting at Garmische-Partenkirchen. Ibid., 619. His February 17 meeting with Hitler, and the assurance he was to be no "Trojan horse," predated Hitler's speech to the Reichstag suggesting he was about to rescue Germans living in Austria and Czechoslovakia. Ibid., 619, 620. Skubl also testified that Seyss admitted that he was, at least at that point, a National Socialist but insisted he had never been a leader of the Nazis. Ibid., 177.

79. Toland, *Adolf Hitler*, 330, 352. Accordingly, as dangerous as it was to loosen the Austrian government's crackdown on the Nazis, to legalize the party once again, and to allow certain Nazis into the Fatherland Front and to be restored to their state jobs, the fact was that Hitler was soon to take Austria one way or another, and the conquest was not caused by the Berchtesgaden agreement or by any real or perceived breach of that agreement. Beller, *Concise History*, 229.

80. Brook-Shepherd, *The Anschluss*, 19; Schuschnigg, *Brutal Takeover*, 208.

81. Schuschnigg, *Brutal Takeover*, 163.

82. Toland, *Adolf Hitler*, 436.

83. John A. Lukacs, *The Great Powers and Eastern Europe* (New York: American Book Company, 1953), 118.

84. Brook-Shepherd, *The Anschluss*, 206.

85. Lynne Olson, *Troublesome Young Men* (New York: Farrar, Straus and Giroux, 2007), 5, 95.

86. Lukacs, *The Great Powers*, 107.

87. Lukacs, *The Great Powers*, 106.

88. Olson, *Troublesome Young Men*, 5, 95.

89. Lukacs, *The Great Powers*, 80, 114.

90. William Manchester, *The Last Lion*, vol. 2, *Alone, 1932–1940* (Boston: Little, Brown, 1988), 283.

91. Manchester, *The Last Lion*, 2:248, 2:249, 2:283, 2:284.

92. Olson, *Troublesome Young Men*, 202, 203.

93. Shirer, *Rise/Fall*, 286.

94. Shirer, *Rise/Fall*, 287.

95. Toland, *Adolf Hitler*, 330, 352, 438.

96. Toland, *Adolf Hitler*, 438.

97. Toland, *Adolf Hitler*, 438.

98. Toland, *Adolf Hitler*, 439; Brook-Shepherd, *The Anschluss*, 10. The end of the speech is quoted as "Bis in der Tod! Rot-Weiss-Rot!" ("Red-White-Red until we're dead"). Manchester, *The Last Lion*, 2:273.

99. Toland, *Adolf Hitler*, 439.

100. Brook-Shepherd, *The Anschluss*, 73.

101. Brook-Shepherd, *The Anschluss*, 102; Toland, *Adolf Hitler*, 439.

102. Brook-Shepherd, *The Anschluss*, 105. The Nazi effort to have their policies adopted in the nationalistic Volkspolitische Offices was a galling affront to Schuschnigg's face-to-face refusal to accept Hitler's demand to jointly announce the compatibility of Nazism and Austrian policy. Schuschnigg, *Brutal Takeover*, 263.

103. Charles A. Gulick, *Austria from Habsburg to Hitler*, vol. 2, *Fascism's Subversion of Democracy* (Oakland: University of California Press, 1948), 1817. The socialists were undoubtedly motivated less by acceptance of Schuschnigg than by intense hatred of Hitler. Schuschnigg, *Brutal Takeover*, 123, 124.

104. Gordon Brook-Shepherd, *Prelude to Infamy: The Story of Chancellor Dollfuss of Austria* (New York: Ivan Obolensky, 1961), 146.

105. Gulick, *Austria from Habsburg to Hitler*, 2:1817.

106. Brook-Shepherd, *The Anschluss*, 120; Toland, *Adolf Hitler*, 442.

107. Schuschnigg, *Brutal Takeover*, 225.

108. Schuschnigg, *Austrian Requiem*, 110.

109. Schuschnigg, *Austrian Requiem*, 15.

110. Schuschnigg, *Brutal Takeover*, 119, 137. Skubl testified that the announcement of the plebiscite had the effect of a "bombshell" on the Nazis. IMT, vol. 16, June 13, 1946, 178. The Nazis feared they were about to suffer a "great defeat" by an "overwhelming majority." Ibid., 179. Nazi Gauleiter Friedrich Rainer testified that the speech was like a "spark in a powder barrel" and threw the election analysis into turmoil because it revealed a very unexpected attitude among the Austrian people. Ibid., June 12, 1946, 126.

111. Freidenreich, *Jewish Politics in Vienna*, 202.

112. Alexander Lassner and Günter Bischof, introduction to *The Dollfuss/Schuschnigg Era in Austria: A Reassessment*, eds. Günter Bischof, Anton Pelinka, and Alexander Lassner, Contemporary Austrian Studies 11 (Abington on Thames: Routledge, 2003), 179.

113. Brook-Shepherd, *The Anschluss*, 118, 119.

114. Toland, *Adolf Hitler*, 442; Thompson, foreword to Schuschnigg, *My Austria*, xix, xxi; Shirer, *Rise/Fall*, 337.

115. Thompson, foreword to Schuschnigg, *My Austria*, xxi.

116. Thompson, foreword to Schuschnigg, *My Austria*, xix.

117. IMT, Nuremberg Trial Proceedings, vol. 2, Thursday, November 29, 1945, 409.

118. Thompson, foreword to Schuschnigg, *My Austria*, xix; Toland, *Adolf Hitler*, 442.

119. Schuschnigg, *Brutal Takeover*, 4.

120. Brook-Shepherd, *The Anschluss*, 122.

121. Brook-Shepherd, *The Anschluss*, 124; Toland, *Adolf Hitler*, 443. It is difficult to conclude that, if Seyss were a full conspirator with the Nazis at that crucial juncture, he would have agreed. However, he admitted in his Nuremberg testimony that, while he had raised some objections and warnings about the plebiscite in discussing it with Schuschnigg, nevertheless, he did, as Schuschnigg has reported, agree that he would support Schuschnigg in the plebiscite. IMT, Nuremberg Trial Proceedings, vol. 15, testimony of Arthur Seyss-Inquart, 625. It was not until May 13, 1938, that Seyss joined the Nazi Party. Ibid., 615.

CHAPTER 9

1. Gordon Brook-Shepherd, *The Anschluss* (Philadelphia and New York: Lippincott, 1963), 134.

2. John Toland, *Adolf Hitler* (New York: Anchor, 1976), 445.

3. Brook-Shepherd, *The Anschluss*, 134.

4. Toland, *Adolf Hitler*, 442. A total equivalent to three army corps plus the air force were mobilized to attack Austria. William L. Shirer, *The Rise and Fall of the Third Reich* (New York: Simon & Schuster, 1960), 355. How many more troops Germany had at that moment can be estimated by later confirmation that Hitler ordered universal military service on March 16, 1935, and directed that it should consist of an army of twelve corps and thirty-six divisions totaling 500,000 men, and by 1939, it was up to fifty divisions. Shirer, *Rise/Fall*, 284, 489. The Luftwaffe by then also had 260,000 men of its own. Ibid.

5. Brook-Shepherd, *The Anschluss*, 135.

6. Brook-Shepherd, *The Anschluss*, 135.

7. Brook-Shepherd, *The Anschluss*, 137, 138. Skubl learned that "unusually alarming troop movements were taking place on the Austrian border." IMT, vol. 16, June 13, 1946.

8. Toland, *Adolf Hitler*, 444.

9. John A. Lukacs, *The Great Powers and Eastern Europe* (New York: American Book Company, 1953), 119.

10. Brook-Shepherd, *The Anschluss*, 66.

11. Brook-Shepherd, *The Anschluss*, 139; Toland, *Adolf Hitler*, 444.

12. Toland, *Adolf Hitler*, 445.

13. Toland, *Adolf Hitler*, 444–46.

14. Toland, *Adolf Hitler*, 446; Kurt von Schuschnigg, *The Brutal Takeover* (New York: Atheneum, 1971), 279.

15. Toland, *Adolf Hitler*, 440.

16. Lukacs, *The Great Powers*, 112, 721fn18.

17. William Manchester, *The Last Lion*, vol. 2, *Alone, 1932–1940* (Boston: Little, Brown, 1988), 145, 247.

18. Manchester, *The Last Lion*, 2:273.

19. Manchester, *The Last Lion*, 2:273, 2:275.

20. Brook-Shepherd, *The Anschluss*, 141.

21. Brook-Shepherd, *The Anschluss*, 142.

22. Toland, *Adolf Hitler*, 445.

23. Brook-Shepherd, *The Anschluss*, 149.

24. Toland, *Adolf Hitler*, 447. Göring told Seyss that the rationale was that Schuschnigg "had broken the agreement." IMT, Nuremberg testimony of Arthur Seyss-Inquart, 626. This was hardly a basis for a conquest, and it was ironic since Hitler had proposed such an idea while in a taunting mood at Berchtesgaden. Göring directed that Seyss be made chancellor. Ibid., 627.

25. Brook-Shepherd, *The Anschluss*, 150, 151.

26. William L. Shirer, *Berlin Diary: The Journal of a Foreign Correspondent 1934–1941* (New York: Knopf, 1941), 104.

27. One report about the hectic messages of March 11 suggests that perhaps Hitler himself called Schuschnigg. Dorothy Thompson, foreword to Kurt von Schuschnigg, *My Austria* (New York: Knopf, 1938), viii. Such a call is not, however, mentioned by Schuschnigg himself and thus may simply be a paraphrased synopsis of the many calls relaying Hitler's and Göring's demands that day.

28. Brook-Shepherd, *The Anschluss*, 152.

29. Brook-Shepherd, *The Anschluss*, 152.

30. Lukacs, *The Great Powers*, 119.

31. Brook-Shepherd, *The Anschluss*, 153, 154; Toland, *Adolf Hitler*, 446.

32. Brook-Shepherd, *The Anschluss*, 158.

33. Brook-Shepherd, *The Anschluss*, 165.

34. Lukacs, *The Great Powers*, 724fn24.

35. Lukacs, *The Great Powers*, 108.

36. Schuschnigg, *Brutal Takeover*, 273, 274.

37. Schuschnigg, *Brutal Takeover*, 274.

38. Shirer, *Berlin Diary*, 25.

39. Schuschnigg, *Brutal Takeover*, 271.

40. Shirer, *Berlin Diary*, 29.

41. Toland, *Adolf Hitler*, 442; Shirer, *Rise/Fall*, 284, 355, 489.

42. Toland, *Adolf Hitler*, 442; Shirer, *Rise/Fall*, 284, 355, 489. See, generally, Feldgrau.com.

43. Manchester, *The Last Lion*, 2:271, 2:277, 2:278.

44. Toland, *Adolf Hitler*, 442; Shirer, *Rise/Fall*, 284, 355, 489.

45. Schuschnigg, *Brutal Takeover*, 274.

46. Brook-Shepherd, *The Anschluss*, 166, 167.

47. Brook-Shepherd, *The Anschluss*, 167, 168.

48. Brook-Shepherd, *The Anschluss*, 169.

49. Hansard, March 14, 1938, *Documents on British Foreign Policy*, 3rd ser., 1, no. 79.

50. Manchester, *The Last Lion*, 2:283.

51. Manchester, *The Last Lion*, 2:283, 2:284.

52. Toland, *Adolf Hitler*, 448.

53. Schuschnigg, *Brutal Takeover*, 280.

54. Brook-Shepherd, *The Anschluss*, 172.

55. IMT, Nuremberg Trial Proceedings, vol. 2, Thursday, November 29, 1945, 423. Days later, Göring was still directing Ribbentrop to tell the British that story. Ibid., 423.

56. Brook-Shepherd, *The Anschluss*, 173; Toland, *Adolf Hitler*, 447, 448. Even before the main invasion on the morning of March 12, in the late evening of March 11, Gauleiter Klausner gave the order to Austrian Nazis to seize power. He sent forty SS men to march in and occupy the chancellery. Before they could seize the broadcasting equipment, Schuschnigg commandeered the microphone and delivered his broadcast. IMT, vol. 16, July 12, 1945, 128.

57. Shirer, *Rise/Fall*, 341.

58. Shirer, *Berlin Diary*, 99. "I declare before the world that the reports launched in Germany . . . are lies from A to Z. [W]e have yielded to force. . . . [W]e have decided to order the troops to offer no resistance." Shirer, *Berlin Diary*, 99.

Gordon Brook-Shepherd translates the speech to say the reports were "invented from A to Z." Brook-Shepherd, *The Anschluss*, 173.

59. Shirer, *Berlin Diary*, 99.

60. The full text of Schuschnigg's speech in English is at Shirer, *Berlin Diary*, 99.

61. Shirer, *Rise/Fall*, 331. Later, Miklas signed a directive accepting Schuschnigg's resignation.

62. Lukacs, *The Great Powers*, 116.

63. Maria Augusta Trapp, *The Story of the Trapp Family Singers* (Philadelphia: Lippincott, 1949), 113.

64. Trapp, *The Story of the Trapp Family Singers*, 113.

65. Brook-Shepherd, *The Anschluss*, 177.

66. Brook-Shepherd, *The Anschluss*, 177; Toland, *Adolf Hitler*, 448.

67. Brook-Shepherd, *The Anschluss*, 177, 178; Toland, *Adolf Hitler*, 449. Transcripts seized from the Germans show that Göring insisted to Keppler that the phony telegram inviting the Nazis to come to Austria's rescue should still be sent. The Nazis thought that was necessary to fool the appeasers—so necessary that Göring ignored Keppler's firsthand report that there was no violence and thus no need of a rescue. But Göring only compounded the lie; he assured Keppler that Seyss merely had to say he had sent the telegram. Schuschnigg, *Brutal Takeover*, 308, 309.

68. IMT, Nuremberg Trial Proceedings, vol. 2, Thursday, November 29, 1945, 423. Hitler's directive located after the war accentuates the severity of the lie by ordering that resistance "must be broken ruthlessly by force of arms." Ibid. Exhibit USA–74, Document W102 at 409.

69. Manchester, *The Last Lion*, 2:282.

70. Schuschnigg refused the offer to have a plane readied at Aspern Airfield to take him out of Austria and another offer to move him to safety at the Hungarian embassy in Vienna. Brook-Shepherd, *The Anschluss*, 183; Kurt von Schuschnigg, *Austrian Requiem* (New York: Putnam, 1946), 54. The SS men who came to the office that night took no action to arrest Schuschnigg, perhaps by plan, or perhaps because some well-armed Austrian soldiers were in the immediate area. IMT, Nuremberg Trial Proceedings, vol. 15, testimony of Arthur Seyss-Inquart, 629.

71. Shirer, *Berlin Diary*, 103.

72. Brook-Shepherd, *The Anschluss*, 183.

73. Schuschnigg, *Austrian Requiem*, 54–56.

74. David Faber, *Munich: The 1938 Appeasement Crisis* (London: Pocket Books, 2009), 132, 135; Toland, *Adolf Hitler*, 448.

75. Faber, *Munich*, 138.

76. Toland, *Adolf Hitler*, 450.

77. Schuschnigg, *Brutal Takeover*, 266.

78. Toland, *Adolf Hitler*, 456.

79. Manchester, *The Last Lion*, 2:280.

80. Thompson, foreword to Schuschnigg, *My Austria*, xxii.

81. Mary Fulbrook, *A Concise History of Germany*, 2nd ed. (Cambridge: Cambridge University Press, 1991), 191.

82. Toland, *Adolf Hitler*, 457.

83. Steven Beller, *A Concise History of Austria* (Cambridge: Cambridge University Press, 2006), 232.

84. Beller, *Concise History*, 232, 233.

85. Shirer called the Anschluss "one of the biggest stories of my life." Shirer, *Berlin Diary*, 95.

86. Roger Moorhouse, *Killing Hitler: The Plots, the Assassins, and the Dictator Who Cheated Death* (New York: Bantam, 2006), 95.

87. Manchester, *The Last Lion*, 2:281.

88. Manchester, *The Last Lion*, 2:271, 2:272.

89. Shirer, *Rise/Fall*, 350–52.

90. Shirer, *Rise/Fall*, 345–52.

91. Shirer, *Rise/Fall*, 350.

92. Toland, *Adolf Hitler*, 452. When Seyss stepped down, Josef Bürckel became the senior Nazi of Austria, named Reich commissioner for the Reunion. IMT, Nuremberg testimony of Arthur Seyss-Inquart, 633.

93. Faber, *Munich*, 137.

94. Zara Steiner, *The Triumph of the Dark: European International History 1933–1939* (Oxford: Oxford University Press, 2013), 554.

95. Manchester, *The Last Lion*, 2:281.

96. Shirer, *Berlin Diary*, 110, 111. Many slogans of the Schuschnigg plebiscite had been scrawled on pavements, and Jews were forced to wash them away. Monroe Price, *Objects of Remembrance: A Memoir of American Opportunities and Viennese Dreams* (Budapest: Central European University Press, 2009), 24.

97. Manchester, *The Last Lion*, 2:281.

98. Toland, *Adolf Hitler*, 454.

99. Marjorie Perloff, *The Vienna Paradox: A Memoir* (New York: New Directions, 2004), 35.

100. Brook-Shepherd, *The Anschluss*, 198.

101. Lisa Silverman, *Becoming Austrians: Jews and Culture between the World Wars* (Oxford: Oxford University Press, 2012), 172, 173.

102. George S. Messersmith, letter from Alan S. Rogers, April 1, 1938, Rome, Italy, University of Delaware 19716/6948.

103. Shirer, *Berlin Diary*, 108.

104. Shirer, *Berlin Diary*, 110; Beller, *Concise History*, 235.

105. Shirer, *Berlin Diary*, 109.

106. Manchester, *The Last Lion*, 2:281.

107. Kurt von Schuschnigg, with Janet von Schuschnigg, *When Hitler Took Austria* (San Francisco, CA: Ignatius, 2012), 113, 114.

108. Beller, *Concise History*, 234, 235. Many refugees, however, were badly restricted in their choices of havens. Some wound up in Czechoslovakia or France, only to be confronted by the Nazis again. Ibid.

109. Shirer, *Berlin Diary*, 103.

110. Harriet Pass Freidenreich, *Jewish Politics in Vienna, 1918 to 1938* (Bloomington and Indianapolis: Indiana University Press, 1991), 206.

111. Freidenreich, *Jewish Politics in Vienna*, 206.

112. An eyewitness account of the swarm of uniformed Nazis at the polls dramatizes the pressure on voters. Julia Boyd, *Travelers in the Third Reich: The Rise of Fascism: 1919–1945* (Berkeley, CA: Pegasus, 2018), 291. See also Toland, *Adolf Hitler*, 457; Brook-Shepherd, *The Anschluss*, 202, 203. A modern historical analysis prepared for the US Department of the Army by the Library of Congress concluded that there was broad support for the Nazis in the plebiscite, but its outcome was indeed influenced by intimidation. Eric Solsten and David E. McClave, eds., "Austria, a Country Study," Federal Research Division, vol. 5, series 6 (sponsored by the Department of the Army) (Washington, DC: Library of Congress, December 1993; 2nd ed., 1994), 45.

113. Shirer, *Berlin Diary*, 112. The end of Austria had been certified. Long before Churchill used his famous phrase after the war, Schuschnigg had already written in 1938: "The iron curtain of History had been rung down." Kurt von Schuschnigg, *My Austria* (New York: Knopf, 1938), 39.

114. Schuschnigg, *Austrian Requiem*, 82, 107. Once Schuschnigg was in the custody of the Nazis, Innitzer began offering criticism of him to the Nazi officials. Schuschnigg, *Austrian Requiem*, 63.

115. Schuschnigg, *Austrian Requiem*, 82, 107.

116. Brook-Shepherd, *The Anschluss*, 211.

117. Lukacs, *The Great Powers*, 121.

118. Schuschnigg, *Brutal Takeover*, 314.

119. Schuschnigg, *Brutal Takeover*, 314.

120. Schuschnigg, *Brutal Takeover*, 266.

121. Schuschnigg, *Brutal Takeover*, 314.

122. Economic success followed in due course, and unemployment disappeared; but Austria's phenomenal rebound was heavily subsidized by use of slave labor and facilitated by the Third Reich's need to locate wartime munitions factories and major hydroelectric projects in Austria rather than Germany to put them beyond the range of Allied bombers. Beller, *Concise History*, 225, 237, 240. One trade-off to this prosperity was that Austria's very substantial gold reserves and securities were all confiscated. *Brutal Takeover*, 294. At no time after the Anschluss was Austria treated like a conquered nation, nor were Austrians abused as an occupied people other than the targets of Nazi racial and similar policies. Beller, *Concise History*, 237.

CHAPTER 10

1. Kurt von Schuschnigg, with Janet von Schuschnigg, *When Hitler Took Austria* (San Francisco, CA: Ignatius, 2012), 99.
2. William L. Shirer, *The Rise and Fall of the Third Reich* (New York: Simon & Schuster, 1960), 430, 431.
3. Shirer, *Rise/Fall*, 431.
4. Shirer, *Rise/Fall*, 430.
5. Monroe Price, *Objects of Remembrance: A Memoir of American Opportunities and Viennese Dreams* (Budapest: Central European University Press, 2009), 28.
6. Hans Rothfels, *The German Opposition to Hitler: An Appraisal* (Chicago: Henry Regnery, 1948, rev. ed. 1961, 1963), 32.
7. Michael Mann, *Fascists* (Cambridge: Cambridge University Press, 2003), 215.
8. Rothfels, *German Opposition*, 33, 34.
9. Shirer, *Rise/Fall*, 1024, 1072.
10. Martin Gilbert, *The Righteous: The Unsung Heroes of the Holocaust* (New York: Henry Holt, 2003), xvi.

CHAPTER 11

1. Gordon Brook-Shepherd, *The Anschluss* (Philadelphia and New York: Lippincott, 1963), 183; Kurt von Schuschnigg, *Austrian Requiem* (New York: Putnam, 1946), 54.
2. John Toland, *Adolf Hitler* (New York: Anchor, 1976), 448.
3. Schuschnigg, *Austrian Requiem*, 62; Dorothy Thompson, foreword to *My Austria*, by Kurt von Schuschnigg (New York: Knopf, 1938), v.
4. Schuschnigg, *Austrian Requiem*, 62–67.
5. Schuschnigg, *Austrian Requiem*, 62–67.
6. Schuschnigg, *Austrian Requiem*, 214.
7. David Faber, *Munich: The 1938 Appeasement Crisis* (London: Pocket Books, 2009), 41, 42.
8. Schuschnigg, *Austrian Requiem*, 62–70.
9. Schuschnigg, *When Hitler Took Austria*, 103.
10. Schuschnigg, *When Hitler Took Austria*, 105.
11. Schuschnigg, *When Hitler Took Austria*, 107.
12. Schuschnigg, *Austrian Requiem*, 82, 83.
13. Schuschnigg, *When Hitler Took Austria*, 100.
14. Schuschnigg, *When Hitler Took Austria*, 100.
15. Schuschnigg, *Austrian Requiem*, 92.
16. Schuschnigg, *Austrian Requiem*, 218.
17. Schuschnigg, *Austrian Requiem*, 74.
18. Schuschnigg, *Austrian Requiem*, 219.
19. Schuschnigg, *Austrian Requiem*, 222.
20. Schuschnigg, *Austrian Requiem*, 223.
21. Schuschnigg, *When Hitler Took Austria*, 107.
22. Schuschnigg, *Austrian Requiem*, 224, 244.
23. Kurt von Schuschnigg, interview by Gerhard Jagschitz, 1972–1974, Saint Louis University Archives, DOC MSS 69.6.2, 62.

24. Schuschnigg, interview by Jagschitz, 62.

25. Schuschnigg, *Austrian Requiem*, 2.

26. Schuschnigg, *Austrian Requiem*, 75.

27. Schuschnigg, *When Hitler Took Austria*, 105.

28. Roger Moorhouse, *Killing Hitler: The Plots, the Assassins, and the Dictator Who Cheated Death* (New York: Bantam, 2006), 92. Hostility to Hitler had quickly given rise to conspiratorial discussions and memos and a meeting as early as December 1933. Franz von Papen's office was one focus of this turmoil. His writer-consultant Edgar Jung was aggressively critical and, at that early date, already favored killing Hitler. Jung wrote a dangerous speech for Papen. The vice chancellor saw that it could get him assassinated but gave the speech anyway, and it led to Jung's murder in the Long Knives events. Benjamin Carter Hett, *The Death of Democracy* (New York: Henry Holt, 2018), 217–19.

29. Moorhouse, *Killing Hitler*, 92.

30. Moorhouse, *Killing Hitler*, 96.

31. Hans Bernd Gisevius, *To the Bitter End*, trans. Richard and Clara Winston (Santa Barbara, CA: Greenwood, 1947), xiii; Moorhouse, *Killing Hitler*, 97.

32. Moorhouse, *Killing Hitler*, 99.

33. Moorhouse, *Killing Hitler*, 100.

34. Shirer, *Rise/Fall*, 380, 381, 404–8.

35. Moorhouse, *Killing Hitler*, 92, 100, 101.

36. Moorhouse, *Killing Hitler*, 92.

37. Andrew Nagorski, *Hitlerland: American Eyewitnesses to the Nazi Rise to Power* (New York: Simon & Schuster, 2012), 238.

38. Nagorski, *Hitlerland*, 238.

39. Kurt von Schuschnigg, *The Brutal Takeover* (New York: Atheneum, 1971), 351n3.

40. Nagorski, *Hitlerland*, 239.

41. Schuschnigg, *Brutal Takeover*, 6.

42. Schuschnigg, *Brutal Takeover*, 6.

43. Lynne Olson, *Troublesome Young Men* (New York: Farrar, Straus and Giroux, 2007), 156.

44. Olson, *Troublesome Young Men*, 133.

45. William L. Shirer, *Berlin Diary: The Journal of a Foreign Correspondent 1934–1941* (New York: Knopf, 1941), 130–35.

46. Shirer, *Berlin Diary*, 140.

47. Shirer, *Rise/Fall*, 385, 386.

48. Shirer, *Berlin Diary*, 136. Poland succeeded in obtaining a sizable portion of land it had long sought, Teschen, a valuable industrial and agricultural border area within Czechoslovakia. Lynne Olson, *Last Hope Island* (New York: Random House, 2017), 231.

49. Faber, *Munich*, 344.

50. Faber, *Munich*, 348.

51. Faber, *Munich*, 346.

52. Shirer, *Berlin Diary*, 138–40.

53. Shirer, *Berlin Diary*, 145.

54. Olson, *Troublesome Young Men*, 157.

55. Olson, *Troublesome Young Men*, 133.

56. Shirer, *Berlin Diary*, 146.

57. Shirer, *Berlin Diary*, 146.

58. Shirer, *Berlin Diary*, 147, 148. The more prevalent view of the British public was expressed by member of Parliament Sir Henry Channon who wrote that "the whole world rejoices whilst only a few malcontents jeer." Henry Channon, *Chips: The Diaries of Sir Henry Channon*, ed. R. R. James (London: Weidenfeld & Nicholson, 1967), 172, 173.

59. The Churchill Center offers several letters with different versions of this quotation.

60. William Manchester, *The Last Lion*, vol. 2, *Alone, 1932–1940* (New York: Little, Brown, 1988), 334, quoting letter to Lord Moyne: "The government had to choose between war and shame. They chose shame. They will get War too." See also Martin Gilbert, *Churchill: A Life* (New York: Henry Holt, 1991), 595, recounting a September 11, 1938, letter to Lord Moyne (Walter Guinness) ("My feeling is that we shall choose shame, and then have war thrown in a little later, on even more adverse terms than at present").

61. Moorhouse, *Killing Hitler*, 103, 104.

62. Nagorski, *Hitlerland*, 239.

63. Nagorski, *Hitlerland*, 239.

64. Faber, *Munich*, 434, 437.

65. Olson, *Troublesome Young Men*, 157.

66. Maria Augusta Trapp, *The Story of the Trapp Family Singers* (Philadelphia: Lippincott, 1949), 120.

67. Nagorski, *Hitlerland*, 236.

68. Nagorski, *Hitlerland*, 236.

69. Dorothy Thompson, "Goodbye to Germany," *Harper's Magazine*, December 1934.

70. Trapp, *The Story of the Trapp Family Singers*, 121.

71. Trapp, *The Story of the Trapp Family Singers*, 122.

72. Trapp, *The Story of the Trapp Family Singers*, 122, 123.

73. Trapp, *The Story of the Trapp Family Singers*, 127.

74. Schuschnigg, *When Hitler Took Austria*, 159–64.

75. Schuschnigg, *When Hitler Took Austria*, 206–13, 214, 217.

76. Schuschnigg, *When Hitler Took Austria*, 165–67.

77. Schuschnigg, *When Hitler Took Austria*, 206–17.

CHAPTER 12

1. Stephen Harding, *The Last Battle* (Boston: Da Capo, 2013), 45.

2. Harding, *Last Battle*, 26.

3. Harding, *Last Battle*, 26.

4. Harding, *Last Battle*, 26.

5. Harding, *Last Battle*, 27.

6. Harding, *Last Battle*, 27.

7. Harding, *Last Battle*, 27.

8. Harding, *Last Battle*, 34, 35.

9. Harding, *Last Battle*, 28.

10. Harding, *Last Battle*, 28.

11. Harding, *Last Battle*, 28.

12. Harding, *Last Battle*, 31.

13. Harding, *Last Battle*, 31.

14. Harding, *Last Battle*, 32.

15. Harding, *Last Battle*, 34.

16. Kurt von Schuschnigg, with Janet von Schuschnigg, *When Hitler Took Austria* (San Francisco, CA: Ignatius, 2012), 246–50, 256, 285–87.

17. Kurt von Schuschnigg, *Austrian Requiem* (New York: Putnam, 1946), 251.

18. Schuschnigg, *When Hitler Took Austria*, 136.

19. Schuschnigg, *Austrian Requiem*, 242, 249.

20. Schuschnigg, *Austrian Requiem*, 242.

21. Schuschnigg, *Austrian Requiem*, 242.

22. Schuschnigg, *Austrian Requiem*, 246, 249.

23. Schuschnigg, *When Hitler Took Austria*, 293; Harding, *Last Battle*, 69, 87, 91–94; William L. Shirer, *The Rise and Fall of the Third Reich* (New York: Simon & Schuster, 1960), 1024, 1072, 1115; H. R. Trevor-Roper, *The Last Days of Hitler* (London: Pan Macmillan, 2013), 124–27.

24. Kurt von Schuschnigg, interview by Gerhard Jagschitz, 1972–1974, Saint Louis University Archives, DOC MSS 69.6.2, 65–71, 75.

25. Schuschnigg, interview by Jagschitz, 70.

26. Schuschnigg, interview by Jagschitz, 65, 70, 71.

27. Schuschnigg, *Austrian Requiem*, 275.

28. Schuschnigg, *Austrian Requiem*, 278.

29. Schuschnigg, *Austrian Requiem*, 285.

30. Schuschnigg, *When Hitler Took Austria*, 293.

31. Kurt von Schuschnigg, *The Brutal Takeover* (New York: Atheneum, 1971), 17.

32. Schuschnigg, *Brutal Takeover*, 16.

33. Shirer, *Rise/Fall*, 1113–15.

34. Trevor-Roper, *Last Days*, 124, 126–27; Shirer, *Rise/Fall*, 1115.

35. Schuschnigg, *When Hitler Took Austria*, 305. The jewelry was never recovered; however, surprisingly a Vermeer painting Vera had secreted for a time was found after the war, and it still hangs in a Vienna museum. Schuschnigg, *When Hitler Took Austria*, 305.

36. Schuschnigg, *Brutal Takeover*, 18.

37. Ian Sayer and Jeremy Dronfield, *Hitler's Last Plot* (New York: Da Capo, 2019), 187–90.

38. Schuschnigg, *Brutal Takeover*, 18.

39. Schuschnigg, *Austrian Requiem*, 288.

40. Schuschnigg, *Brutal Takeover*, 17.

41. Sayer and Dronfield, *Hitler's Last Plot*, 59.

42. Sayer and Dronfield, *Hitler's Last Plot*, 238, 258.

43. Sayer and Dronfield, *Hitler's Last Plot*, 58, 59.

44. Harding, *Last Battle*, 112.

45. Harding, *Last Battle*, 146–60.

46. Harding, *Last Battle*, 150.

47. Schuschnigg, *Brutal Takeover*, 17.

48. Sayer and Dronfield, *Hitler's Last Plot*, 97, 155.

49. Schuschnigg, *When Hitler Took Austria*, 292.

50. Schuschnigg, *Austrian Requiem*, 287.

51. Sayer and Dronfield, *Hitler's Last Plot*, 169.

52. Sayer and Dronfield, *Hitler's Last Plot*, 166, 167, 189.

53. Sayer and Dronfield, *Hitler's Last Plot*, 194–96.

54. Sayer and Dronfield, *Hitler's Last Plot*, 188; Peter Churchill, *The Spirit in the Cage* (London: Hodder and Stoughton, 1954), 218; Sydney Smith, *Wings Day: The Man Who Led the RAF's Epic Battle in German Captivity* (London: Collins, 1968), 234.

55. Sayer and Dronfield, *Hitler's Last Plot*, 214, 215.

56. Sayer and Dronfield, *Hitler's Last Plot*, 220, 231, 235.

57. Sayer and Dronfield, *Hitler's Last Plot*, 230, 236, 259, 260.

58. Sayer and Dronfield, *Hitler's Last Plot*, 87, 230, 231, 235, 236, 259, 260.

59. Sayer and Dronfield, *Hitler's Last Plot*, 230, 260, 272.

60. Sayer and Dronfield, *Hitler's Last Plot*, 238, 239, 244, 268, 270.

61. Schuschnigg, *Brutal Takeover*, 22.

62. William Manchester, *The Last Lion*, vol. 2, *Alone, 1932–1940* (Boston: Little, Brown, 1988), 281.

63. Shirer, *Rise/Fall*, 1074.

64. Schuschnigg, *Austrian Requiem*, 289.

65. Schuschnigg, *Austrian Requiem*, 288.

66. Schuschnigg, *Brutal Takeover*, 17.

67. At a later date, Schuschnigg concluded that the Tyrol resistance fighters had played a very significant role in the salvation of the special prisoners. Schuschnigg, *Brutal Takeover*, 20–22.

68. Schuschnigg, *Brutal Takeover*, 18, 20.

69. Schuschnigg, *Brutal Takeover*, 21.

70. Schuschnigg, *When Hitler Took Austria*, 293; Nuremberg testimony confirmed that Admiral Canaris was executed at Flossenbürg on April 9, 1945. Shirer, *Rise/Fall*, 1073.

71. Steven Beller, *A Concise History of Austria* (Cambridge: Cambridge University Press, 2006), 248.

72. Karl Renner was still an Austro-Marxist, and he agreed to set up the postwar provisional government under the tight fist of the Soviet occupying forces. Beller, *Concise History*, 247.

73. Günter Bischof, *Allied Plans and the Occupation of Austria 1938–1955* (New Brunswick, NJ: Transaction, 2009), 162–89; Matthew Paul Berg, "Caught between Iwan and Weihnachsmann: Occupation, the Marshall Plan and Austrian Identity," in Bischof, *Allied Plans*, 156–84.

74. Schuschnigg, interview by Jagschitz, 80.

75. Harriet Pass Freidenreich, *Jewish Politics in Vienna, 1918 to 1938* (Bloomington and Indianapolis: Indiana University Press, 1991), 207–9.

CHAPTER 13

1. Raymond J. Derrig, SJ, "Kurt von Schuchnigg: Christian Statesman and Scholar,"*Jesuit Bulletin*, Vol. 46, no. 2, April 1967, 3-4; SLU Archive, series 2, folder 31.

2. Statement of the mayor of Mutters in a church newspaper from Innsbruck, SLU Archive, clippings, folder 84, DOC MSS 69.2.84.

3. *Wochenpresse* (Vienna), November 23, 1977, SLU Archive clippings, folder 75, DOC MSS 69.2.75.

4. Hans Huebner, *Die Furche* (Vienna), November 25, 1977, SLU Archive, clippings, folder 79, DOC MSS 69.2.79.

5. SLU Archive, clippings, folder 83, DOC MSS 69.2.83.

6. SLU Archive, clippings, folder 49, DOC MSS 69.2.49. The author of the report was referring to Schuschnigg's final radio broadcast on March 11, 1938, from the chancellery announcing to the world that Austria was yielding to force; the broadcast ended "God protect Austria."

7. William L. Shirer, *The Rise and Fall of the Third Reich* (New York: Simon & Schuster, 1960), 371.

Select Bibliography

Bader, William B. *Austria between East and West*. Palo Alto, CA: Stanford University Press, 1966.

Barker, Elizabeth. *Austria 1918–1972*. Miami, FL: University of Miami Press, 1973.

Bartley, Peter. *Catholics Confronting Hitler: The Catholic Church and the Nazis*. San Francisco, CA: Ignatius, 2016.

Beller, Steven. *A Concise History of Austria*. Cambridge: Cambridge University Press, 2006.

———. *Vienna and the Jews, 1867–1938: A Cultural History*. Cambridge: Cambridge University Press, 1989.

Berg, Matthew Paul. "Caught between Iwan and Weihnachsmann: Occupation, the Marshall Plan and Austrian Identity." In *Allied Plans and the Occupation of Austria 1938–1955*, edited by Günter Bischof. New Brunswick, NJ: Transaction, 2009.

Bischof, Günter. *Allied Plans and the Occupation of Austria 1938–1955*. New Brunswick, NJ: Transaction, 2009.

Bischof, Günter, Anton Pelinka, and Alexander Lassner, eds. *The Dollfuss/Schuschnigg Era in Austria: A Reassessment*. Contemporary Austrian Studies 11. Abington on Thames: Routledge, 2003.

Blum, John Morton. *Woodrow Wilson and the Politics of Morality*. Boston: Little, Brown, 1956.

Boyd, Julia. *Travelers in the Third Reich: The Rise of Fascism: 1919–1945*. Berkeley, CA: Pegasus, 2018.

Brook-Shepherd, Gordon. *The Anschluss*. Philadelphia and New York: Lippincott, 1963.

———. *The Last Habsburg*. London: Garden City, 1968.

———. *Prelude to Infamy: The Story of Chancellor Dollfuss of Austria*. New York: Ivan Obolensky, 1961.

Bullock, Jamie. *Karl Renner, Austria; Makers of the Modern World*. London: Haus Histories, 2009.

Carsten, F. L. *The First Austrian Republic 1918–1938*. Middlesex, UK: Tower/Maurice Temple Smith, 1986.

Clements, Kendrick A. *Woodrow Wilson, World Statesman*. Chicago: Ivan R. Dee, 1999.

Cornwell, John G. *Hitler's Pope: The Secret History of Pius XII*. New York: Penguin, 2008.

Dalin, David G. *The Myth of Hitler's Pope*. Washington, DC: Regnery History, 2005.

Dorpalen, Andreas. *Hindenburg and the Weimar Republic*. Princeton, NJ: Princeton University Press, 1964.

Eberle, Henrik, and Matthias Uhl, eds. *The Hitler Book: The Secret Dossier Prepared for Stalin*. Translated by G. MacDonagh. London: John Murray, 2005.

Eisner, Peter. *The Pope's Last Crusade: How an American Jesuit Helped Pope Pius XI's Campaign to Stop Hitler*. New York: William Morrow, 2014.

Evans, Richard J. *The Third Reich at War: How the Nazis Led Germany from Conquest to Disaster*. New York: Penguin, 2008.

Faber, David. *Munich: The 1938 Appeasement Crisis*. London: Pocket Books, 2009.

Fest, Joachim. *Plotting Hitler's Death: The German Resistance to Hitler 1933–1945*. London: Weidenfeld & Nicolson, 1996.

Freidenreich, Harriet Pass. *Jewish Politics in Vienna, 1918 to 1938*. Bloomington and Indianapolis: Indiana University Press, 1991.

Fulbrook, Mary. *A Concise History of Germany*. 2nd ed. Cambridge: Cambridge University Press, 1991.

Fullilove, Michael. *Rendezvous with Destiny*. New York: Penguin, 2013.

Gilbert, Martin. *The Righteous: The Unsung Heroes of the Holocaust*. New York: Henry Holt, 2003.

Gisevius, Hans Bernd. *To the Bitter End*. Translated by Richard and Clara Winston. Santa Barbara, CA: Greenwood, 1947.

Gulick, Charles A. *Austria from Habsburg to Hitler*. Vol. 2, *Fascism's Subversion of Democracy*. Oakland: University of California Press, 1948.

Harding, Stephen. *The Last Battle*. Boston: Da Capo, 2013.

Hett, Benjamin Carter. *The Death of Democracy*. New York: Henry Holt, 2018.

Hildebrand, Dietrich von. *My Battle against Hitler: Faith, Truth, and Defiance in the Shadow of the Third Reich*. New York: Image, 2014.

Hitler, Adolf. *Mein Kampf*. Translated by James Murphy. 2nd ed. Reprint, Stockholm: White Wolf, 2014. Originally published 1925–1926.

John, Michael. "We Do Not Even Possess Ourselves: On Identity and Ethnicity in Austria, 1880–1937." In *Austrian History Yearbook*, vol. 30. Minneapolis: Center for Austrian Studies, University of Minnesota, 1999.

Kershaw, Ian. *Fateful Choices*. New York: Penguin, 2007.

———. *Hitler: A Biography*. New York: Norton, 2008.

———. *Hitler 1889–1936: Hubris*. New York: Norton, 1998.

———. *Hitler 1936–1945: Nemesis*. New York: Norton, 2000.

Kertzer, David. *The Pope and Mussolini: The Secret History of Pius XI and the Rise of Fascism in Europe*. New York: Random House, 2014.

Kinderman, Gottfried-Karl. *Hitler's Defeat in Austria 1933–1934: Europe's First Containment of Nazi Expansionism*. Boulder, CO: Westview, 1988.

Kubizek, August. *The Young Hitler I Knew*. Boston: Houghton Mifflin, 1955.

Large, David Clay. *Between Two Fires: Europe's Path in the 1930s*. New York: Norton, 1990.

Lassner, Alexander, and Günter Bischof. Introduction to *The Dollfuss/Schuschnigg Era in Austria: A Reassessment*. Edited by Günter Bischof, Anton Pelinka, and Alexander Lassner. Contemporary Austrian Studies 11. Abington on Thames: Routledge, 2003.

Lukacs, John A. *The Great Powers and Eastern Europe*. New York: American Book Company, 1953.

Luther, Martin. *Von den Juden und iren Lügen* [On the Jews and their lies]. Wittenberg, 1543.

MacMillan, Margaret. *Paris 1919: Six Months That Changed the World*. New York: Random House, 2003.

Manchester, William. *The Last Lion*. Vol. 2, *Alone, 1932–1940*. Boston: Little, Brown, 1988.

Mann, Michael. *Fascists*. Cambridge: Cambridge University Press, 2003.

Messenger, Johann, trans. *The Death of Dollfuss*. London: Denis Archer, 1935.

Meyer, G. J. *A World Undone: The Story of the Great War, 1914 to 1918*. New York: Delacorte, 2006.

Moe, Richard. *Roosevelt's Second Act*. New York: Oxford University Press, 2013.

Moorhouse, Roger. *Killing Hitler: The Plots, the Assassins, and the Dictator Who Cheated Death*. New York: Bantam, 2006.

Nagorski, Andrew. *Hitlerland: American Eyewitnesses to the Nazi Rise to Power*. New York: Simon & Schuster, 2012.

Norwich, John Julius. *Absolute Monarchs: A History of the Papacy*. New York: Random House, 2011.

Olson, Lynne. *Troublesome Young Men*. New York: Farrar, Straus & Giroux, 2007.

Perloff, Marjorie. *The Vienna Paradox: A Memoir*. New York: New Directions, 2004.

Pocock, Tom. *Stopping Napoleon: War and Intrigue in the Mediterranean*. London: Thistle, 2004.

Price, Monroe. *Objects of Remembrance: A Memoir of American Opportunities and Viennese Dreams*. Budapest: Central European University Press, 2009.

Rath, R. John. "The Dollfuss Ministry: The Intensification of Animosities and the Drift toward Authoritarianism." In *Austrian History Yearbook*, vol. 30. Minneapolis: Center for Austrian Studies, University of Minnesota, 1999.

Roberts, Andrew. *The Holy Fox: A Biography of Lord Halifax*. London: Weidenfeld & Nicholson, 1991.

Roberts, Stephen Henry. *The House That Hitler Built*. Whitefish, MT: Kessinger, 1938. Reprint, Redland, MD: Gordon Press, 2007.

Sayer, Ian, and Jeremy Dronfield. *Hitler's Last Plot*. New York: Da Capo, 2019.

Schmidt, Paul. *Hitler's Interpreter*. Edited by R. Steed. London: Heinemann, 1951.

Schuschnigg, Kurt von. *Austrian Requiem*. New York: Putnam, 1946.

———. *The Brutal Takeover*. New York: Atheneum, 1971.

———. *Farewell Austria*. New York: Cassell, 1938.

———. *My Austria*. New York: Knopf, 1938.

Schuschnigg, Kurt von, with Janet von Schuschnigg. *When Hitler Took Austria*. San Francisco, CA: Ignatius, 2012.

Scott, Joan W. "The Evidence of Experience." *Critical Inquiry* 17, no. 4 (Summer 1991): 773–97.

Senft, Gerhard. "Economic Development and Economic Policies in the *Ständestaat* Era." In *The Dollfuss/Schuschnigg Era in Austria: A Reassessment*, edited by Günter Bischof, Anton Pelinka, and Alexander Lassner. Contemporary Austrian Studies 11. Abington on Thames: Routledge, 2003.

Seppelt, Francis X., and Clement Loffler. *A Short History of the Popes*. St. Louis, MO: Herder, 1932.

Seton-Watson, Hugh. "Fascism, Right and Left." *Journal of Contemporary History* 1, no. 1, 183–215 (1966).

Shedel, James. *Art and Society: The New Art Movement in Vienna, 1897–1914*. Vienna: Sposs, 1981.

Shirer, William L. *Berlin Diary: The Journal of a Foreign Correspondent 1934–1941*. New York: Knopf, 1941.

———. *The Rise and Fall of the Third Reich*. New York: Simon & Schuster, 1960.

Showalter, Dennis E., and William J. Astore. *Hindenburg, Icon of German Militarism*. Lincoln, NE: Potomac, 2005.

Silverman, Lisa. *Becoming Austrians: Jews and Culture between the World Wars*. Oxford: Oxford University Press, 2012.

Solsten, Eric, and David E. McClave, eds. "Austria, a Country Study." Federal Research Division. Vol. 5. Series 6. Sponsored by the Department of the Army. Washington, DC: Library of Congress, December 1993; 2nd ed., 1994.

Spector, Robert M. *World without Civilization: Mass Murder and the Holocaust, History and Analysis*. Vol. 1. Lanham, MD: University Press of America, 2004.

Spiel, Hilde. *Vienna's Golden Autumn, 1866–1938*. London: Weidenfeld & Nicolson, 1987.

Sprecher, Drexel A. *Inside the Nuremberg Trial: A Prosecutor's Comprehensive Account*. 2 vols. Lanham, MD: University Press of America, 1999.

Stadler, Karl R. *Austria*. Santa Barbara, CA: Praeger, 1971.

Steinacher, Gerald. *Nazis on the Run*. Oxford: Oxford University Press, 2011.

Steiner, Zara. *The Triumph of the Dark: European International History 1933–1939*. Oxford: Oxford University Press, 2013.

Steininger, Rolf, Günter Bischof, and Michael Gehler, eds. *Austria in the Twentieth Century*. Piscataway, NJ: Transaction, 2002.

Thorpe, Julie. *Education and the Austrofascist State: Das Dollfuss/Schuschnigg-Regime 1933–1938*. Vienna: Bohlau Verlag Wien, 2013.

Toland, John. *Adolf Hitler*. New York: Anchor, 1976.

Trapp, Maria Augusta. *The Story of the Trapp Family Singers*. Philadelphia: Lippincott, 1949.

Trevor-Roper, H. R. *Hitler's Secret Conversations, 1941–1944*. New York: Signet, 1953.

Trevor-Roper, H. R. *The Last Days of Hitler*. London: Pan Macmillan, 2013.

Vital, David. *A People Apart: A Political History of the Jews in Europe 1789–1939*. Oxford: Oxford University Press, 1997.

Von der Golt, Anna. *Hindenburg: Power, Myth and the Rise of the Nazis*. Oxford: Oxford University Press, 2009.

Vuillard, Erik. *The Order of the Day*. Translated by Mark Polizzotti. New York: Other Press, 2017.

Warren, John. "Cultural Decline in Vienna in the 1930s." In *Interwar Vienna: Culture between Tradition and Modernity*, edited by Deborah Holmes and Lisa Silverman. Rochester, NY: Camden House, 2009.

Wasserman, Janek. *Black Vienna: The Radical Right in the Red City, 1918–1938*. Ithaca, NY: Cornell University Press, 2013.

Wheatcroft, Andrew. *The Habsburgs, Embodying Empire*. New York: Penguin, 1996.

Willebrands, Johannes G. M. *Church and Jewish People: New Considerations*. Mahwah, NJ: Paulist, 1999.

Zweig, Stefan. *The World of Yesterday*. New York: Viking, 1943.

Index

Roosevelt, Franklin Delano, 87, 173
Rosenberg, Alfred, 106, 243
Rothschild, 99, 103

SA. *See* Sturmabteilung
Sachsenhausen, 210
Saint Louis University, 238–41
Salazar, Antonio, 85
Salzburg, 157, 168, 183, 219
Savoy, House of, 138
Schacht, Hjalmar, 84, 212, 226
Schiff, Hotel, 90, 91
Schilhawsky, General, 186
Schirach, Baldur von, 97, 98
Schlamperei, 195
Schleicher, General Kurt von, 53, 55–
    64, 68, 69, 84, 134
Schloss Itter, 222, 227, 231
Schmidt, Guido, 129, 135, *139*, 146,
    159–68, 187
Schmitz, Richard, 105, 110, 111
Schöber, Johannes, 40
Schönerer, Georg von, 253n5
Schuebner-Richter, Max Erwin von, 49
Schuschnigg, Anna von (Kurt von
    Schuschnigg's mother), 13
Schuschnigg, General Artur von (Kurt
    von Schuschnigg's father), 13, 16,
    207, 209
Schuschnigg, Artur von, Jr. (Kurt von
    Schuschnigg's brother), 13
Schuschnigg, Herma von (Kurt von
    Schuschnigg's first wife), 23 24, 117,
    118
Schuschnigg, Chancellor Kurt von;
    and Abkommen, 144–46, 158; and
    Anschluss, 187–97; assassination
    attempts, 6, 114, 117–19; and
    Austria, return to, 241; becoming
    chancellor, 6–11; and Buresch, Karl,
    41, 42; in Buresch cabinet, 41, 42;
    captivity after World War I, 16; as
    chancellor, 8, 104–21; character,
    11–12, 268n173; Christian Social
    Party, relations with, 41–42; and

conscription, 129; Dachau captivity,
226–29; death of, 241; and Dollfuss,
Engelbert, 42–44; and Dollfuss,
Engelbert, assassination of, 6–10;
in Dollfuss, Engelbert, cabinet,
42–43; education, 22–23; election
to the Diet, 41; family, 117, 210,
211; Gestapo captivity in Vienna,
208–9; Gestapo captivity in Munich,
209–10; and Hess, Rudolph, 71;
and Himmler, Heinrich, 71, 208–9;
and Hindenburg, 59, 60; and Hitler,
Berchtesgaden meeting with, 157–
68; and Innitzer, Cardinal Theodor,
138, 162, 194; and Jewish leaders,
relations with, 104–06, 174–79;
liberation, 234–35; marriage,
23–24; as minister of justice, 42; as
minister of education, 42; music,
love of, 12–14, 24, 117, 224; and
Mussolini, Benito, relations with,
123, 132, 137, 185, 191; opponent
of totalitarianism, 117; oratorical
style of, 11–12, 174–77; and Pacelli,
Cardinal, 138, 193; and Papen,
Franz von, 131–34, 153; and Pius
XI, Pope, 101; plebiscite, 176–86;
"Red-White-Red" speech (March
1938), 174–75; reputation, 11–12,
268n173; Sachsenhausen captivity,
210–11; at Saint Louis University,
238–41; and Schuschnigg, Herma
von (first wife), 23, 24, 117–*18;*
and Schuschnigg, Herma von, death
of, *118*–19; and Schuschnigg, Kurti
von (son with Herma), *118,* 211,
220; and Schuschnigg, Maria (Sissi)
von (daughter with Vera), 210*, 237,
239;* and Schuschnigg, Vera von
(second wife), 129–30, 208–9, *237;*
and Seipel, Ignaz, 41; and Seyss-
Inquart, Arthur, 131–34, 179, 184–
85, 190, *197;* South Tyrol captivity,
226–34; and Starhemberg, Prince
Ernst von, 6–9, 129; and study of

law, 23; and visits to Germany, 59,
60, 71; in World War I, 15–23;
youth of, 12–15
Schuschnigg, Kurt (Kurti) von (Kurt
von Schuschnigg's son), *118,* 208,
211, 223–24, 232, 245, 256
Schuschnigg, Maria (Sissi) von (Kurt von
Schuschnigg's daughter), 210, *237,*
239, 245
Schuschnigg, Vera von (Kurt von
Schuschnigg's second wife), 117, 130,
208–9, *237,* 240
Schutzbund, 29, 34, 36, 83, 88, 90–93
Schutzstaffel (SS), 65–67, 159, 165, 190,
198, 226–36
Seipel, Ignaz, 5, 40, 42, 43, 88
Selassie, Haile, 140
Seyss-Inquart, Arthur; and anschluss,
183–97, *196, 197;* chancellor,
190; Catholicism of, 131; death
of, 243; minister of the interior,
166, 170; and music, appreciation
of, 131, 171; Nazi sympathies of,
131–35, 171; Nuremberg trial of,
243; and Schuschnigg, relations
with, 131, 171, 179; and support for
Schuschnigg's plebiscite, 179
Shirer, William, 187–90, 200, 242
Skubl, Police President Michael, 5, 170,
186
Social Democratic Party, 24–26, 31, 36,
43, 102–05
Somme, the, 15
South Tyrol, 23, 230–32, 235
Spanish Civil War, 84, 141
Spartacists, 21
Squadristi, 135, 142
Ständestaat, 80, 84, 86, 116, 264n72
Starhemberg, Prince Ernst von; and
anschluss, 190; and assassination
of Dollfuss, 8–9; in cabinet of
Dollfuss, 7; death of, 242; dismissal
by Schuschnigg, 129; and fascism,
129; and Heimwehr, 8–10, 29, 35,

42, 43, 85, 92; and Hitler, 8; and
Mussolini, 8, 135–36; personal style,
85; and Rintelen, Anton, 41; and
Schuschnigg, 8, 129; in wartime,
243
Stauffenberg, Colonel Claus von, 228
Steeruwitz, Ernst, 41
Steidle, Richard, 34, 35
Stella Matutina, 14
Sterneckerbrau, 22
St. Germaine, Treaty of, 11, 29, 186
St. Gilgen, 117
Stiller, Edgar, 233
Stoyadinovic, Milan, 284n72
Straffner, Sepp, 78
Strasser, Otto, 50
Strasser, Gregor, 58, 68
Strauss, Johann, 11
Stresa, Treaty of. *See* Stresa Front
Stresa Front, 136, 172
Stresemann, Gustav, 52, 84
SS. *See* Schutzstaffel
Stürgkh, Count Karl von, 5, 32, 89
Sturmabteilung (SA), 35, 65–68, 159,
187
Styria, 10, 34–36, 41, 90, 176
Sudetenland, *212,* 213–18
Syrový, General Jan, 216

Tannenberg, Battle of, 60
Tavs, Leopold, 39, 114, 128, 169
Theresienstadt, 205, 237
Third Reich, 65–67, 127
Thompson, Dorothy, 272n80
Thule Society, 21
Time, xvii, 190
Toller, Ernst, 21
Trapp, Georg von, 119–22, 189,
218–20
Trapp, Maria von, 119, *122,* 189,
218–20
Trapp, Rupert von, 219
Trianon, Treaty of, 143
Tyrol, 13, 24, 174, 234